# SUPERMAN
## ACTION COMICS
### VOL. 2 LEVIATHAN RISING

# SUPERMAN
## ACTION COMICS
### VOL. 2 LEVIATHAN RISING

**BRIAN MICHAEL BENDIS**
writer

**STEVE EPTING**
YANICK PAQUETTE
artists

**BRAD ANDERSON**
NATHAN FAIRBAIRN
colorists

**JOSH REED**
ROB LEIGH
DAVE SHARPE
ALW'S TROY PETERI
letterers

**STEVE EPTING**
collection cover artist

**SUPERMAN** created by **JERRY SIEGEL** and **JOE SHUSTER**
By special arrangement with the Jerry Siegel family

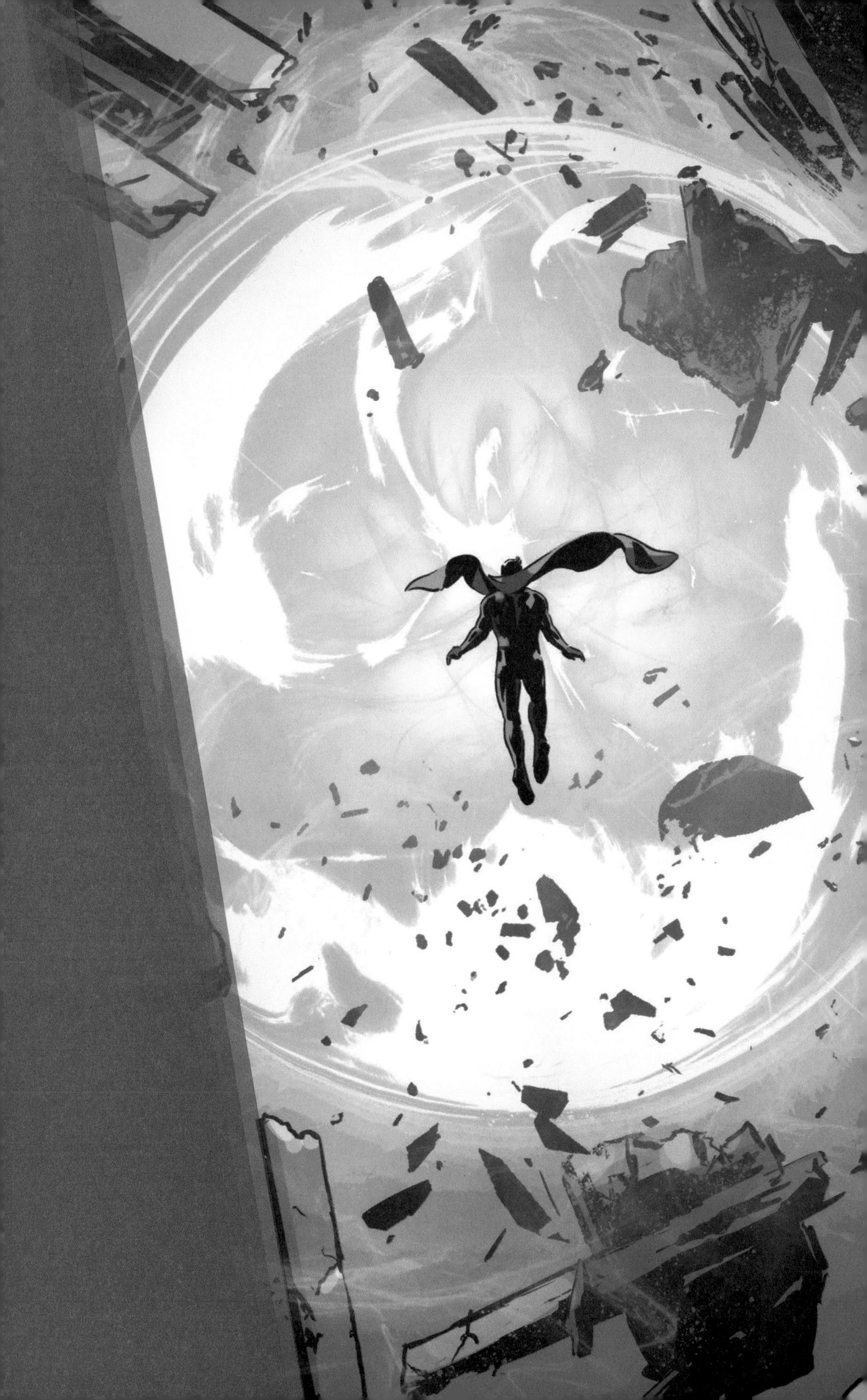

MIKE COTTON Editor – Original Series
JESSICA CHEN Associate Editor – Original Series
JEB WOODARD Group Editor – Collected Editions
ROBIN WILDMAN Editor – Collected Edition
STEVE COOK Design Director – Books
MONIQUE NARBONETA Publication Design
CHRISTY SAWYER Publication Production

BOB HARRAS Senior VP – Editor-in-Chief, DC Comics
PAT McCALLUM Executive Editor, DC Comics

DAN DiDIO Publisher
JIM LEE Publisher & Chief Creative Officer
BOBBIE CHASE VP – New Publishing Initiatives & Talent Development
DON FALLETTI VP – Manufacturing Operations & Workflow Management
LAWRENCE GANEM VP – Talent Services
ALISON GILL Senior VP – Manufacturing & Operations
HANK KANALZ Senior VP – Publishing Strategy & Support Services
DAN MIRON VP – Publishing Operations
NICK J. NAPOLITANO VP – Manufacturing Administration & Design
NANCY SPEARS VP – Sales
MICHELE R. WELLS VP & Executive Editor, Young Reader

SUPERMAN: ACTION COMICS VOL. 2: LEVIATHAN RISING



DC Comics, 2900 West Alameda Ave., Burbank, CA 91505
Printed by LSC Communications, Kendallville, IN, USA. 10/4/19. First Printing.
ISBN: 978-1-4012-9480-9

Library of Congress Cataloging-in-Publication Data is available.

PEFC Certified
This product is from sustainably managed forests and controlled sources
www.pefc.org
PEFC/29-31-337

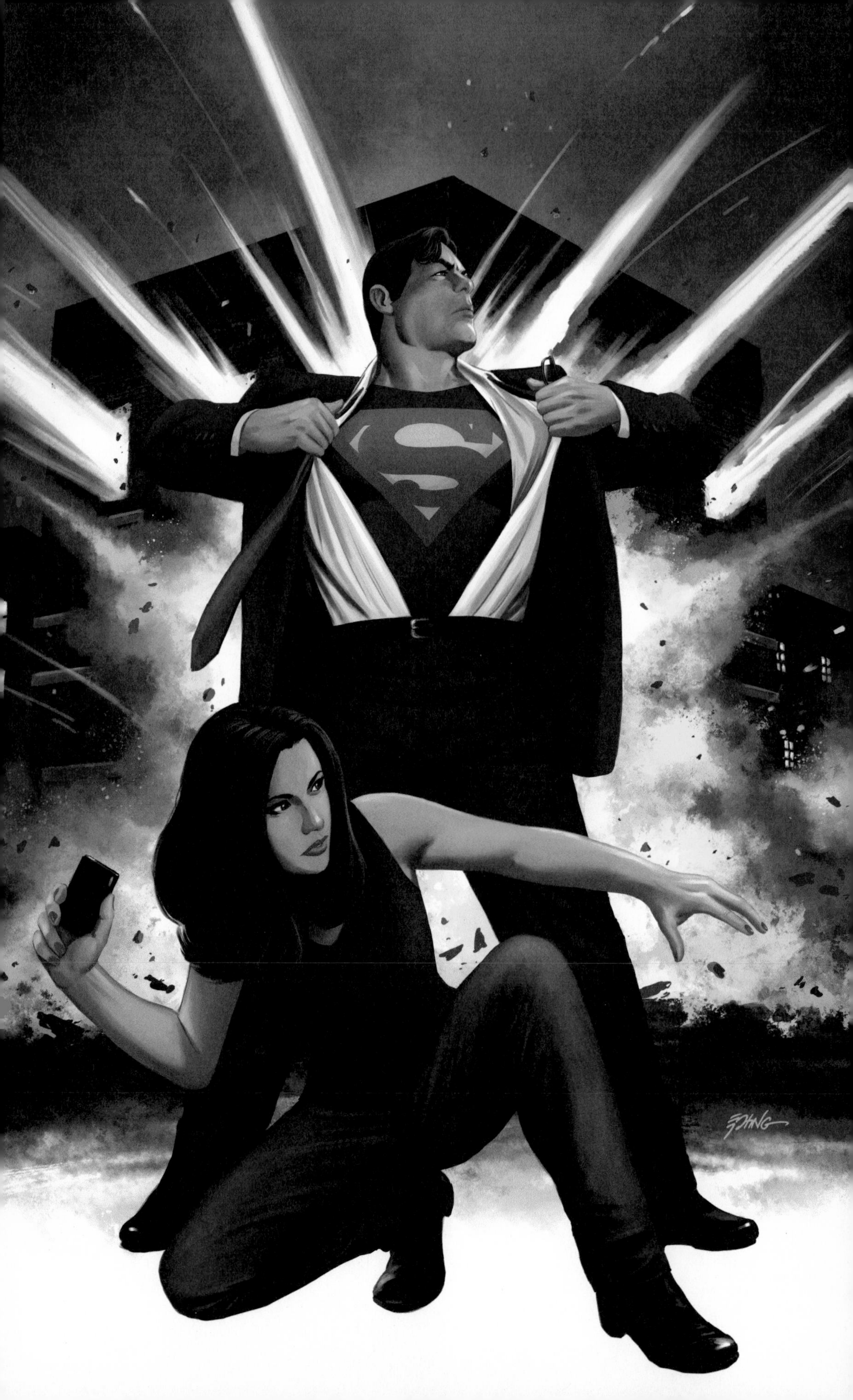

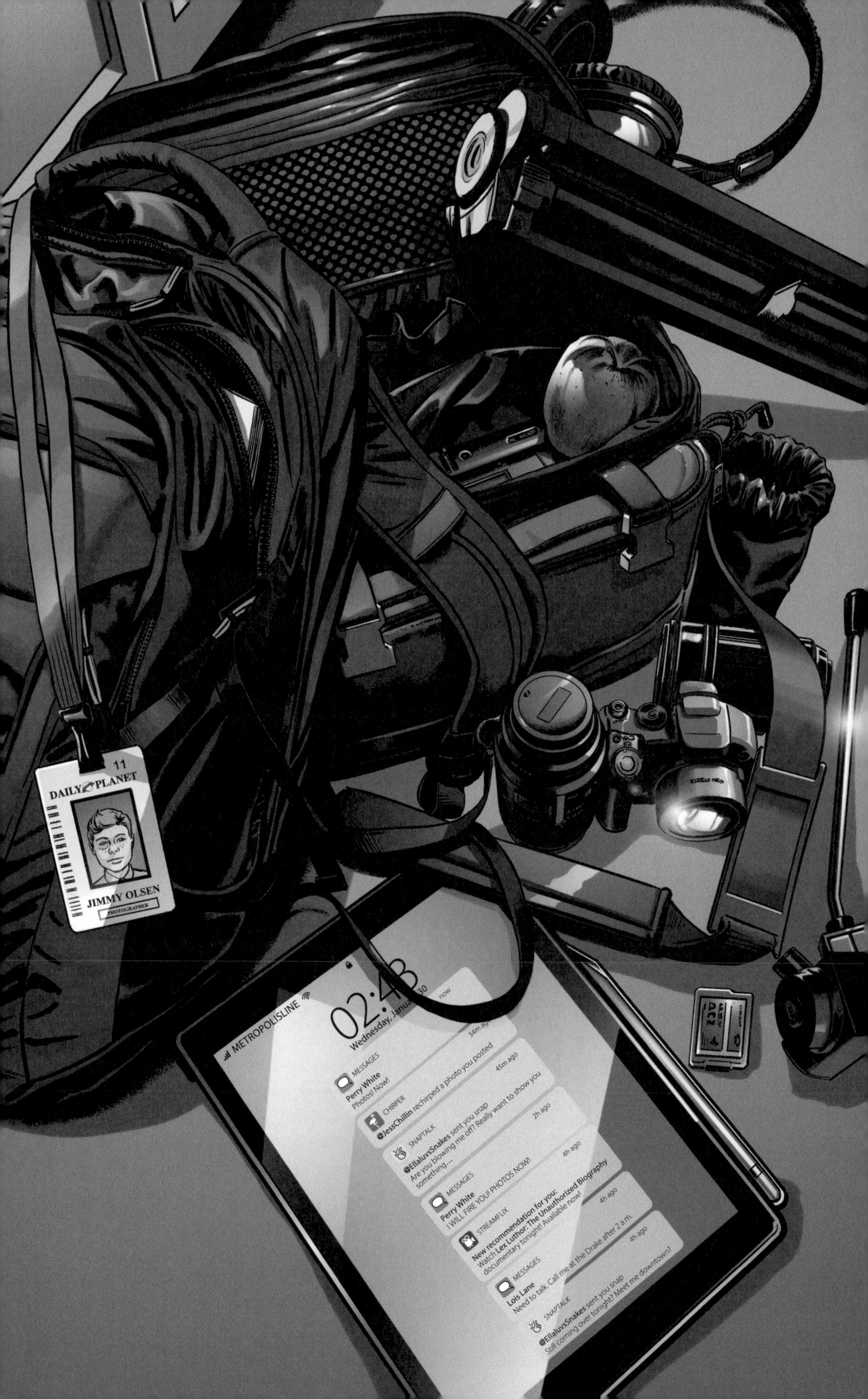
11
DAILY PLANET
JIMMY OLSEN
PHOTOGRAPHER
METROPOLISLINE
02:43
now
MESSAGES 34m ago
Perry White
Photos! Now!
CHIRPER 45m ago
@JessChillin rechirped a photo you posted
SNAPTALK 2h ago
@EllaluvsSnakes sent you snap
Are you blowing me off? Really want to show you something...
MESSAGES 4h ago
Perry White
I WILL FIRE YOU! PHOTOS NOW!
STREAMFLIX 4h ago
New recommendation for you:
Watch Lex Luthor: The Unauthorized Biography documentary tonight! Available now!
MESSAGES 4h ago
Lois Lane
Need to talk. Call me at the Drake after 2 a.m.
SNAPTALK
@EllaluvsSnakes sent you snap
Still coming over tonight? Meet me downtown?

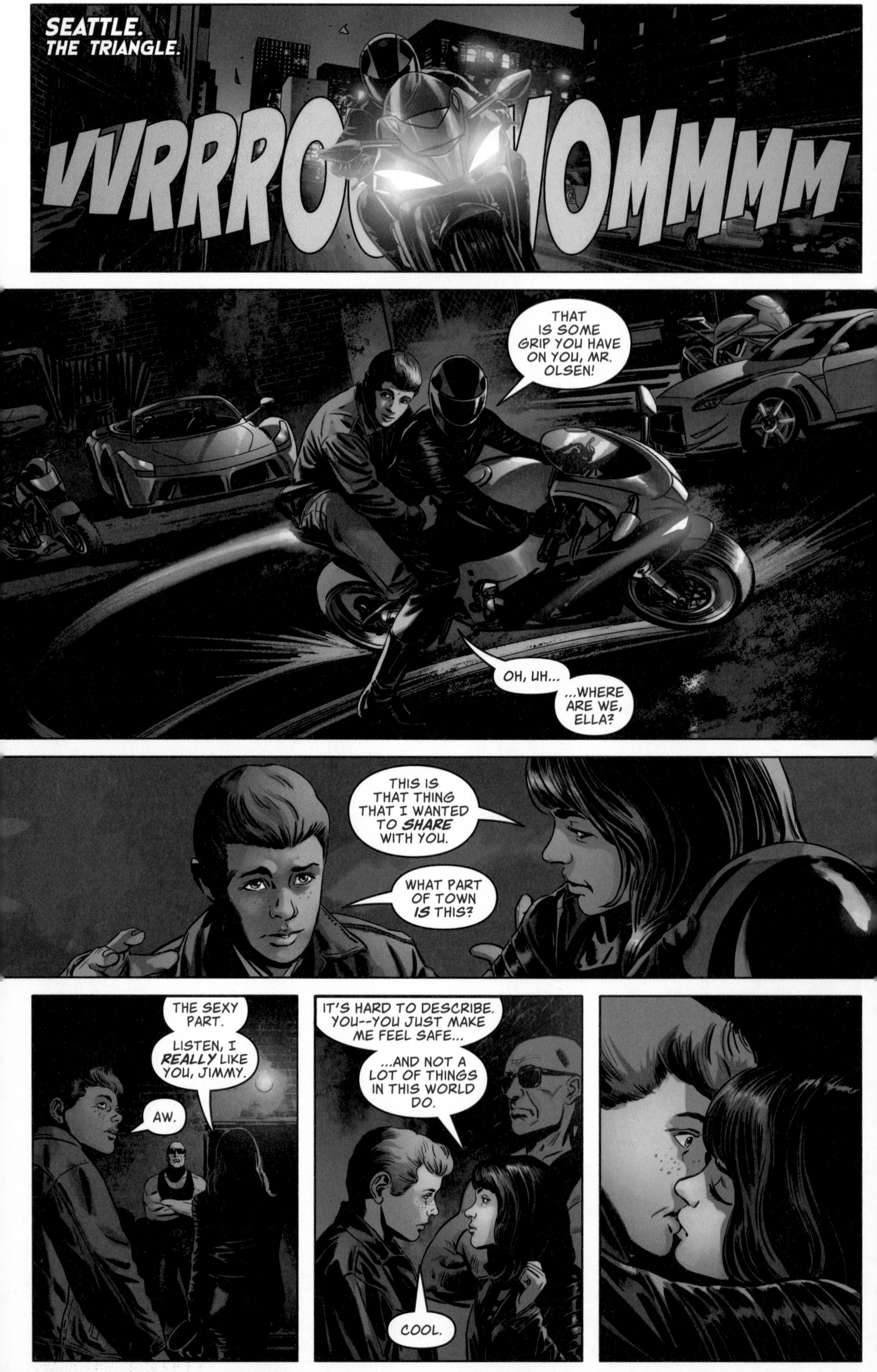
SEATTLE.
THE TRIANGLE.
VVRRROOOOMMMMM
THAT IS SOME GRIP YOU HAVE ON YOU, MR. OLSEN!
OH, UH...
...WHERE ARE WE, ELLA?
THIS IS THAT THING THAT I WANTED TO SHARE WITH YOU.
WHAT PART OF TOWN IS THIS?
THE SEXY PART.
LISTEN, I REALLY LIKE YOU, JIMMY.
AW.
IT'S HARD TO DESCRIBE. YOU--YOU JUST MAKE ME FEEL SAFE...
...AND NOT A LOT OF THINGS IN THIS WORLD DO.
COOL.

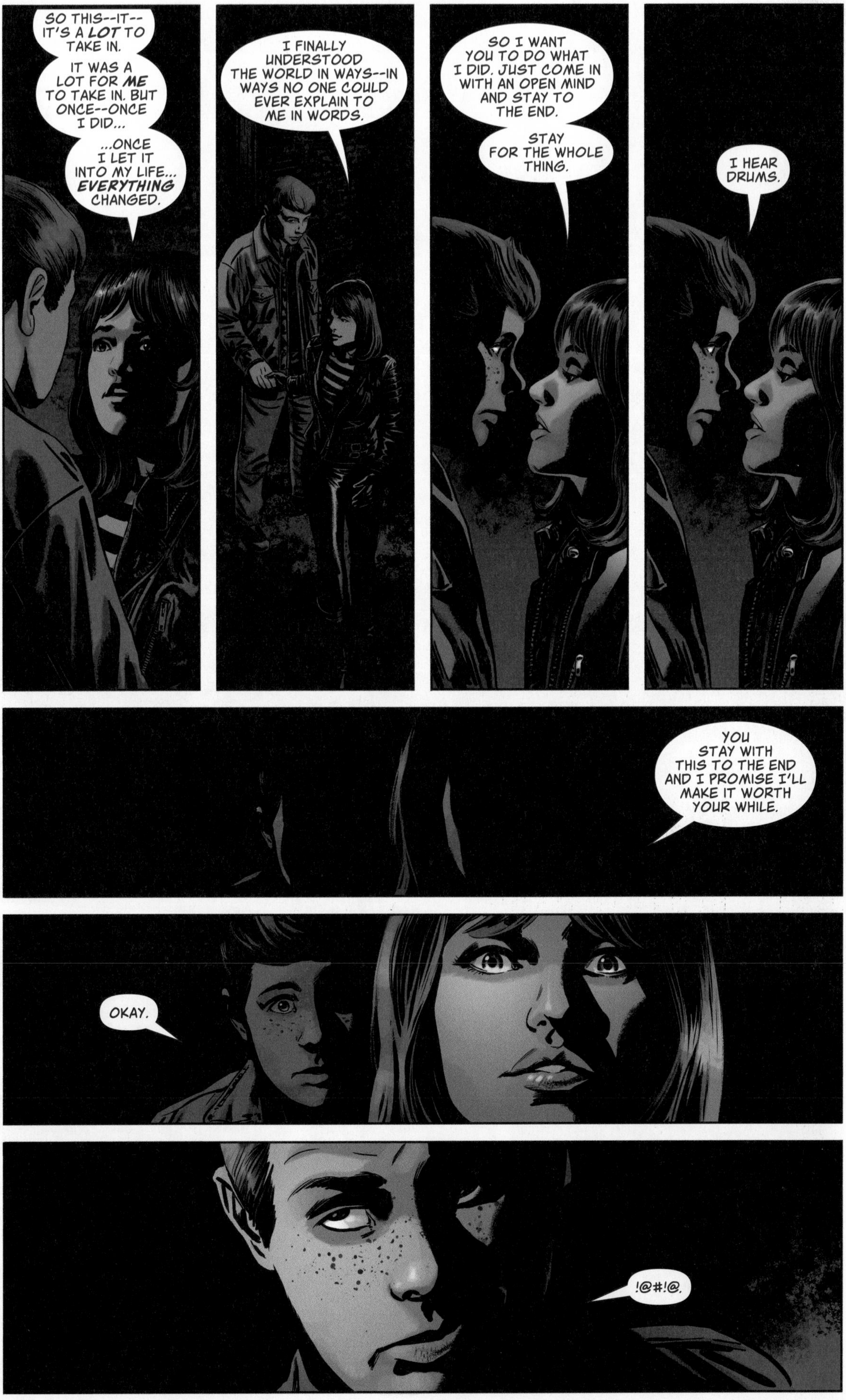
SO THIS--IT--IT'S A *LOT* TO TAKE IN.
IT WAS A LOT FOR *ME* TO TAKE IN. BUT ONCE--ONCE I DID...
...ONCE I LET IT INTO MY LIFE... *EVERYTHING* CHANGED.
I FINALLY UNDERSTOOD THE WORLD IN WAYS--IN WAYS NO ONE COULD EVER EXPLAIN TO ME IN WORDS.
SO I WANT YOU TO DO WHAT I DID. JUST COME IN WITH AN OPEN MIND AND STAY TO THE END.
STAY FOR THE WHOLE THING.
I HEAR DRUMS.
YOU STAY WITH THIS TO THE END AND I PROMISE I'LL MAKE IT WORTH YOUR WHILE.
OKAY.
!@#!@.

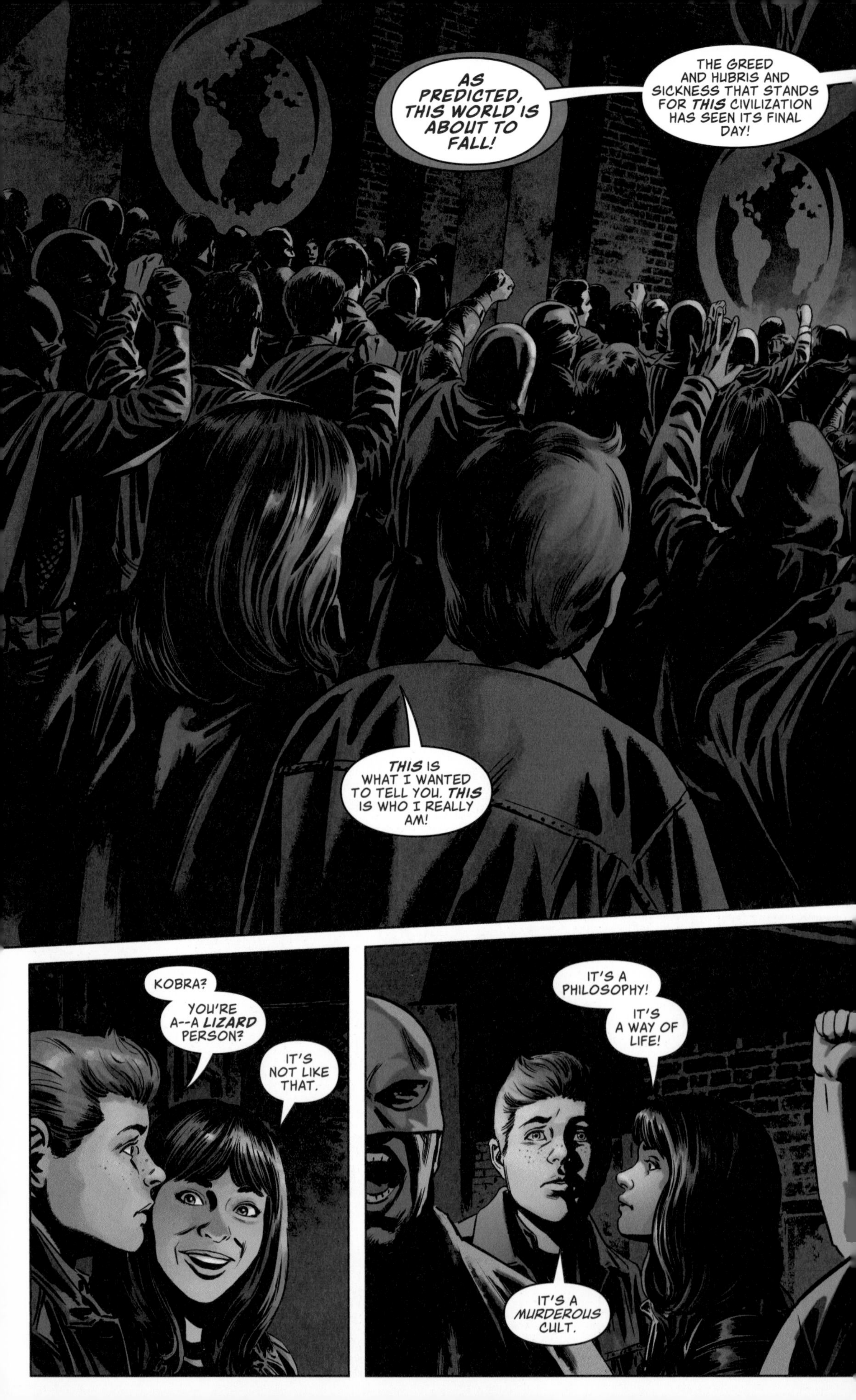
AS PREDICTED, THIS WORLD IS ABOUT TO FALL!
THE GREED AND HUBRIS AND SICKNESS THAT STANDS FOR THIS CIVILIZATION HAS SEEN ITS FINAL DAY!
THIS IS WHAT I WANTED TO TELL YOU. THIS IS WHO I REALLY AM!
KOBRA?
YOU'RE A--A LIZARD PERSON?
IT'S NOT LIKE THAT.
IT'S A PHILOSOPHY!
IT'S A WAY OF LIFE!
IT'S A MURDEROUS CULT.

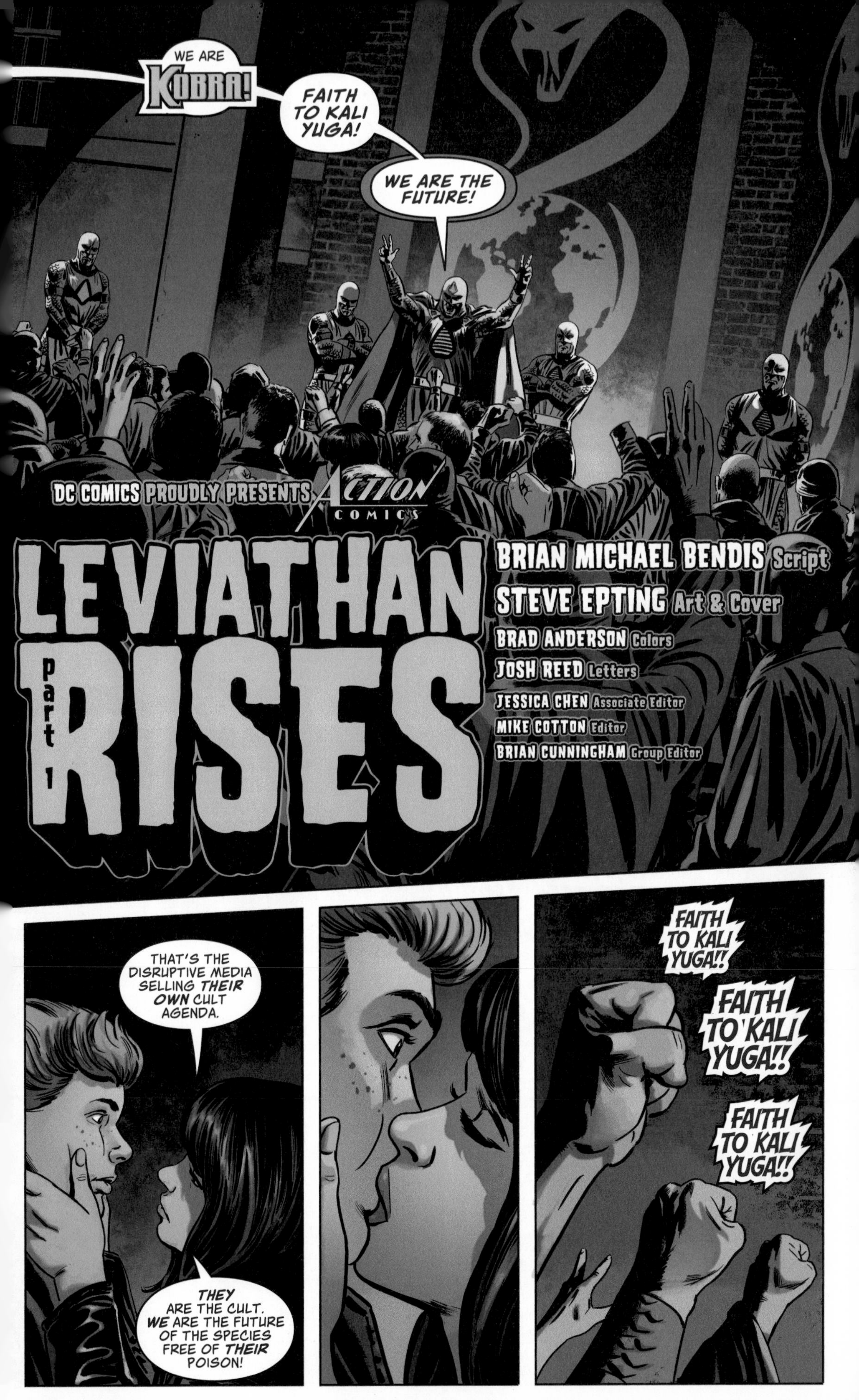
WE ARE KOBRA!
FAITH TO KALI YUGA!
WE ARE THE FUTURE!
DC COMICS PROUDLY PRESENTS ACTION COMICS
LEVIATHAN RISES part 1
BRIAN MICHAEL BENDIS Script
STEVE EPTING Art & Cover
BRAD ANDERSON Colors
JOSH REED Letters
JESSICA CHEN Associate Editor
MIKE COTTON Editor
BRIAN CUNNINGHAM Group Editor
THAT'S THE DISRUPTIVE MEDIA SELLING THEIR OWN CULT AGENDA.
THEY ARE THE CULT. WE ARE THE FUTURE OF THE SPECIES FREE OF THEIR POISON!
FAITH TO KALI YUGA!!
FAITH TO KALI YUGA!!
FAITH TO KALI YUGA!!

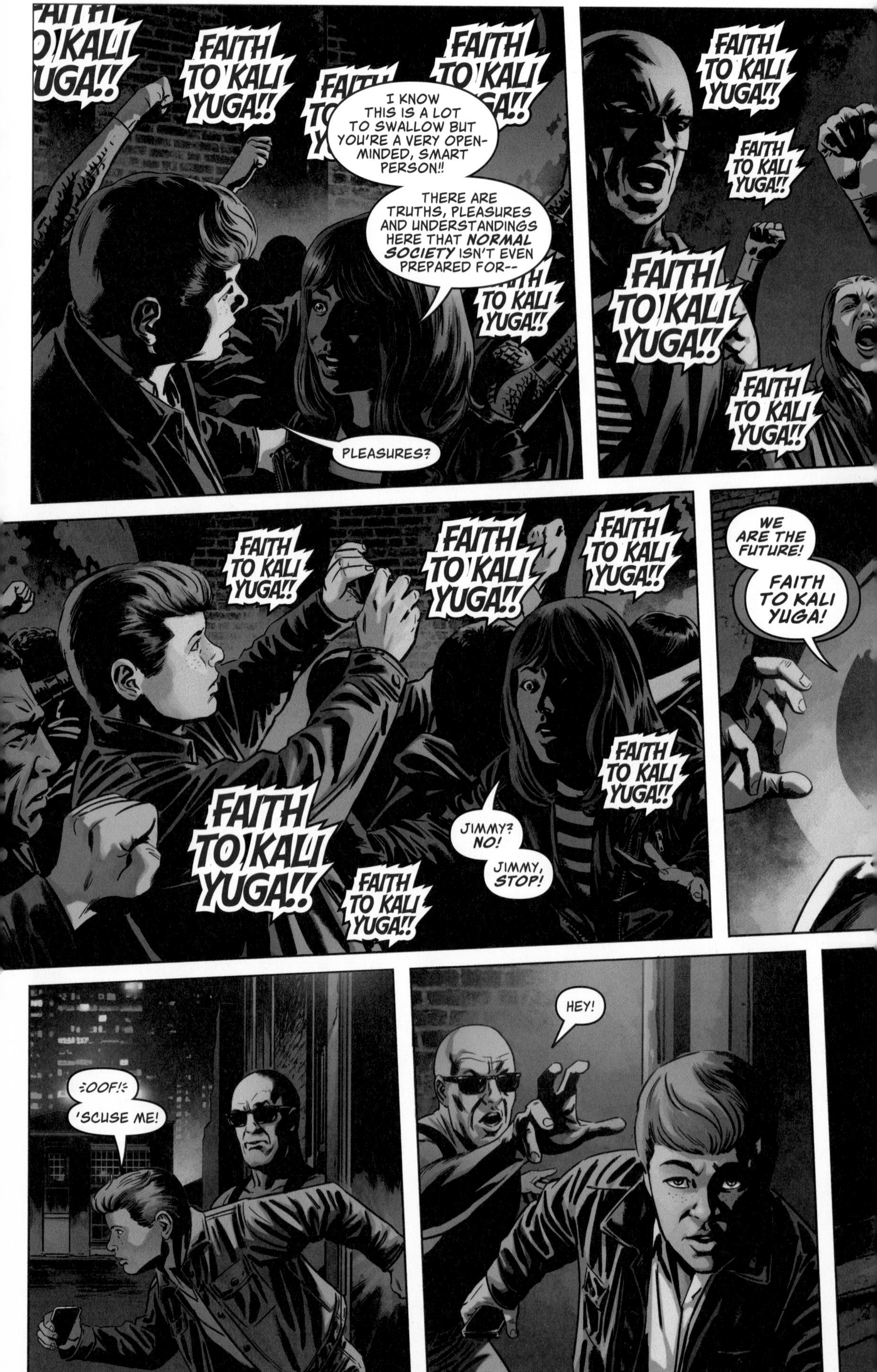
FAITH TO KALI YUGA!!
FAITH TO KALI YUGA!!
FAITH TO KALI YUGA!!
I KNOW THIS IS A LOT TO SWALLOW BUT YOU'RE A VERY OPEN-MINDED, SMART PERSON!!
THERE ARE TRUTHS, PLEASURES AND UNDERSTANDINGS HERE THAT NORMAL SOCIETY ISN'T EVEN PREPARED FOR--
FAITH TO KALI YUGA!!
PLEASURES?
FAITH TO KALI YUGA!!
FAITH TO KALI YUGA!!
FAITH TO KALI YUGA!!
FAITH TO KALI YUGA!!
FAITH TO KALI YUGA!!
FAITH TO KALI YUGA!!
FAITH TO KALI YUGA!!
FAITH TO KALI YUGA!!
FAITH TO KALI YUGA!!
JIMMY? NO!
JIMMY, STOP!
FAITH TO KALI YUGA!!
WE ARE THE FUTURE!
FAITH TO KALI YUGA!
OOF!
'SCUSE ME!
HEY!

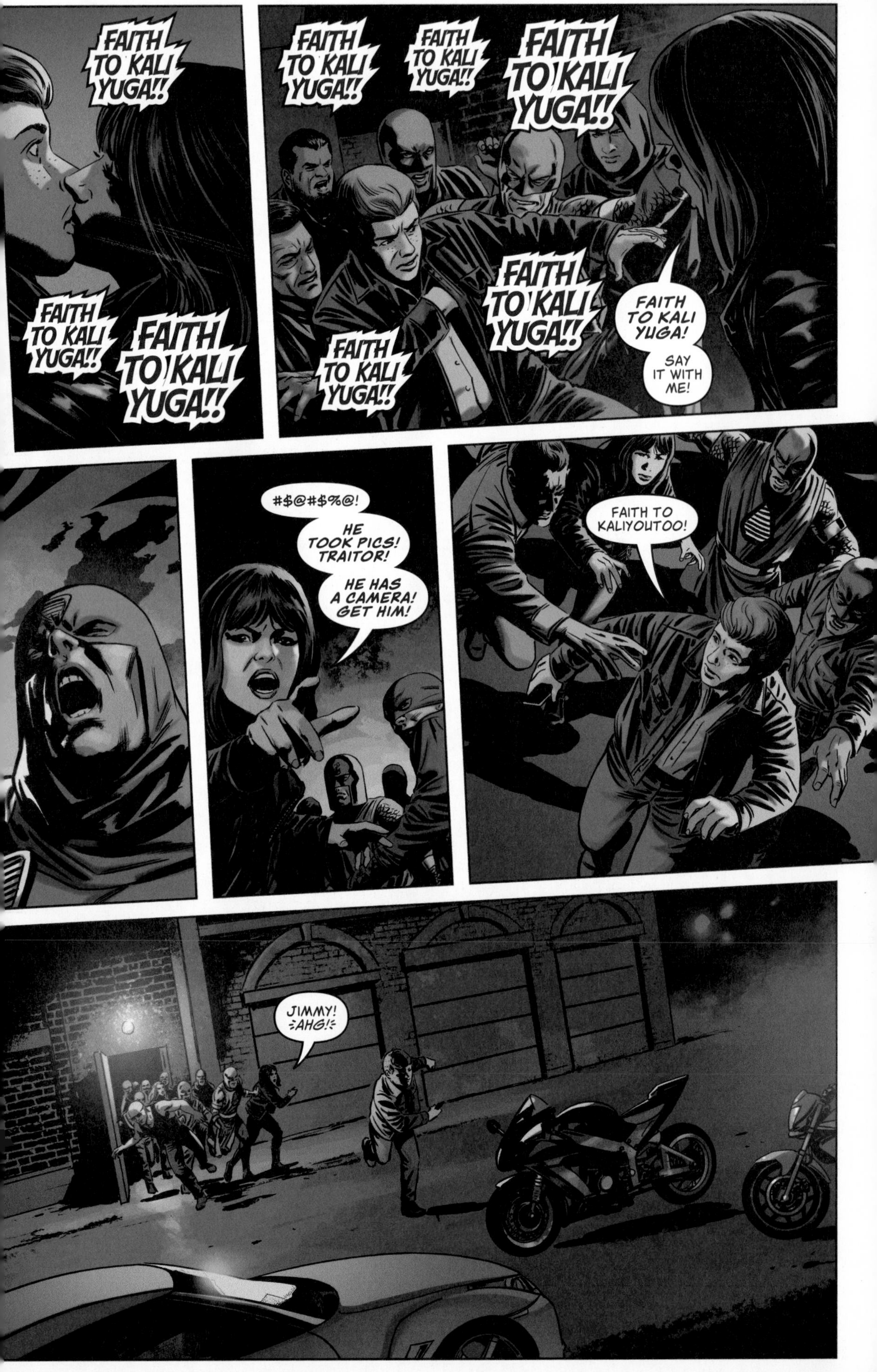
FAITH TO KALI YUGA!!
FAITH TO KALI YUGA!!
FAITH TO KALI YUGA!!
FAITH TO KALI YUGA!!
FAITH TO KALI YUGA!!
FAITH TO KALI YUGA!!
FAITH TO KALI YUGA!!
FAITH TO KALI YUGA!!
FAITH TO KALI YUGA!
SAY IT WITH ME!
#$@#$%@!
HE TOOK PICS! TRAITOR!
HE HAS A CAMERA! GET HIM!
FAITH TO KALIYOUTOO!
JIMMY!
AHG!

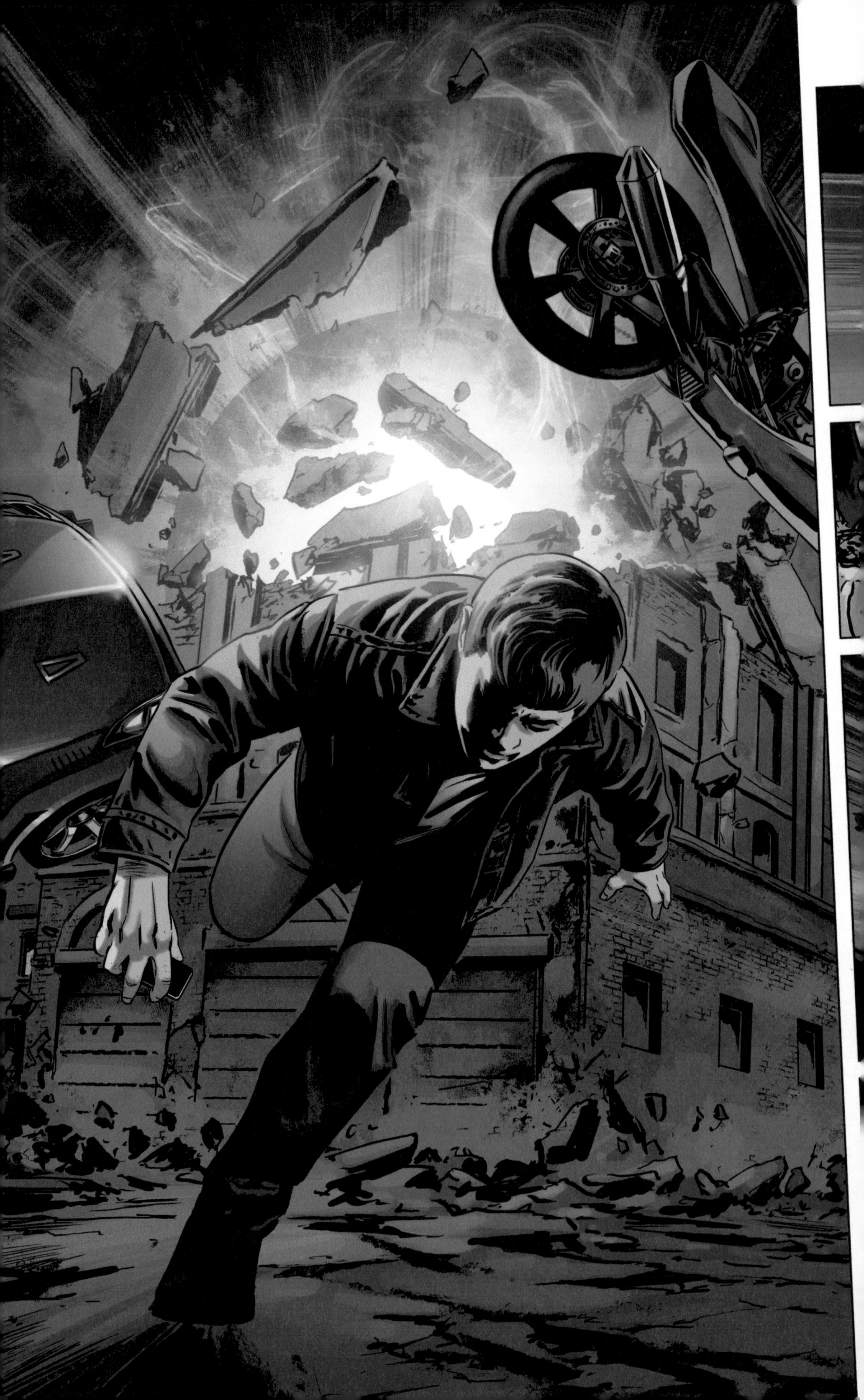

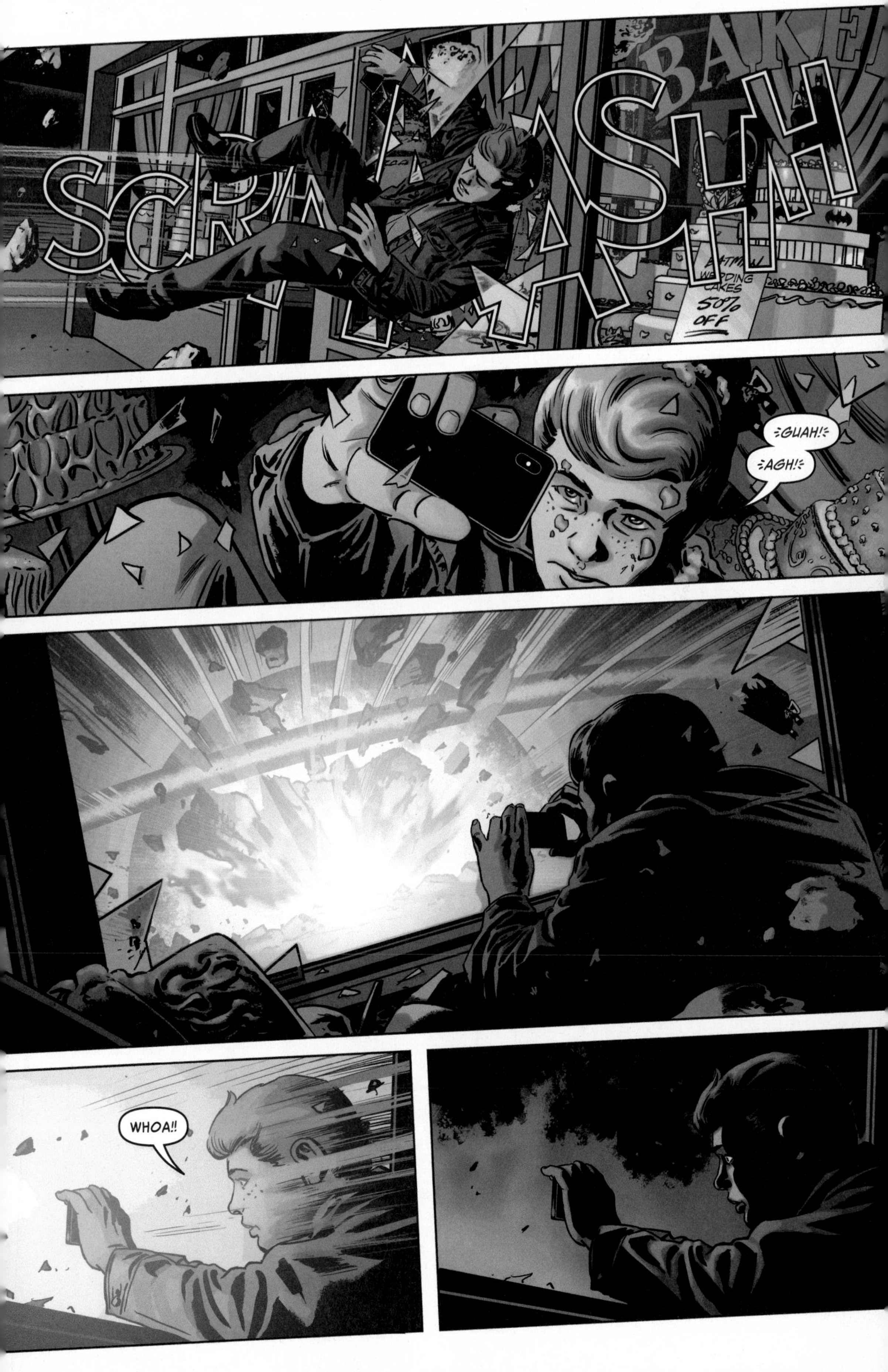
SCRAASHH
WEDDING CAKES 50% OFF
GUAH!
AGH!
WHOA!!

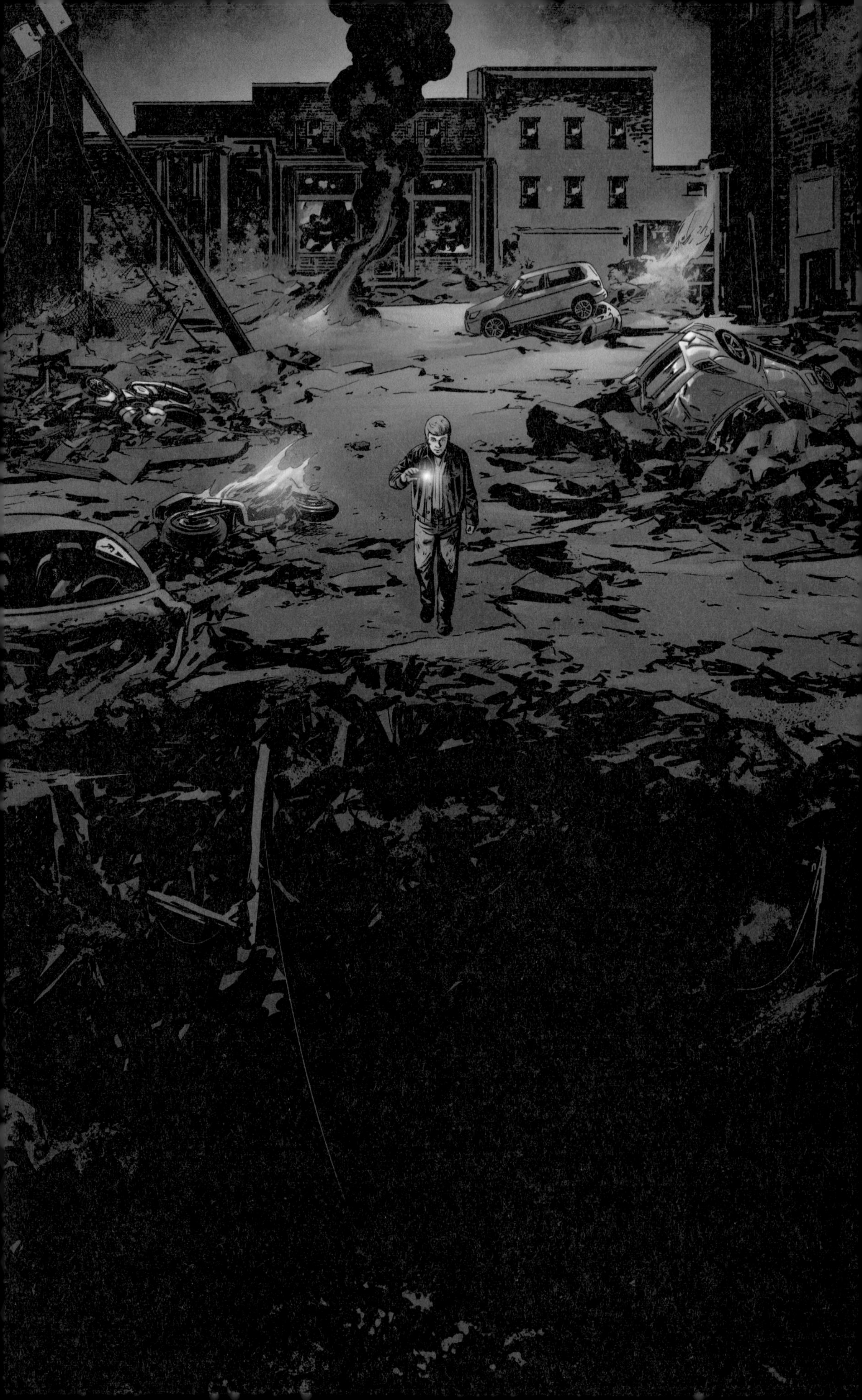

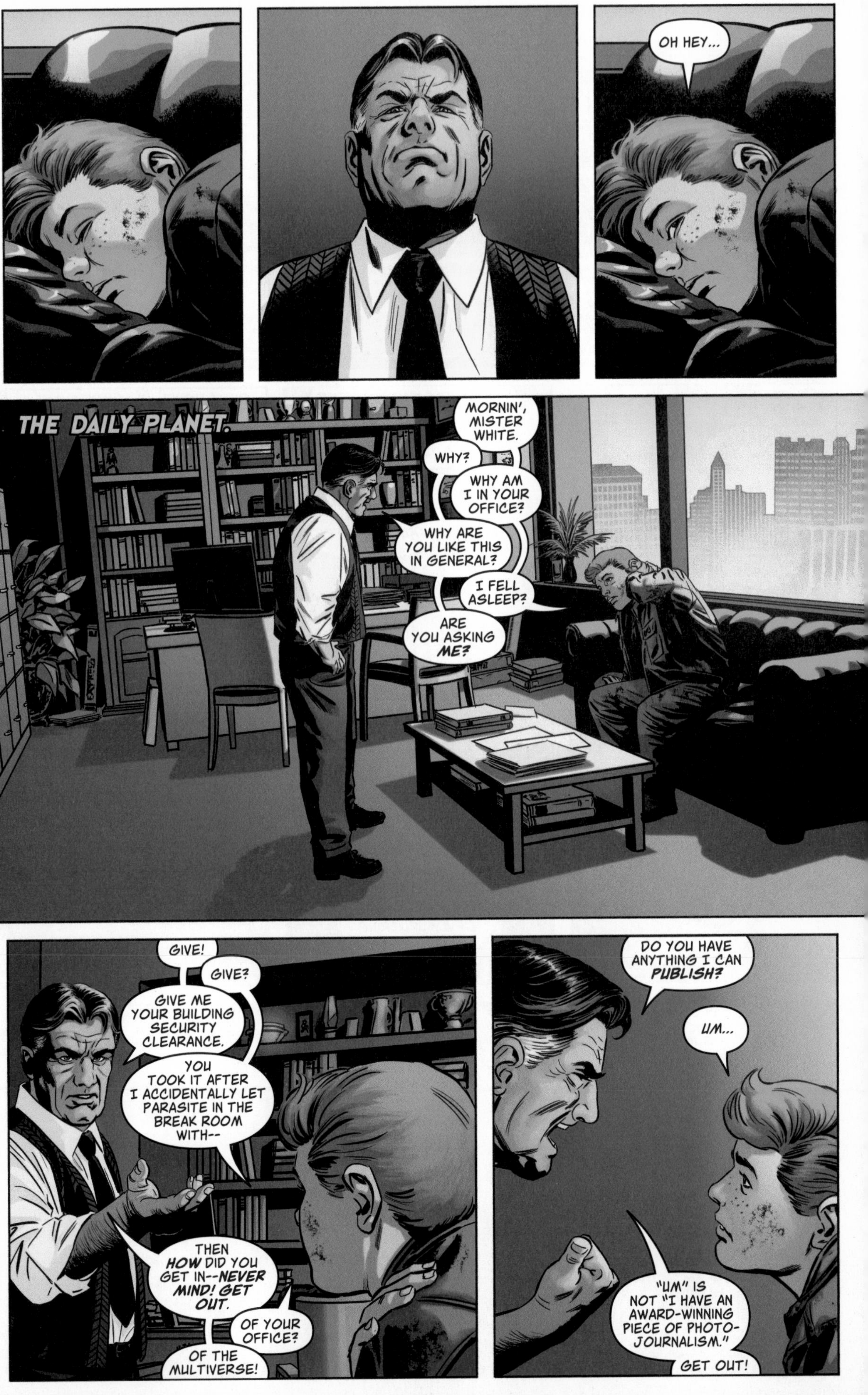
OH HEY...
THE DAILY PLANET.
MORNIN', MISTER WHITE.
WHY?
WHY AM I IN YOUR OFFICE?
WHY ARE YOU LIKE THIS IN GENERAL?
I FELL ASLEEP?
ARE YOU ASKING ME?
GIVE!
GIVE?
GIVE ME YOUR BUILDING SECURITY CLEARANCE.
YOU TOOK IT AFTER I ACCIDENTALLY LET PARASITE IN THE BREAK ROOM WITH--
THEN HOW DID YOU GET IN--NEVER MIND! GET OUT.
OF YOUR OFFICE?
OF THE MULTIVERSE!
DO YOU HAVE ANYTHING I CAN PUBLISH?
UM...
"UM" IS NOT "I HAVE AN AWARD-WINNING PIECE OF PHOTO-JOURNALISM."
GET OUT!

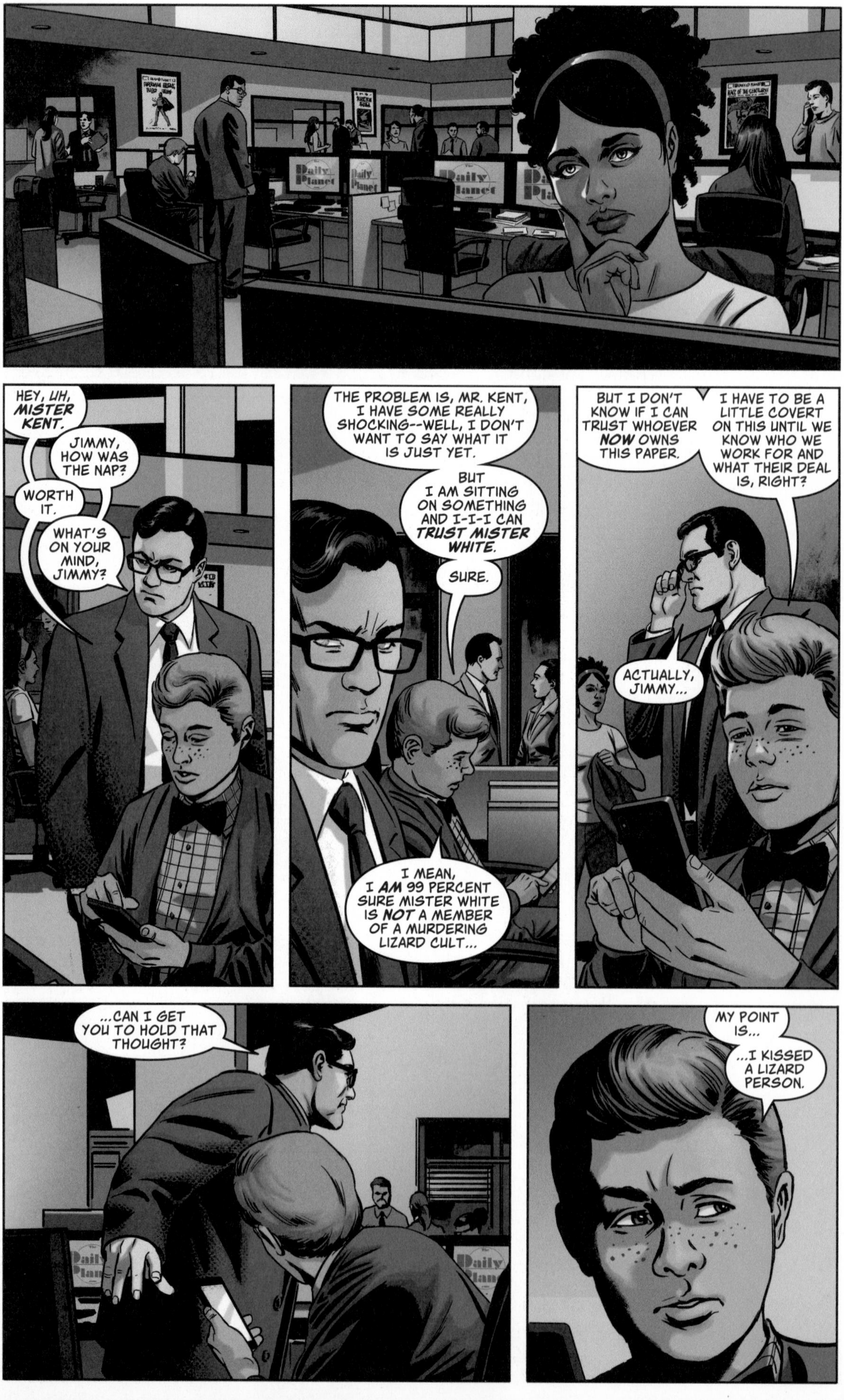
HEY, UH, MISTER KENT.
JIMMY, HOW WAS THE NAP?
WORTH IT.
WHAT'S ON YOUR MIND, JIMMY?
THE PROBLEM IS, MR. KENT, I HAVE SOME REALLY SHOCKING--WELL, I DON'T WANT TO SAY WHAT IT IS JUST YET.
BUT I AM SITTING ON SOMETHING AND I-I-I CAN TRUST MISTER WHITE.
SURE.
I MEAN, I AM 99 PERCENT SURE MISTER WHITE IS NOT A MEMBER OF A MURDERING LIZARD CULT...
BUT I DON'T KNOW IF I CAN TRUST WHOEVER NOW OWNS THIS PAPER.
I HAVE TO BE A LITTLE COVERT ON THIS UNTIL WE KNOW WHO WE WORK FOR AND WHAT THEIR DEAL IS, RIGHT?
ACTUALLY, JIMMY...
...CAN I GET YOU TO HOLD THAT THOUGHT?
MY POINT IS...
...I KISSED A LIZARD PERSON.

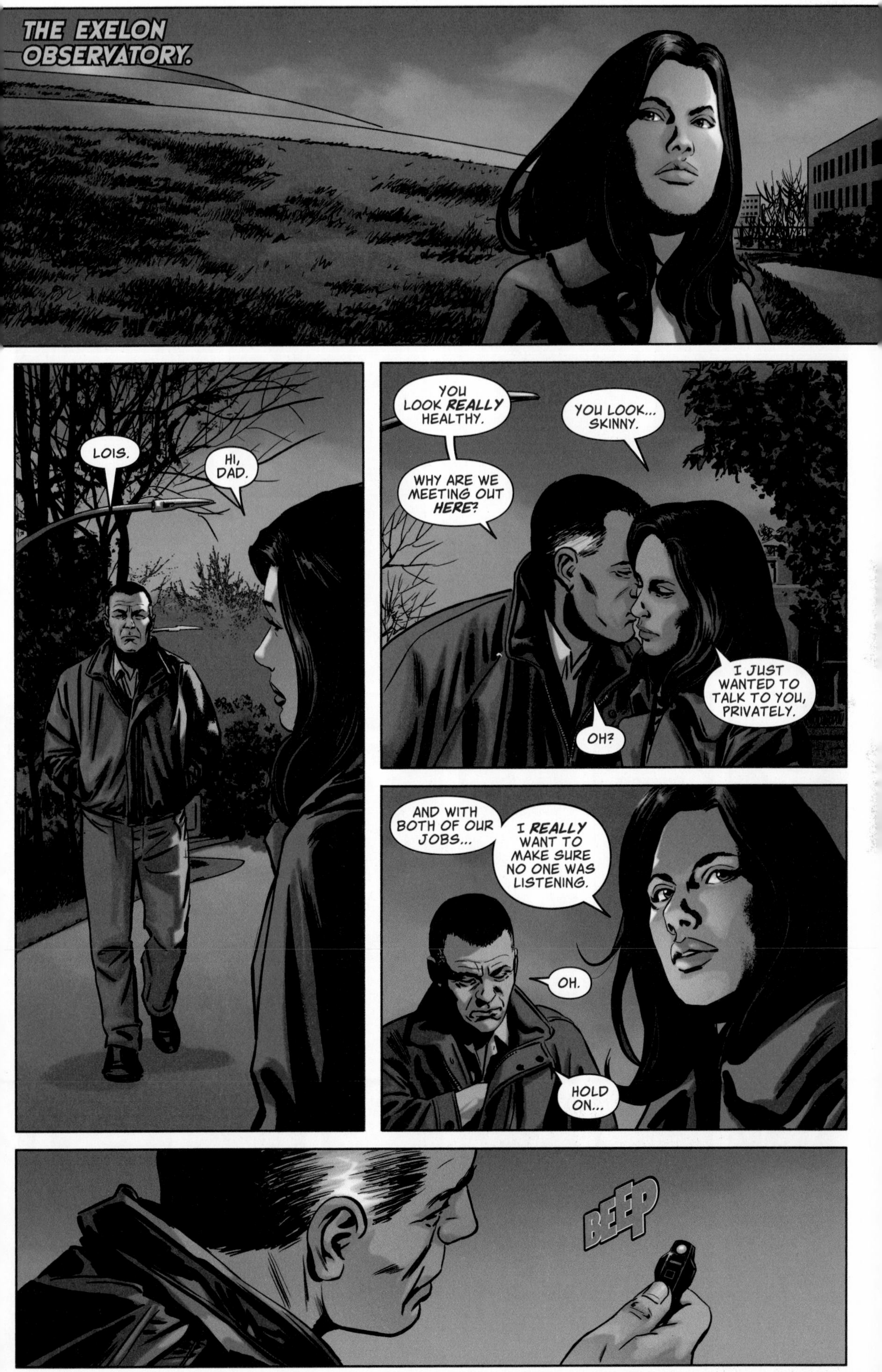
THE EXELON OBSERVATORY.
LOIS.
HI, DAD.
YOU LOOK REALLY HEALTHY.
WHY ARE WE MEETING OUT HERE?
YOU LOOK... SKINNY.
I JUST WANTED TO TALK TO YOU, PRIVATELY.
OH?
AND WITH BOTH OF OUR JOBS...
I REALLY WANT TO MAKE SURE NO ONE WAS LISTENING.
OH.
HOLD ON...
BEEP

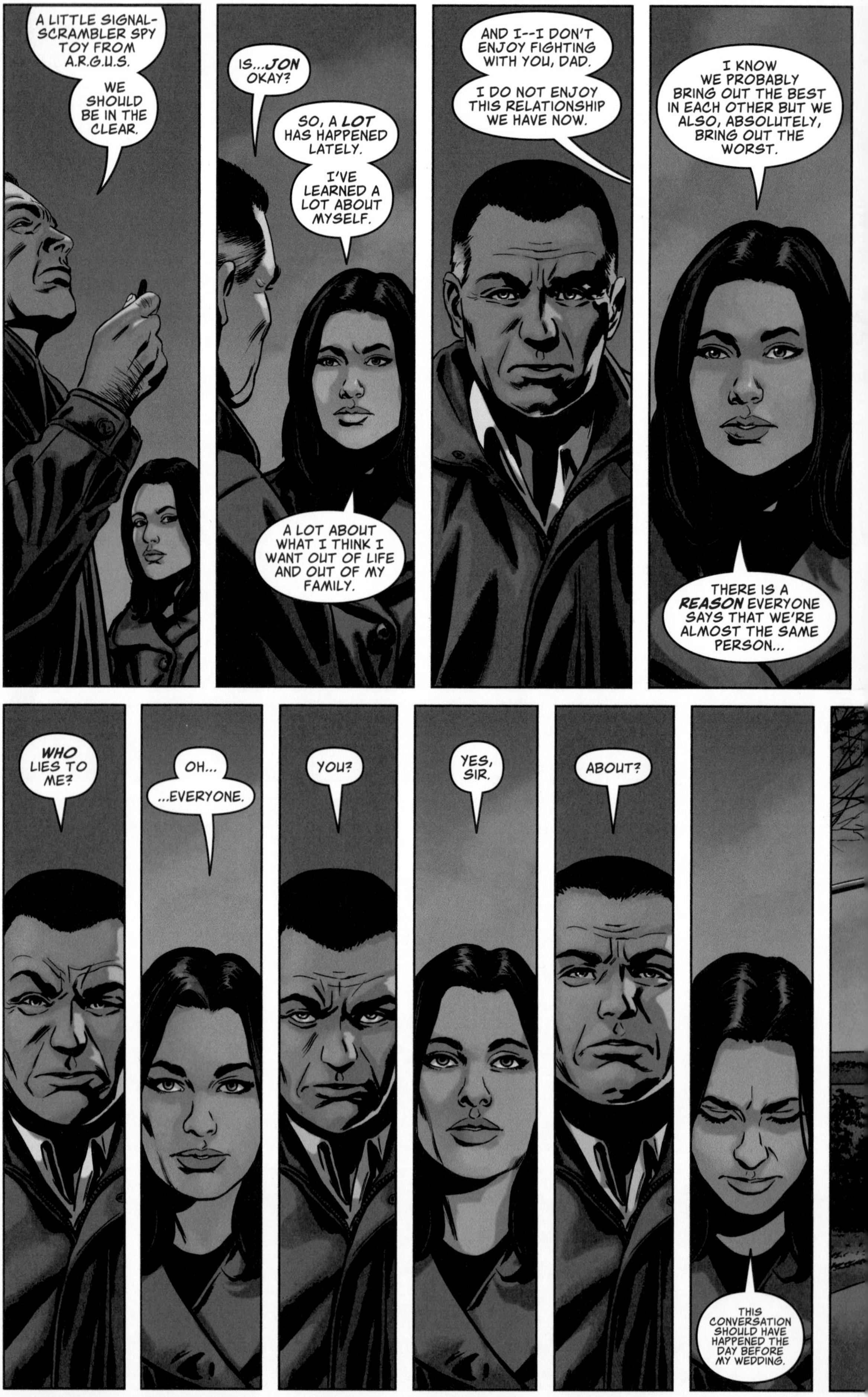
A LITTLE SIGNAL-SCRAMBLER SPY TOY FROM A.R.G.U.S.
WE SHOULD BE IN THE CLEAR.
IS...JON OKAY?
SO, A LOT HAS HAPPENED LATELY.
I'VE LEARNED A LOT ABOUT MYSELF.
A LOT ABOUT WHAT I THINK I WANT OUT OF LIFE AND OUT OF MY FAMILY.
AND I--I DON'T ENJOY FIGHTING WITH YOU, DAD.
I DO NOT ENJOY THIS RELATIONSHIP WE HAVE NOW.
I KNOW WE PROBABLY BRING OUT THE BEST IN EACH OTHER BUT WE ALSO, ABSOLUTELY, BRING OUT THE WORST.
THERE IS A REASON EVERYONE SAYS THAT WE'RE ALMOST THE SAME PERSON...
WHO LIES TO ME?
OH...
...EVERYONE.
YOU?
YES, SIR.
ABOUT?
THIS CONVERSATION SHOULD HAVE HAPPENED THE DAY BEFORE MY WEDDING.

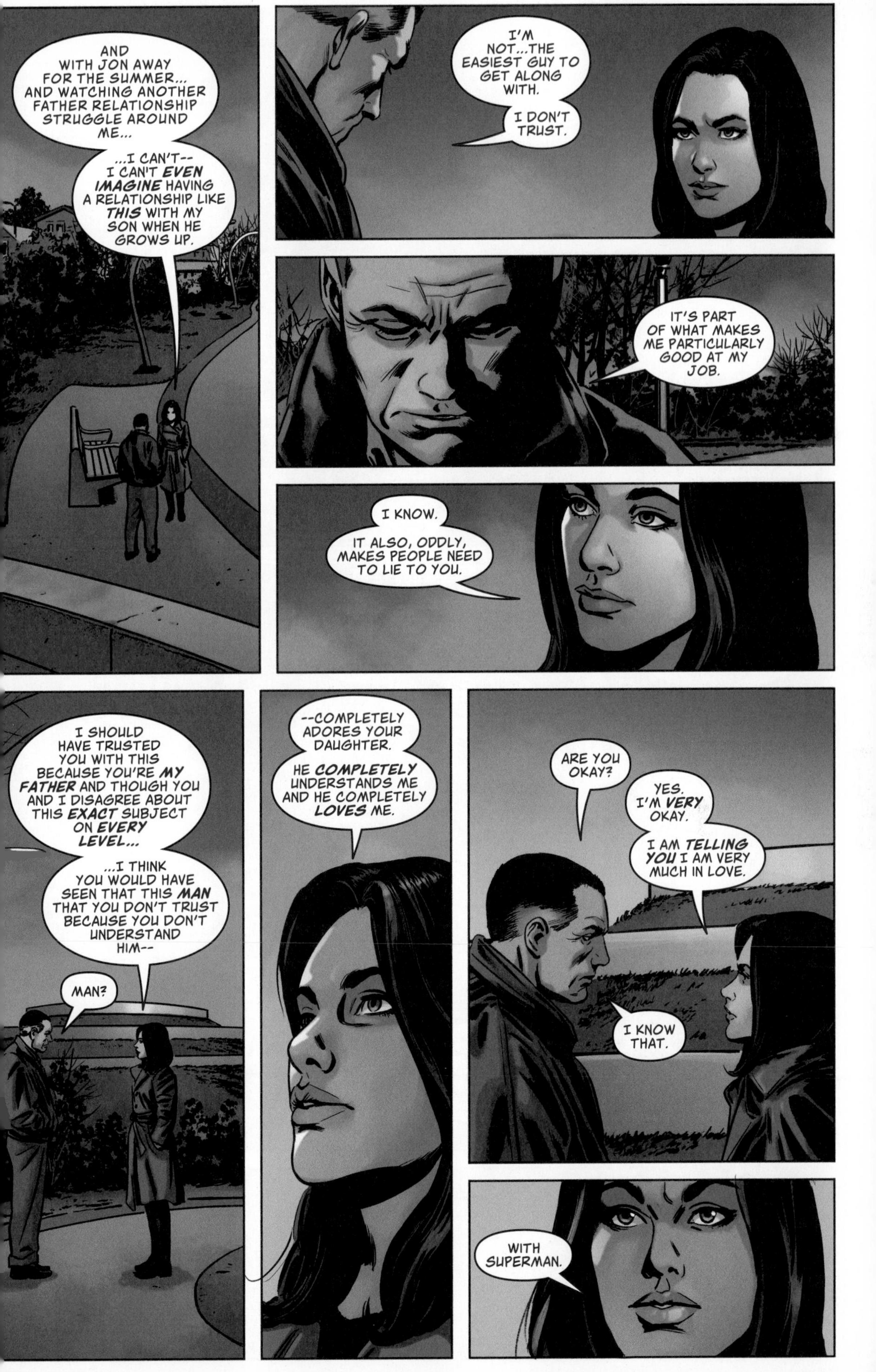
AND WITH JON AWAY FOR THE SUMMER... AND WATCHING ANOTHER FATHER RELATIONSHIP STRUGGLE AROUND ME...
...I CAN'T-- I CAN'T EVEN IMAGINE HAVING A RELATIONSHIP LIKE THIS WITH MY SON WHEN HE GROWS UP.
I'M NOT...THE EASIEST GUY TO GET ALONG WITH.
I DON'T TRUST.
IT'S PART OF WHAT MAKES ME PARTICULARLY GOOD AT MY JOB.
I KNOW.
IT ALSO, ODDLY, MAKES PEOPLE NEED TO LIE TO YOU.
I SHOULD HAVE TRUSTED YOU WITH THIS BECAUSE YOU'RE MY FATHER AND THOUGH YOU AND I DISAGREE ABOUT THIS EXACT SUBJECT ON EVERY LEVEL...
...I THINK YOU WOULD HAVE SEEN THAT THIS MAN THAT YOU DON'T TRUST BECAUSE YOU DON'T UNDERSTAND HIM--
MAN?
--COMPLETELY ADORES YOUR DAUGHTER.
HE COMPLETELY UNDERSTANDS ME AND HE COMPLETELY LOVES ME.
ARE YOU OKAY?
YES. I'M VERY OKAY.
I AM TELLING YOU I AM VERY MUCH IN LOVE.
I KNOW THAT.
WITH SUPERMAN.

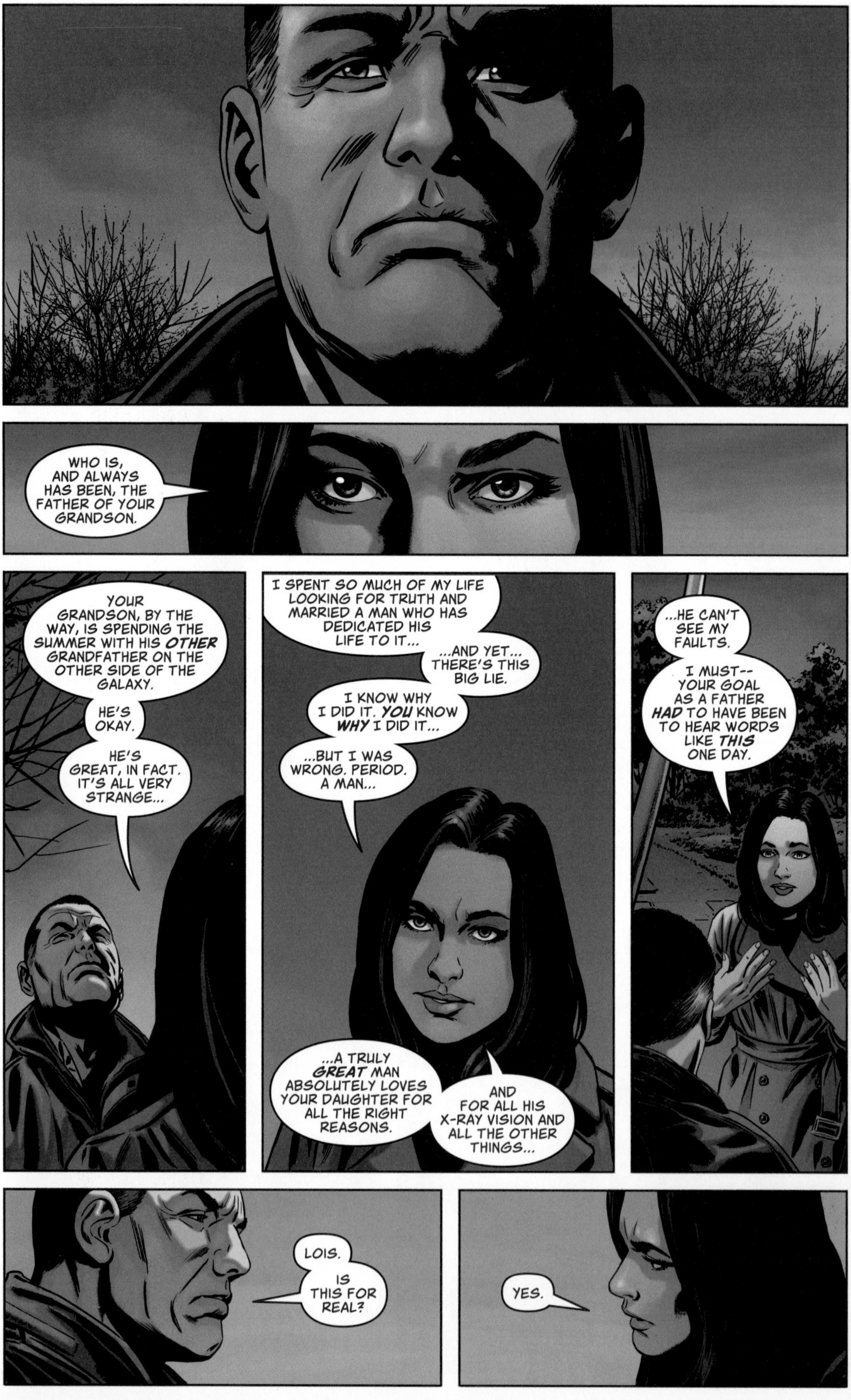
WHO IS, AND ALWAYS HAS BEEN, THE FATHER OF YOUR GRANDSON.
YOUR GRANDSON, BY THE WAY, IS SPENDING THE SUMMER WITH HIS OTHER GRANDFATHER ON THE OTHER SIDE OF THE GALAXY.
HE'S OKAY.
HE'S GREAT, IN FACT. IT'S ALL VERY STRANGE...
I SPENT SO MUCH OF MY LIFE LOOKING FOR TRUTH AND MARRIED A MAN WHO HAS DEDICATED HIS LIFE TO IT...
...AND YET... THERE'S THIS BIG LIE.
I KNOW WHY I DID IT. YOU KNOW WHY I DID IT...
...BUT I WAS WRONG. PERIOD. A MAN...
...A TRULY GREAT MAN ABSOLUTELY LOVES YOUR DAUGHTER FOR ALL THE RIGHT REASONS.
AND FOR ALL HIS X-RAY VISION AND ALL THE OTHER THINGS...
...HE CAN'T SEE MY FAULTS.
I MUST-- YOUR GOAL AS A FATHER HAD TO HAVE BEEN TO HEAR WORDS LIKE THIS ONE DAY.
LOIS.
IS THIS FOR REAL?
YES.

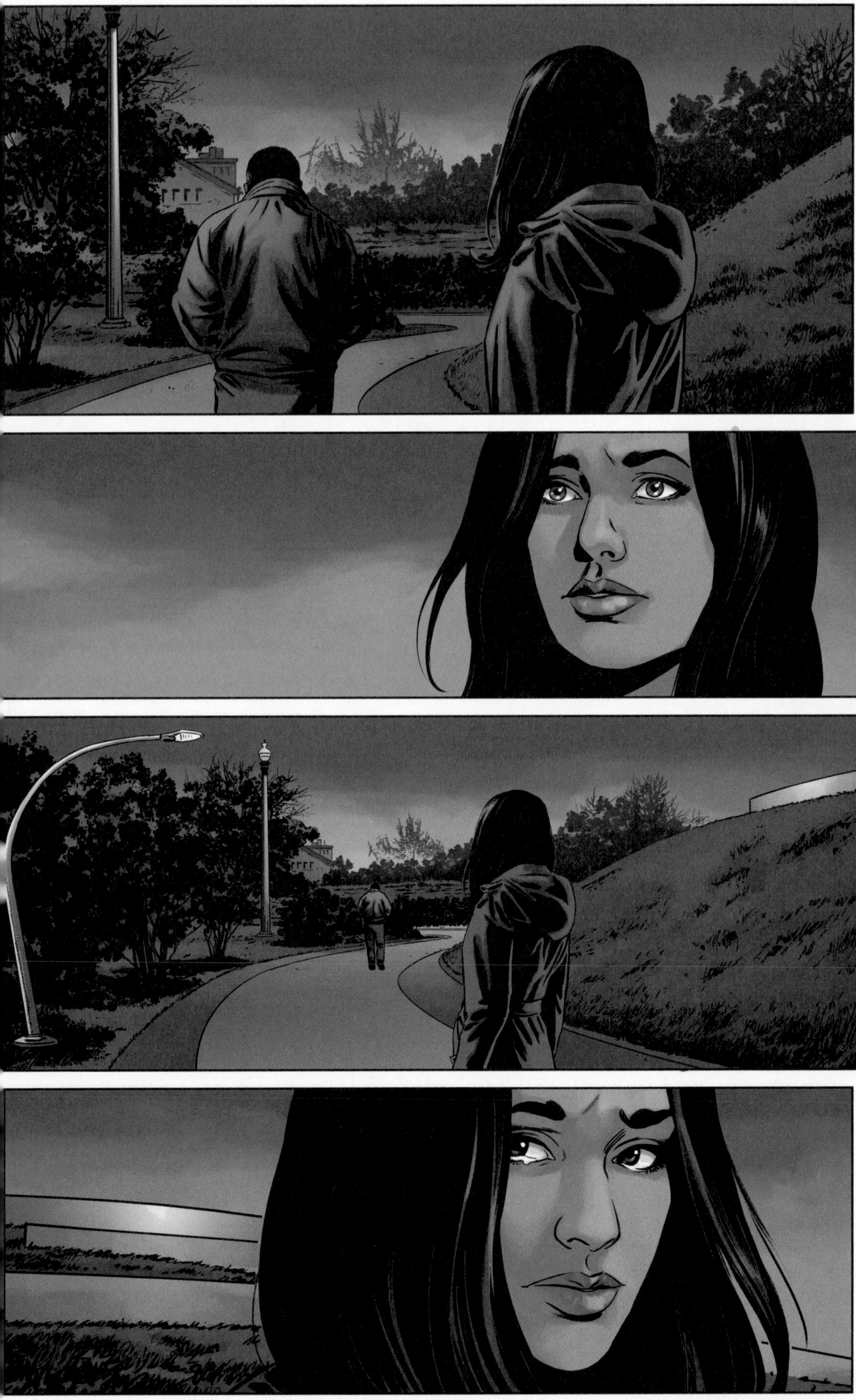

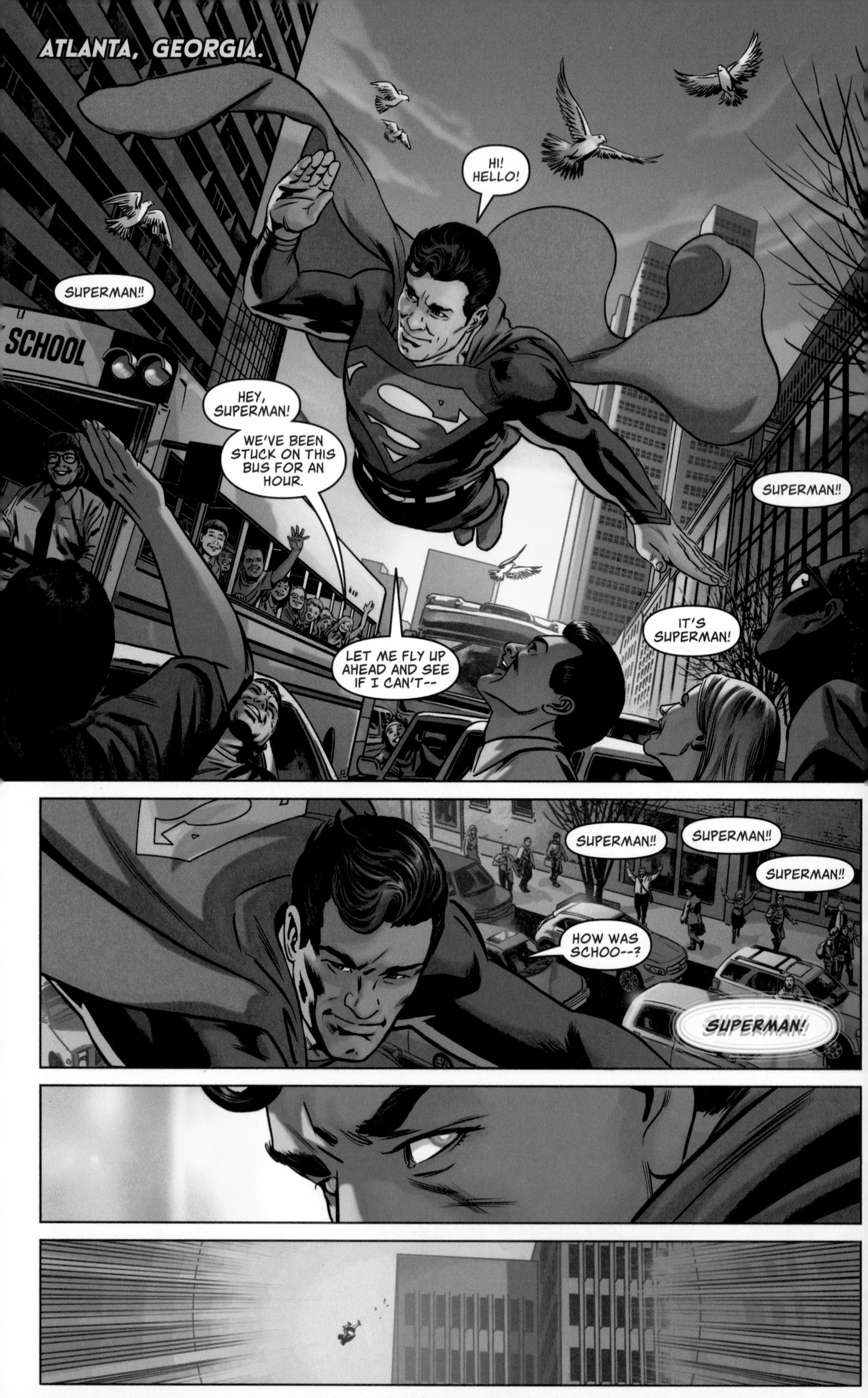
ATLANTA, GEORGIA.
SCHOOL
HI! HELLO!
SUPERMAN!!
HEY, SUPERMAN!
WE'VE BEEN STUCK ON THIS BUS FOR AN HOUR.
LET ME FLY UP AHEAD AND SEE IF I CAN'T--
IT'S SUPERMAN!
SUPERMAN!!
SUPERMAN!!
SUPERMAN!!
SUPERMAN!!
HOW WAS SCHOO--?
SUPERMAN!

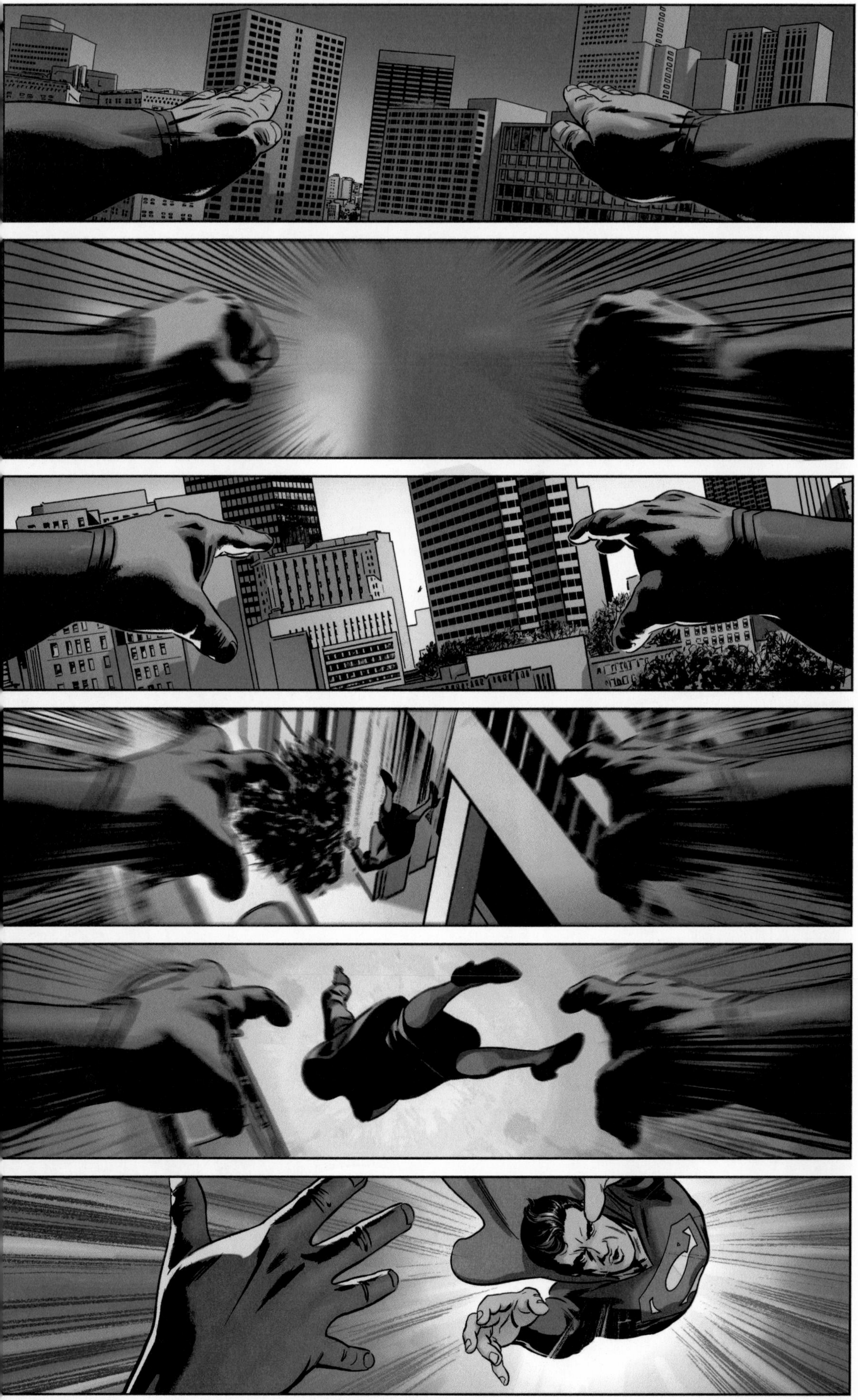

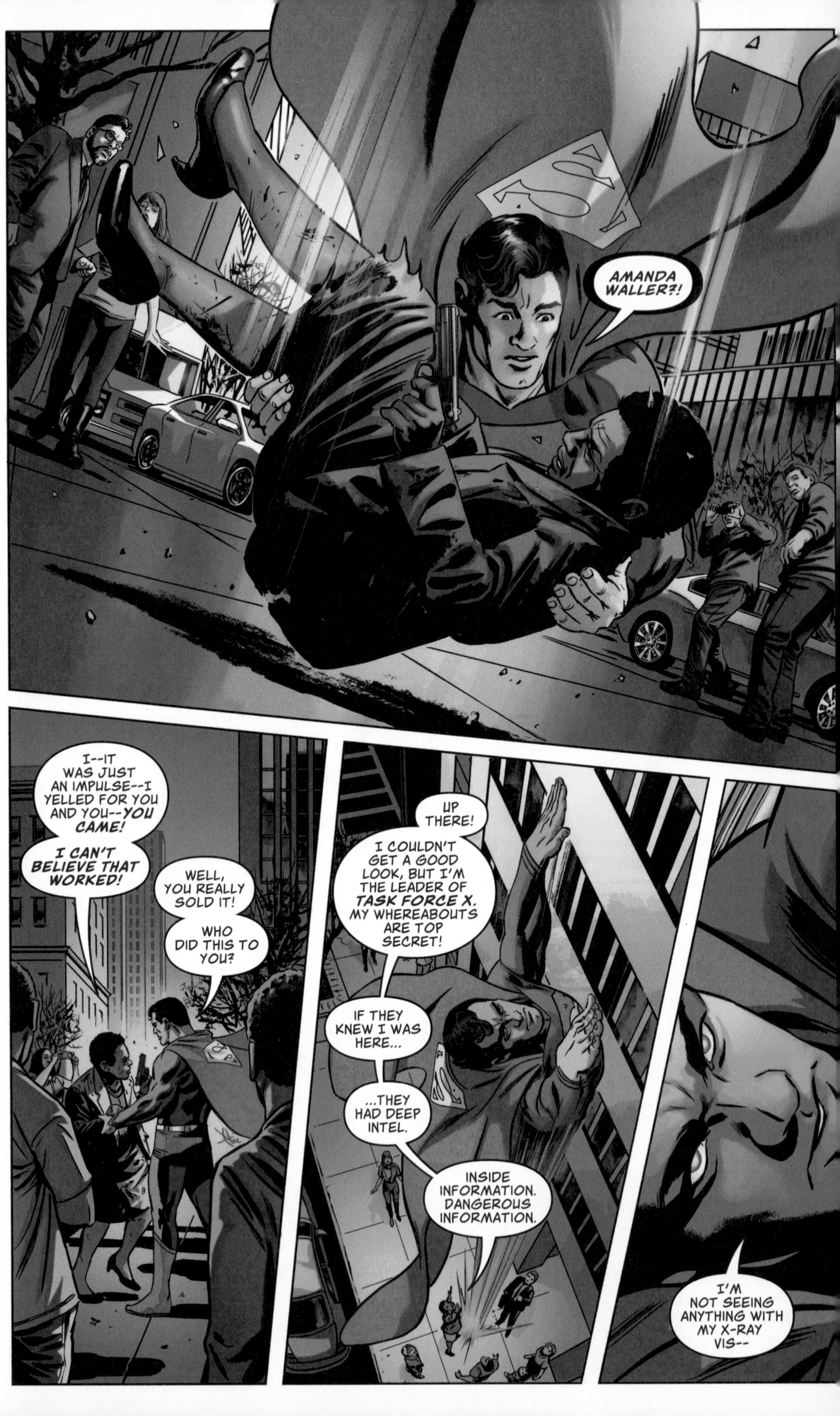

AMANDA WALLER?!
I--IT WAS JUST AN IMPULSE--I YELLED FOR YOU AND YOU--YOU CAME!
I CAN'T BELIEVE THAT WORKED!
WELL, YOU REALLY SOLD IT!
WHO DID THIS TO YOU?
UP THERE!
I COULDN'T GET A GOOD LOOK, BUT I'M THE LEADER OF TASK FORCE X. MY WHEREABOUTS ARE TOP SECRET!
IF THEY KNEW I WAS HERE...
...THEY HAD DEEP INTEL.
INSIDE INFORMATION. DANGEROUS INFORMATION.
I'M NOT SEEING ANYTHING WITH MY X-RAY VIS--

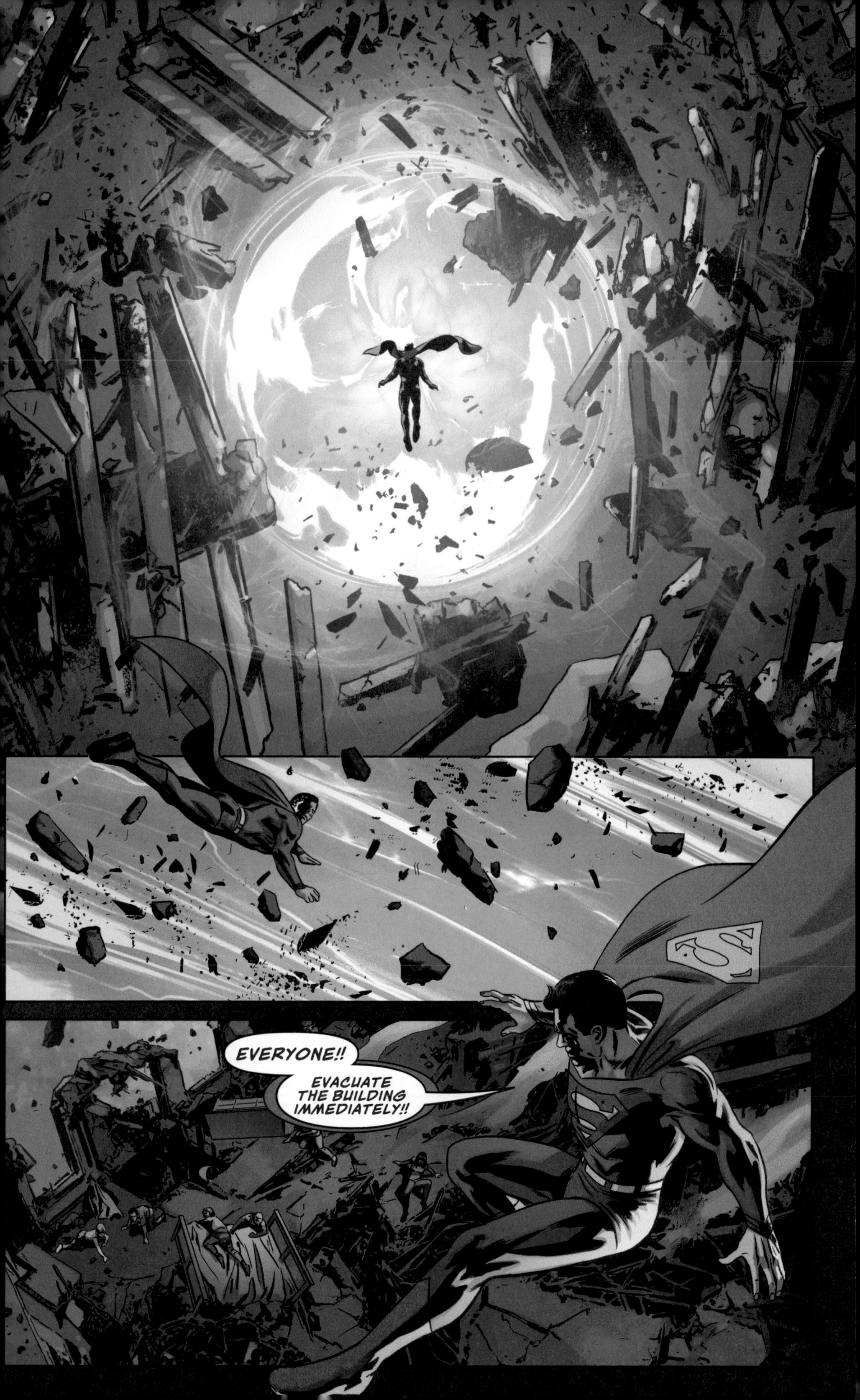
EVERYONE!!
EVACUATE THE BUILDING IMMEDIATELY!!

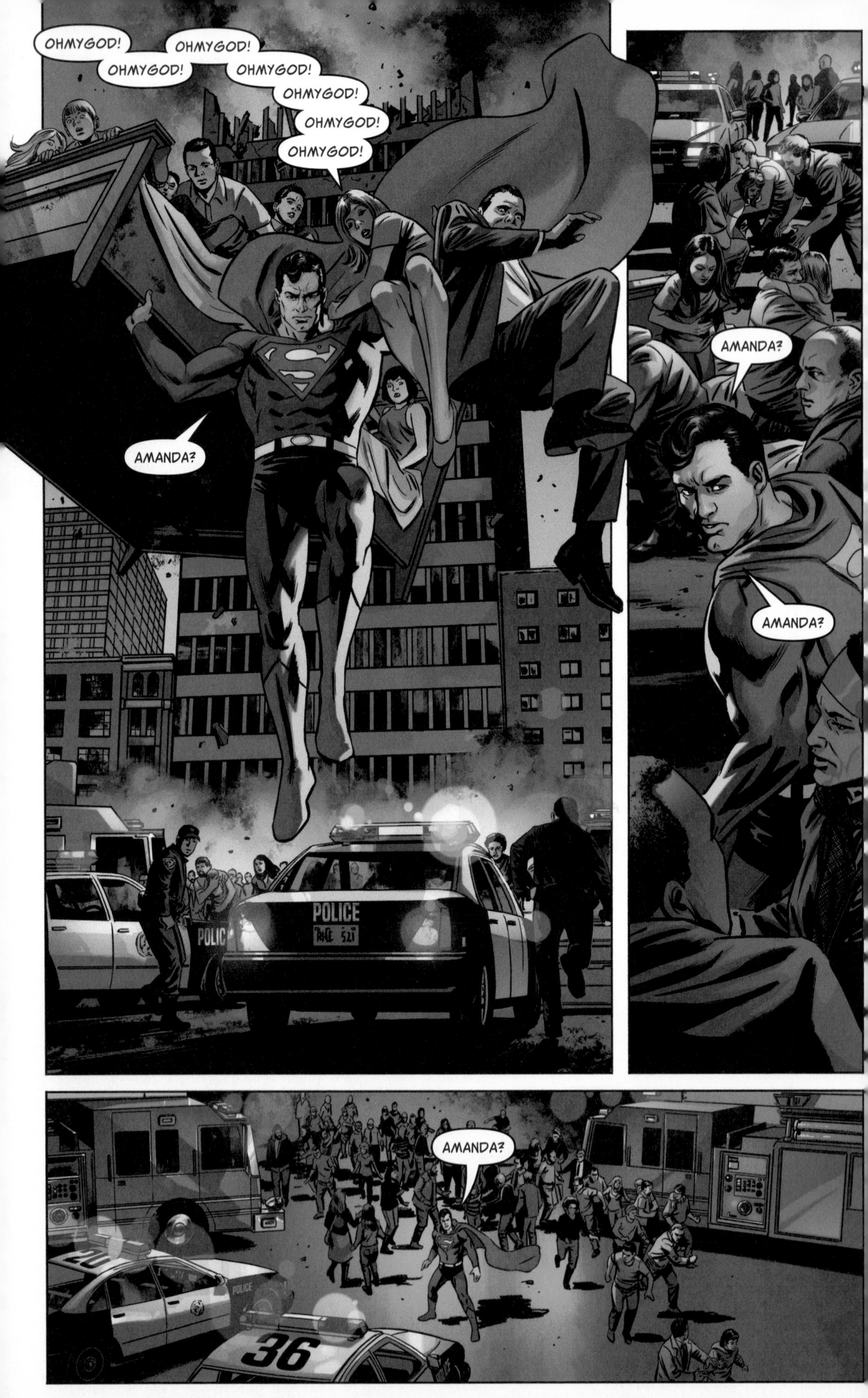
OHMYGOD!
OHMYGOD!
OHMYGOD!
OHMYGOD!
OHMYGOD!
OHMYGOD!
OHMYGOD!
AMANDA?
AMANDA?
AMANDA?
AMANDA?

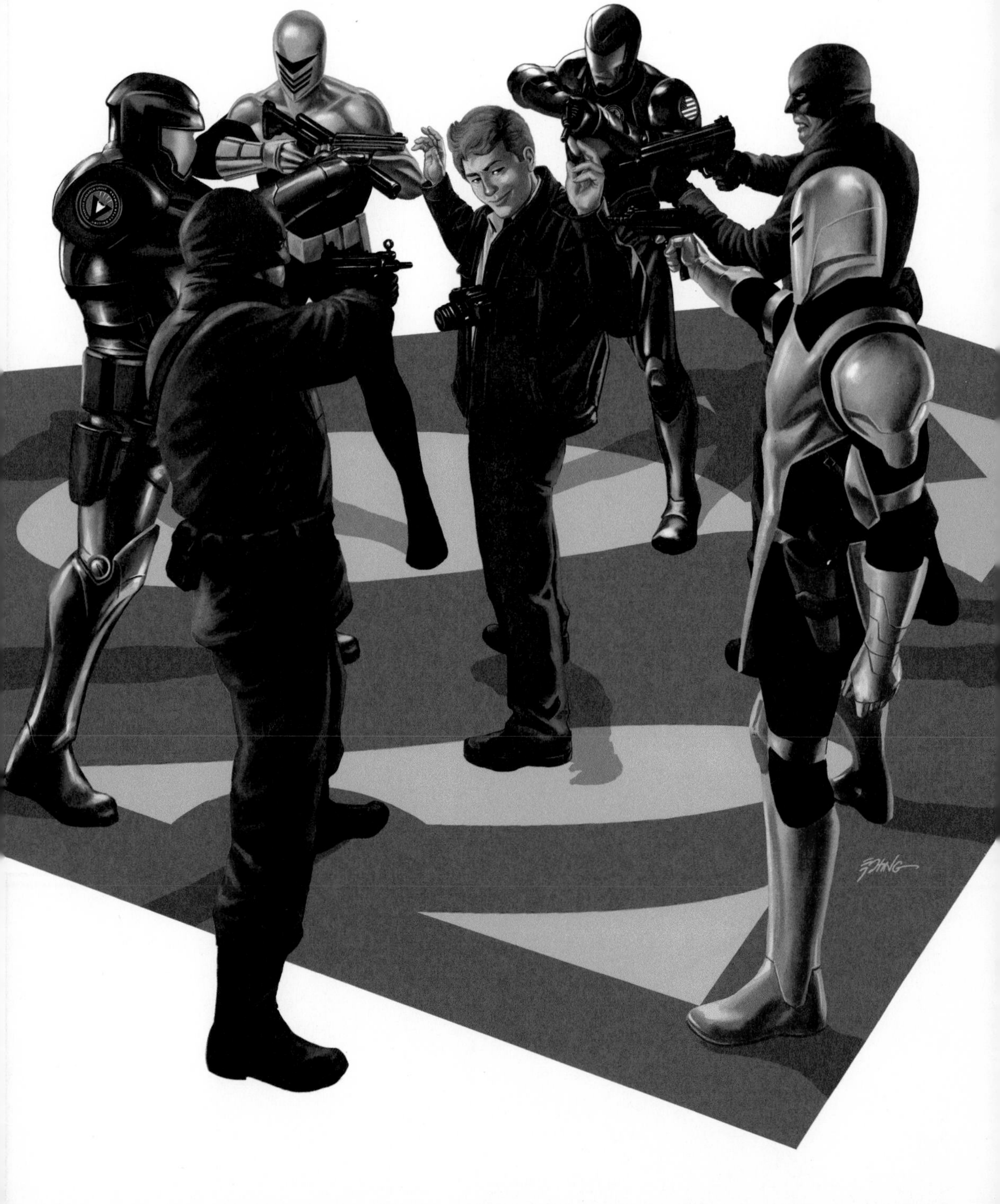

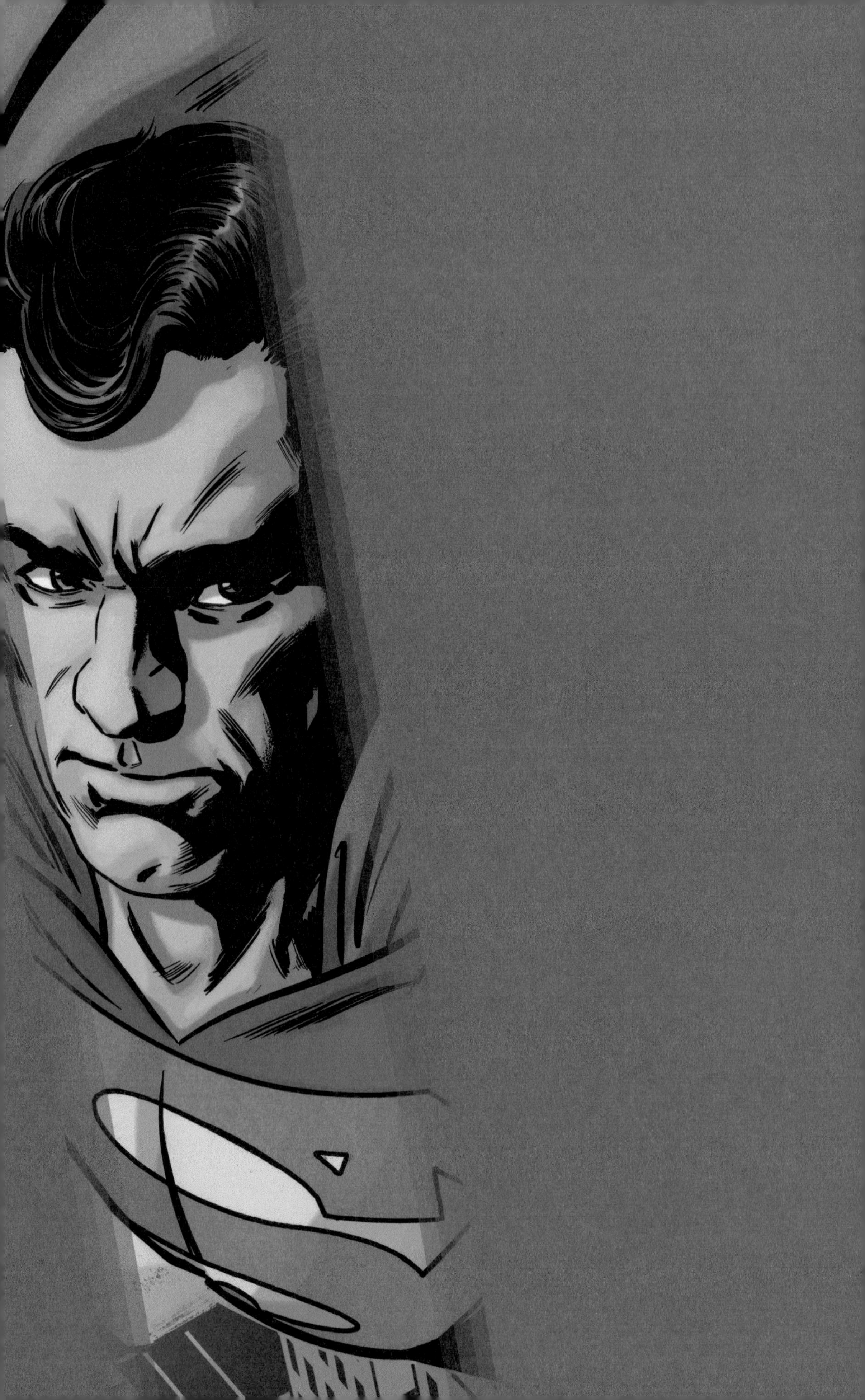

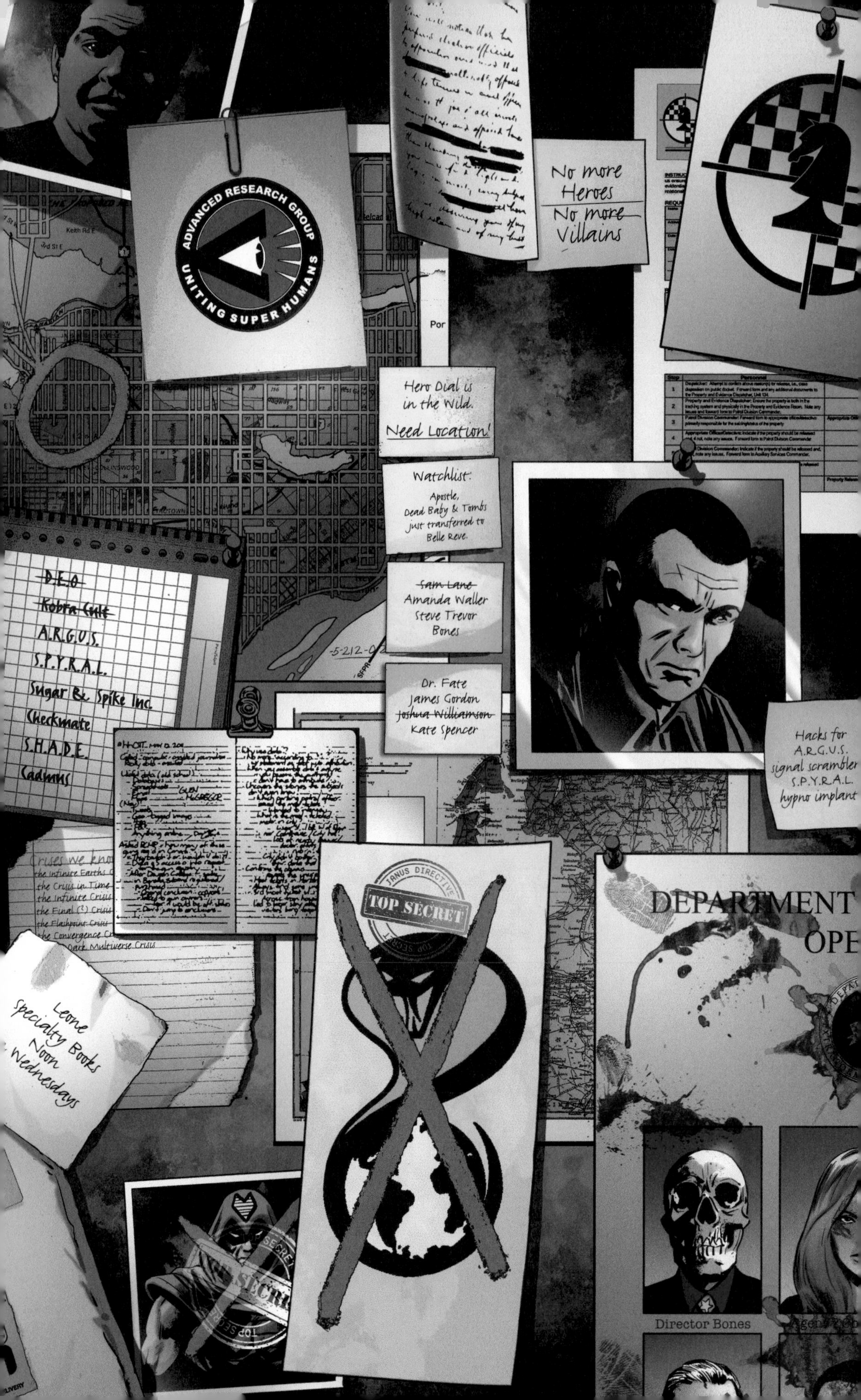

ADVANCED RESEARCH GROUP
UNITING SUPER HUMANS
No more Heroes
No more Villains
Hero Dial is in the Wild.
Need Location!
Watchlist:
Apostle, Dead Baby & Tombs just transferred to Belle Reve.
Sam Lane
Amanda Waller
Steve Trevor
Bones
Dr. Fate
James Gordon
Joshua Williamson
Kate Spencer
D.E.O
Kobra Cult
A.R.G.U.S.
S.P.Y.R.A.L.
Sugar & Spike Inc.
Checkmate
S.H.A.D.E.
Cadmus
Hacks for A.R.G.U.S. signal scrambler
S.P.Y.R.A.L. hypno implant
Leone Specialty Books
Noon Wednesdays
JANUS DIRECTIVE
TOP SECRET
DEPARTMENT
Director Bones

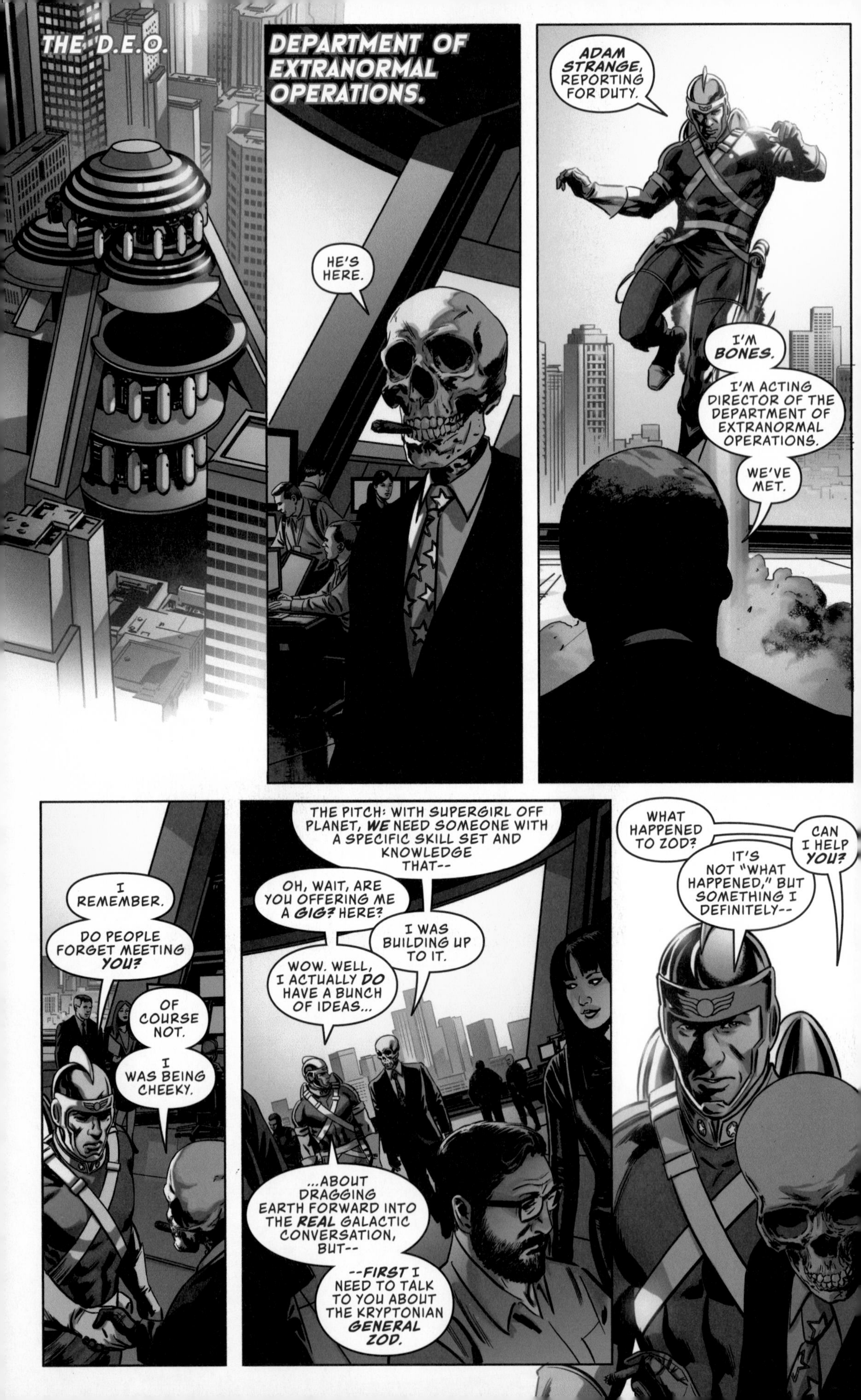
THE D.E.O.
DEPARTMENT OF EXTRANORMAL OPERATIONS.
HE'S HERE.
ADAM STRANGE, REPORTING FOR DUTY.
I'M BONES.
I'M ACTING DIRECTOR OF THE DEPARTMENT OF EXTRANORMAL OPERATIONS.
WE'VE MET.
I REMEMBER.
DO PEOPLE FORGET MEETING YOU?
OF COURSE NOT.
I WAS BEING CHEEKY.
THE PITCH: WITH SUPERGIRL OFF PLANET, WE NEED SOMEONE WITH A SPECIFIC SKILL SET AND KNOWLEDGE THAT--
OH, WAIT, ARE YOU OFFERING ME A GIG? HERE?
I WAS BUILDING UP TO IT.
WOW. WELL, I ACTUALLY DO HAVE A BUNCH OF IDEAS...
...ABOUT DRAGGING EARTH FORWARD INTO THE REAL GALACTIC CONVERSATION, BUT--
--FIRST I NEED TO TALK TO YOU ABOUT THE KRYPTONIAN GENERAL ZOD.
WHAT HAPPENED TO ZOD?
CAN I HELP YOU?
IT'S NOT "WHAT HAPPENED," BUT SOMETHING I DEFINITELY--

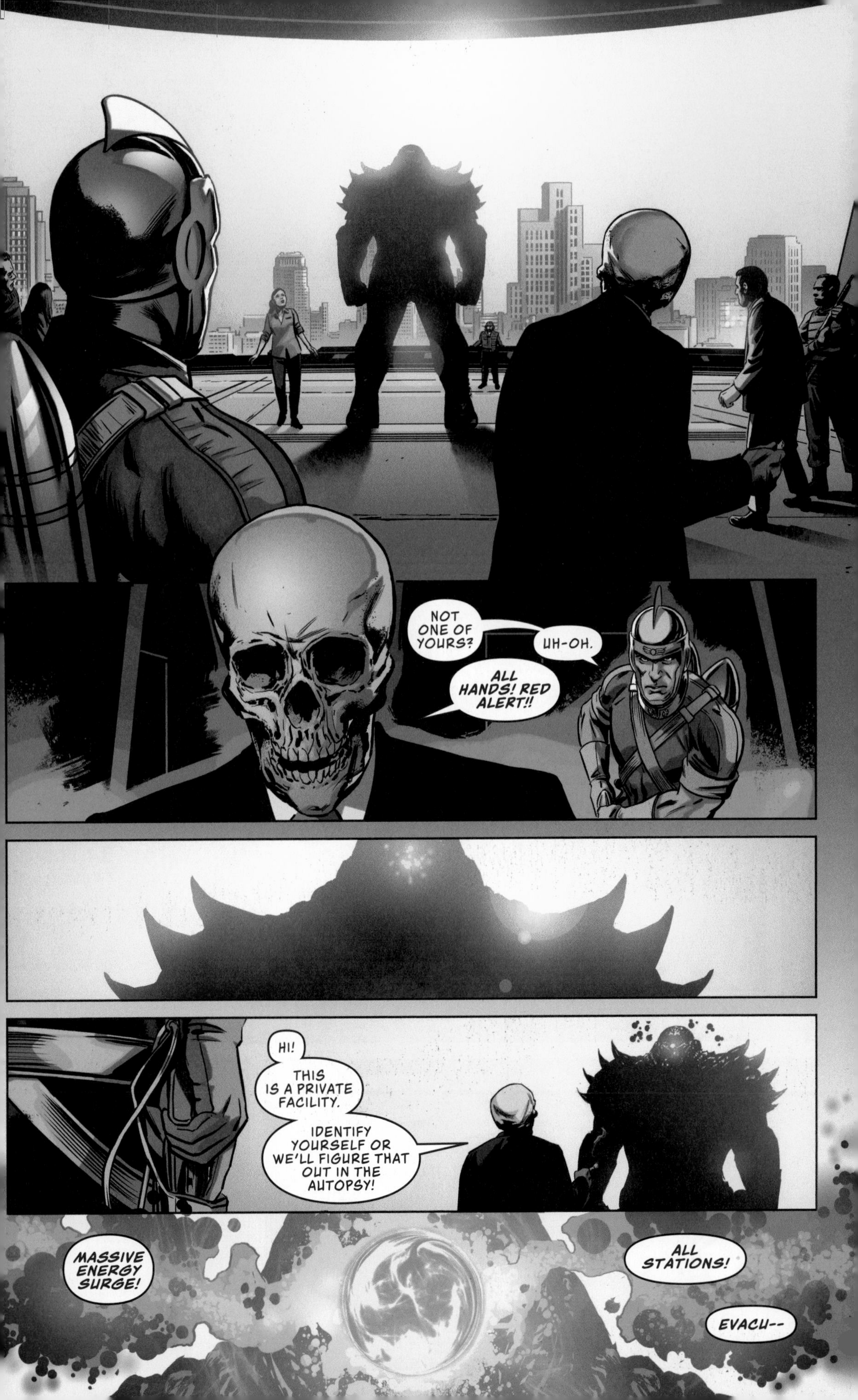
NOT ONE OF YOURS?
UH-OH.
ALL HANDS! RED ALERT!!
HI!
THIS IS A PRIVATE FACILITY.
IDENTIFY YOURSELF OR WE'LL FIGURE THAT OUT IN THE AUTOPSY!
MASSIVE ENERGY SURGE!
ALL STATIONS!
EVACU--

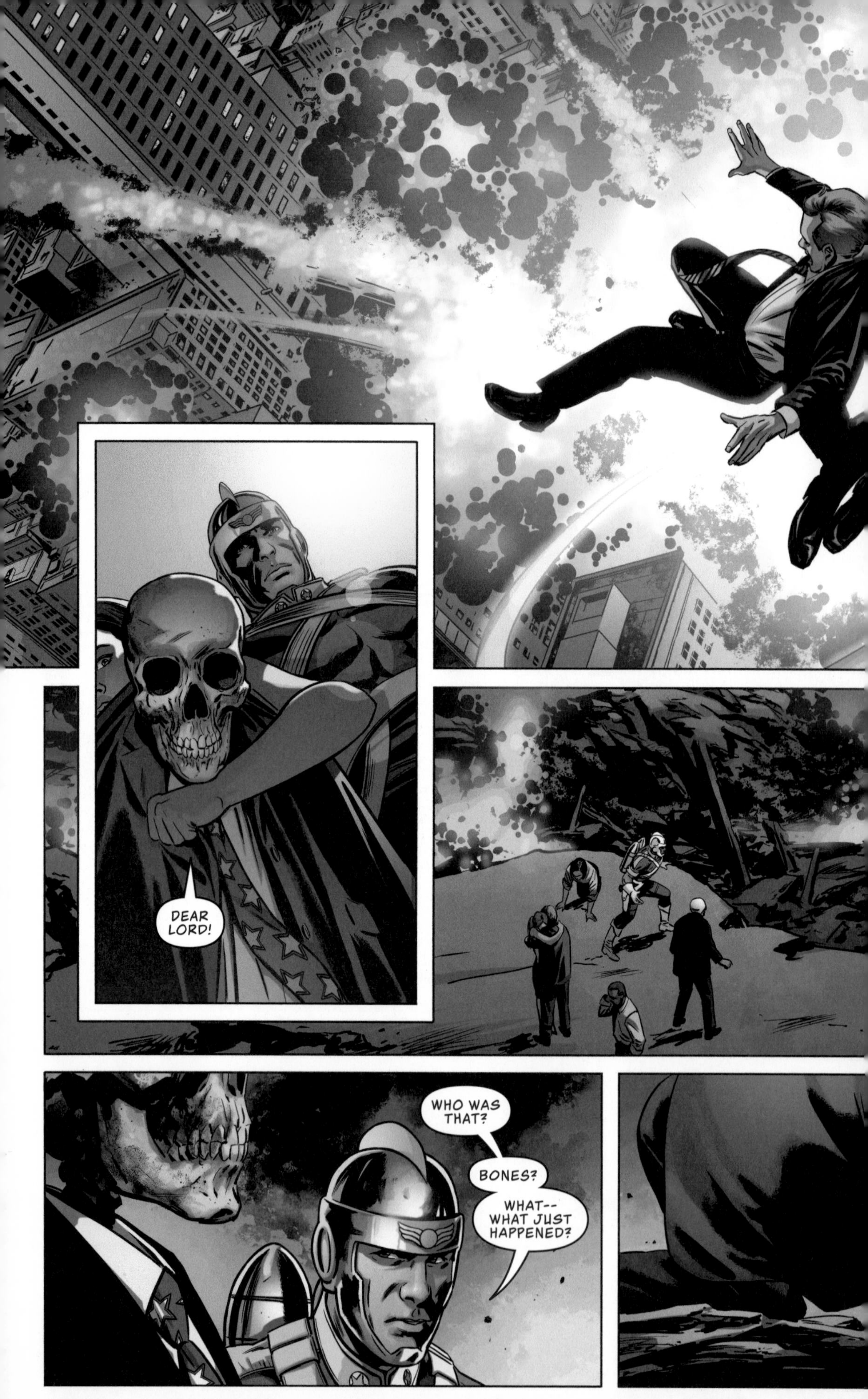
DEAR LORD!
WHO WAS THAT?
BONES?
WHAT-- WHAT JUST HAPPENED?

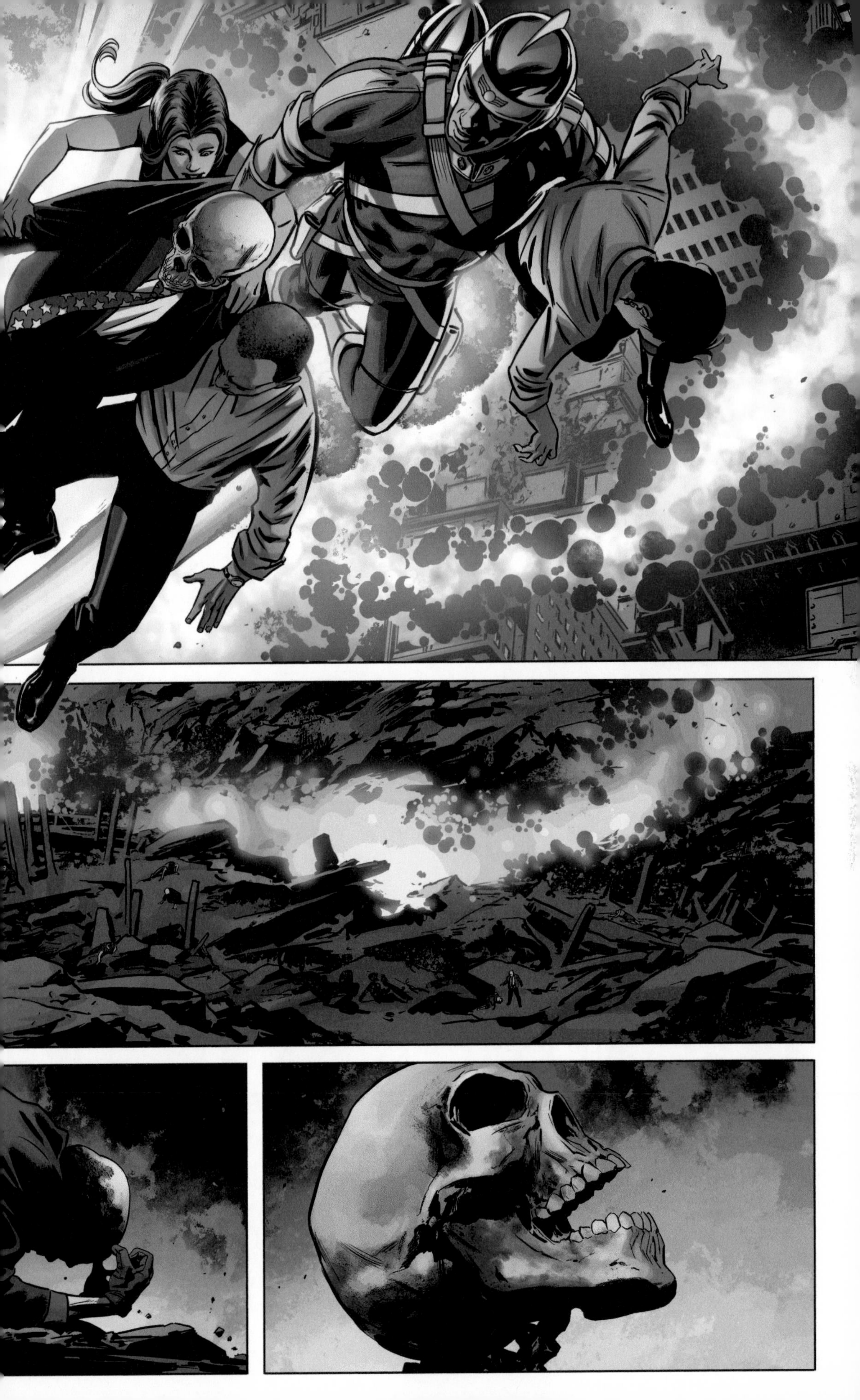

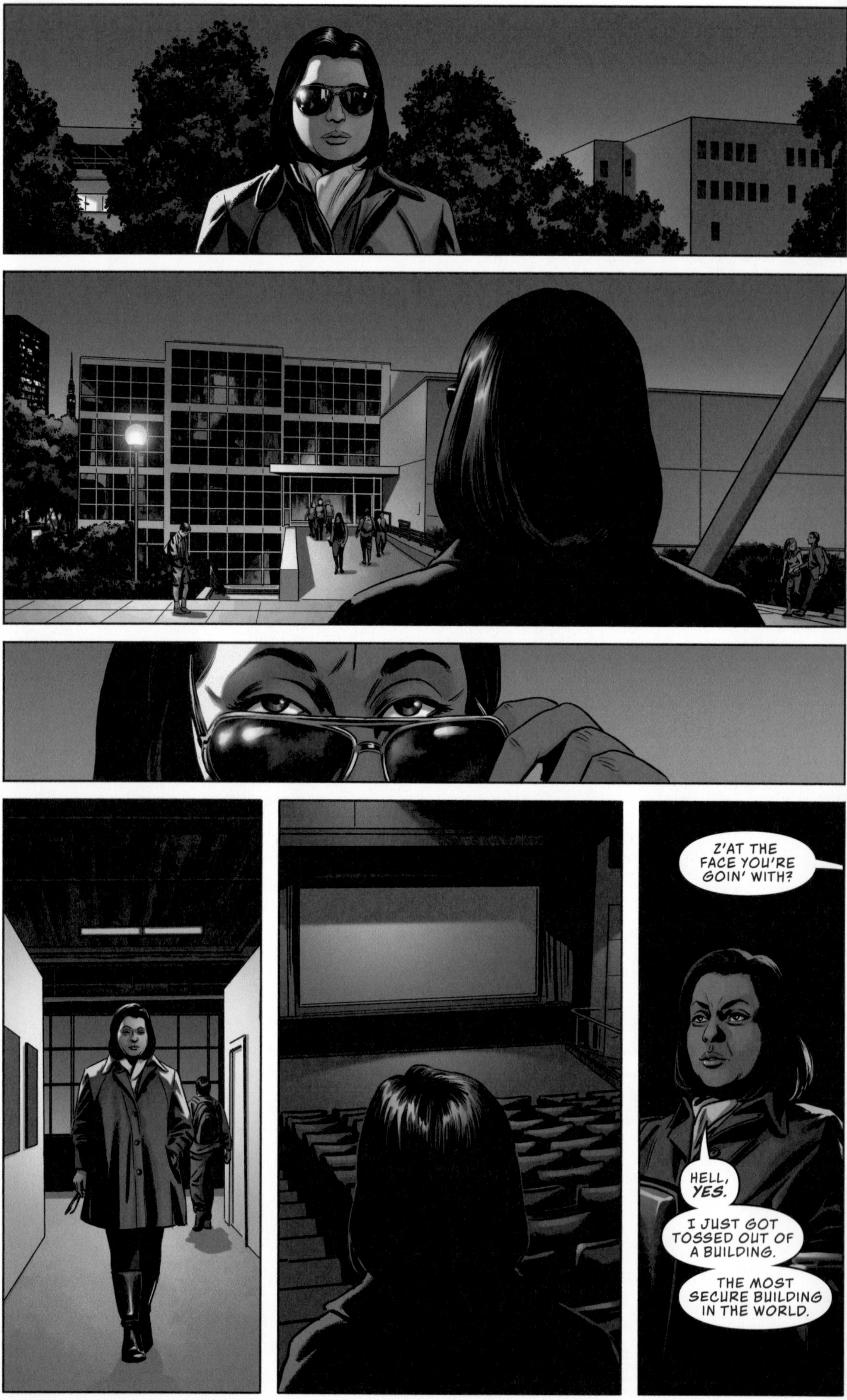
Z'AT THE FACE YOU'RE GOIN' WITH?
HELL, *YES.*
I JUST GOT TOSSED OUT OF A BUILDING.
THE MOST SECURE BUILDING IN THE WORLD.

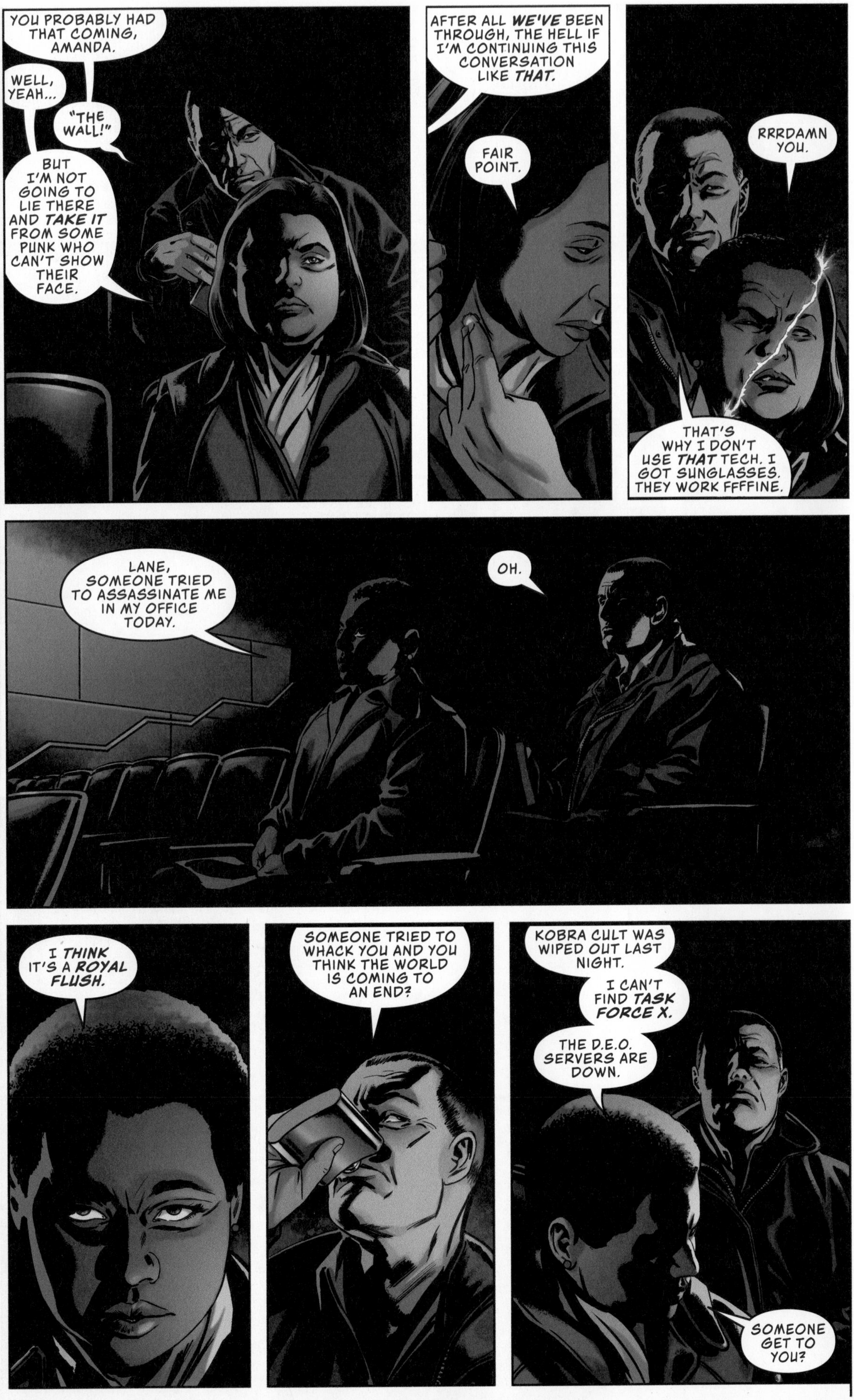
YOU PROBABLY HAD THAT COMING, AMANDA.
WELL, YEAH...
"THE WALL!"
BUT I'M NOT GOING TO LIE THERE AND *TAKE IT* FROM SOME PUNK WHO CAN'T SHOW THEIR FACE.
AFTER ALL *WE'VE* BEEN THROUGH, THE HELL IF I'M CONTINUING THIS CONVERSATION LIKE *THAT.*
FAIR POINT.
RRRDAMN YOU.
THAT'S WHY I DON'T USE *THAT* TECH. I GOT SUNGLASSES. THEY WORK FFFFINE.
LANE, SOMEONE TRIED TO ASSASSINATE ME IN MY OFFICE TODAY.
OH.
I *THINK* IT'S A *ROYAL FLUSH.*
SOMEONE TRIED TO WHACK YOU AND YOU THINK THE WORLD IS COMING TO AN END?
KOBRA CULT WAS WIPED OUT LAST NIGHT.
I CAN'T FIND *TASK FORCE X.*
THE D.E.O. SERVERS ARE DOWN.
SOMEONE GET TO YOU?

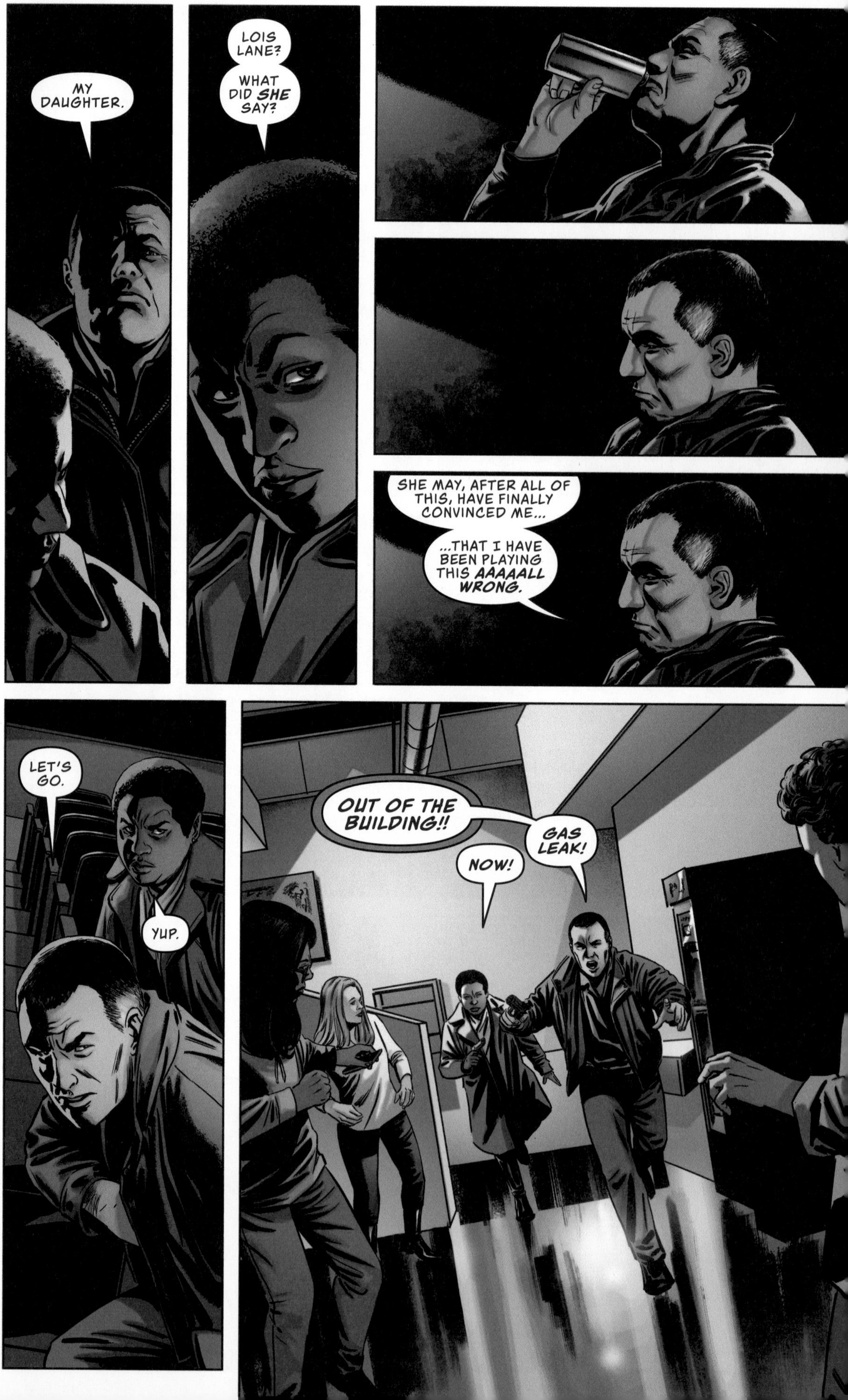
MY DAUGHTER.
LOIS LANE?
WHAT DID SHE SAY?
SHE MAY, AFTER ALL OF THIS, HAVE FINALLY CONVINCED ME...
...THAT I HAVE BEEN PLAYING THIS AAAAALL WRONG.
LET'S GO.
YUP.
OUT OF THE BUILDING!!
GAS LEAK!
NOW!

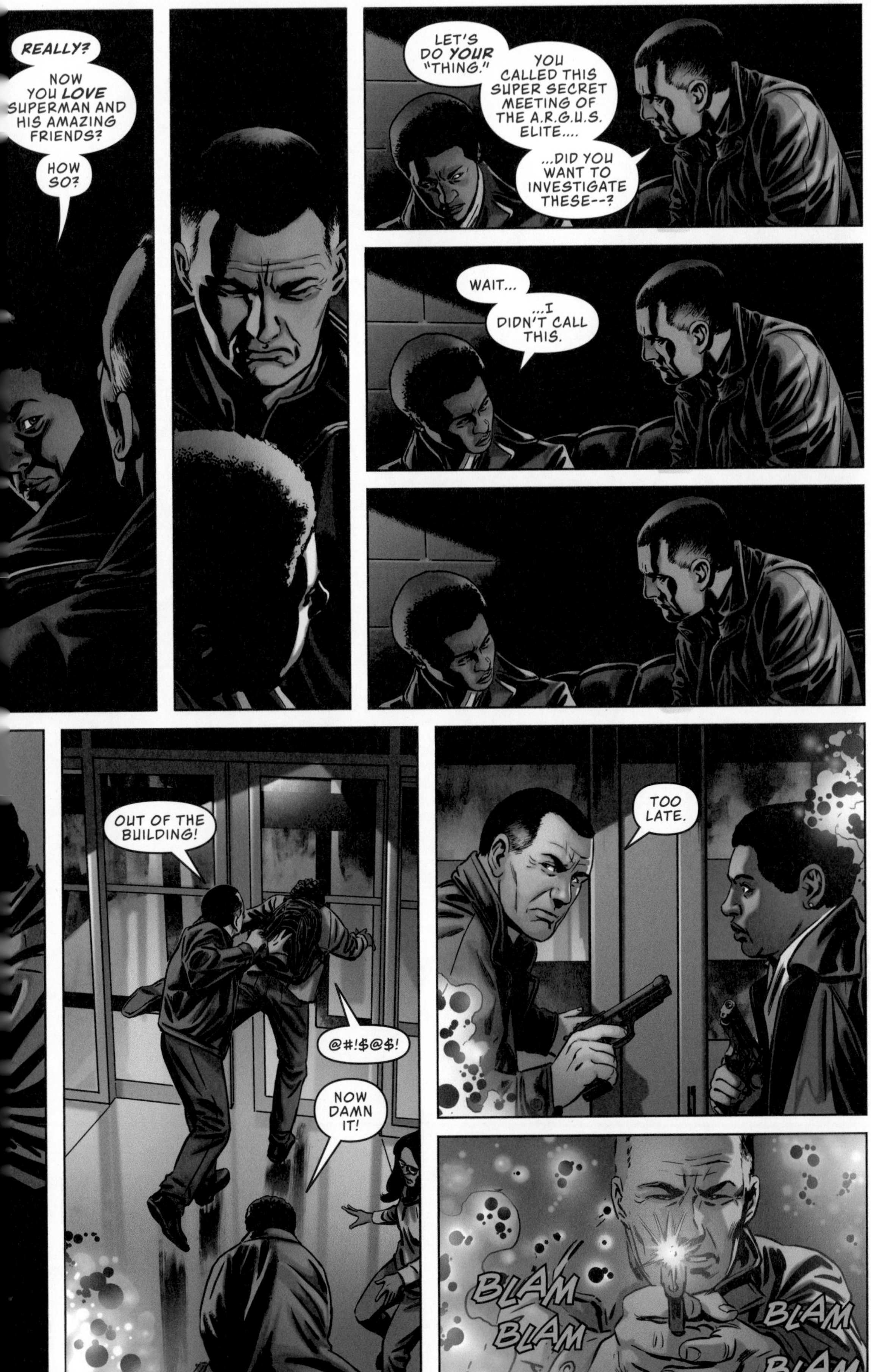
REALLY?
NOW YOU LOVE SUPERMAN AND HIS AMAZING FRIENDS?
HOW SO?
LET'S DO YOUR "THING."
YOU CALLED THIS SUPER SECRET MEETING OF THE A.R.G.U.S. ELITE....
...DID YOU WANT TO INVESTIGATE THESE--?
WAIT...
...I DIDN'T CALL THIS.
OUT OF THE BUILDING!
@#!$@$!
NOW DAMN IT!
TOO LATE.
BLAM
BLAM
BLAM
BLAM

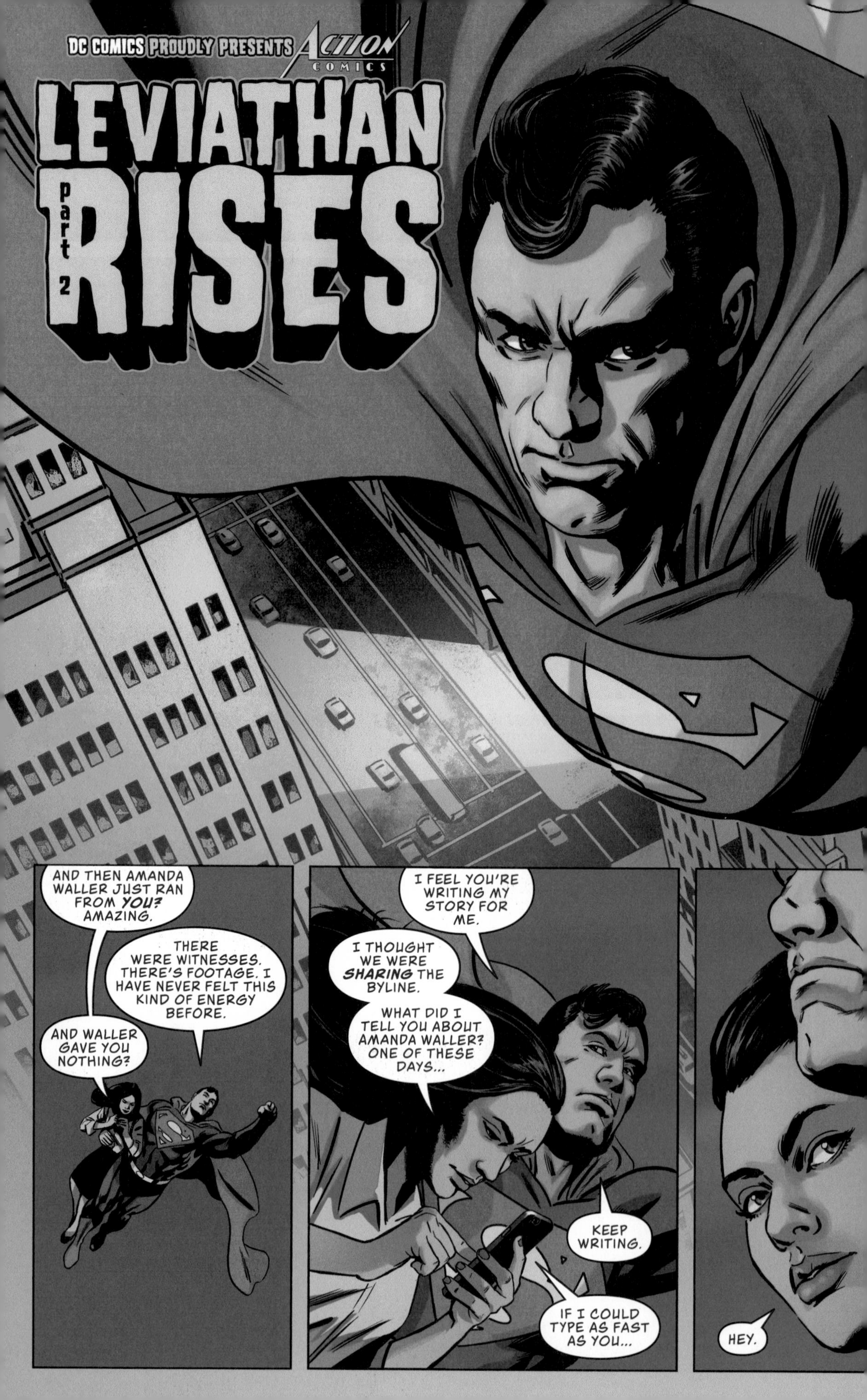
DC COMICS PROUDLY PRESENTS ACTION COMICS
LEVIATHAN RISES part 2
AND THEN AMANDA WALLER JUST RAN FROM YOU? AMAZING.
THERE WERE WITNESSES. THERE'S FOOTAGE. I HAVE NEVER FELT THIS KIND OF ENERGY BEFORE.
AND WALLER GAVE YOU NOTHING?
I FEEL YOU'RE WRITING MY STORY FOR ME.
I THOUGHT WE WERE SHARING THE BYLINE.
WHAT DID I TELL YOU ABOUT AMANDA WALLER? ONE OF THESE DAYS...
KEEP WRITING.
IF I COULD TYPE AS FAST AS YOU...
HEY.

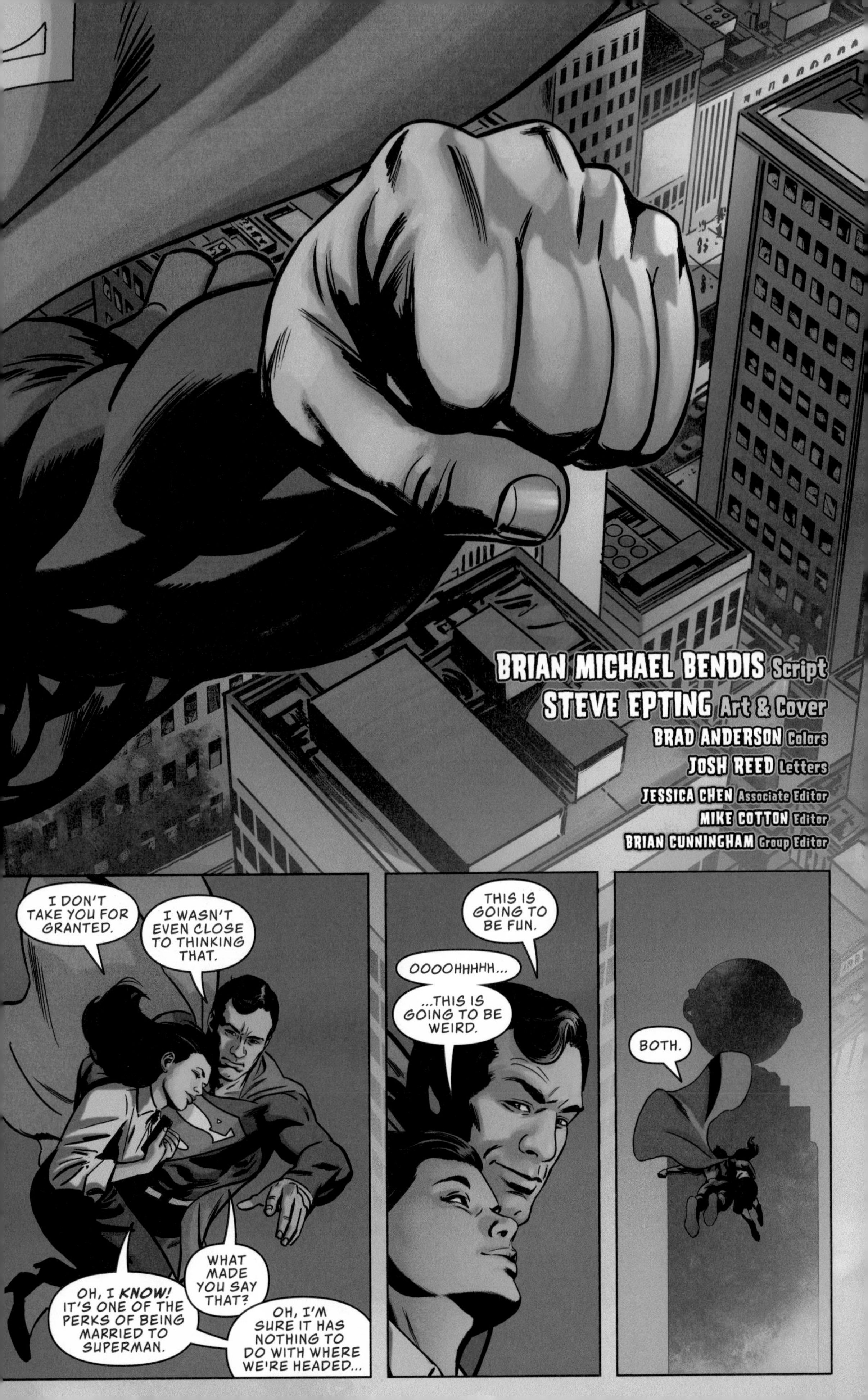

BRIAN MICHAEL BENDIS Script
STEVE EPTING Art & Cover
BRAD ANDERSON Colors
JOSH REED Letters
JESSICA CHEN Associate Editor
MIKE COTTON Editor
BRIAN CUNNINGHAM Group Editor
I DON'T TAKE YOU FOR GRANTED.
I WASN'T EVEN CLOSE TO THINKING THAT.
OH, I **KNOW!** IT'S ONE OF THE PERKS OF BEING MARRIED TO SUPERMAN.
WHAT MADE YOU SAY THAT?
OH, I'M SURE IT HAS NOTHING TO DO WITH WHERE WE'RE HEADED...
THIS IS GOING TO BE FUN.
OOOOHHHHH...
...THIS IS GOING TO BE WEIRD.
BOTH.

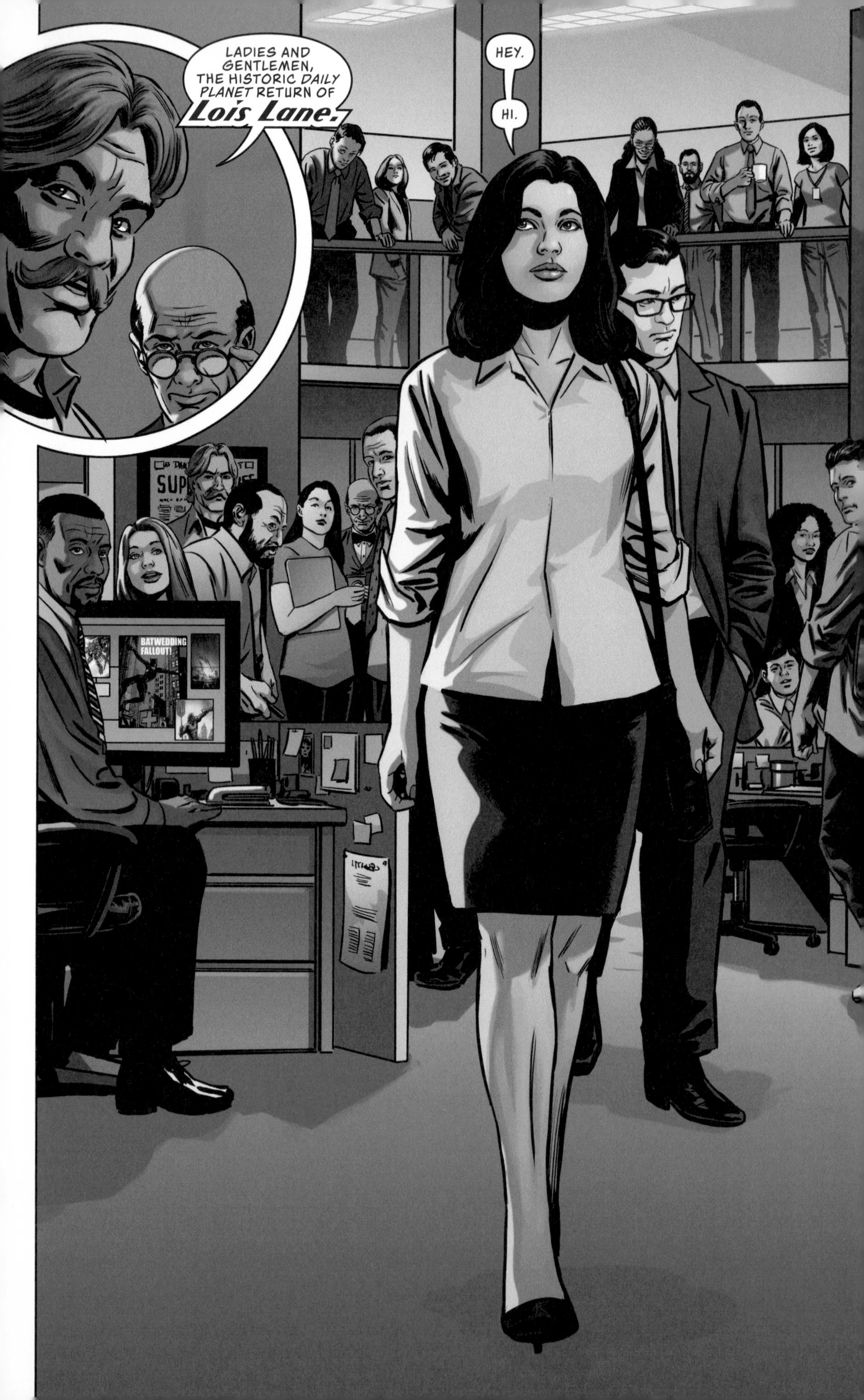
LADIES AND GENTLEMEN, THE HISTORIC *DAILY PLANET* RETURN OF **Lois Lane.**
HEY.
HI.
SUP
BATWEDDING FALLOUT!

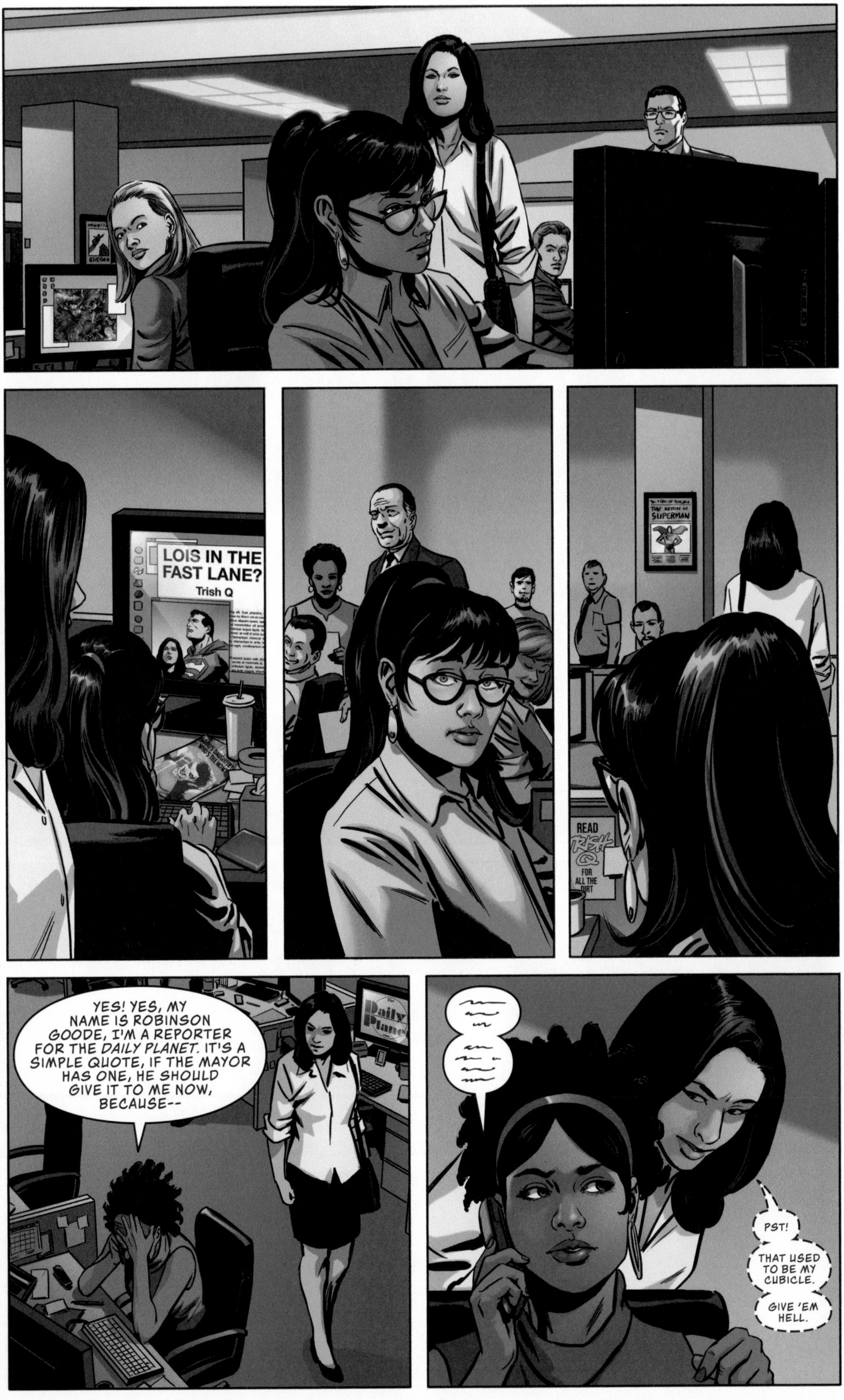
LOIS IN THE FAST LANE?
Trish Q
THE RETURN OF SUPERMAN
READ TRISH Q FOR ALL THE DIRT
Daily Planet
YES! YES, MY NAME IS ROBINSON GOODE, I'M A REPORTER FOR THE *DAILY PLANET*. IT'S A SIMPLE QUOTE, IF THE MAYOR HAS ONE, HE SHOULD GIVE IT TO ME NOW, BECAUSE--
PST!
THAT USED TO BE MY CUBICLE.
GIVE 'EM HELL.

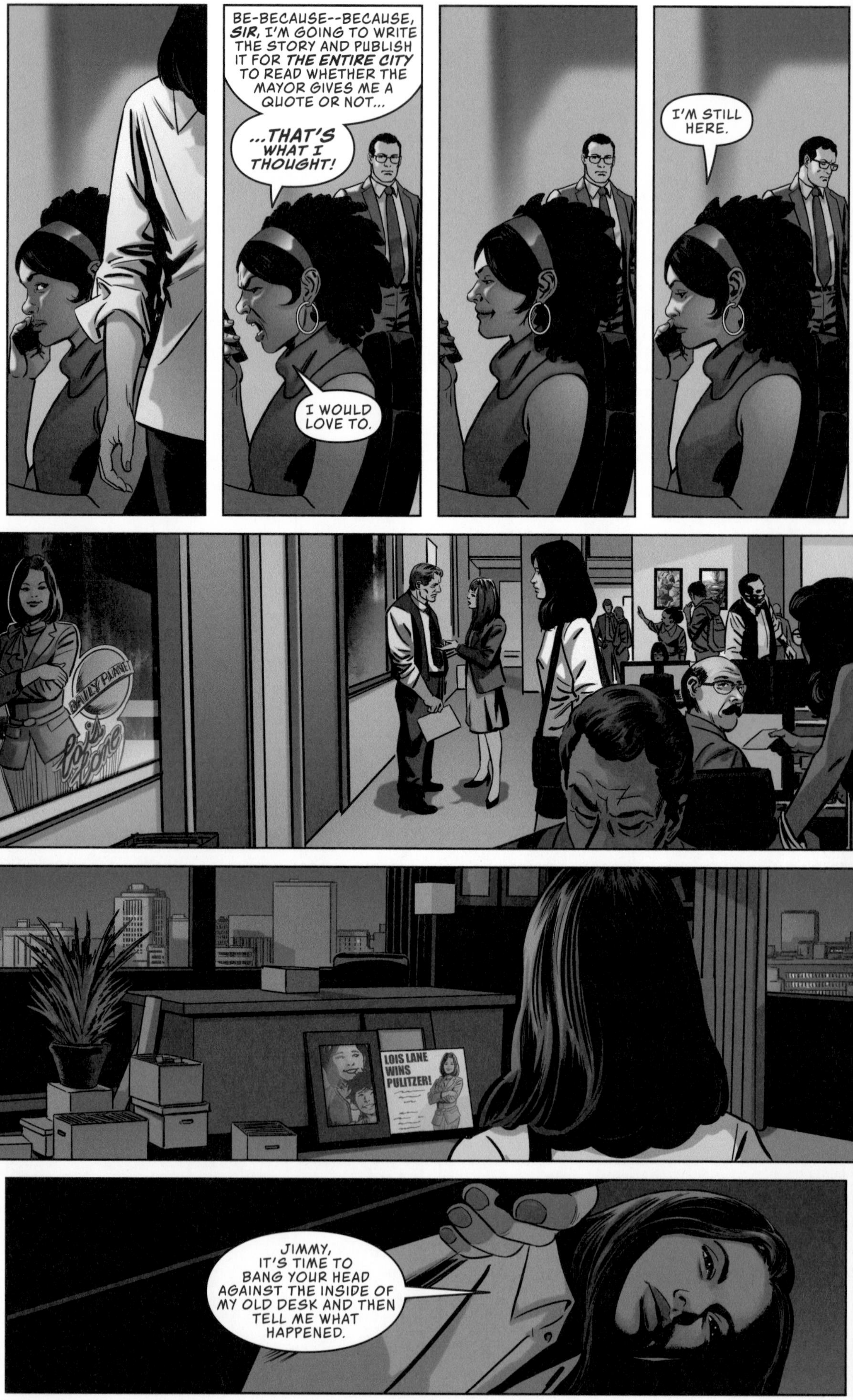
BE-BECAUSE--BECAUSE, SIR, I'M GOING TO WRITE THE STORY AND PUBLISH IT FOR THE ENTIRE CITY TO READ WHETHER THE MAYOR GIVES ME A QUOTE OR NOT...
...THAT'S WHAT I THOUGHT!
I WOULD LOVE TO.
I'M STILL HERE.
DAILY PLANET
lois lane
LOIS LANE WINS PULITZER!
JIMMY, IT'S TIME TO BANG YOUR HEAD AGAINST THE INSIDE OF MY OLD DESK AND THEN TELL ME WHAT HAPPENED.

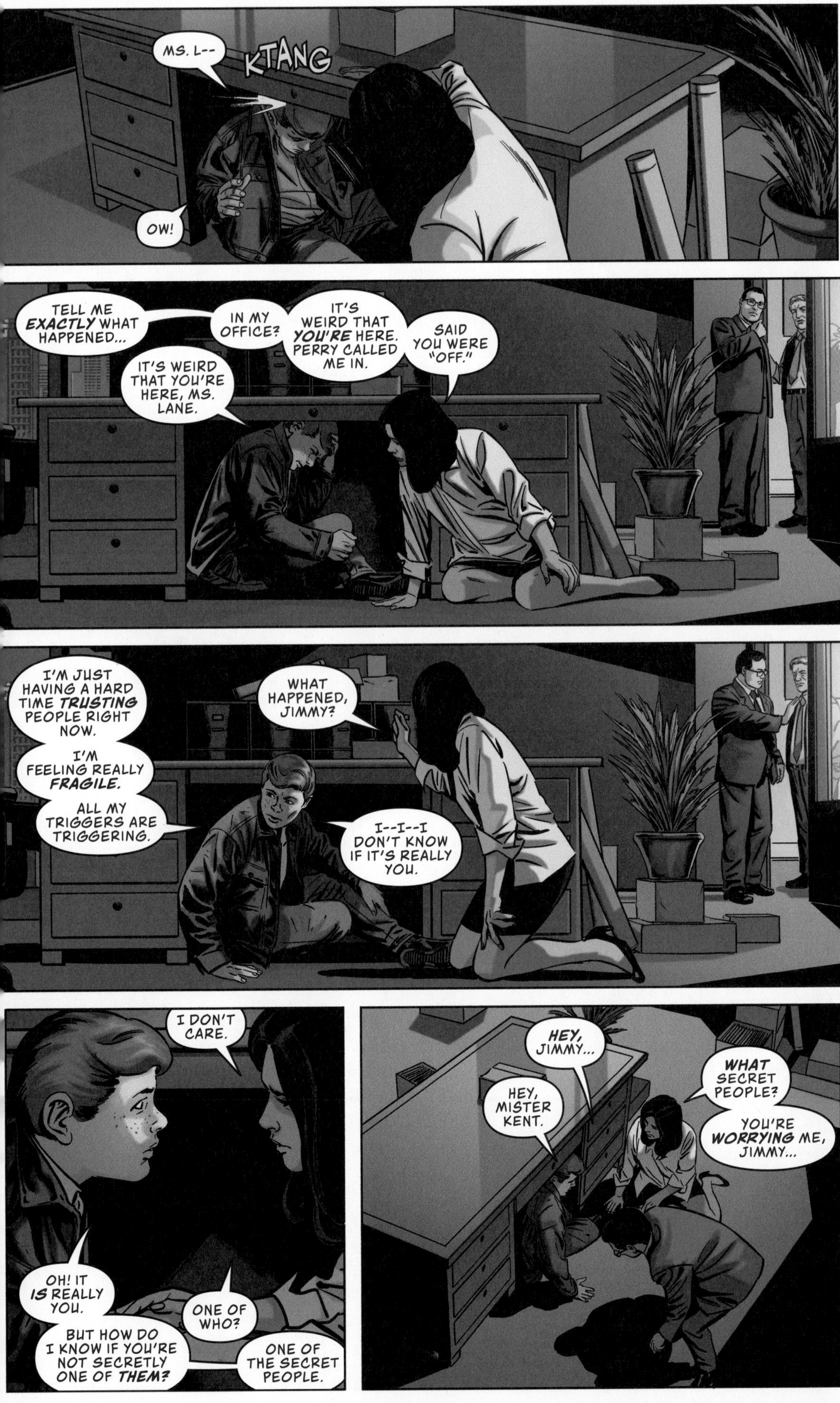

MS. L--
KTANG
OW!
TELL ME EXACTLY WHAT HAPPENED...
IN MY OFFICE?
IT'S WEIRD THAT YOU'RE HERE. PERRY CALLED ME IN.
SAID YOU WERE "OFF."
IT'S WEIRD THAT YOU'RE HERE, MS. LANE.
I'M JUST HAVING A HARD TIME TRUSTING PEOPLE RIGHT NOW.
I'M FEELING REALLY FRAGILE.
ALL MY TRIGGERS ARE TRIGGERING.
WHAT HAPPENED, JIMMY?
I--I--I DON'T KNOW IF IT'S REALLY YOU.
I DON'T CARE.
OH! IT IS REALLY YOU.
ONE OF WHO?
BUT HOW DO I KNOW IF YOU'RE NOT SECRETLY ONE OF THEM?
ONE OF THE SECRET PEOPLE.
HEY, JIMMY...
HEY, MISTER KENT.
WHAT SECRET PEOPLE?
YOU'RE WORRYING ME, JIMMY...

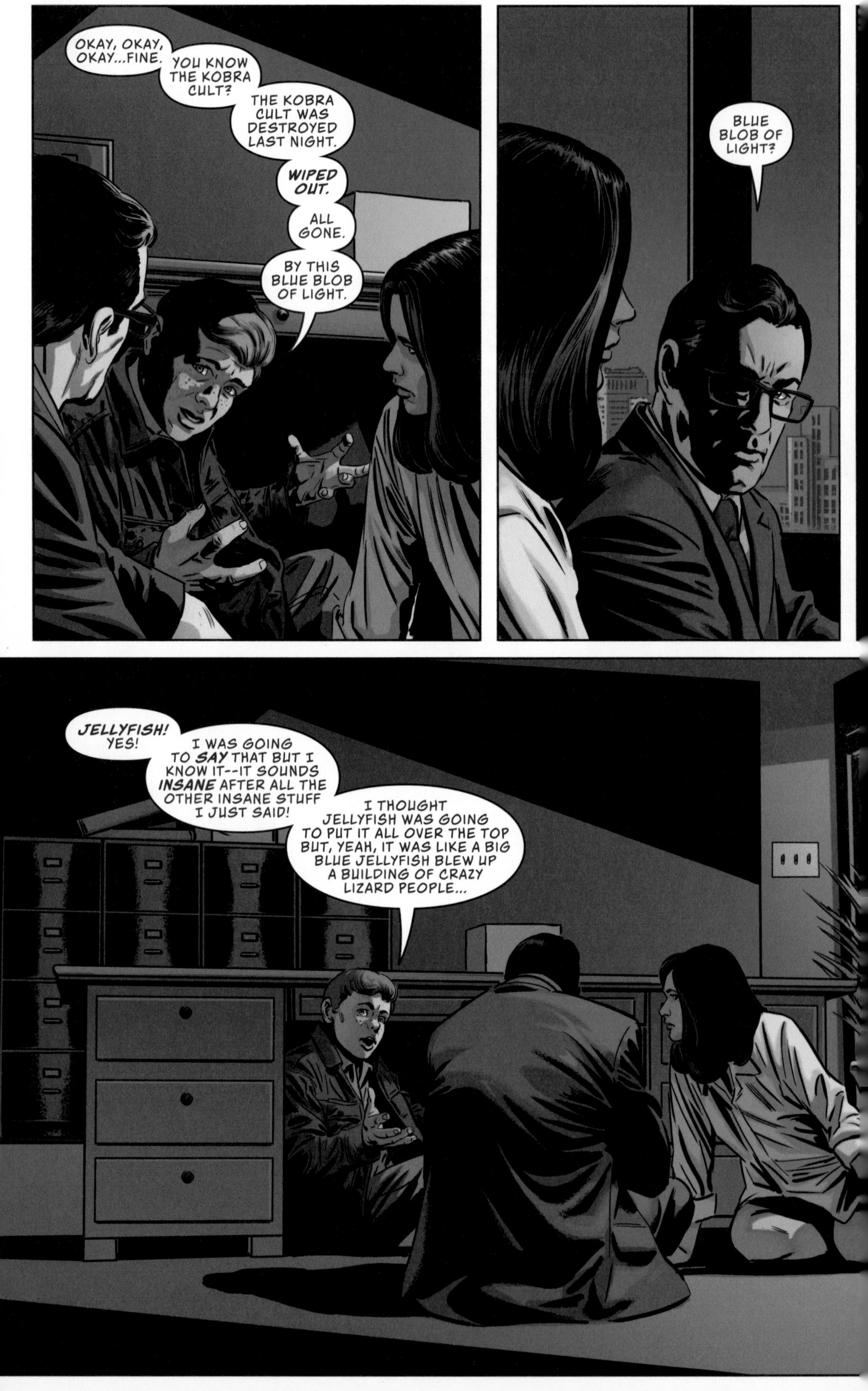
OKAY, OKAY, OKAY...FINE.
YOU KNOW THE KOBRA CULT?
THE KOBRA CULT WAS DESTROYED LAST NIGHT.
WIPED OUT.
ALL GONE.
BY THIS BLUE BLOB OF LIGHT.
BLUE BLOB OF LIGHT?
JELLYFISH! YES!
I WAS GOING TO SAY THAT BUT I KNOW IT--IT SOUNDS INSANE AFTER ALL THE OTHER INSANE STUFF I JUST SAID!
I THOUGHT JELLYFISH WAS GOING TO PUT IT ALL OVER THE TOP BUT, YEAH, IT WAS LIKE A BIG BLUE JELLYFISH BLEW UP A BUILDING OF CRAZY LIZARD PEOPLE...

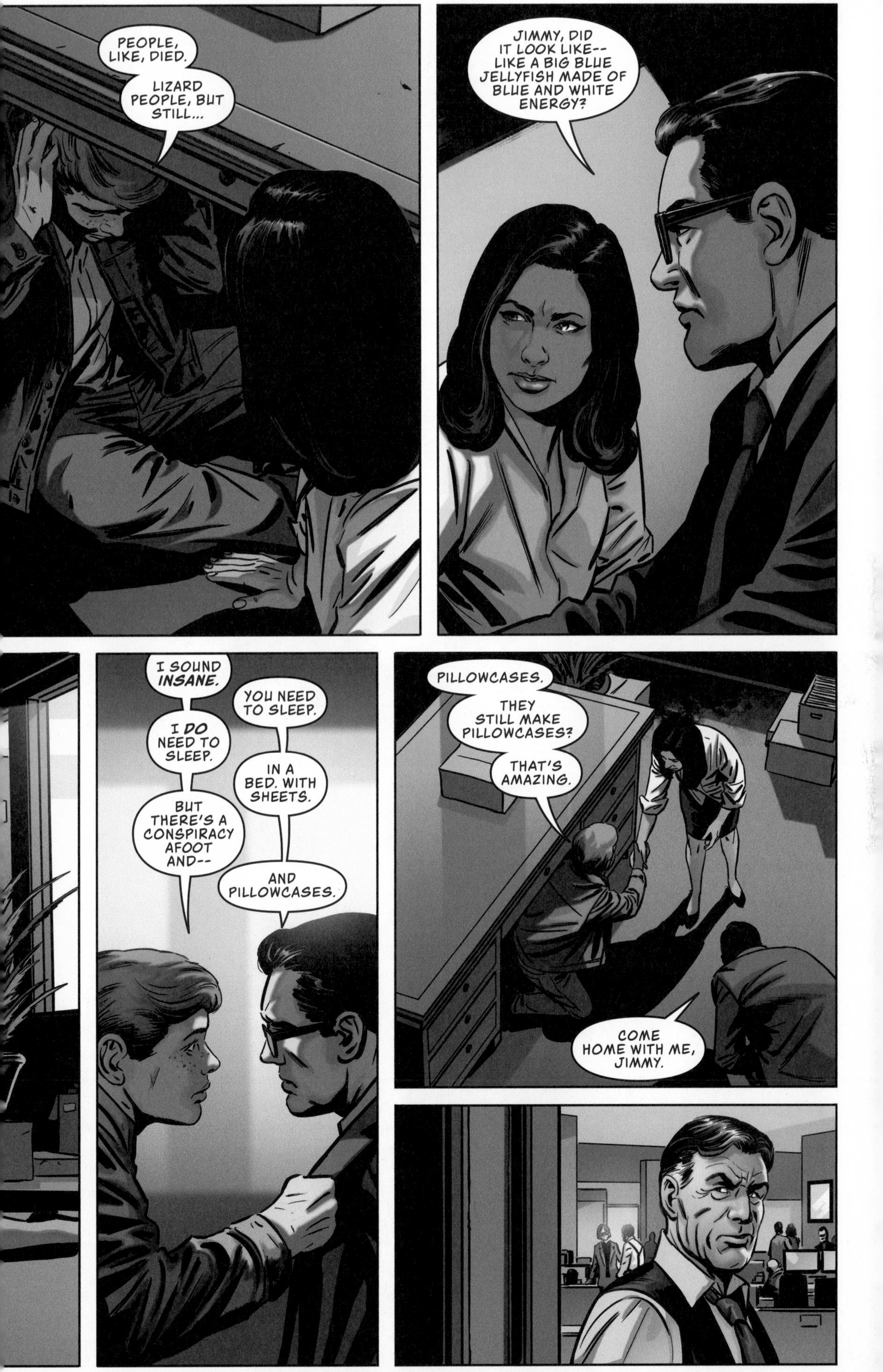
PEOPLE, LIKE, DIED.
LIZARD PEOPLE, BUT STILL...
JIMMY, DID IT LOOK LIKE-- LIKE A BIG BLUE JELLYFISH MADE OF BLUE AND WHITE ENERGY?
I SOUND *INSANE.*
YOU NEED TO SLEEP.
I *DO* NEED TO SLEEP.
IN A BED. WITH SHEETS.
BUT THERE'S A CONSPIRACY AFOOT AND--
AND PILLOWCASES.
PILLOWCASES.
THEY STILL MAKE PILLOWCASES?
THAT'S AMAZING.
COME HOME WITH ME, JIMMY.

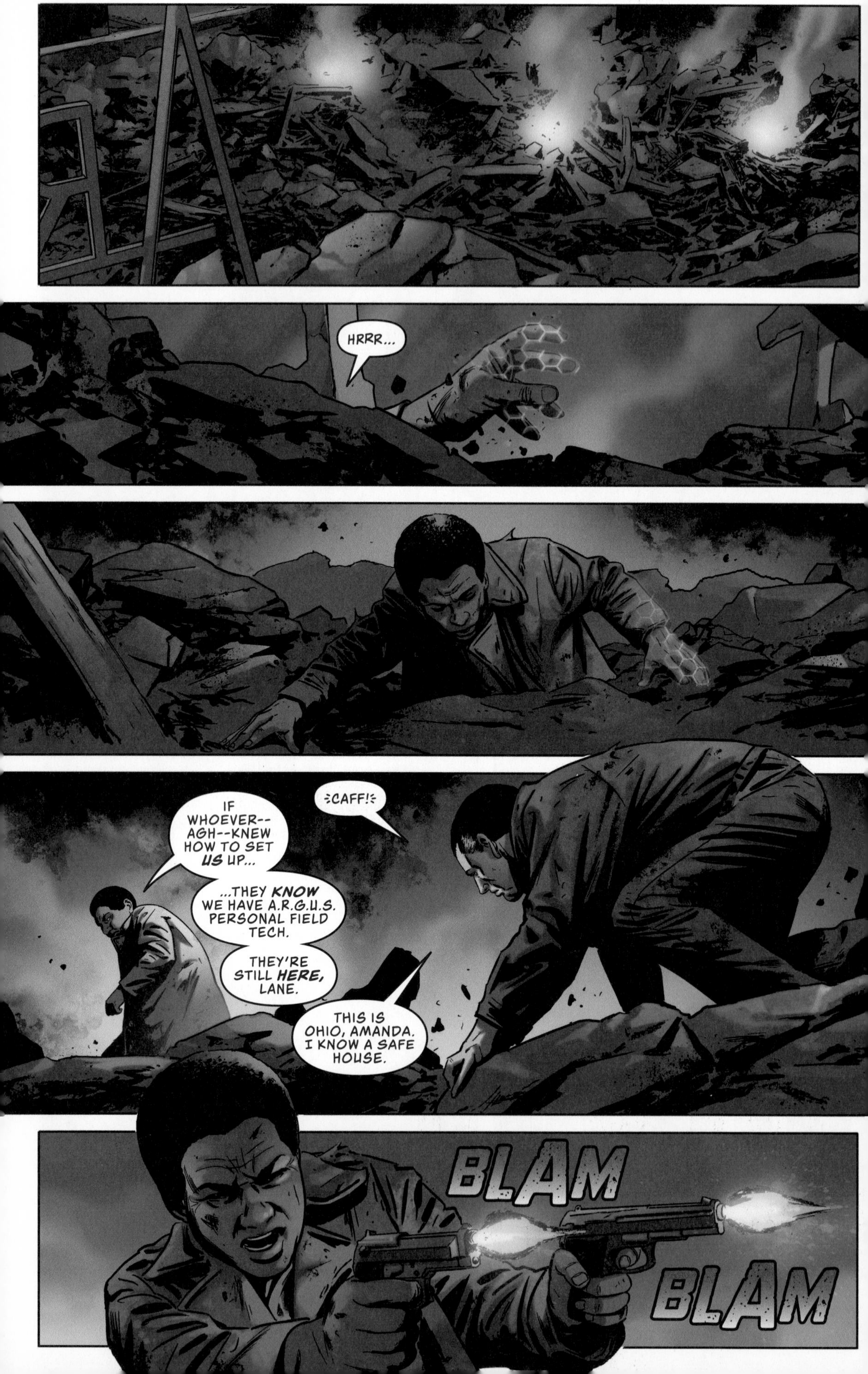
HRRR...
¡CAFF!¡
IF WHOEVER--AGH--KNEW HOW TO SET US UP...
...THEY KNOW WE HAVE A.R.G.U.S. PERSONAL FIELD TECH.
THEY'RE STILL HERE, LANE.
THIS IS OHIO, AMANDA. I KNOW A SAFE HOUSE.
BLAM
BLAM

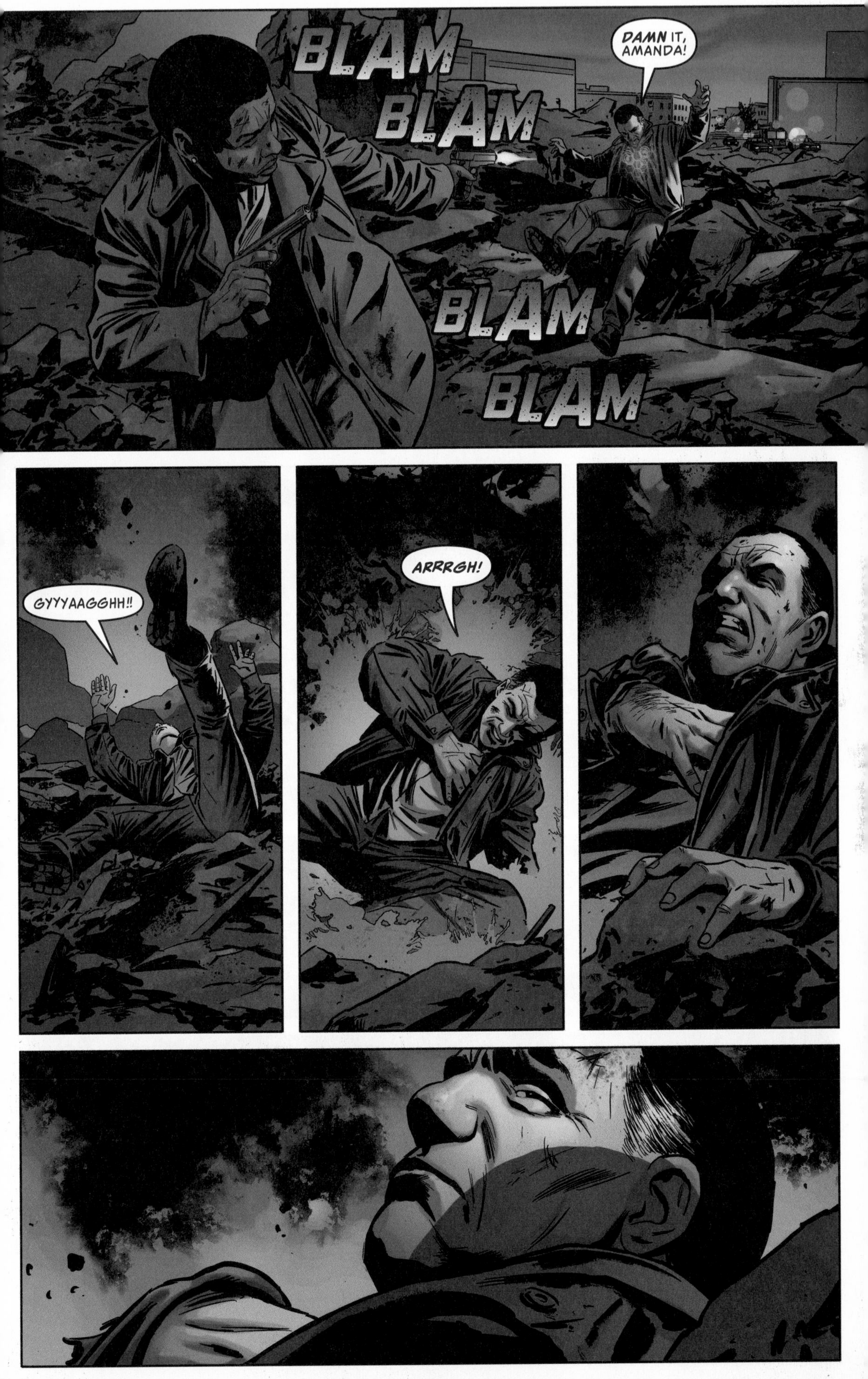
BLAM
BLAM
DAMN IT, AMANDA!
BLAM
BLAM
GYYYAAGGHH!!
ARRRGH!

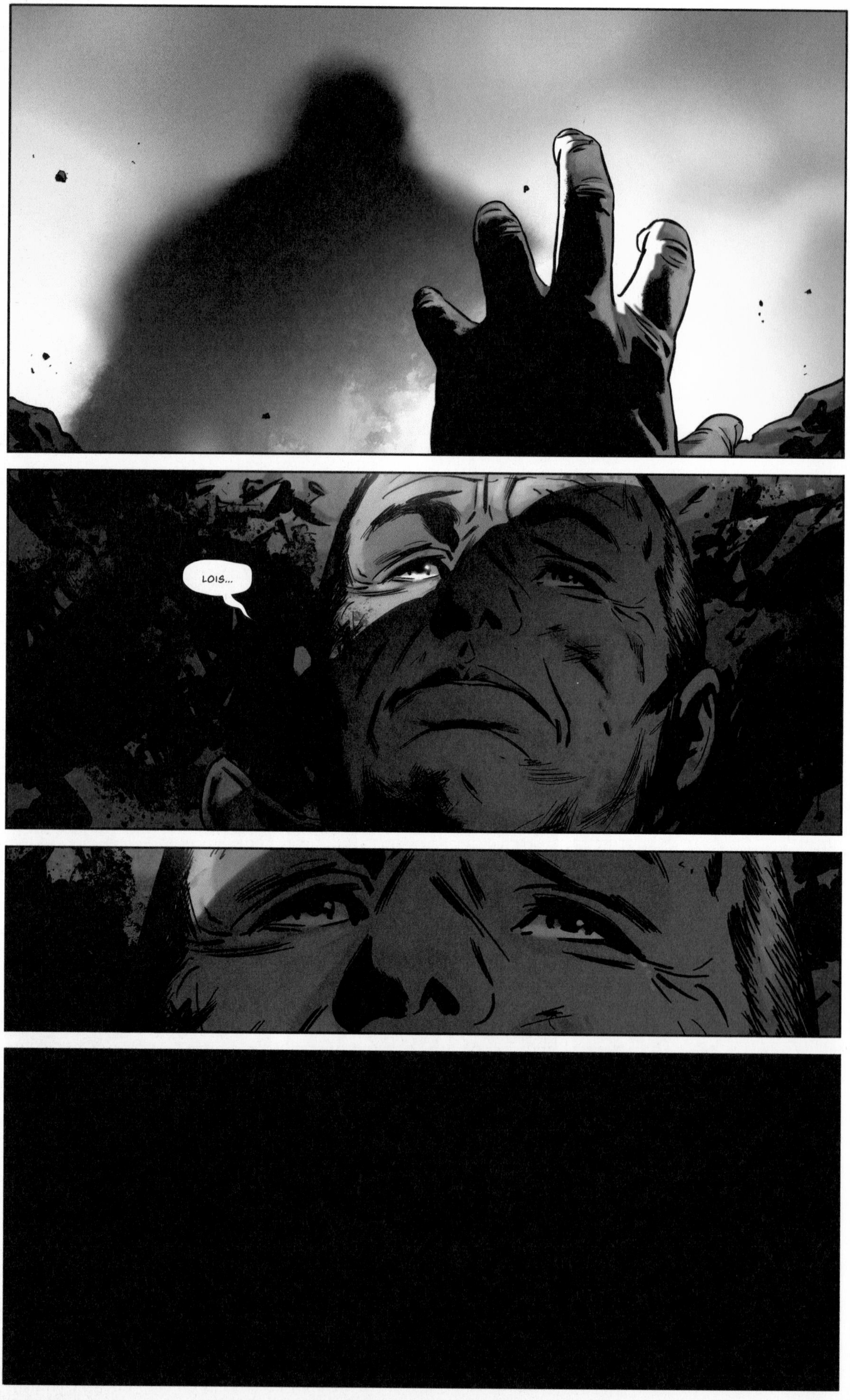
LOIS...

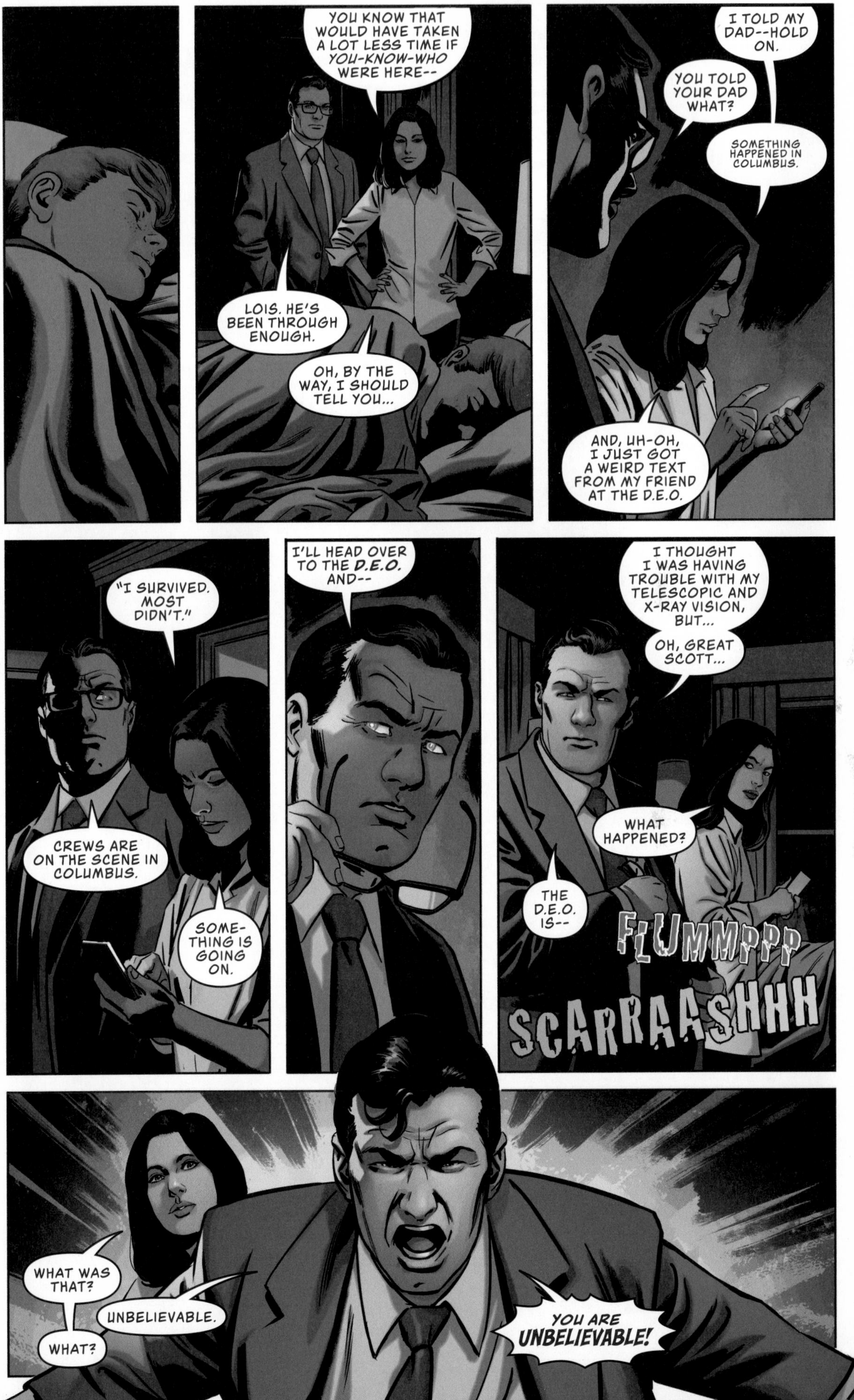

YOU KNOW THAT WOULD HAVE TAKEN A LOT LESS TIME IF YOU-KNOW-WHO WERE HERE--
LOIS. HE'S BEEN THROUGH ENOUGH.
OH, BY THE WAY, I SHOULD TELL YOU...
I TOLD MY DAD--HOLD ON.
YOU TOLD YOUR DAD WHAT?
SOMETHING HAPPENED IN COLUMBUS.
AND, UH-OH, I JUST GOT A WEIRD TEXT FROM MY FRIEND AT THE D.E.O.
"I SURVIVED. MOST DIDN'T."
CREWS ARE ON THE SCENE IN COLUMBUS.
SOME-THING IS GOING ON.
I'LL HEAD OVER TO THE D.E.O. AND--
I THOUGHT I WAS HAVING TROUBLE WITH MY TELESCOPIC AND X-RAY VISION, BUT...
OH, GREAT SCOTT...
WHAT HAPPENED?
THE D.E.O. IS--
FLUMMPPP
SCARRAASHHH
WHAT WAS THAT?
UNBELIEVABLE.
WHAT?
YOU ARE UNBELIEVABLE!

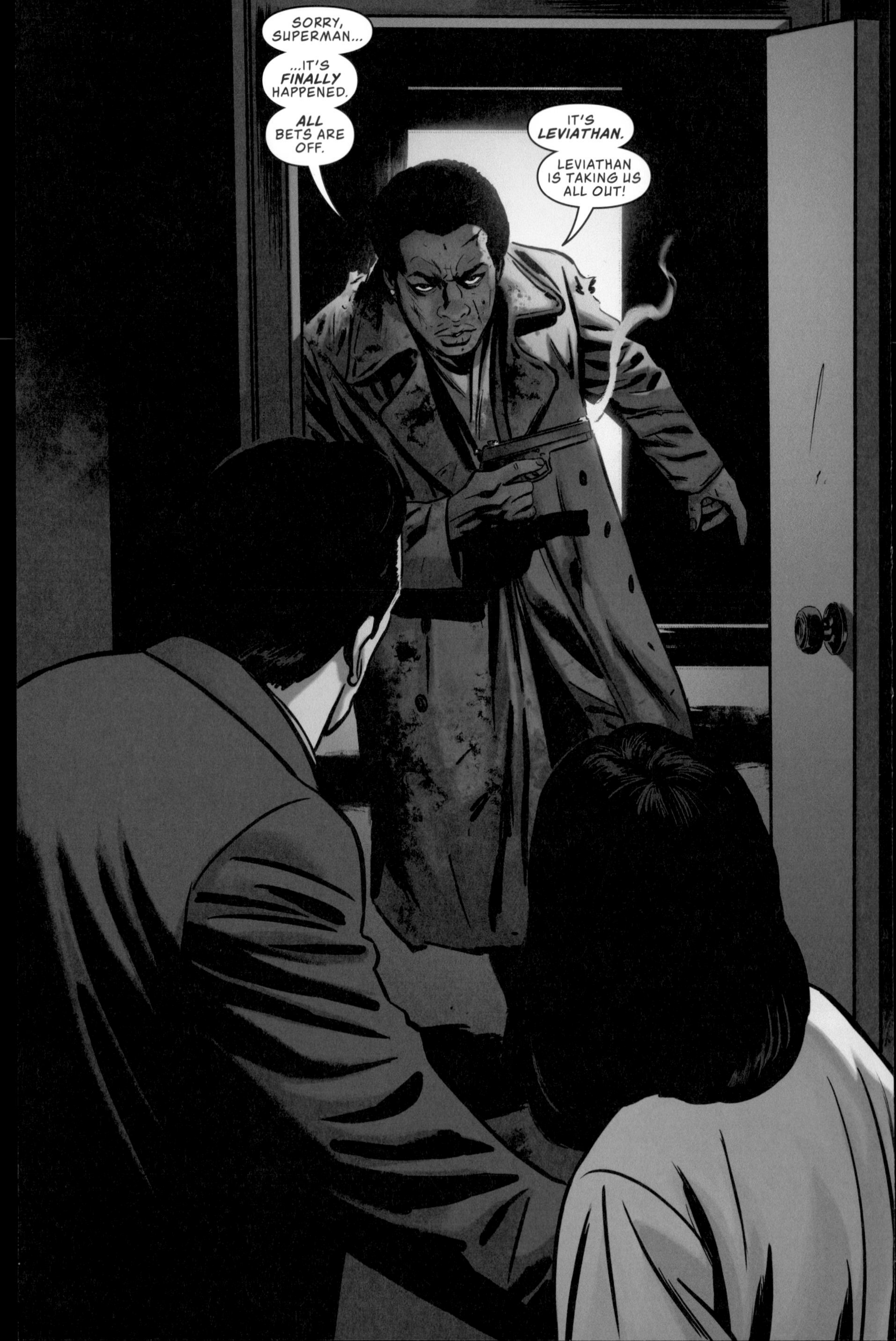
SORRY, SUPERMAN...
...IT'S *FINALLY* HAPPENED.
*ALL* BETS ARE OFF.
IT'S *LEVIATHAN.*
LEVIATHAN IS TAKING US ALL OUT!

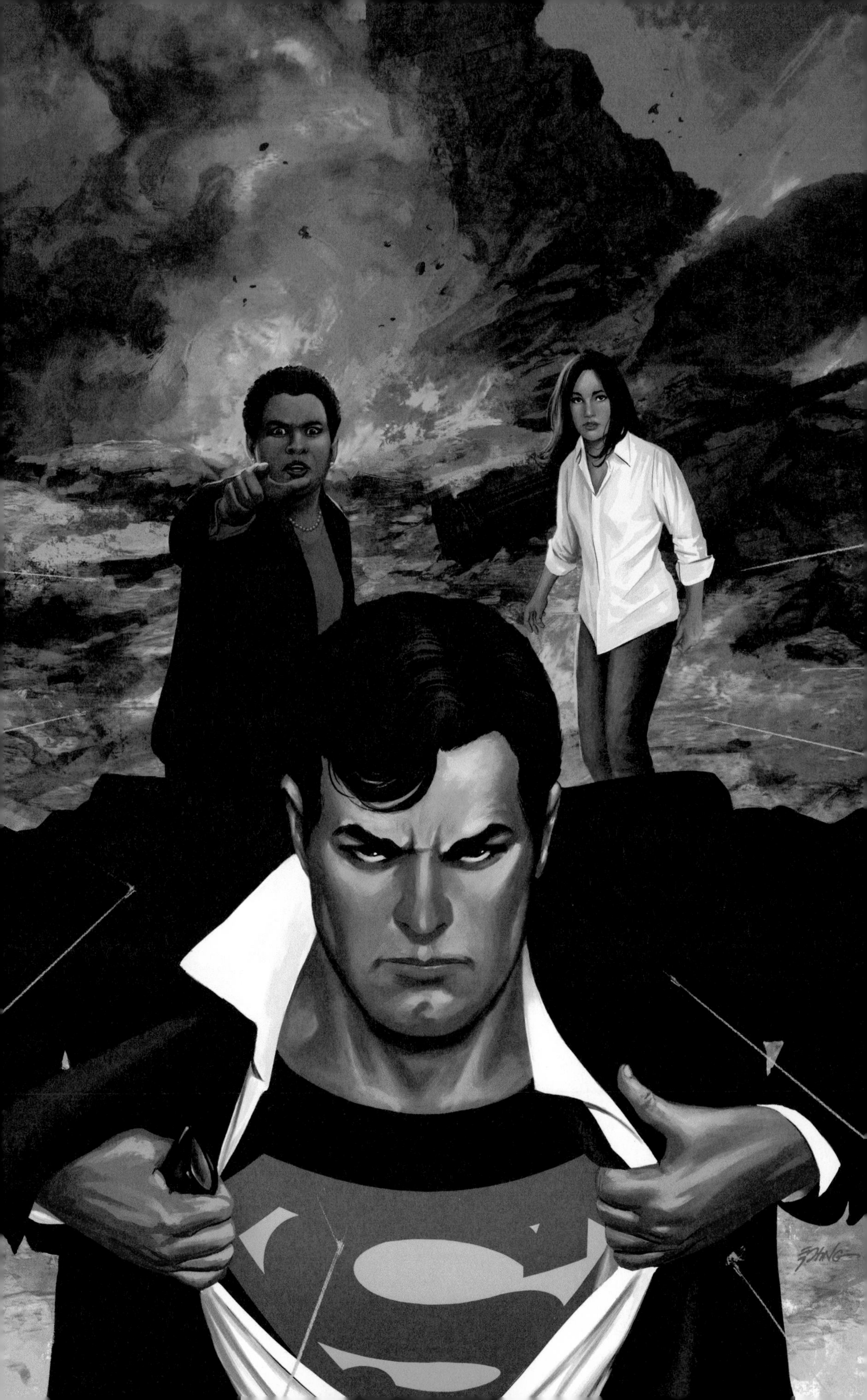

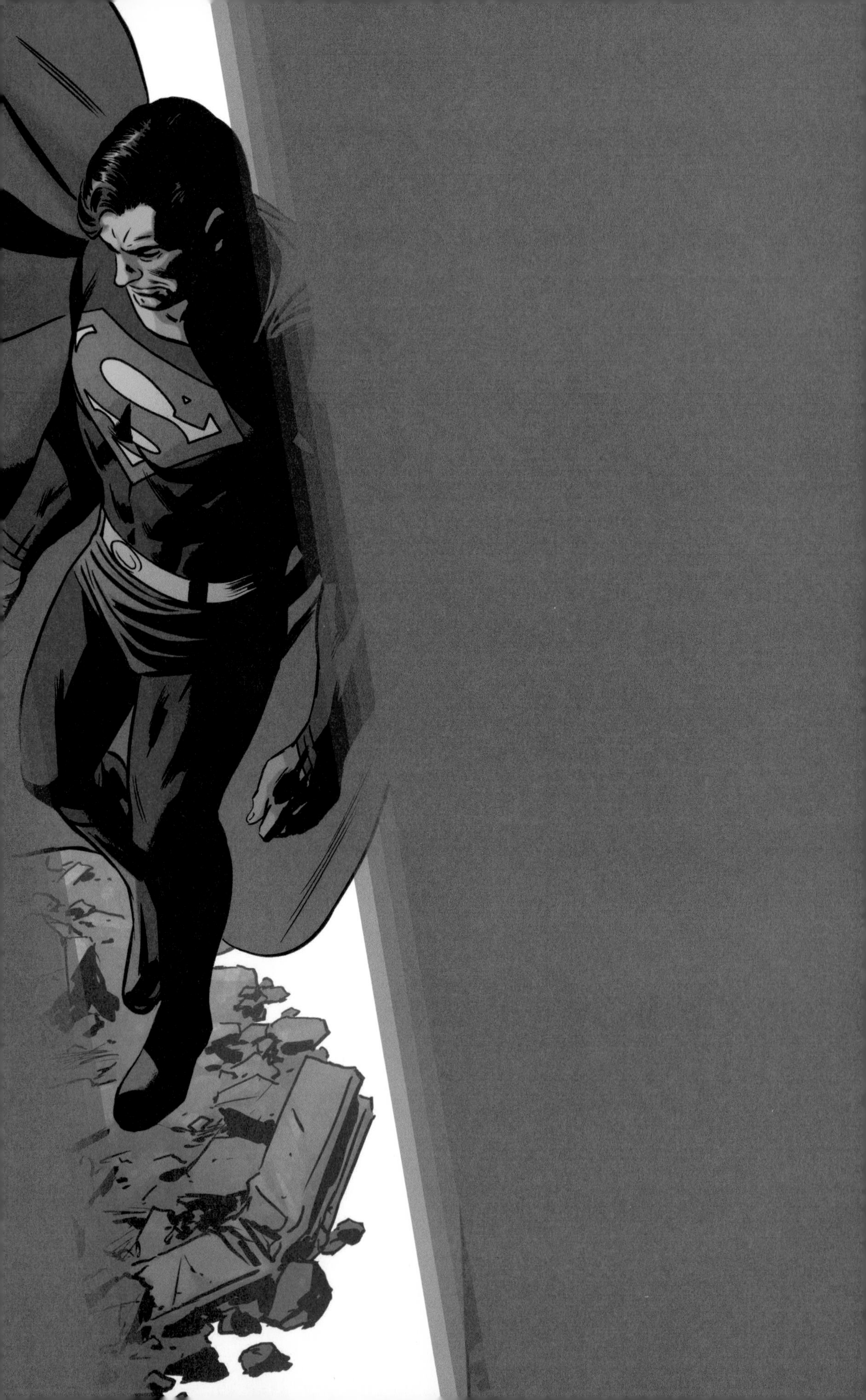

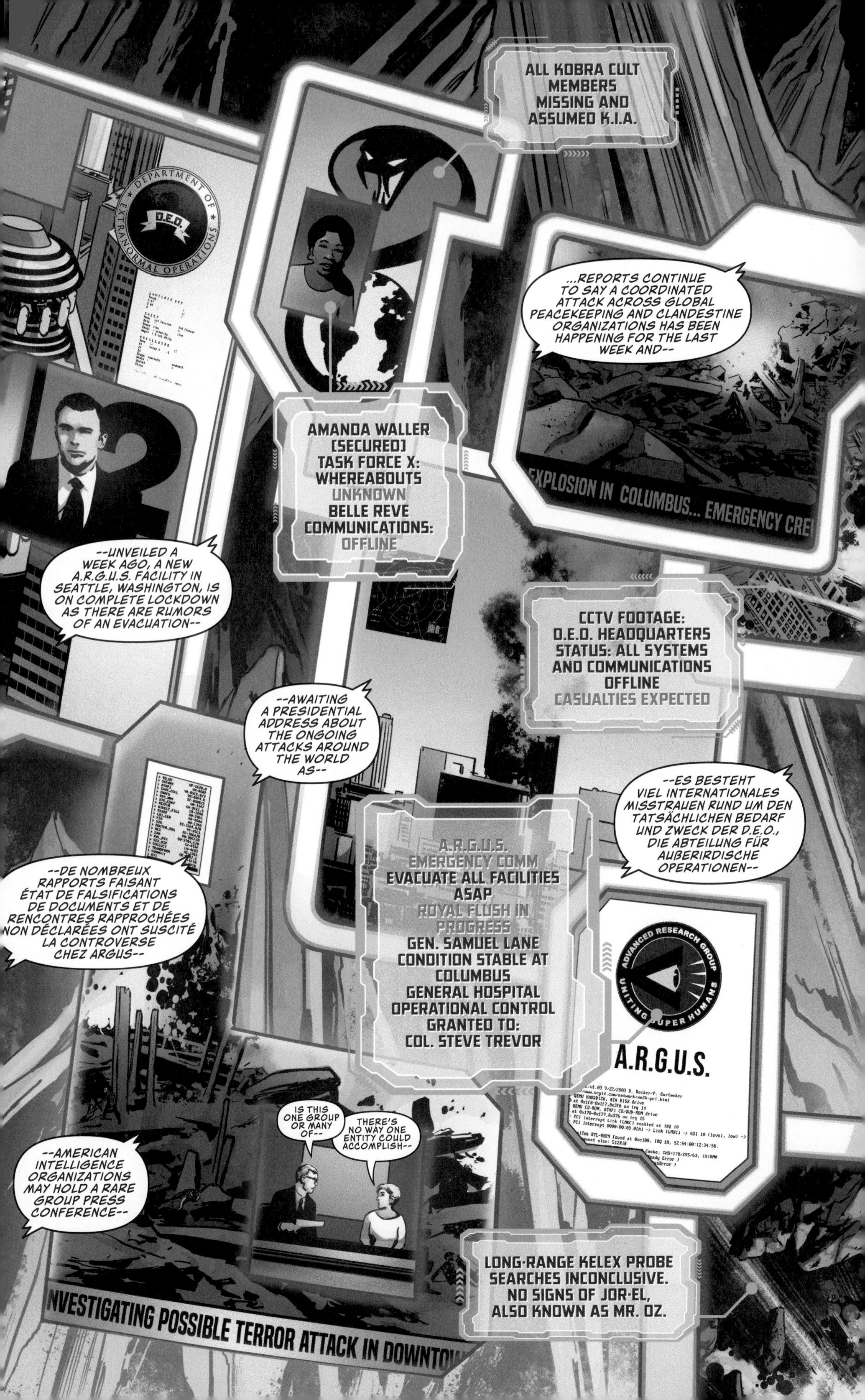
ALL KOBRA CULT MEMBERS MISSING AND ASSUMED K.I.A.
DEPARTMENT OF EXTRANORMAL OPERATIONS
D.E.O.
...REPORTS CONTINUE TO SAY A COORDINATED ATTACK ACROSS GLOBAL PEACEKEEPING AND CLANDESTINE ORGANIZATIONS HAS BEEN HAPPENING FOR THE LAST WEEK AND--
AMANDA WALLER [SECURED] TASK FORCE X: WHEREABOUTS UNKNOWN BELLE REVE COMMUNICATIONS: OFFLINE
EXPLOSION IN COLUMBUS... EMERGENCY CRE
--UNVEILED A WEEK AGO, A NEW A.R.G.U.S. FACILITY IN SEATTLE, WASHINGTON, IS ON COMPLETE LOCKDOWN AS THERE ARE RUMORS OF AN EVACUATION--
CCTV FOOTAGE: D.E.O. HEADQUARTERS STATUS: ALL SYSTEMS AND COMMUNICATIONS OFFLINE CASUALTIES EXPECTED
--AWAITING A PRESIDENTIAL ADDRESS ABOUT THE ONGOING ATTACKS AROUND THE WORLD AS--
--ES BESTEHT VIEL INTERNATIONALES MISSTRAUEN RUND UM DEN TATSÄCHLICHEN BEDARF UND ZWECK DER D.E.O., DIE ABTEILUNG FÜR AUßERIRDISCHE OPERATIONEN--
--DE NOMBREUX RAPPORTS FAISANT ÉTAT DE FALSIFICATIONS DE DOCUMENTS ET DE RENCONTRES RAPPROCHÉES NON DÉCLARÉES ONT SUSCITÉ LA CONTROVERSE CHEZ ARGUS--
A.R.G.U.S. EMERGENCY COMM EVACUATE ALL FACILITIES ASAP ROYAL FLUSH IN PROGRESS GEN. SAMUEL LANE CONDITION STABLE AT COLUMBUS GENERAL HOSPITAL OPERATIONAL CONTROL GRANTED TO: COL. STEVE TREVOR
ADVANCED RESEARCH GROUP UNITING SUPER HUMANS
A.R.G.U.S.
IS THIS ONE GROUP OR MANY OF--
THERE'S NO WAY ONE ENTITY COULD ACCOMPLISH--
--AMERICAN INTELLIGENCE ORGANIZATIONS MAY HOLD A RARE GROUP PRESS CONFERENCE--
LONG-RANGE KELEX PROBE SEARCHES INCONCLUSIVE. NO SIGNS OF JOR-EL, ALSO KNOWN AS MR. OZ.
NVESTIGATING POSSIBLE TERROR ATTACK IN DOWNTO

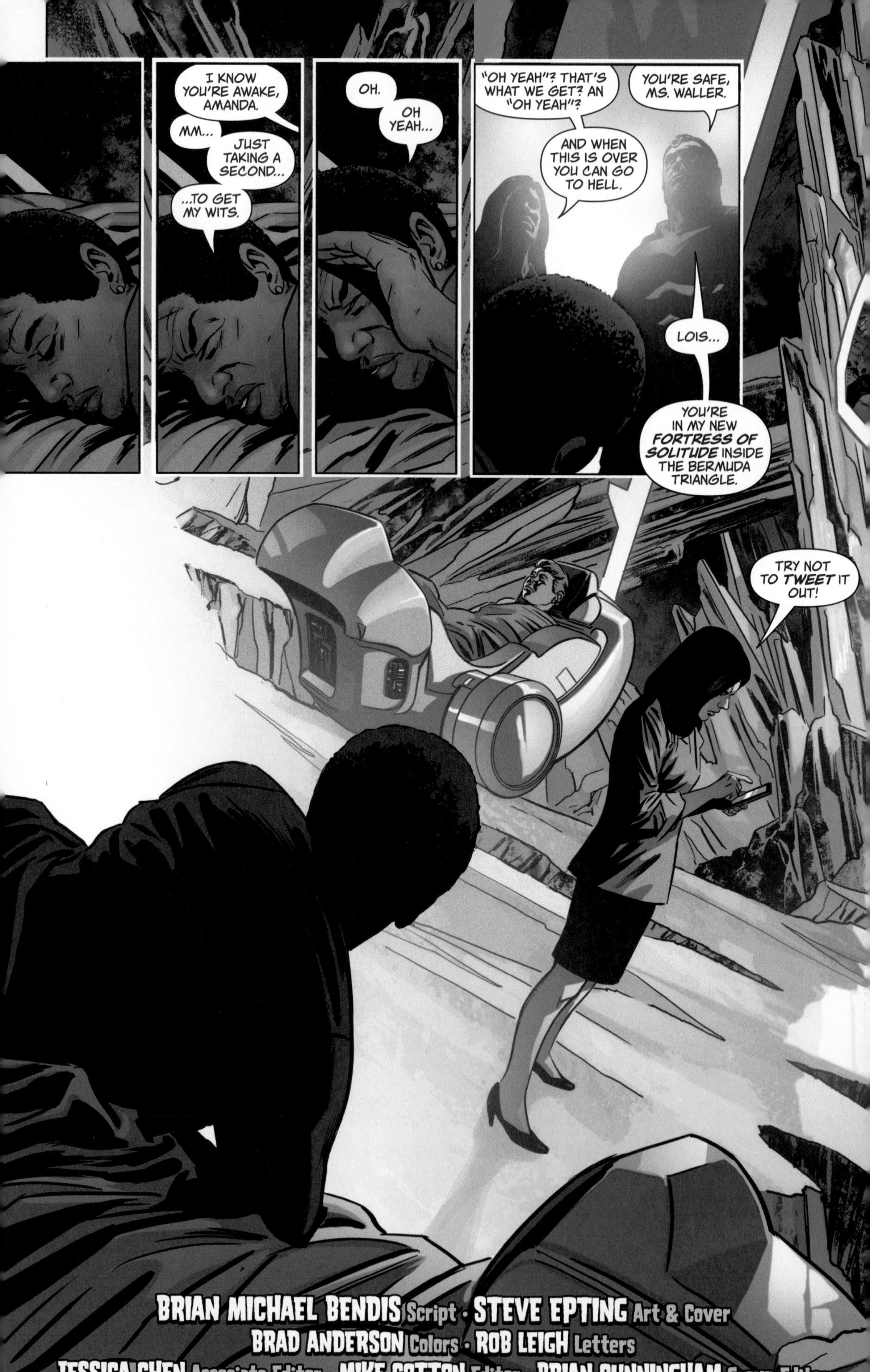
I KNOW YOU'RE AWAKE, AMANDA.
MM...
JUST TAKING A SECOND...
...TO GET MY WITS.
OH.
OH YEAH...
"OH YEAH"? THAT'S WHAT WE GET? AN "OH YEAH"?
AND WHEN THIS IS OVER YOU CAN GO TO HELL.
YOU'RE SAFE, MS. WALLER.
LOIS...
YOU'RE IN MY NEW FORTRESS OF SOLITUDE INSIDE THE BERMUDA TRIANGLE.
TRY NOT TO TWEET IT OUT!

BRIAN MICHAEL BENDIS Script • STEVE EPTING Art & Cover
BRAD ANDERSON Colors • ROB LEIGH Letters
JESSICA CHEN Associate Editor • MIKE COTTON Editor • BRIAN CUNNINGHAM Group Editor

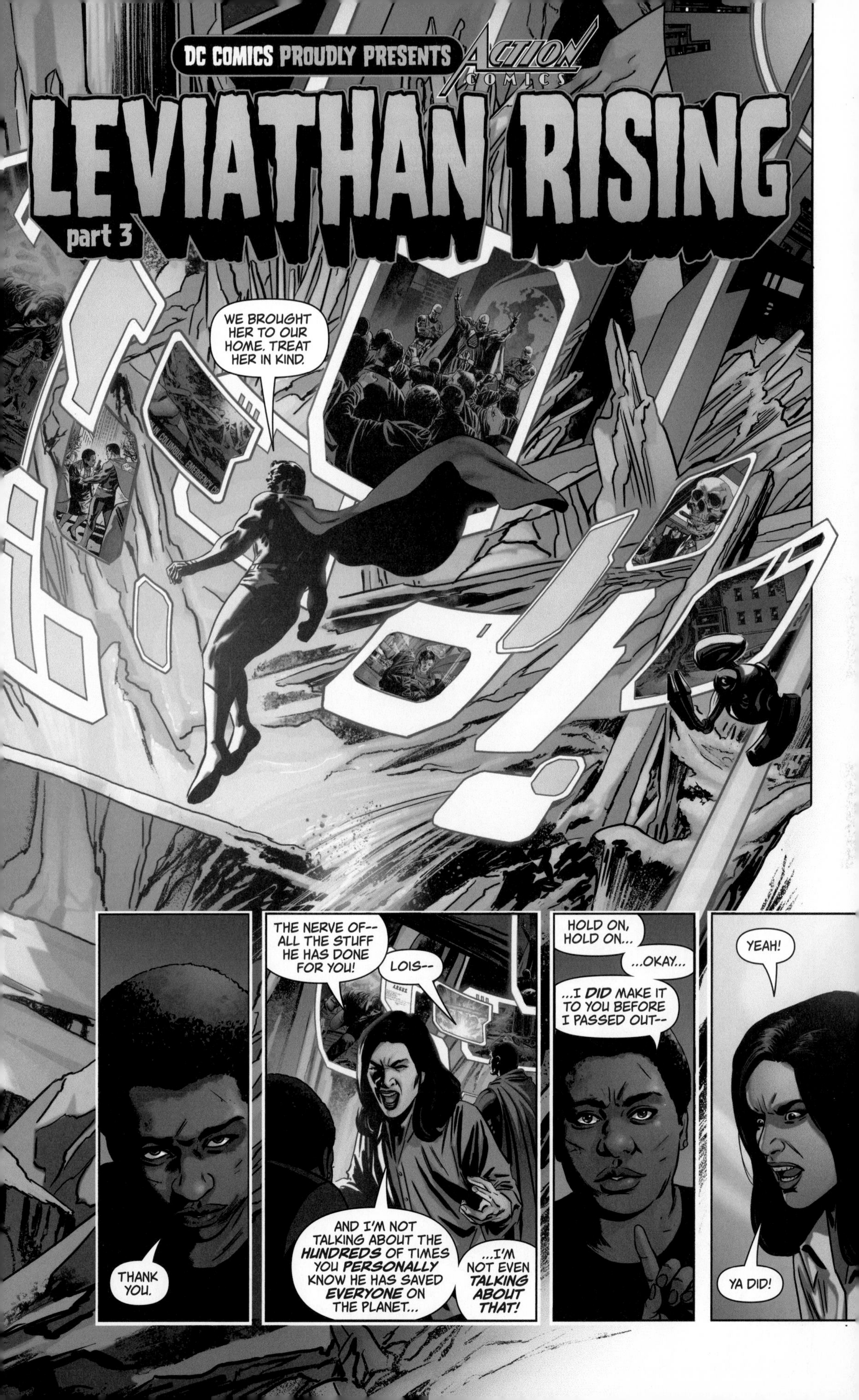

DC COMICS PROUDLY PRESENTS
ACTION COMICS
LEVIATHAN RISING
part 3
WE BROUGHT HER TO OUR HOME. TREAT HER IN KIND.
THANK YOU.
THE NERVE OF-- ALL THE STUFF HE HAS DONE FOR YOU!
LOIS--
AND I'M NOT TALKING ABOUT THE HUNDREDS OF TIMES YOU PERSONALLY KNOW HE HAS SAVED EVERYONE ON THE PLANET...
...I'M NOT EVEN TALKING ABOUT THAT!
HOLD ON, HOLD ON...
...OKAY...
...I DID MAKE IT TO YOU BEFORE I PASSED OUT--
YEAH!
YA DID!

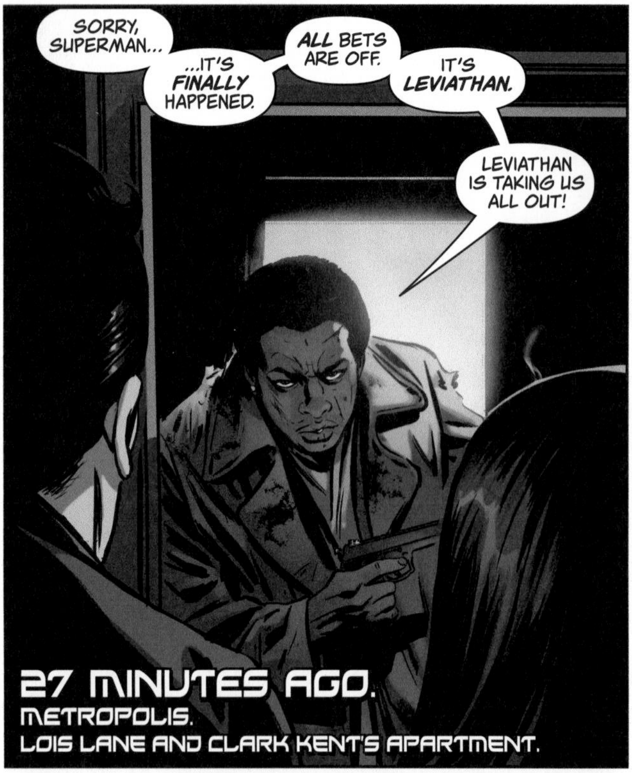
SORRY, SUPERMAN...
...IT'S FINALLY HAPPENED.
ALL BETS ARE OFF.
IT'S LEVIATHAN.
LEVIATHAN IS TAKING US ALL OUT!
27 MINUTES AGO.
METROPOLIS.
LOIS LANE AND CLARK KENT'S APARTMENT.

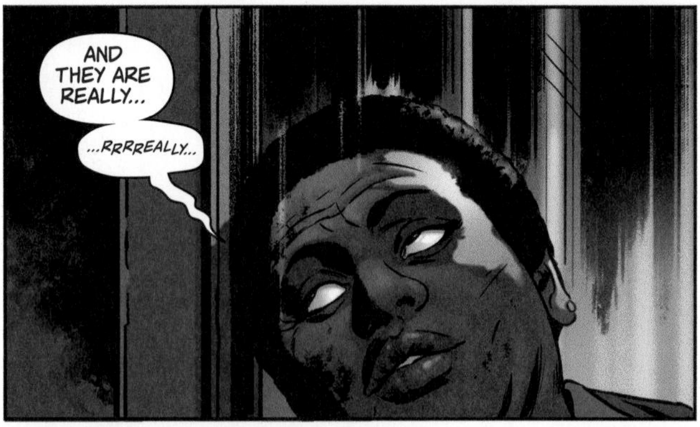
AND THEY ARE REALLY...
...RRRREALLY...

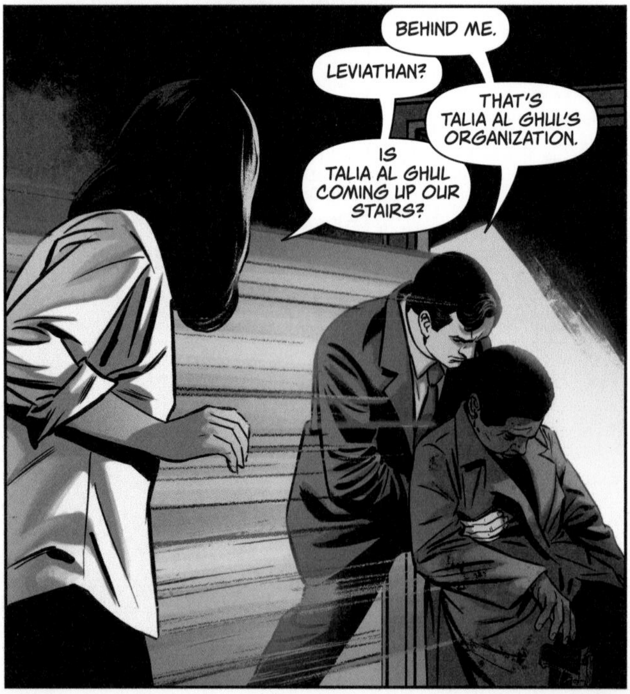
LEVIATHAN?
BEHIND ME.
THAT'S TALIA AL GHUL'S ORGANIZATION.
IS TALIA AL GHUL COMING UP OUR STAIRS?

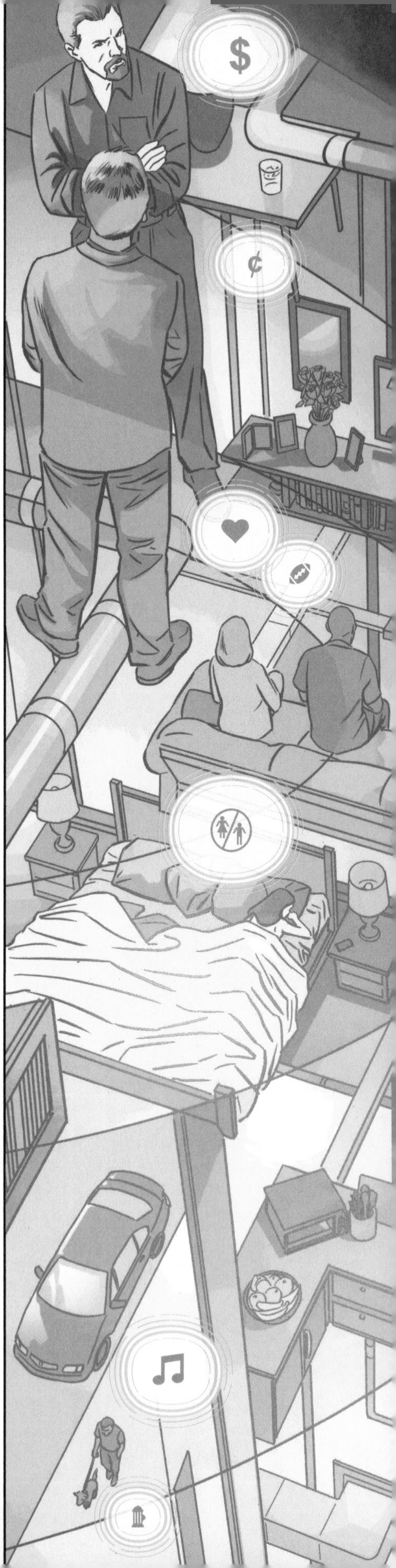

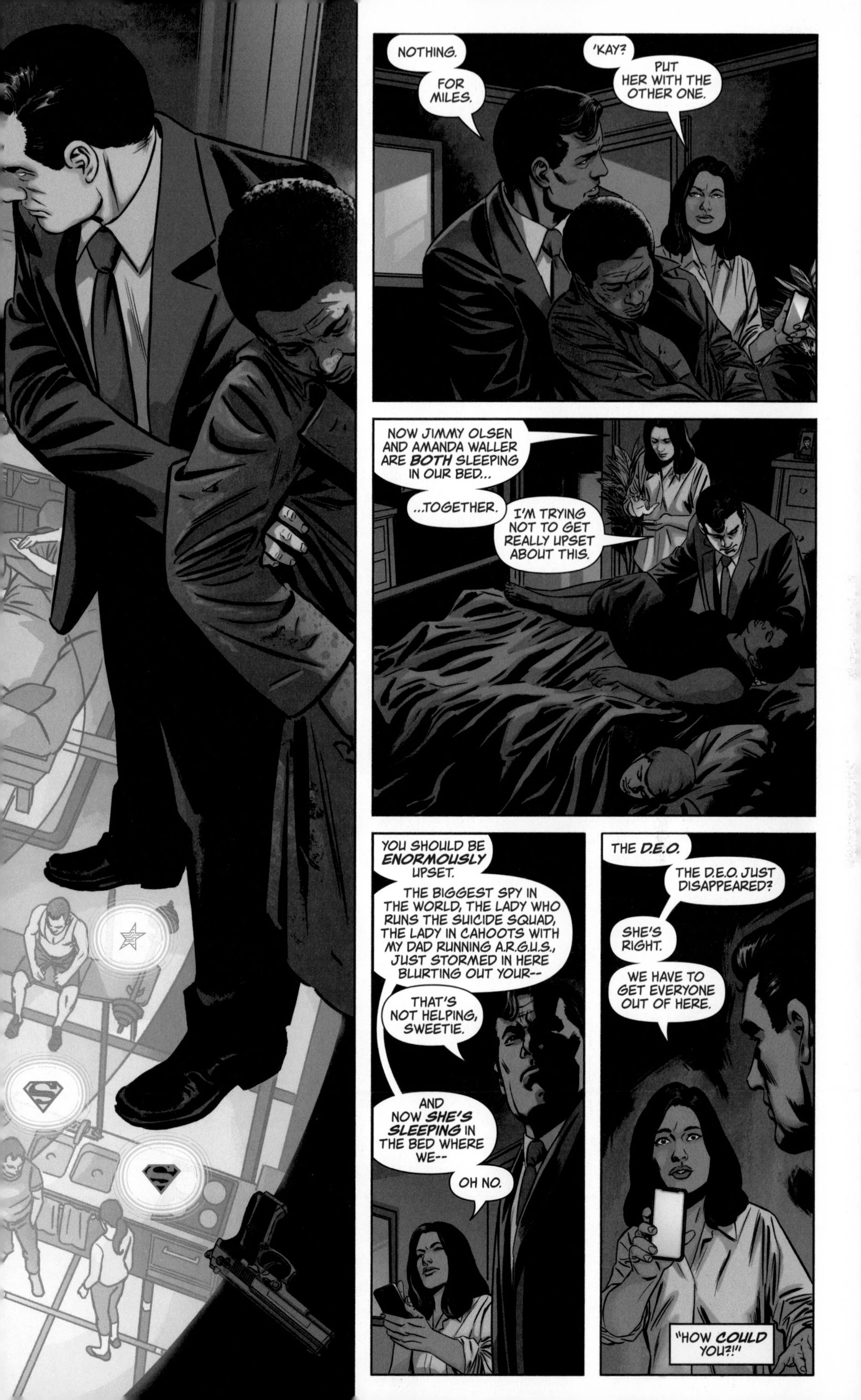
NOTHING.
FOR MILES.
'KAY?
PUT HER WITH THE OTHER ONE.
NOW JIMMY OLSEN AND AMANDA WALLER ARE **BOTH** SLEEPING IN OUR BED...
...TOGETHER.
I'M TRYING NOT TO GET REALLY UPSET ABOUT THIS.
YOU SHOULD BE **ENORMOUSLY** UPSET.
THE BIGGEST SPY IN THE WORLD, THE LADY WHO RUNS THE SUICIDE SQUAD, THE LADY IN CAHOOTS WITH MY DAD RUNNING A.R.G.U.S., JUST STORMED IN HERE BLURTING OUT YOUR--
THAT'S NOT HELPING, SWEETIE.
AND NOW **SHE'S SLEEPING** IN THE BED WHERE WE--
OH NO.
THE ***D.E.O.***
THE D.E.O. JUST DISAPPEARED?
SHE'S RIGHT.
WE HAVE TO GET EVERYONE OUT OF HERE.
"HOW **COULD** YOU?!"

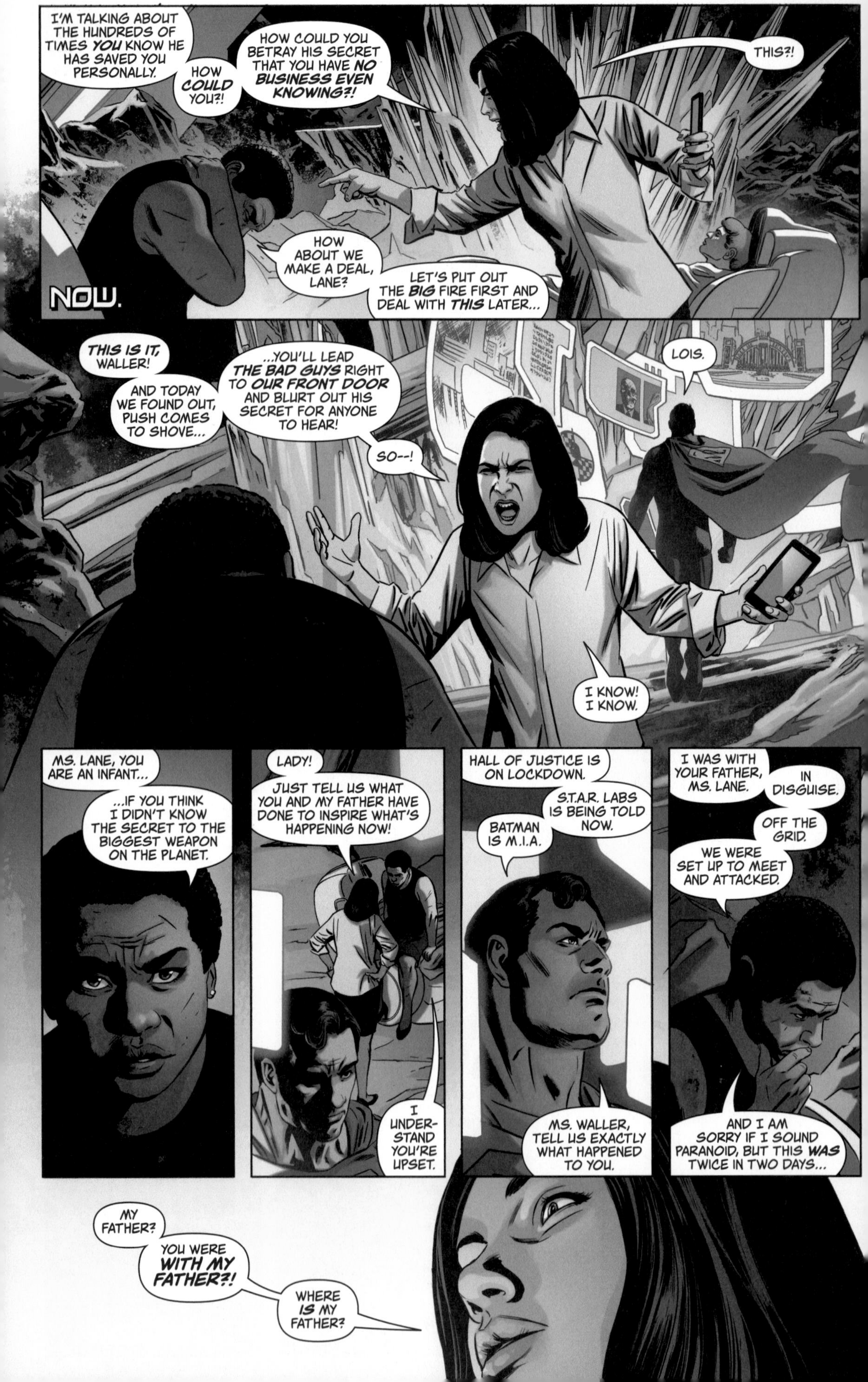

I'M TALKING ABOUT THE HUNDREDS OF TIMES YOU KNOW HE HAS SAVED YOU PERSONALLY.
HOW COULD YOU?!
HOW COULD YOU BETRAY HIS SECRET THAT YOU HAVE NO BUSINESS EVEN KNOWING?!
THIS?!
HOW ABOUT WE MAKE A DEAL, LANE?
LET'S PUT OUT THE BIG FIRE FIRST AND DEAL WITH THIS LATER...
NOW.
THIS IS IT, WALLER!
AND TODAY WE FOUND OUT, PUSH COMES TO SHOVE...
...YOU'LL LEAD THE BAD GUYS RIGHT TO OUR FRONT DOOR AND BLURT OUT HIS SECRET FOR ANYONE TO HEAR!
SO--!
LOIS.
I KNOW! I KNOW.
MS. LANE, YOU ARE AN INFANT...
...IF YOU THINK I DIDN'T KNOW THE SECRET TO THE BIGGEST WEAPON ON THE PLANET.
LADY!
JUST TELL US WHAT YOU AND MY FATHER HAVE DONE TO INSPIRE WHAT'S HAPPENING NOW!
I UNDER-STAND YOU'RE UPSET.
HALL OF JUSTICE IS ON LOCKDOWN.
S.T.A.R. LABS IS BEING TOLD NOW.
BATMAN IS M.I.A.
MS. WALLER, TELL US EXACTLY WHAT HAPPENED TO YOU.
I WAS WITH YOUR FATHER, MS. LANE.
IN DISGUISE.
OFF THE GRID.
WE WERE SET UP TO MEET AND ATTACKED.
AND I AM SORRY IF I SOUND PARANOID, BUT THIS WAS TWICE IN TWO DAYS...
MY FATHER?
YOU WERE WITH MY FATHER?!
WHERE IS MY FATHER?

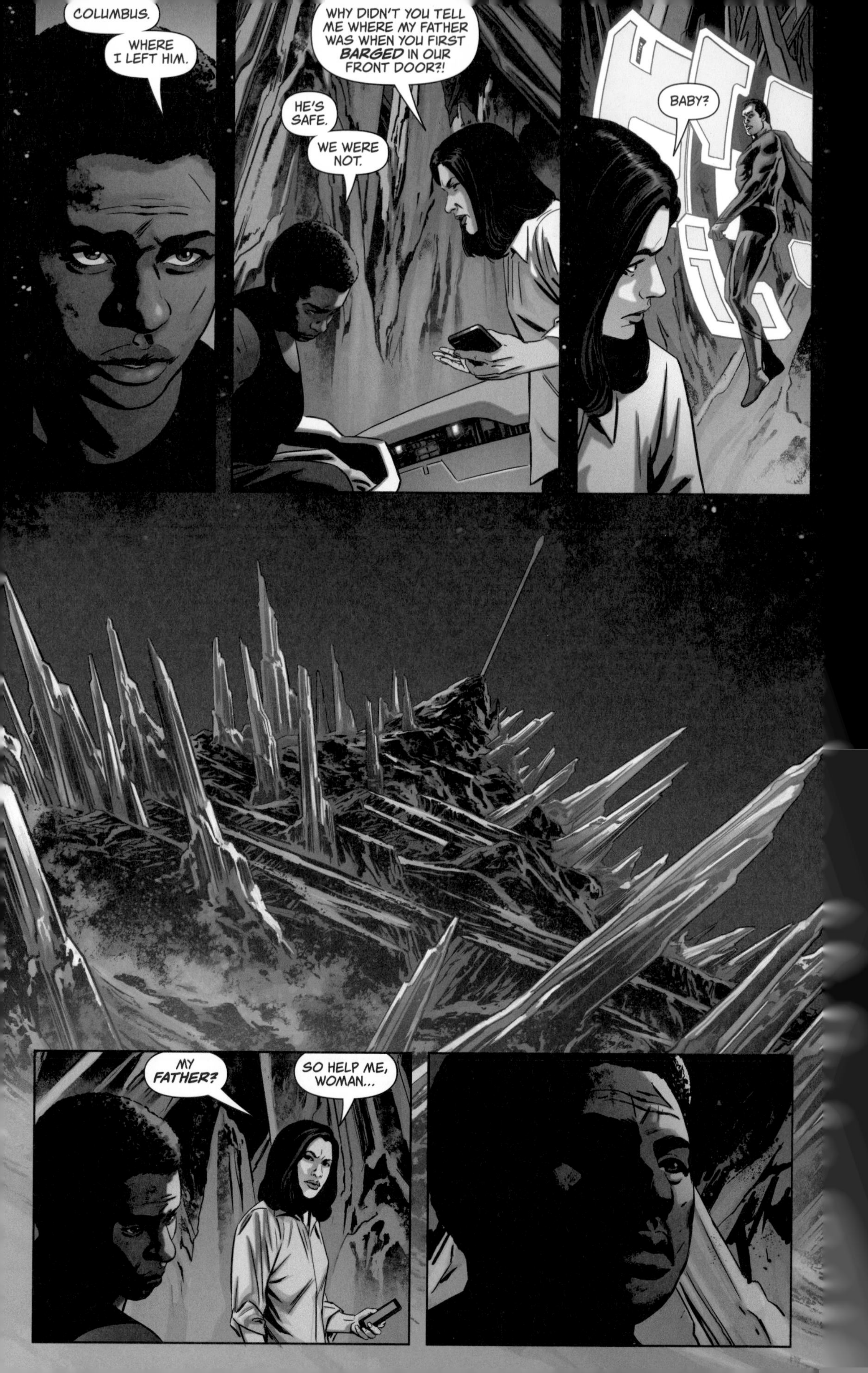
COLUMBUS.
WHERE I LEFT HIM.
WHY DIDN'T YOU TELL ME WHERE MY FATHER WAS WHEN YOU FIRST **BARGED** IN OUR FRONT DOOR?!
HE'S SAFE.
WE WERE NOT.
BABY?
MY *FATHER*?
SO HELP ME, WOMAN...

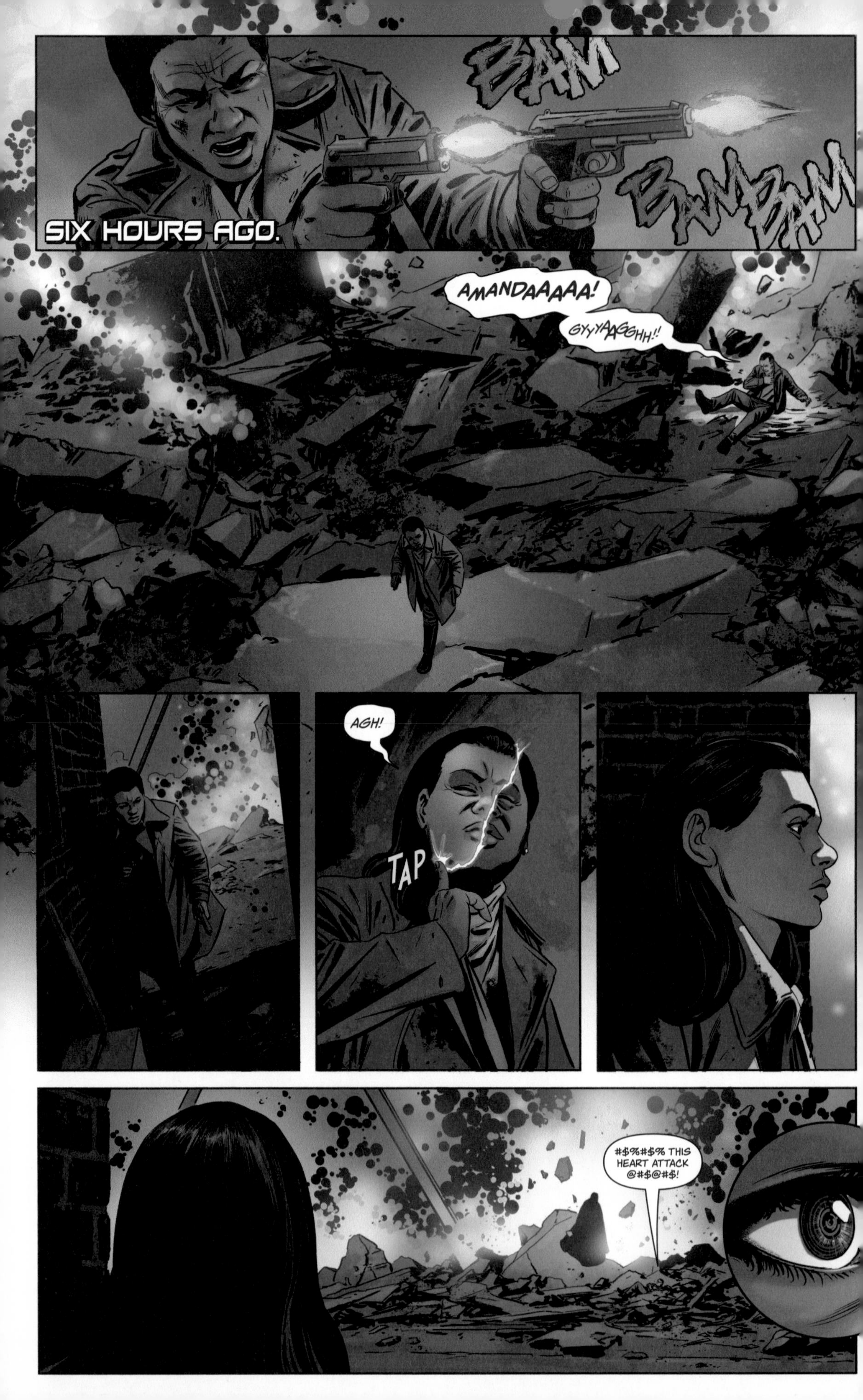
BAM
SIX HOURS AGO.
BAMBAM
AMANDAAAAA!
GYYYAAGGHH!!
AGH!
TAP
#$%#$% THIS HEART ATTACK @#$@#$!

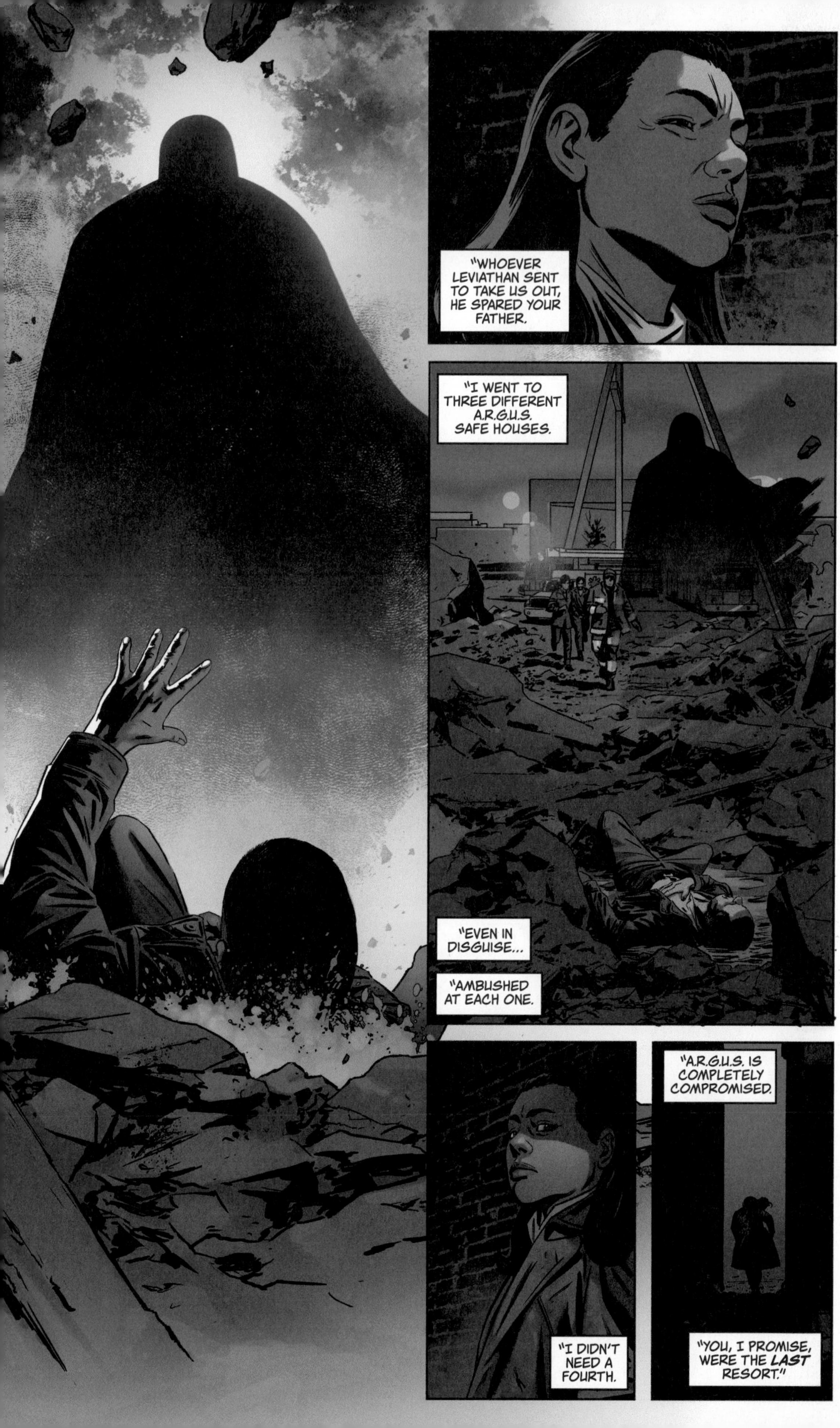
"WHOEVER LEVIATHAN SENT TO TAKE US OUT, HE SPARED YOUR FATHER.
"I WENT TO THREE DIFFERENT A.R.G.U.S. SAFE HOUSES.
"EVEN IN DISGUISE...
"AMBUSHED AT EACH ONE.
"A.R.G.U.S. IS COMPLETELY COMPROMISED.
"I DIDN'T NEED A FOURTH.
"YOU, I PROMISE, WERE THE LAST RESORT."

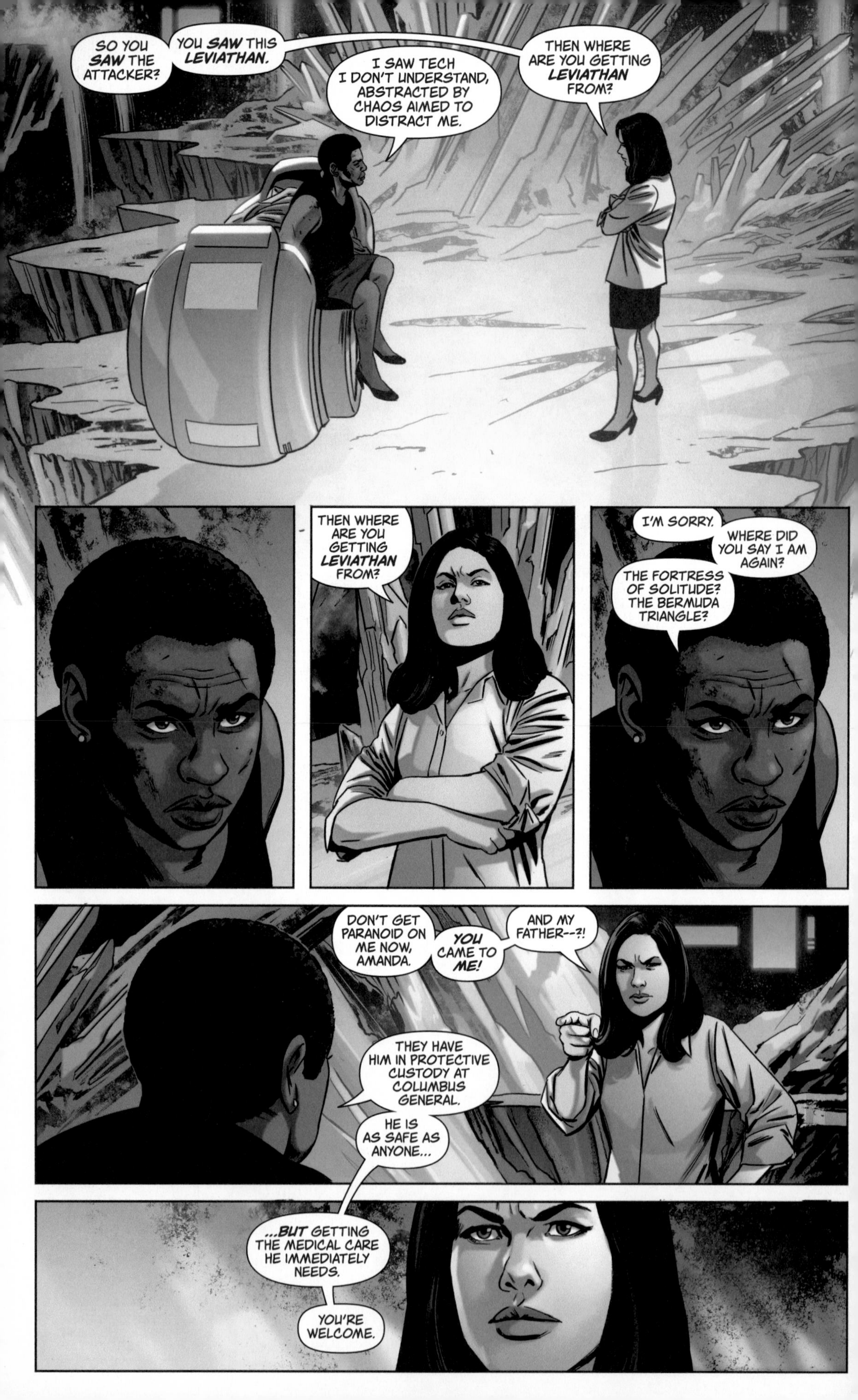
SO YOU SAW THE ATTACKER?
YOU SAW THIS LEVIATHAN.
I SAW TECH I DON'T UNDERSTAND, ABSTRACTED BY CHAOS AIMED TO DISTRACT ME.
THEN WHERE ARE YOU GETTING LEVIATHAN FROM?
THEN WHERE ARE YOU GETTING LEVIATHAN FROM?
I'M SORRY.
WHERE DID YOU SAY I AM AGAIN?
THE FORTRESS OF SOLITUDE? THE BERMUDA TRIANGLE?
DON'T GET PARANOID ON ME NOW, AMANDA.
YOU CAME TO ME!
AND MY FATHER--?!
THEY HAVE HIM IN PROTECTIVE CUSTODY AT COLUMBUS GENERAL.
HE IS AS SAFE AS ANYONE...
...BUT GETTING THE MEDICAL CARE HE IMMEDIATELY NEEDS.
YOU'RE WELCOME.

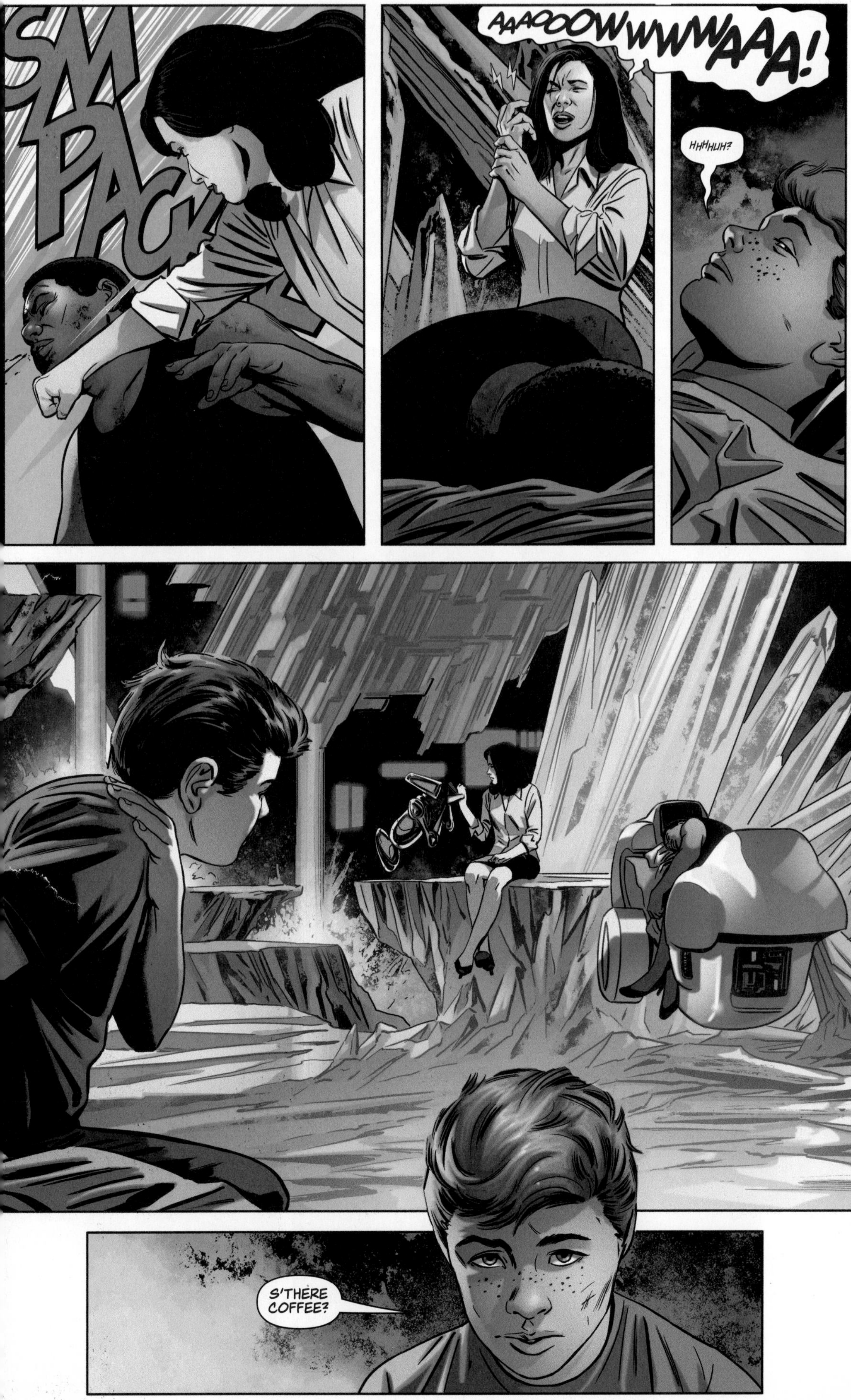
SMPAC
AAAOOOWWWWAAA!
HHHHUH?
S'THERE COFFEE?

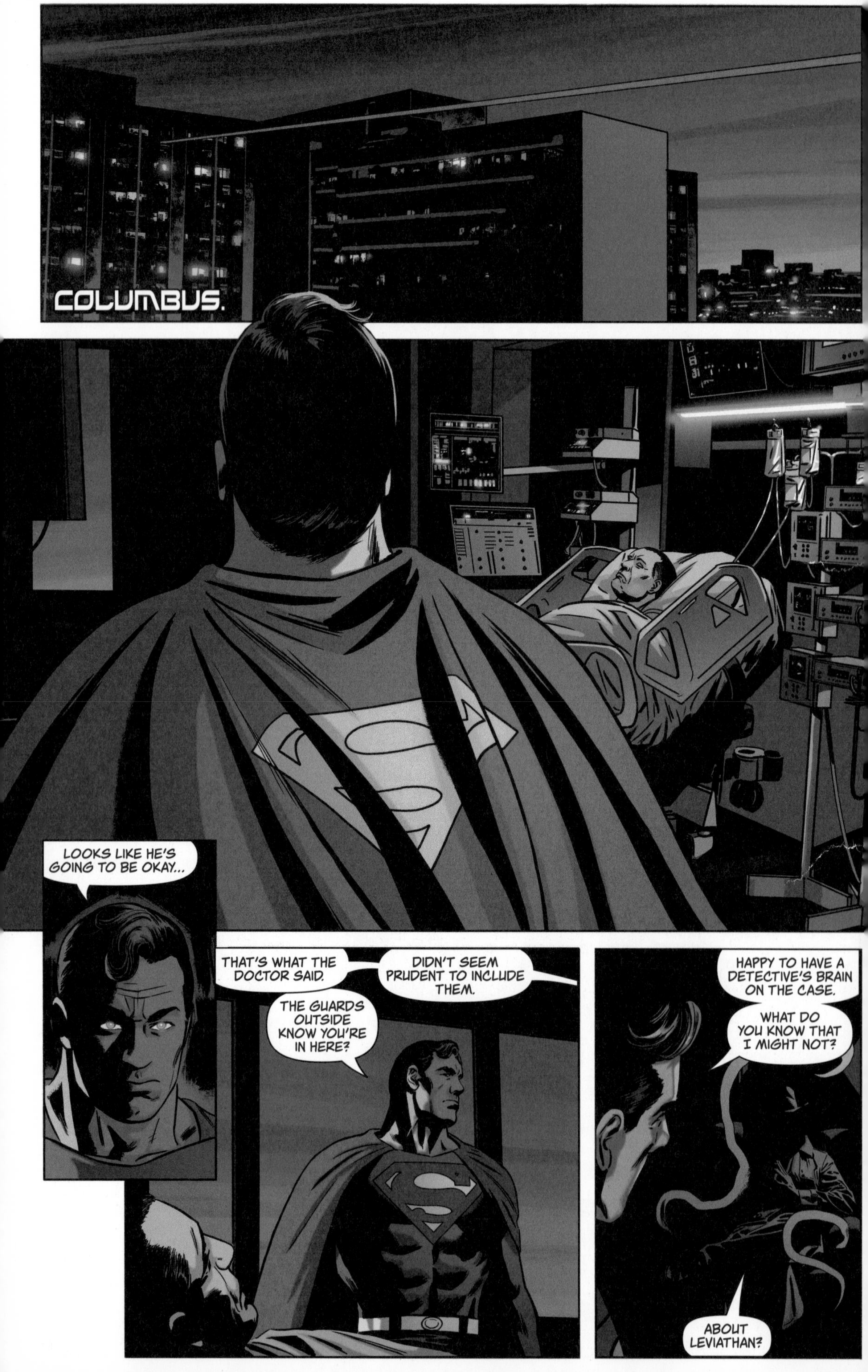
COLUMBUS.
LOOKS LIKE HE'S GOING TO BE OKAY...
THAT'S WHAT THE DOCTOR SAID.
THE GUARDS OUTSIDE KNOW YOU'RE IN HERE?
DIDN'T SEEM PRUDENT TO INCLUDE THEM.
HAPPY TO HAVE A DETECTIVE'S BRAIN ON THE CASE.
WHAT DO YOU KNOW THAT I MIGHT NOT?
ABOUT LEVIATHAN?

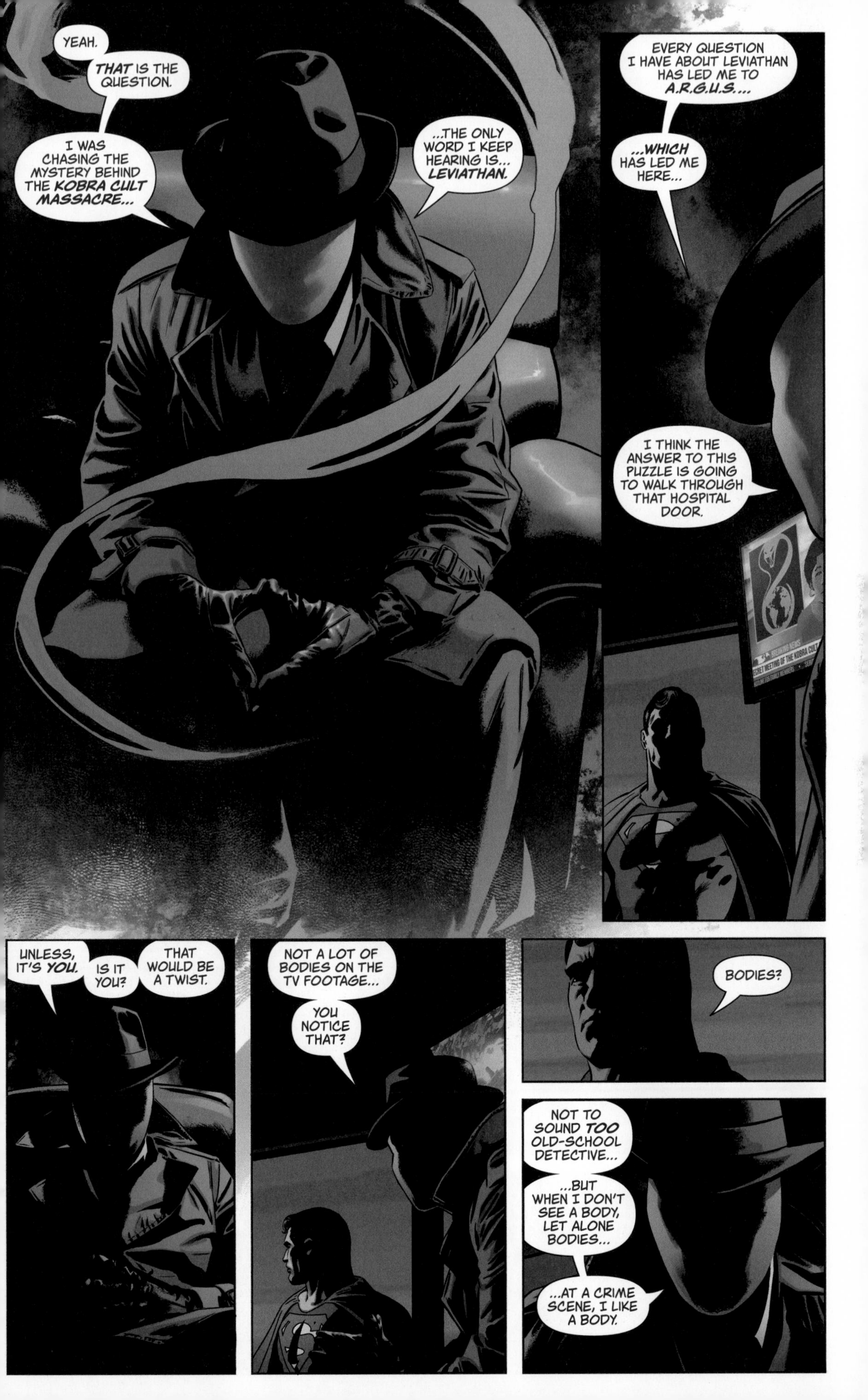
YEAH.
THAT IS THE QUESTION.
I WAS CHASING THE MYSTERY BEHIND THE KOBRA CULT MASSACRE...
...THE ONLY WORD I KEEP HEARING IS... LEVIATHAN.
EVERY QUESTION I HAVE ABOUT LEVIATHAN HAS LED ME TO A.R.G.U.S....
...WHICH HAS LED ME HERE...
I THINK THE ANSWER TO THIS PUZZLE IS GOING TO WALK THROUGH THAT HOSPITAL DOOR.
UNLESS, IT'S YOU.
IS IT YOU?
THAT WOULD BE A TWIST.
NOT A LOT OF BODIES ON THE TV FOOTAGE...
YOU NOTICE THAT?
BODIES?
NOT TO SOUND TOO OLD-SCHOOL DETECTIVE...
...BUT WHEN I DON'T SEE A BODY, LET ALONE BODIES...
...AT A CRIME SCENE, I LIKE A BODY.

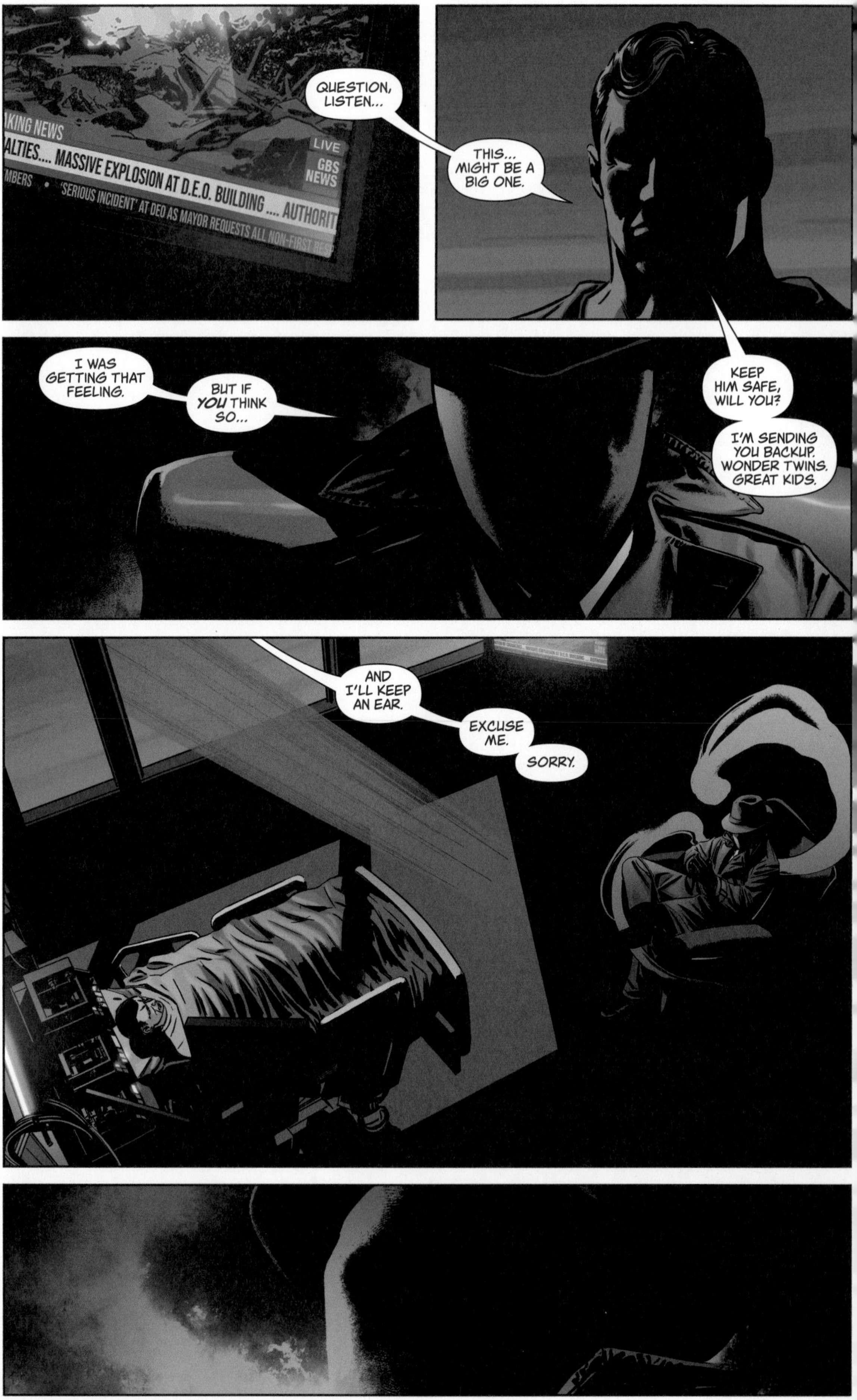

KING NEWS
LIVE
GBS NEWS
ALTIES.... MASSIVE EXPLOSION AT D.E.O. BUILDING .... AUTHORIT
MBERS • 'SERIOUS INCIDENT' AT DEO AS MAYOR REQUESTS ALL NON-FIRST RES
QUESTION, LISTEN...
THIS... MIGHT BE A BIG ONE.
KEEP HIM SAFE, WILL YOU?
I'M SENDING YOU BACKUP. WONDER TWINS. GREAT KIDS.
I WAS GETTING THAT FEELING.
BUT IF *YOU* THINK SO...
AND I'LL KEEP AN EAR.
EXCUSE ME.
SORRY.

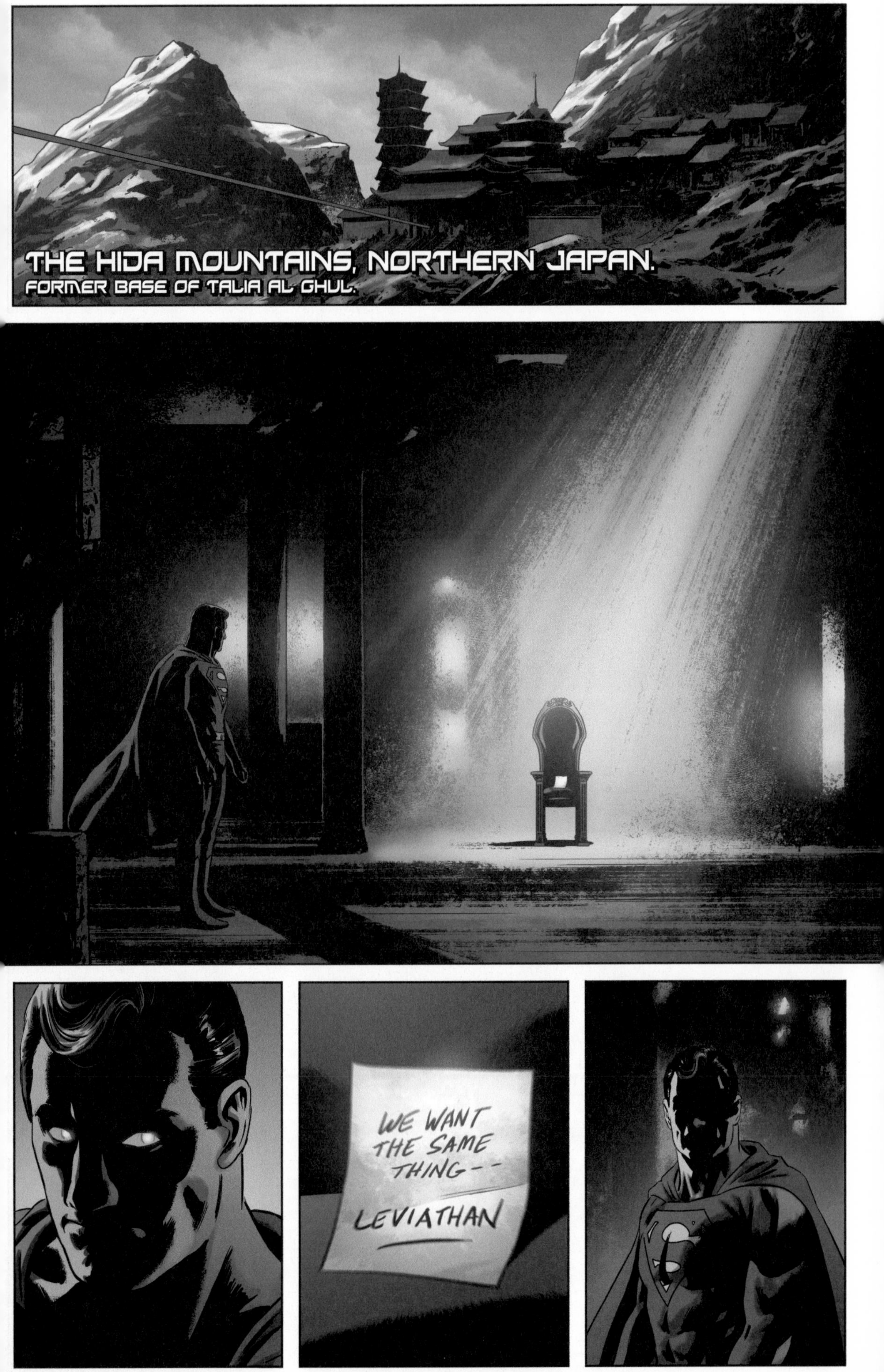
THE HIDA MOUNTAINS, NORTHERN JAPAN.
FORMER BASE OF TALIA AL GHUL.
WE WANT THE SAME THING--
LEVIATHAN

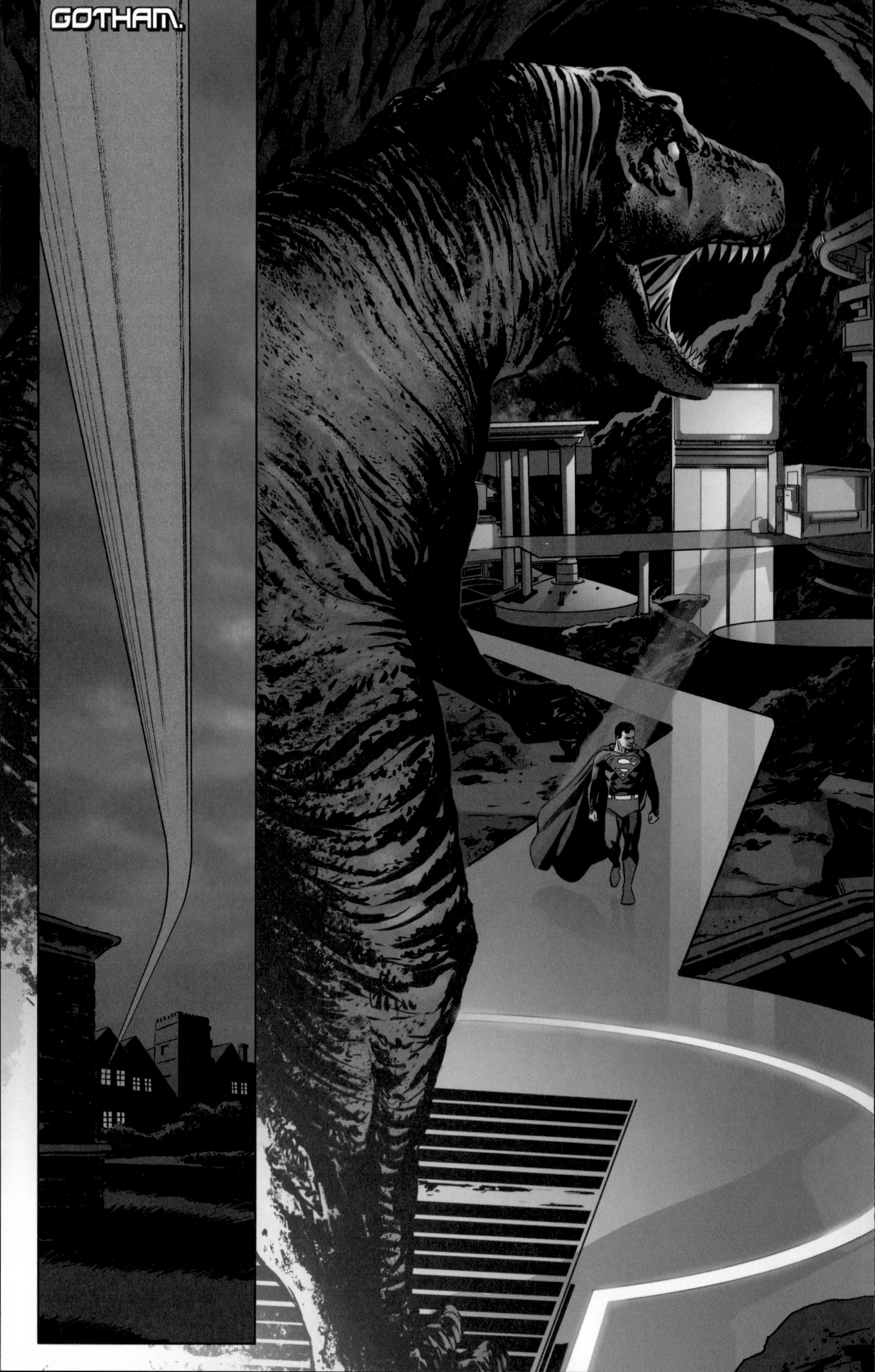
GOTHAM.

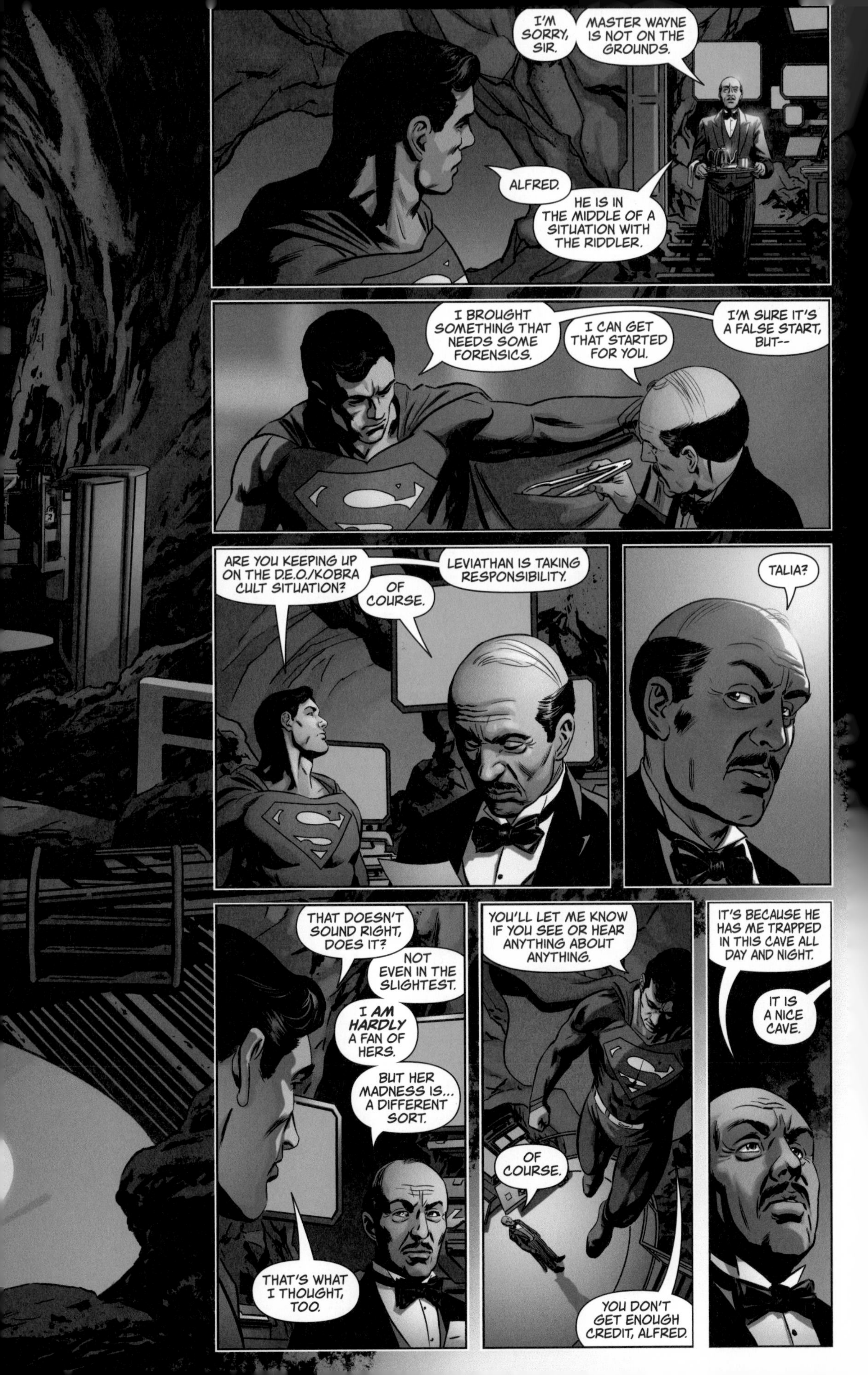
I'M SORRY, SIR.
MASTER WAYNE IS NOT ON THE GROUNDS.
ALFRED.
HE IS IN THE MIDDLE OF A SITUATION WITH THE RIDDLER.
I BROUGHT SOMETHING THAT NEEDS SOME FORENSICS.
I CAN GET THAT STARTED FOR YOU.
I'M SURE IT'S A FALSE START, BUT--
ARE YOU KEEPING UP ON THE D.E.O./KOBRA CULT SITUATION?
OF COURSE.
LEVIATHAN IS TAKING RESPONSIBILITY.
TALIA?
THAT DOESN'T SOUND RIGHT, DOES IT?
NOT EVEN IN THE SLIGHTEST.
I AM HARDLY A FAN OF HERS.
BUT HER MADNESS IS... A DIFFERENT SORT.
THAT'S WHAT I THOUGHT, TOO.
YOU'LL LET ME KNOW IF YOU SEE OR HEAR ANYTHING ABOUT ANYTHING.
OF COURSE.
YOU DON'T GET ENOUGH CREDIT, ALFRED.
IT'S BECAUSE HE HAS ME TRAPPED IN THIS CAVE ALL DAY AND NIGHT.
IT IS A NICE CAVE.

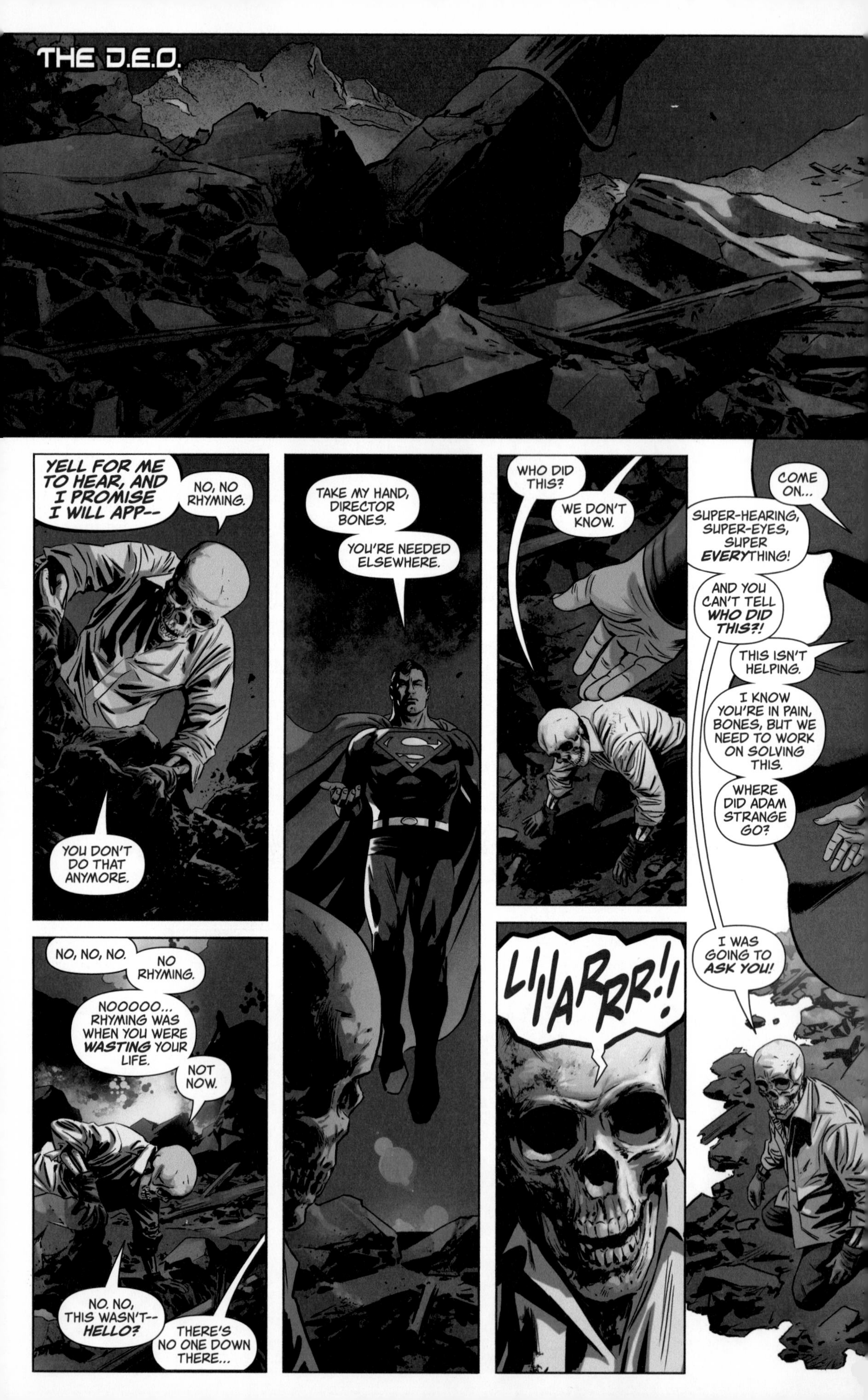
THE D.E.O.
YELL FOR ME TO HEAR, AND I PROMISE I WILL APP--
NO, NO RHYMING.
YOU DON'T DO THAT ANYMORE.
TAKE MY HAND, DIRECTOR BONES.
YOU'RE NEEDED ELSEWHERE.
WHO DID THIS?
WE DON'T KNOW.
COME ON...
SUPER-HEARING, SUPER-EYES, SUPER EVERYTHING!
AND YOU CAN'T TELL WHO DID THIS?!
THIS ISN'T HELPING.
I KNOW YOU'RE IN PAIN, BONES, BUT WE NEED TO WORK ON SOLVING THIS.
WHERE DID ADAM STRANGE GO?
NO, NO, NO.
NO RHYMING.
NOOOOO... RHYMING WAS WHEN YOU WERE WASTING YOUR LIFE.
NOT NOW.
NO. NO, THIS WASN'T-- HELLO?
THERE'S NO ONE DOWN THERE...
LIIIARRR!!
I WAS GOING TO ASK YOU!

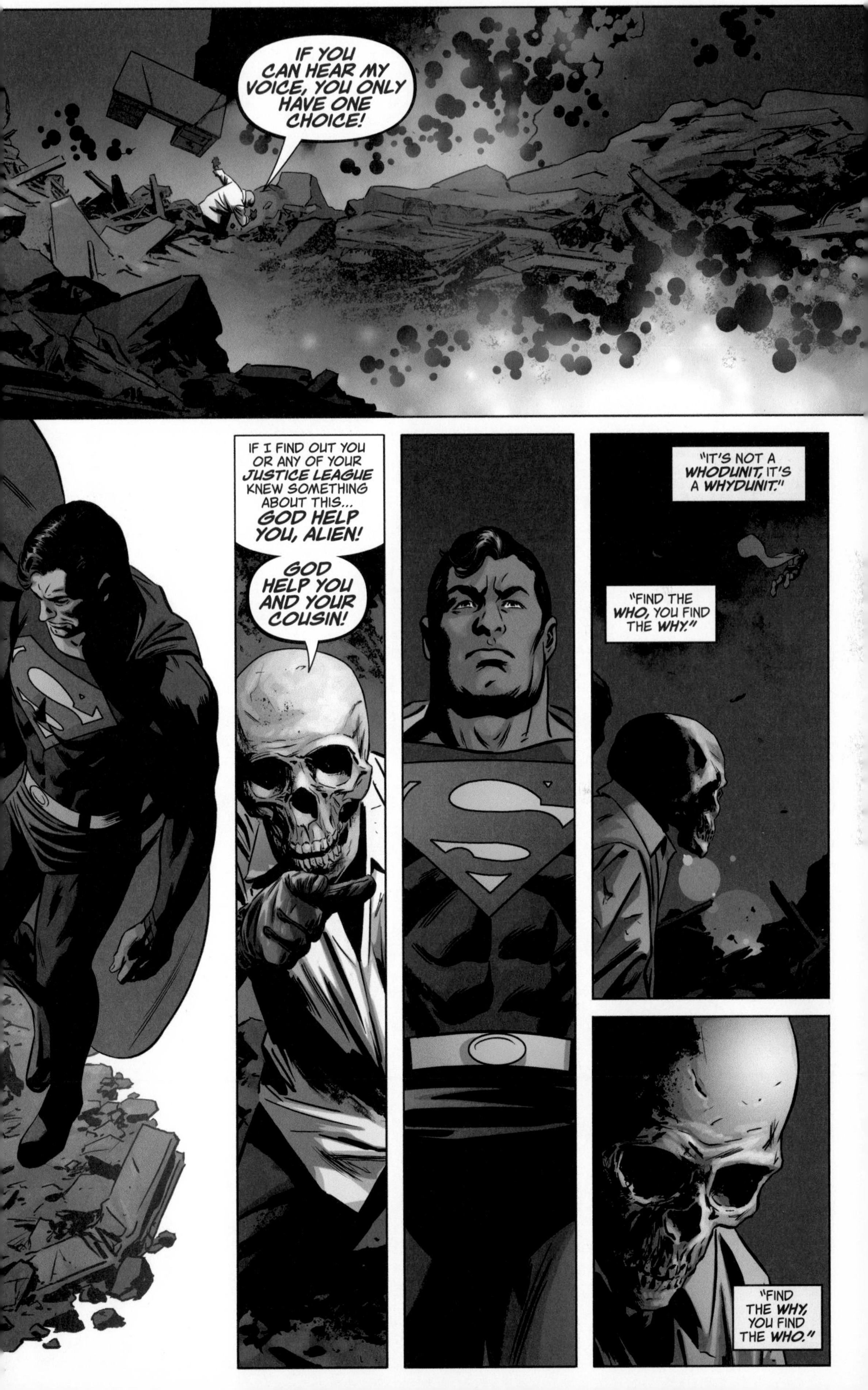
IF YOU CAN HEAR MY VOICE, YOU ONLY HAVE ONE CHOICE!
IF I FIND OUT YOU OR ANY OF YOUR JUSTICE LEAGUE KNEW SOMETHING ABOUT THIS... GOD HELP YOU, ALIEN!
GOD HELP YOU AND YOUR COUSIN!
"IT'S NOT A WHODUNIT, IT'S A WHYDUNIT."
"FIND THE WHO, YOU FIND THE WHY."
"FIND THE WHY, YOU FIND THE WHO."

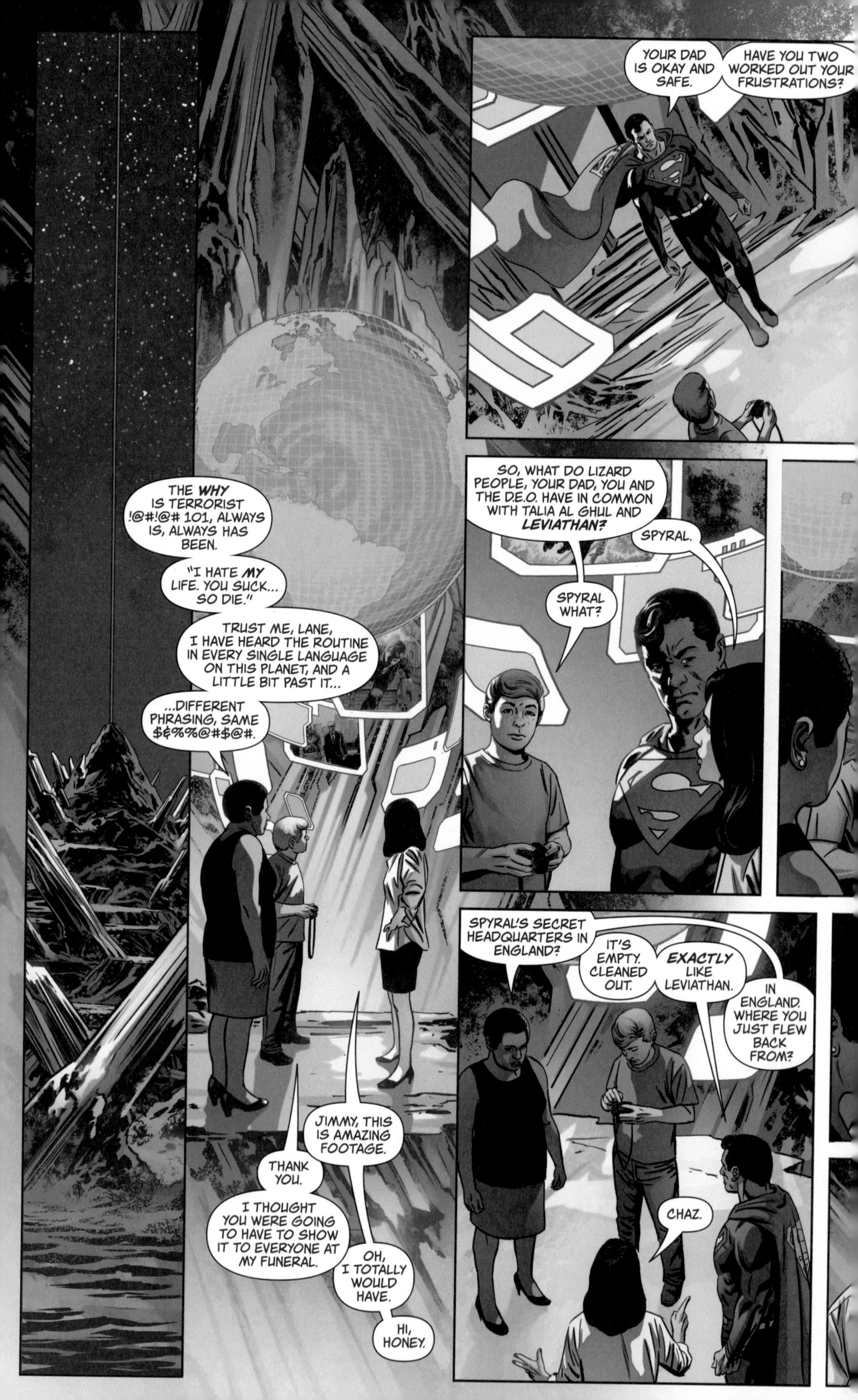
YOUR DAD IS OKAY AND SAFE.
HAVE YOU TWO WORKED OUT YOUR FRUSTRATIONS?
THE WHY IS TERRORIST !@#!@# 101, ALWAYS IS, ALWAYS HAS BEEN.
"I HATE MY LIFE. YOU SUCK... SO DIE."
TRUST ME, LANE, I HAVE HEARD THE ROUTINE IN EVERY SINGLE LANGUAGE ON THIS PLANET, AND A LITTLE BIT PAST IT...
...DIFFERENT PHRASING, SAME $&%%@#$@#.
JIMMY, THIS IS AMAZING FOOTAGE.
THANK YOU.
I THOUGHT YOU WERE GOING TO HAVE TO SHOW IT TO EVERYONE AT MY FUNERAL.
OH, I TOTALLY WOULD HAVE.
HI, HONEY.
SO, WHAT DO LIZARD PEOPLE, YOUR DAD, YOU AND THE D.E.O. HAVE IN COMMON WITH TALIA AL GHUL AND LEVIATHAN?
SPYRAL.
SPYRAL WHAT?
SPYRAL'S SECRET HEADQUARTERS IN ENGLAND?
IT'S EMPTY. CLEANED OUT.
EXACTLY LIKE LEVIATHAN.
IN ENGLAND. WHERE YOU JUST FLEW BACK FROM?
CHAZ.

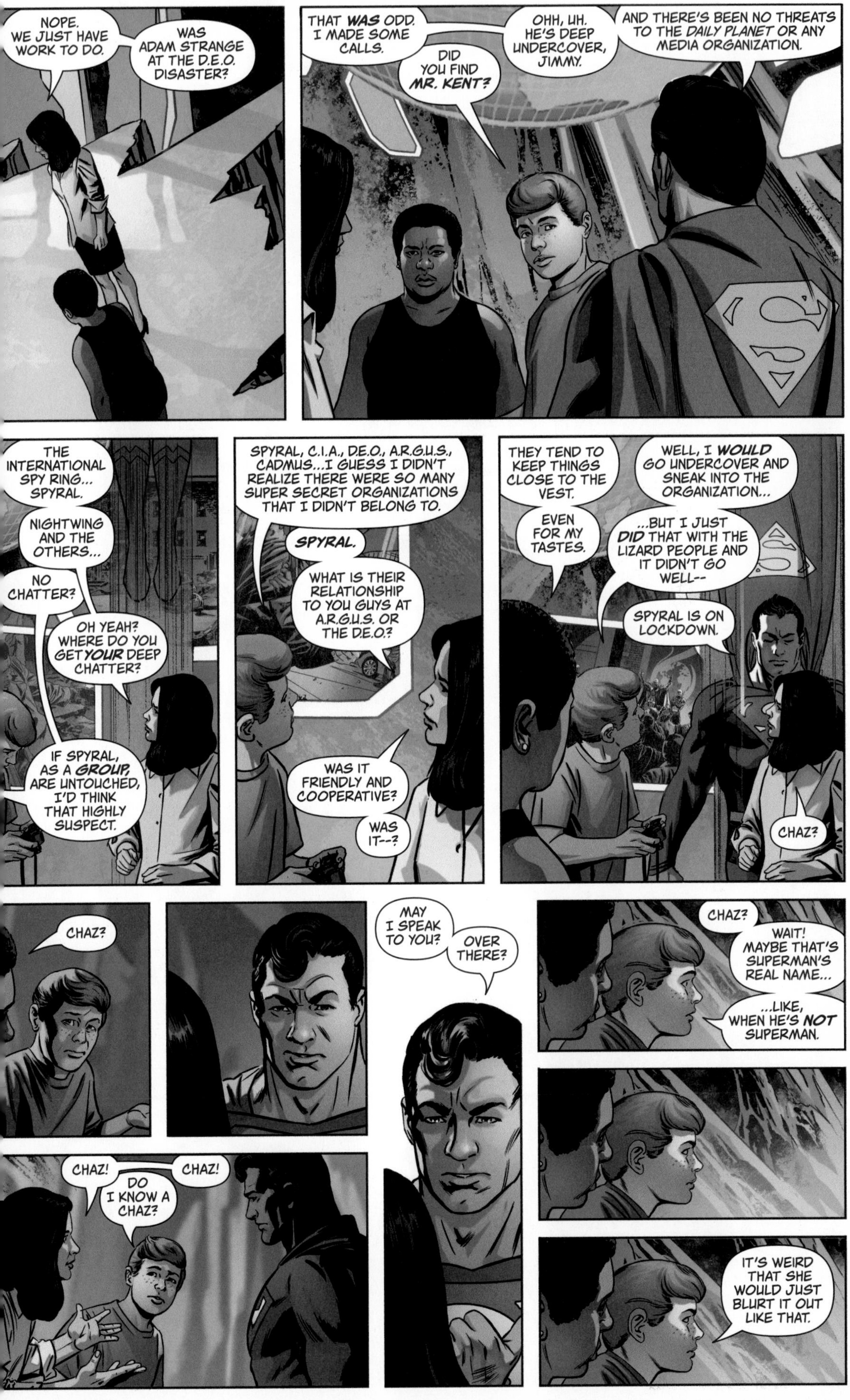
NOPE. WE JUST HAVE WORK TO DO.
WAS ADAM STRANGE AT THE D.E.O. DISASTER?
THAT WAS ODD. I MADE SOME CALLS.
DID YOU FIND MR. KENT?
OHH, UH. HE'S DEEP UNDERCOVER, JIMMY.
AND THERE'S BEEN NO THREATS TO THE DAILY PLANET OR ANY MEDIA ORGANIZATION.
THE INTERNATIONAL SPY RING... SPYRAL.
NIGHTWING AND THE OTHERS...
NO CHATTER?
OH YEAH? WHERE DO YOU GET YOUR DEEP CHATTER?
IF SPYRAL, AS A GROUP, ARE UNTOUCHED, I'D THINK THAT HIGHLY SUSPECT.
SPYRAL, C.I.A., D.E.O., A.R.G.U.S., CADMUS...I GUESS I DIDN'T REALIZE THERE WERE SO MANY SUPER SECRET ORGANIZATIONS THAT I DIDN'T BELONG TO.
SPYRAL.
WHAT IS THEIR RELATIONSHIP TO YOU GUYS AT A.R.G.U.S. OR THE D.E.O.?
WAS IT FRIENDLY AND COOPERATIVE?
WAS IT--?
THEY TEND TO KEEP THINGS CLOSE TO THE VEST.
EVEN FOR MY TASTES.
WELL, I WOULD GO UNDERCOVER AND SNEAK INTO THE ORGANIZATION...
...BUT I JUST DID THAT WITH THE LIZARD PEOPLE AND IT DIDN'T GO WELL--
SPYRAL IS ON LOCKDOWN.
CHAZ?
CHAZ?
MAY I SPEAK TO YOU?
OVER THERE?
CHAZ?
WAIT! MAYBE THAT'S SUPERMAN'S REAL NAME...
...LIKE, WHEN HE'S NOT SUPERMAN.
CHAZ!
DO I KNOW A CHAZ?
CHAZ!
IT'S WEIRD THAT SHE WOULD JUST BLURT IT OUT LIKE THAT.

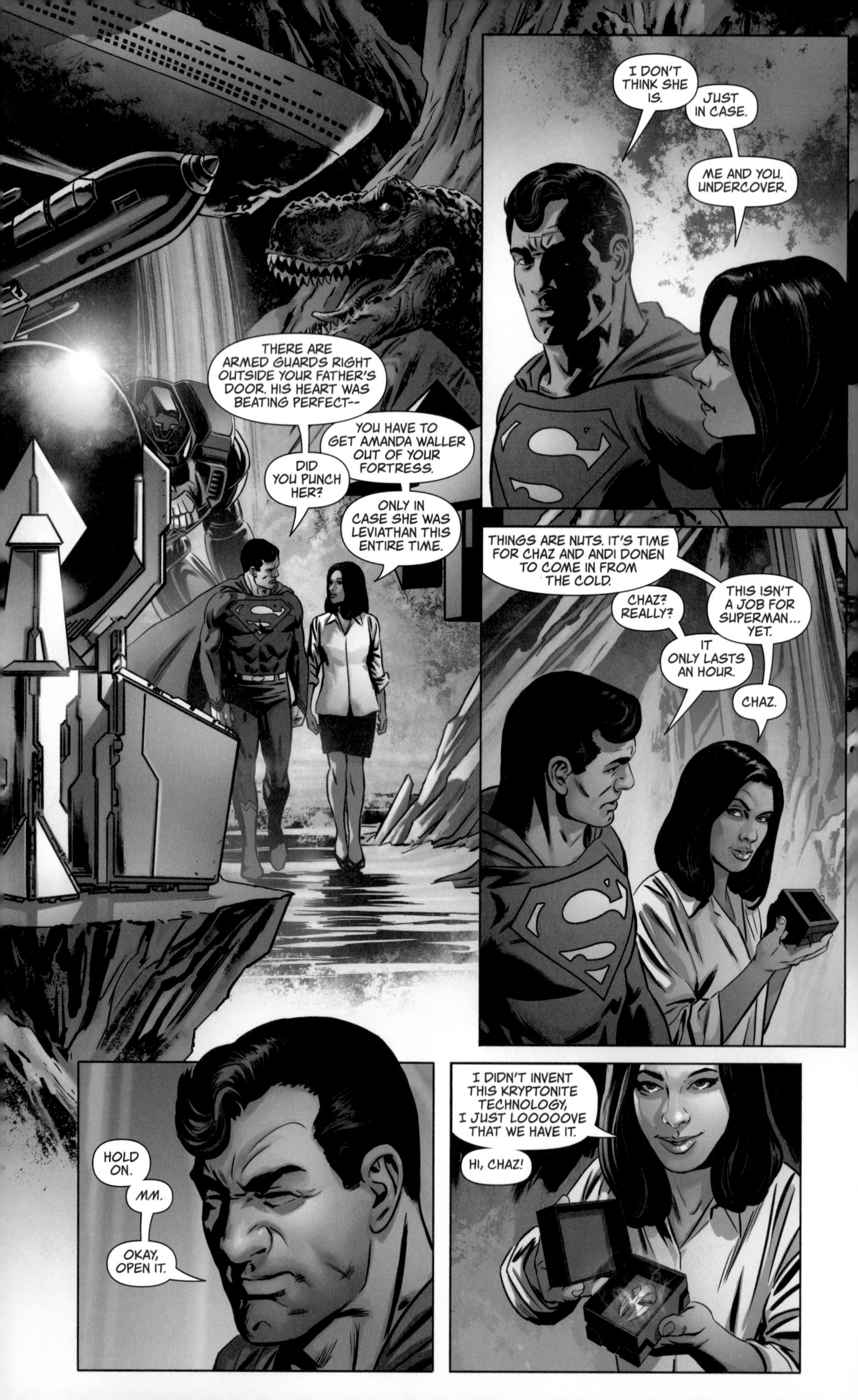
THERE ARE ARMED GUARDS RIGHT OUTSIDE YOUR FATHER'S DOOR. HIS HEART WAS BEATING PERFECT--
YOU HAVE TO GET AMANDA WALLER OUT OF YOUR FORTRESS.
DID YOU PUNCH HER?
ONLY IN CASE SHE WAS LEVIATHAN THIS ENTIRE TIME.
I DON'T THINK SHE IS.
JUST IN CASE.
ME AND YOU. UNDERCOVER.
THINGS ARE NUTS. IT'S TIME FOR CHAZ AND ANDI DONEN TO COME IN FROM THE COLD.
THIS ISN'T A JOB FOR SUPERMAN... YET.
CHAZ? REALLY?
IT ONLY LASTS AN HOUR.
CHAZ.
HOLD ON.
MM.
OKAY, OPEN IT.
I DIDN'T INVENT THIS KRYPTONITE TECHNOLOGY, I JUST LOOOOOVE THAT WE HAVE IT.
HI, CHAZ!

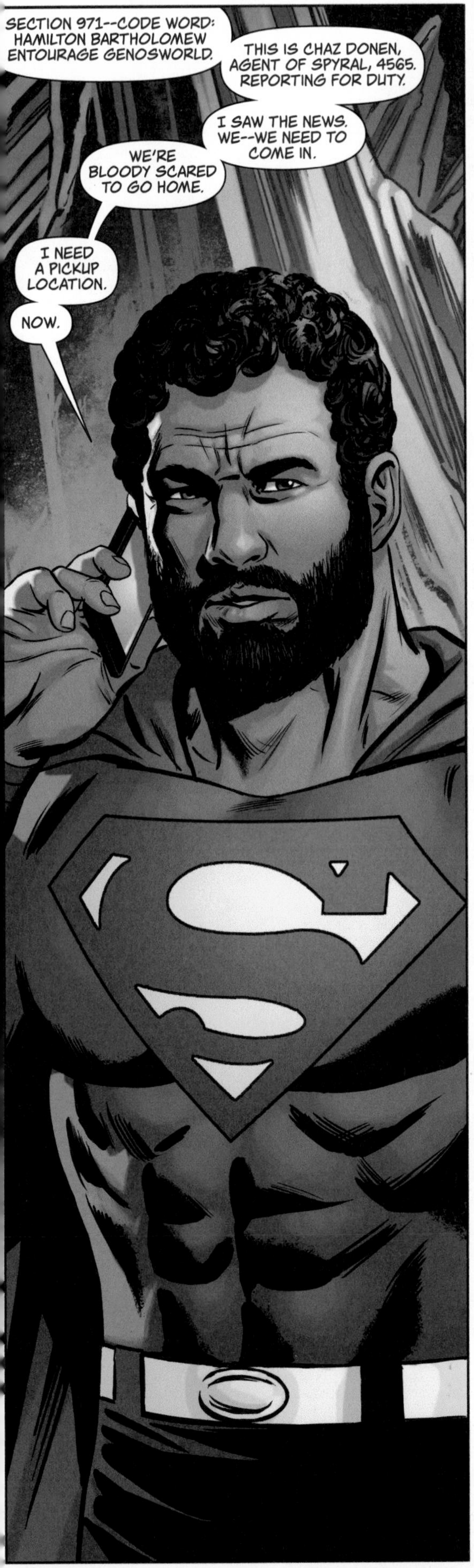
SECTION 971--CODE WORD: HAMILTON BARTHOLOMEW ENTOURAGE GENOSWORLD.
THIS IS CHAZ DONEN, AGENT OF SPYRAL, 4565. REPORTING FOR DUTY.
I SAW THE NEWS. WE--WE NEED TO COME IN.
WE'RE BLOODY SCARED TO GO HOME.
I NEED A PICKUP LOCATION.
NOW.
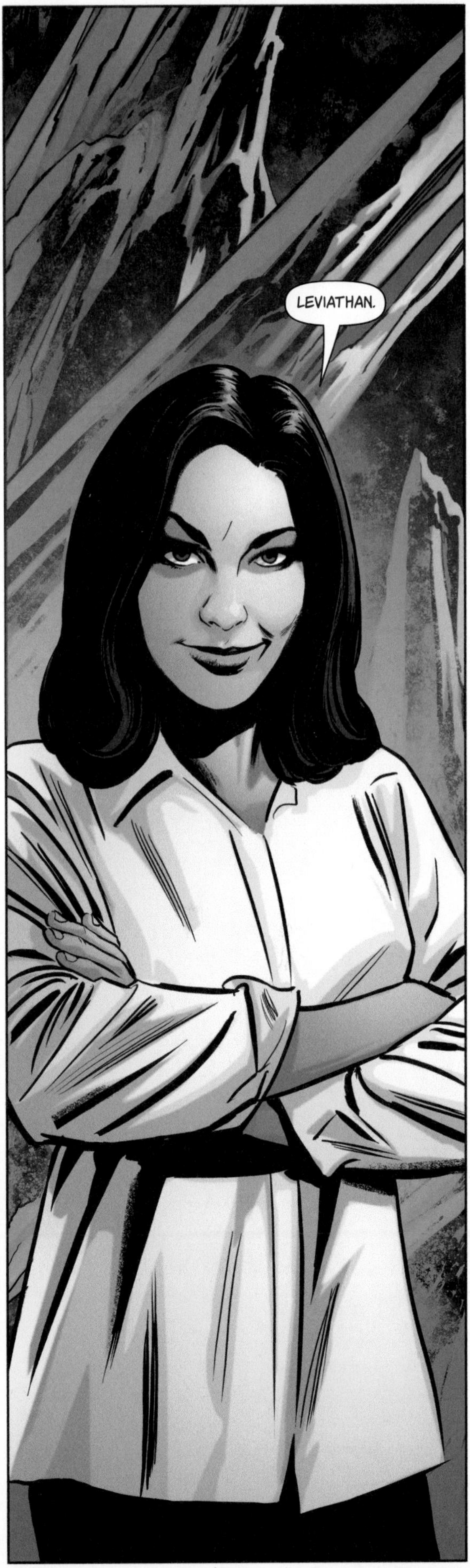
LEVIATHAN.

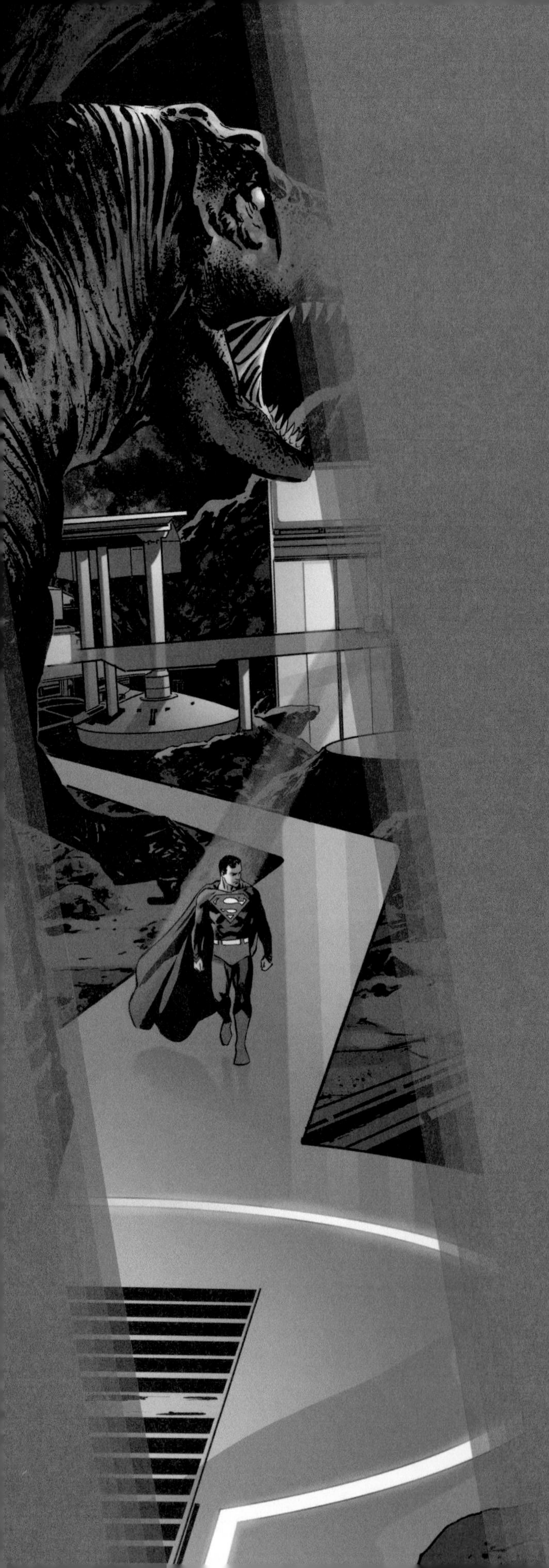

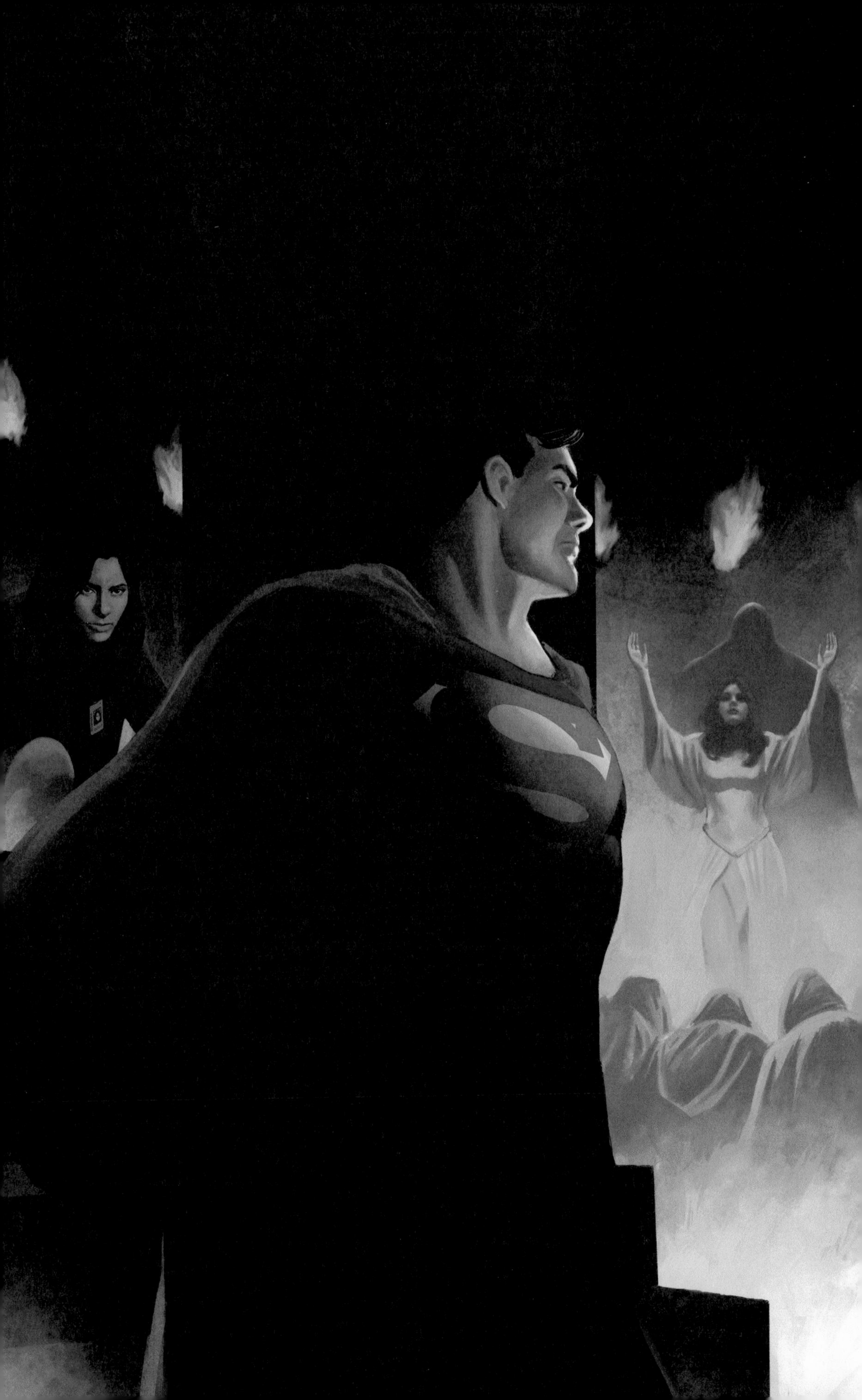

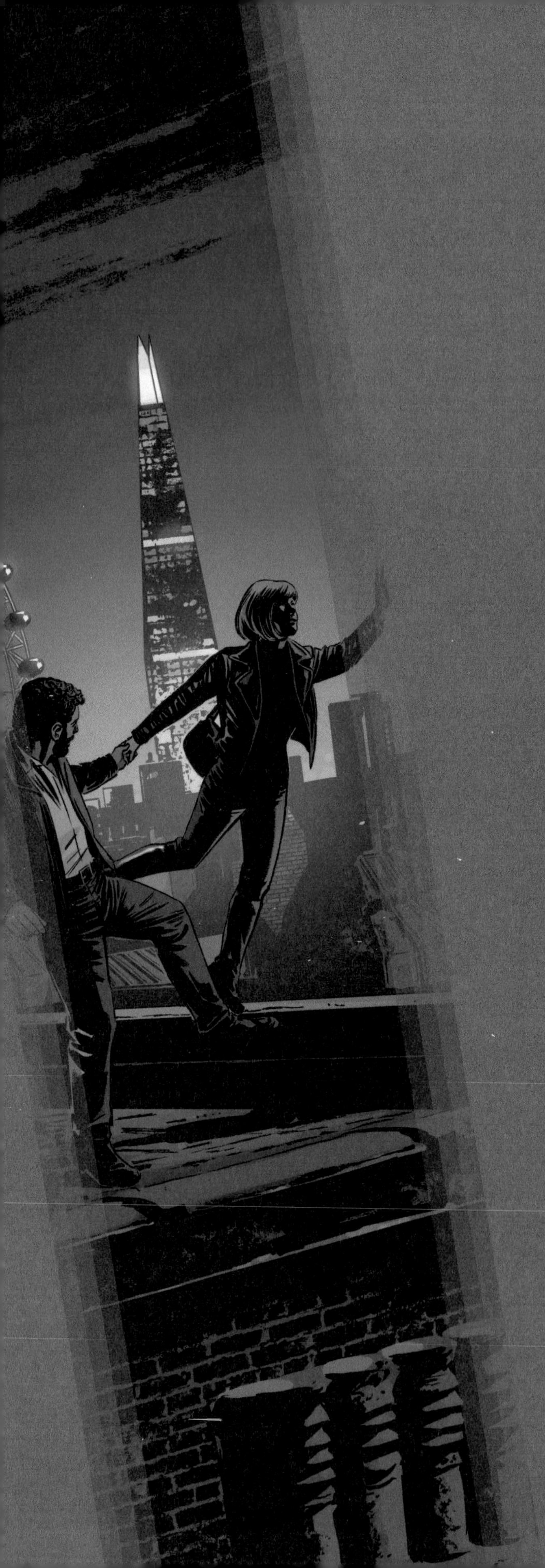

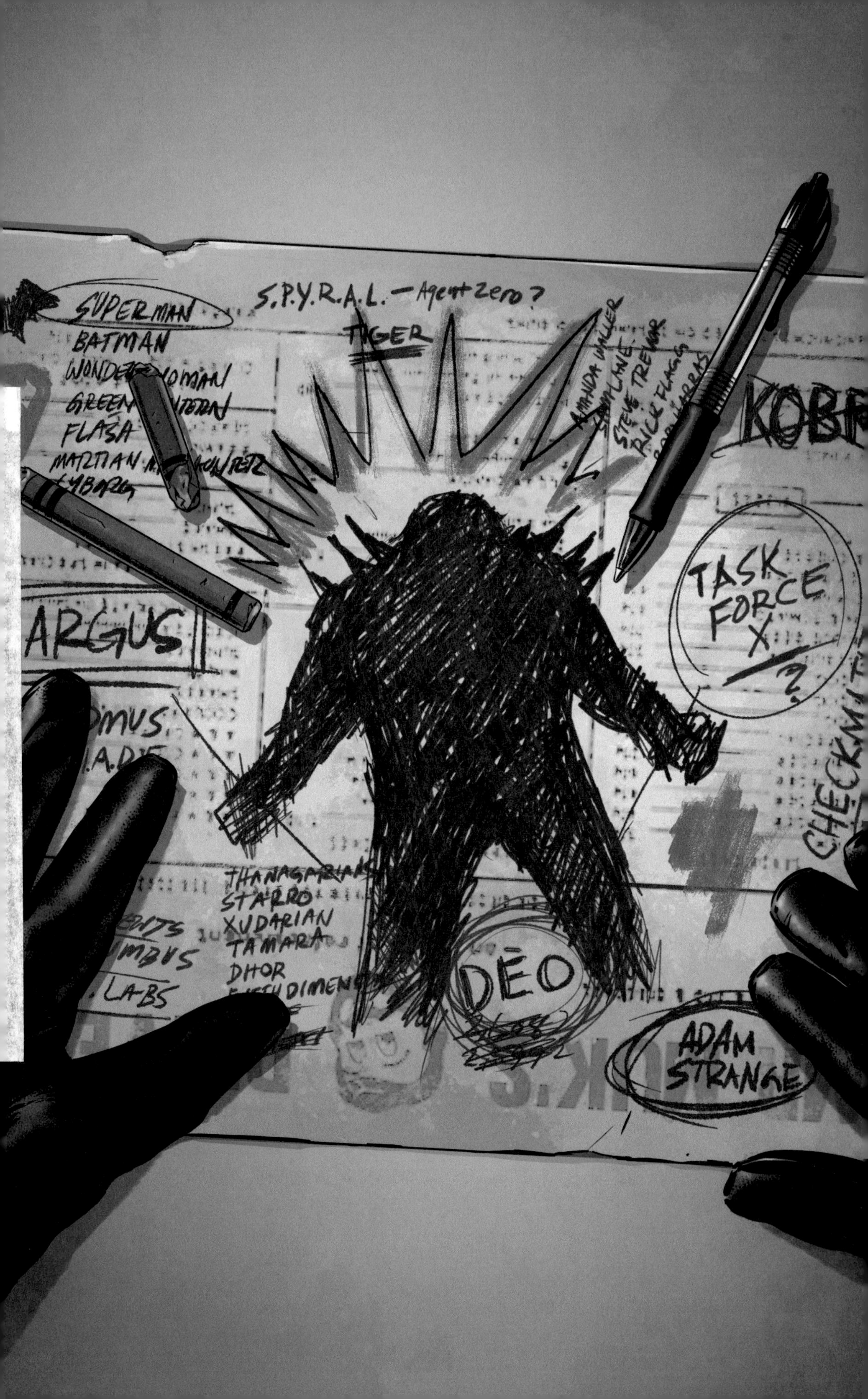

S.P.Y.R.A.L. — Agent Zero?
SUPERMAN
BATMAN
FLASH
TIGER
AMANDA WALLER
STEVE TREVOR
RICK FLAGG
TASK FORCE X
ARGUS
THANAGARIAN
STARRO
XUDARIAN
TAMARA
DHOR
DEO
ADAM STRANGE

D.E.O. DIRECTOR BONES, I AM KATE SPENCER.

I AM *SO* SORRY FOR WHAT YOU HAVE BEEN THROUGH.

I CAN'T EVEN IMAGINE.

CAN YOU TELL ME *EXACTLY* WHAT HAPPENED?

KATE SPENCER. I KNOW YOU.

WHAT ARE *YOU* DOING HERE?

YOU NEED A LAWYER.

A FRIEND OF A FRIEND OF A *FRIEND* CALLED ME.

FOR A SECOND THERE...

...I THOUGHT YOU WERE *THEM.*

COME TO FINISH THE JOB.

WE'VE MET.

I REMEMBER.

I NEED YOU TO TELL ME EXACTLY WHAT HAPPENED TO THE D.E.O. BECAUSE A NARRATIVE IS BEING FORMED IN THE PRESS...

...AND IT IS *NOT* KIND TO YOU.

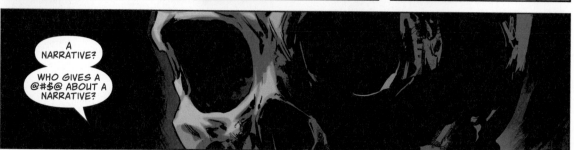

A NARRATIVE?

WHO GIVES A @#$@ ABOUT A NARRATIVE?

THE *TRUTH.*

THE TRUTH CARES.

THEY TOLD ME OUTSIDE--YOU WERE RESCUED BY *ADAM STRANGE?*

*THE* ADAM STRANGE? FROM OUTER SPACE?

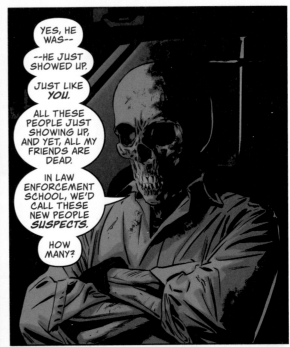

YES, HE WAS--

--HE JUST SHOWED UP.

JUST LIKE *YOU.*

ALL THESE PEOPLE JUST SHOWING UP, AND YET, ALL MY FRIENDS ARE DEAD.

IN LAW ENFORCEMENT SCHOOL, WE'D CALL THESE NEW PEOPLE *SUSPECTS.*

HOW MANY?

HOW MANY PEOPLE ARE *SUSPECTS?*

HOW MANY PEOPLE AT THE D.E.O. DIED HORRIFICALLY UNDER MY PROTECTION TODAY?

I DON'T KNOW.

THEY'RE STILL SIFTING THROUGH IT.

DO YOU--DO YOU HAVE *ANY* IDEA *WHO* DID IT?

WAS IT--*WAS* IT ADAM STRANGE?

I KNOW *EXACTLY* WHO IT WAS.

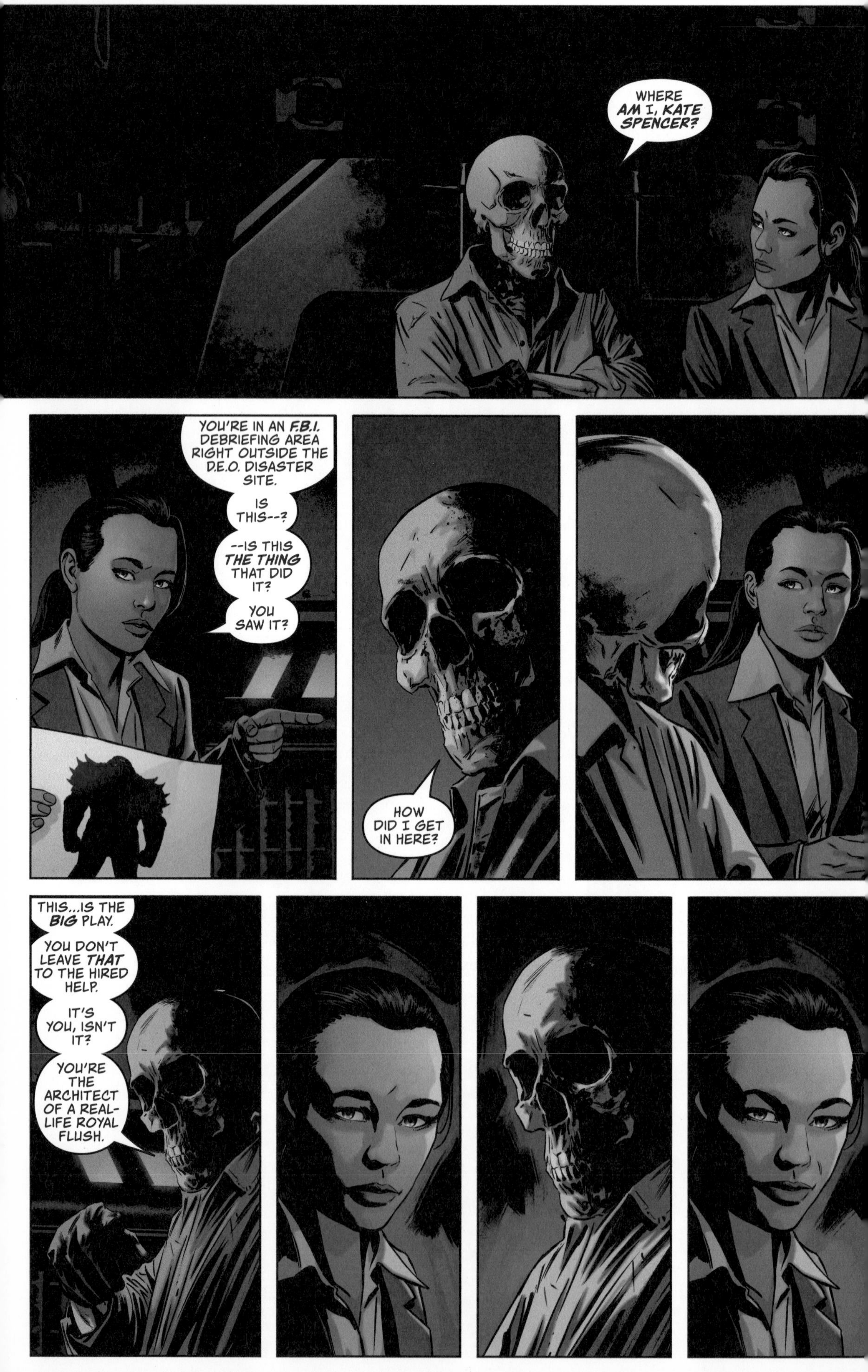
WHERE AM I, KATE SPENCER?
YOU'RE IN AN F.B.I. DEBRIEFING AREA RIGHT OUTSIDE THE D.E.O. DISASTER SITE.
IS THIS--?
--IS THIS THE THING THAT DID IT?
YOU SAW IT?
HOW DID I GET IN HERE?
THIS...IS THE BIG PLAY.
YOU DON'T LEAVE THAT TO THE HIRED HELP.
IT'S YOU, ISN'T IT?
YOU'RE THE ARCHITECT OF A REAL-LIFE ROYAL FLUSH.

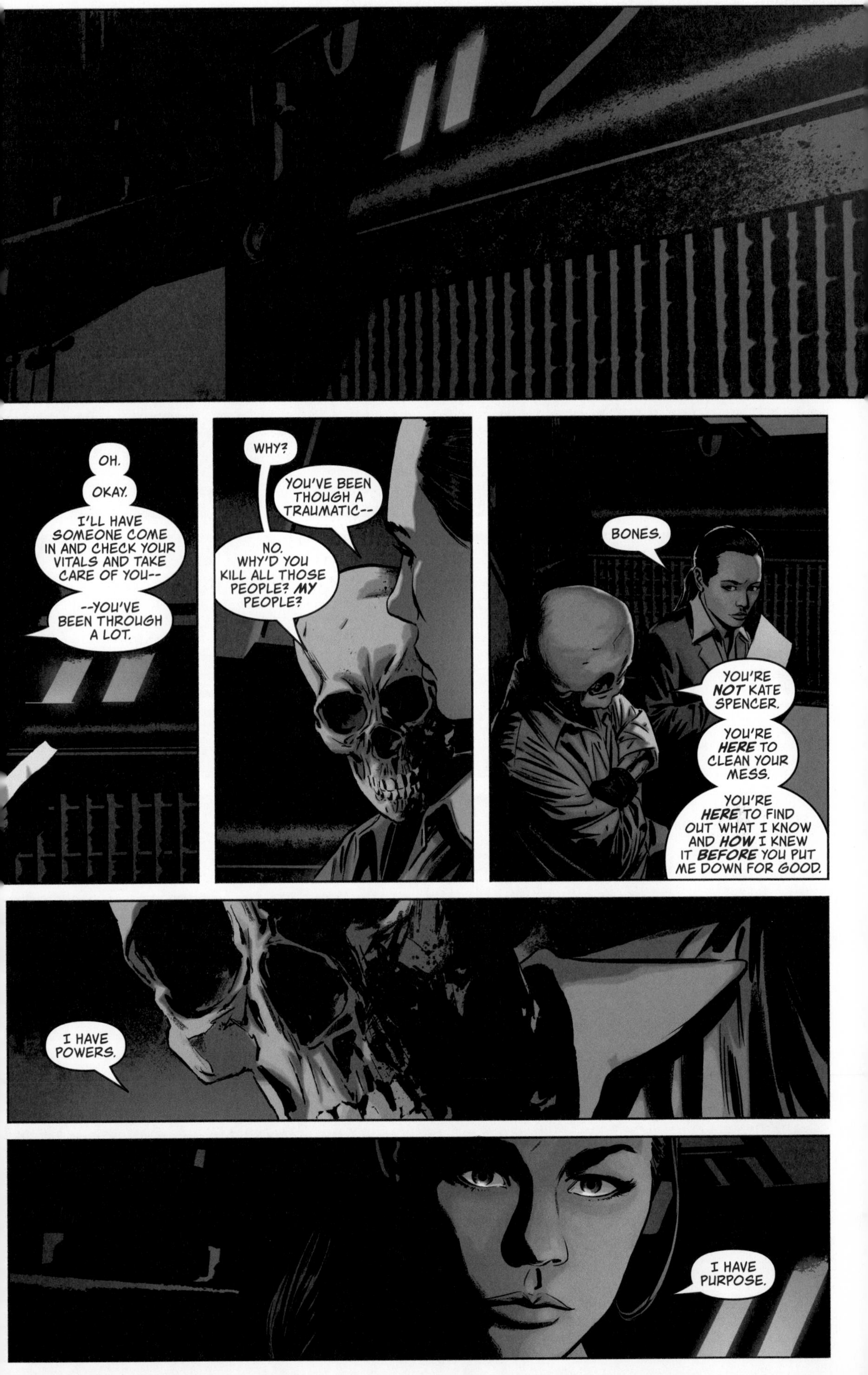
OH.
OKAY.
I'LL HAVE SOMEONE COME IN AND CHECK YOUR VITALS AND TAKE CARE OF YOU--
--YOU'VE BEEN THROUGH A LOT.
WHY?
YOU'VE BEEN THOUGH A TRAUMATIC--
NO. WHY'D YOU KILL ALL THOSE PEOPLE? *MY* PEOPLE?
BONES.
YOU'RE *NOT* KATE SPENCER.
YOU'RE *HERE* TO CLEAN YOUR MESS.
YOU'RE *HERE* TO FIND OUT WHAT I KNOW AND *HOW* I KNEW IT *BEFORE* YOU PUT ME DOWN FOR GOOD.
I HAVE POWERS.
I HAVE PURPOSE.

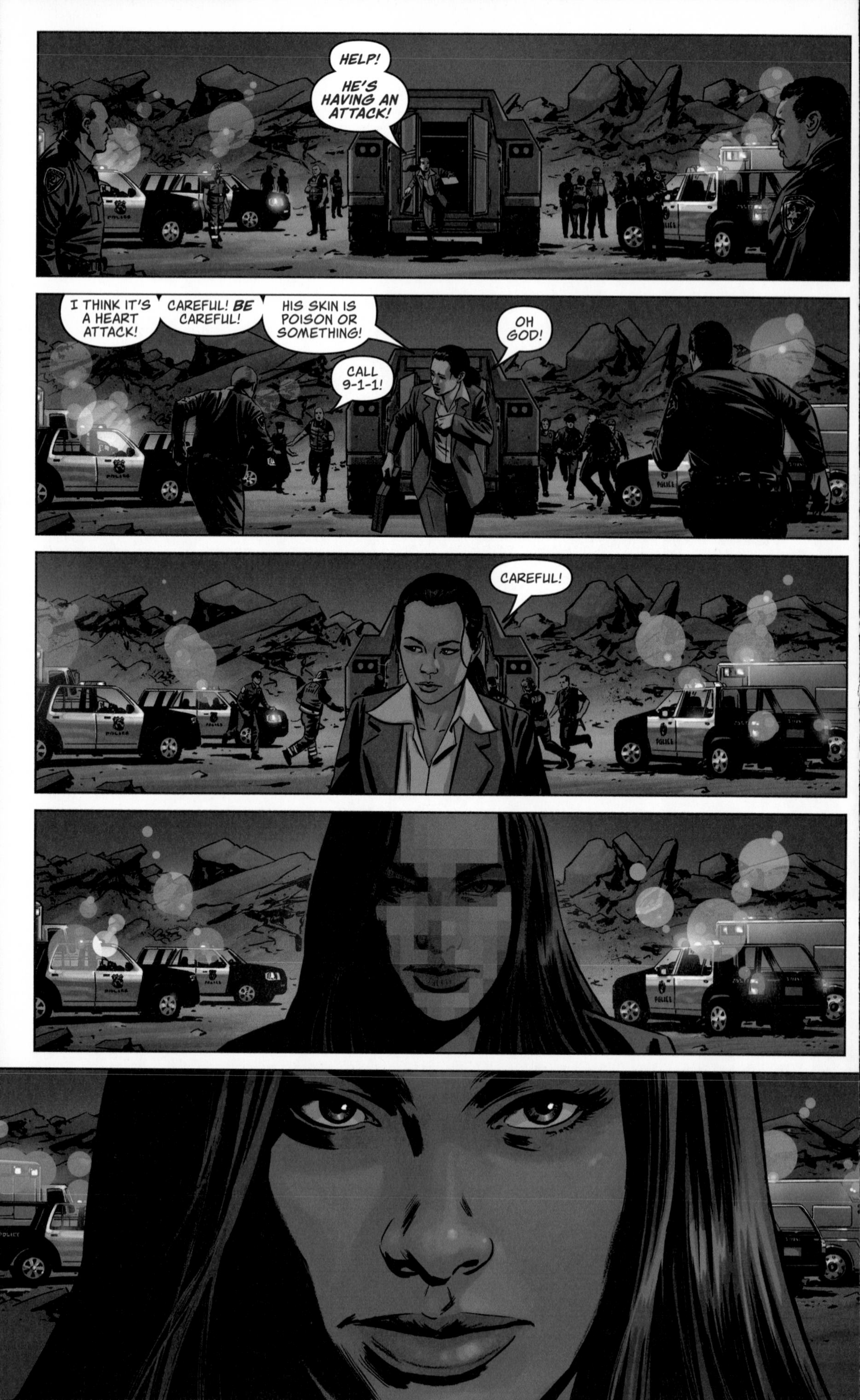
HELP!
HE'S HAVING AN ATTACK!
I THINK IT'S A HEART ATTACK!
CAREFUL! BE CAREFUL!
HIS SKIN IS POISON OR SOMETHING!
OH GOD!
CALL 9-1-1!
CAREFUL!
POLICE

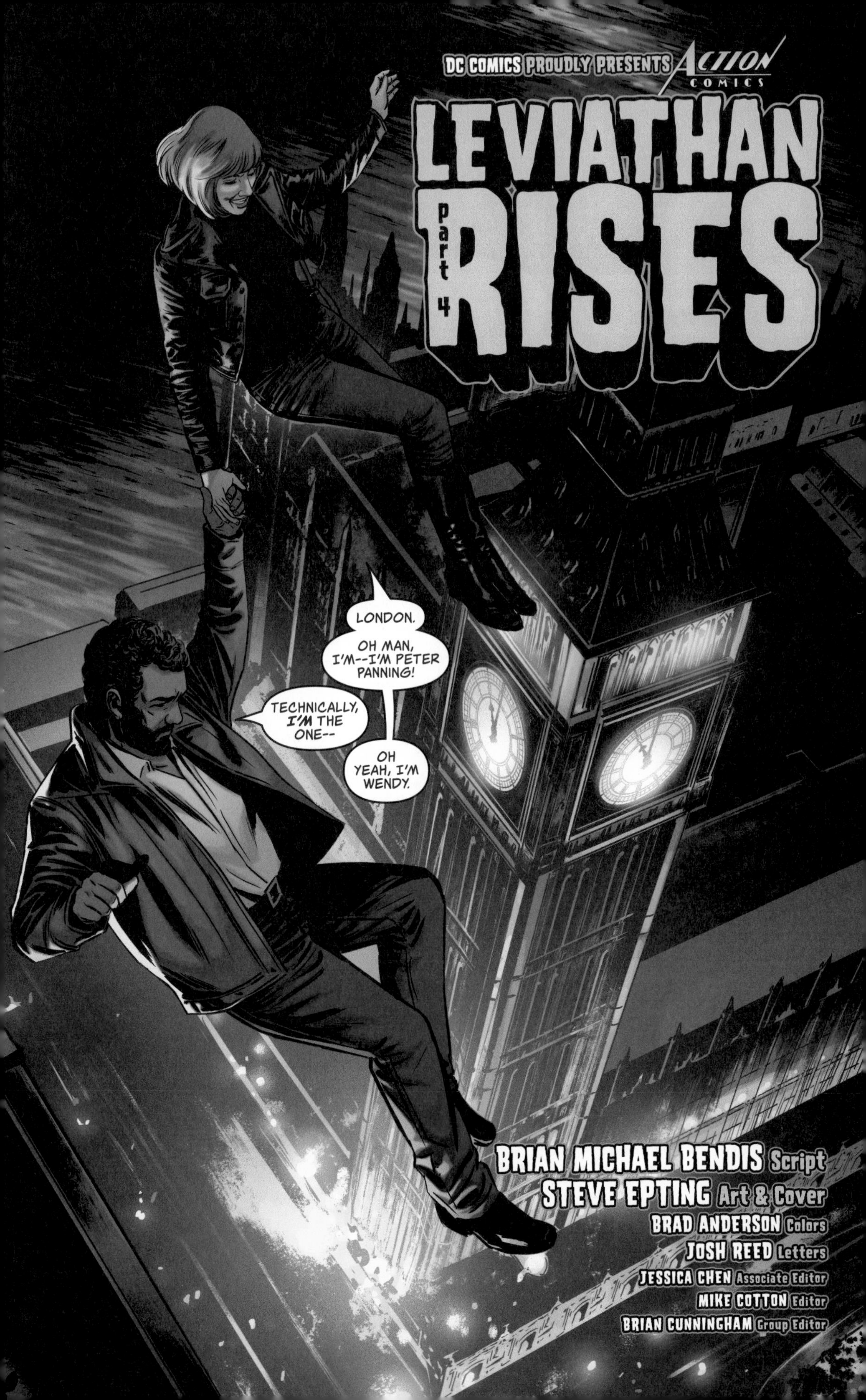

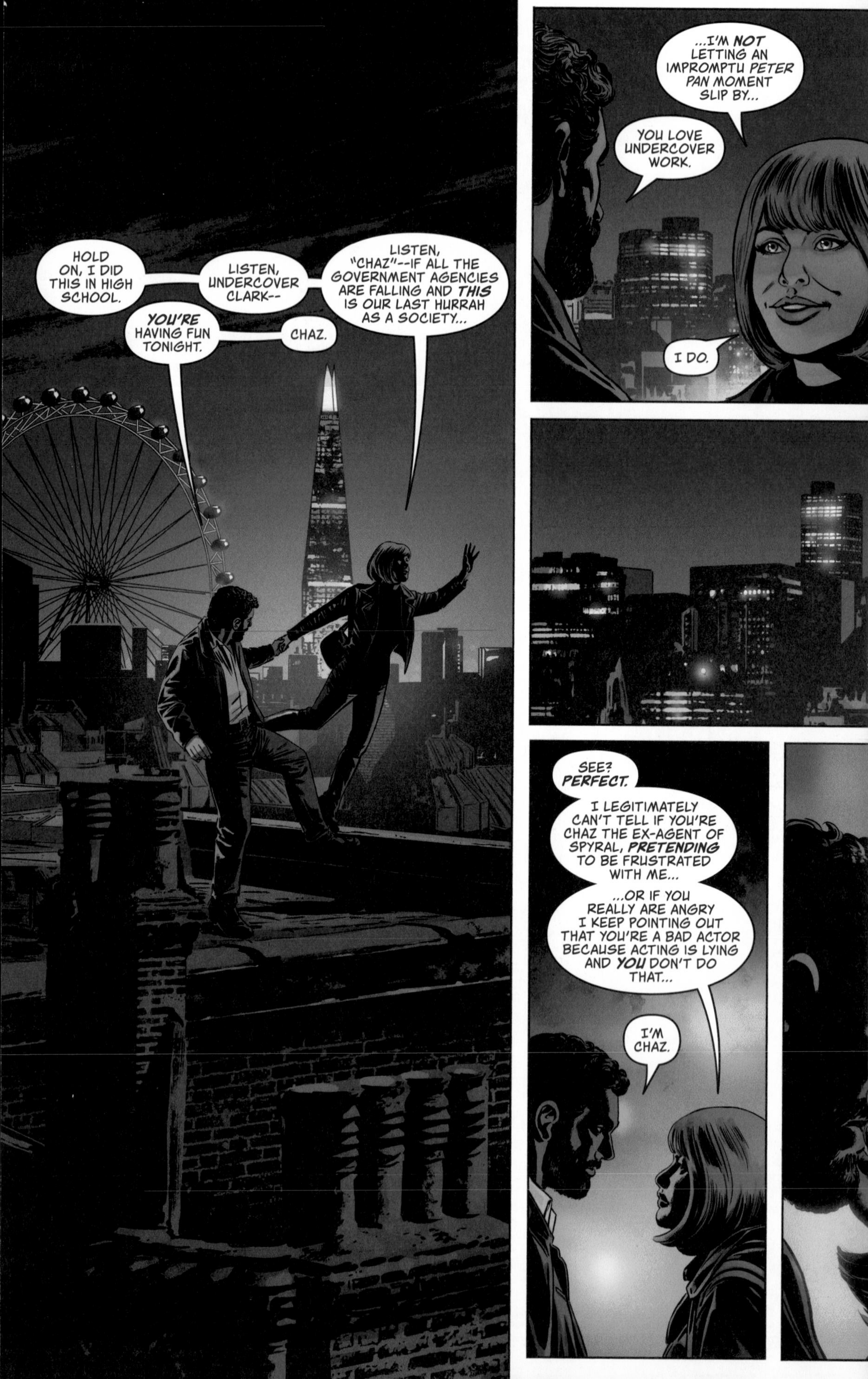
HOLD ON, I DID THIS IN HIGH SCHOOL.
LISTEN, UNDERCOVER CLARK--
LISTEN, "CHAZ"--IF ALL THE GOVERNMENT AGENCIES ARE FALLING AND *THIS* IS OUR LAST HURRAH AS A SOCIETY...
*YOU'RE* HAVING FUN TONIGHT.
CHAZ.
...I'M *NOT* LETTING AN IMPROMPTU *PETER PAN MOMENT* SLIP BY...
YOU LOVE UNDERCOVER WORK.
I DO.
SEE? *PERFECT.*
I LEGITIMATELY CAN'T TELL IF YOU'RE CHAZ THE EX-AGENT OF SPYRAL, *PRETENDING* TO BE FRUSTRATED WITH ME...
...OR IF YOU REALLY ARE ANGRY I KEEP POINTING OUT THAT YOU'RE A BAD ACTOR BECAUSE ACTING IS LYING AND *YOU* DON'T DO THAT...
I'M CHAZ.

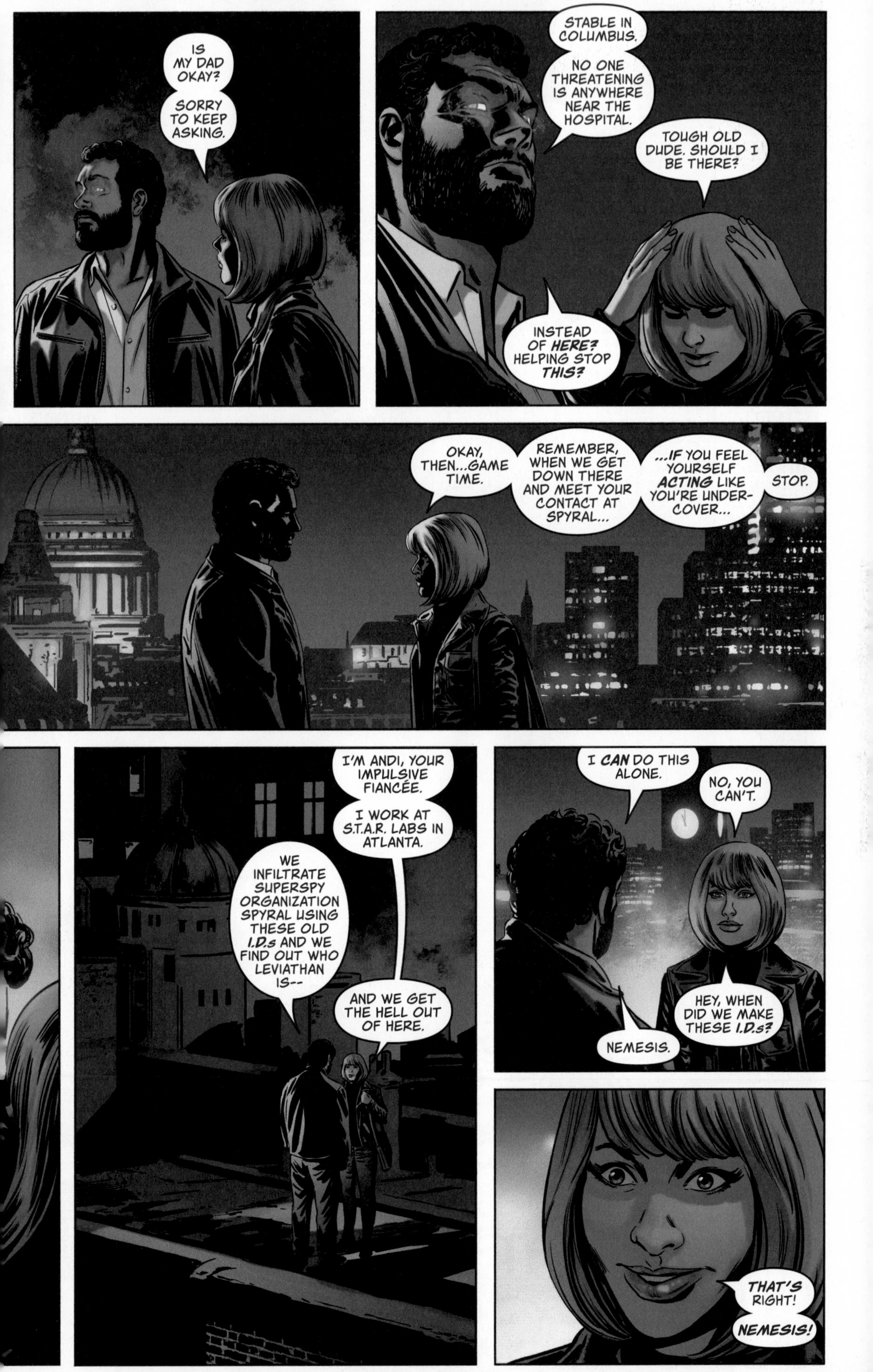

IS MY DAD OKAY?
SORRY TO KEEP ASKING.
STABLE IN COLUMBUS.
NO ONE THREATENING IS ANYWHERE NEAR THE HOSPITAL.
TOUGH OLD DUDE. SHOULD I BE THERE?
INSTEAD OF HERE? HELPING STOP THIS?
OKAY, THEN...GAME TIME.
REMEMBER, WHEN WE GET DOWN THERE AND MEET YOUR CONTACT AT SPYRAL...
...IF YOU FEEL YOURSELF ACTING LIKE YOU'RE UNDER-COVER...
STOP.
I'M ANDI, YOUR IMPULSIVE FIANCÉE.
I WORK AT S.T.A.R. LABS IN ATLANTA.
WE INFILTRATE SUPERSPY ORGANIZATION SPYRAL USING THESE OLD I.D.s AND WE FIND OUT WHO LEVIATHAN IS--
AND WE GET THE HELL OUT OF HERE.
I CAN DO THIS ALONE.
NO, YOU CAN'T.
HEY, WHEN DID WE MAKE THESE I.D.s?
NEMESIS.
THAT'S RIGHT!
NEMESIS!

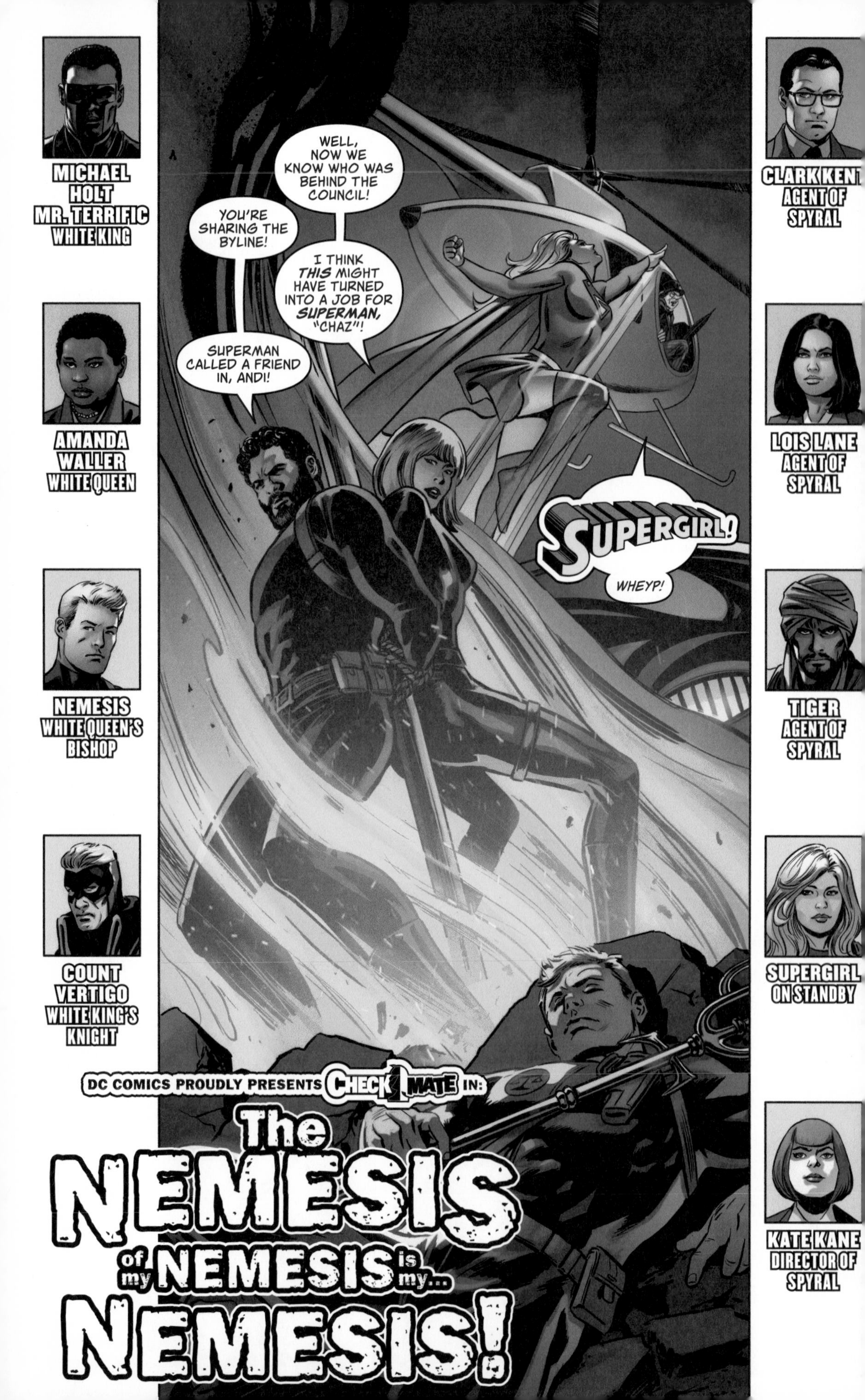
MICHAEL HOLT MR. TERRIFIC WHITE KING
AMANDA WALLER WHITE QUEEN
NEMESIS WHITE QUEEN'S BISHOP
COUNT VERTIGO WHITE KING'S KNIGHT
WELL, NOW WE KNOW WHO WAS BEHIND THE COUNCIL!
YOU'RE SHARING THE BYLINE!
I THINK *THIS* MIGHT HAVE TURNED INTO A JOB FOR *SUPERMAN,* "CHAZ"!
SUPERMAN CALLED A FRIEND IN, ANDI!
SUPERGIRL!
WHEYP!
CLARK KENT AGENT OF SPYRAL
LOIS LANE AGENT OF SPYRAL
TIGER AGENT OF SPYRAL
SUPERGIRL ON STANDBY
KATE KANE DIRECTOR OF SPYRAL
DC COMICS PROUDLY PRESENTS CHECKMATE IN:
The NEMESIS of my NEMESIS is my... NEMESIS!

THAT *WAS* FUN.

THAT WAS A GOOD STORY.

WHAT IF SPYRAL IS BEHIND THIS?

SPYRAL?

*BEHIND* THIS?

WHAT IF SPYRAL *IS* LEVIATHAN?

I HADN'T CONSIDERED *THAT*.

THAT'S ALSO BECAUSE YOU'RE YOU.

TO BE FAIR, YOU TEND TO GO *THERE* QUICKLY.

*THAT'S* BECAUSE OF *MY* DAD.

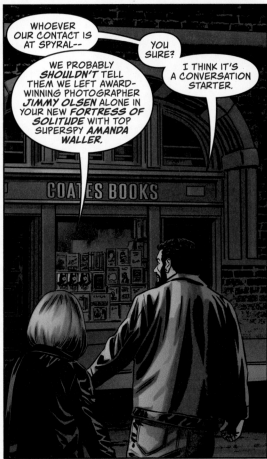

WHOEVER OUR CONTACT IS AT SPYRAL--

YOU SURE?

I THINK IT'S A CONVERSATION STARTER.

WE PROBABLY *SHOULDN'T* TELL THEM WE LEFT AWARD-WINNING PHOTOGRAPHER *JIMMY OLSEN* ALONE IN YOUR NEW *FORTRESS OF SOLITUDE* WITH TOP SUPERSPY *AMANDA WALLER*.

COATES BOOKS

"I WANT TO SAY IT AGAIN SO I KNOW YOU HEARD IT--

"AMANDA WALLER IS *IN* THE FORTRESS OF SOLITUDE.

"UNATTENDED."

"I TRUST HER."

YOU'RE KELEX?

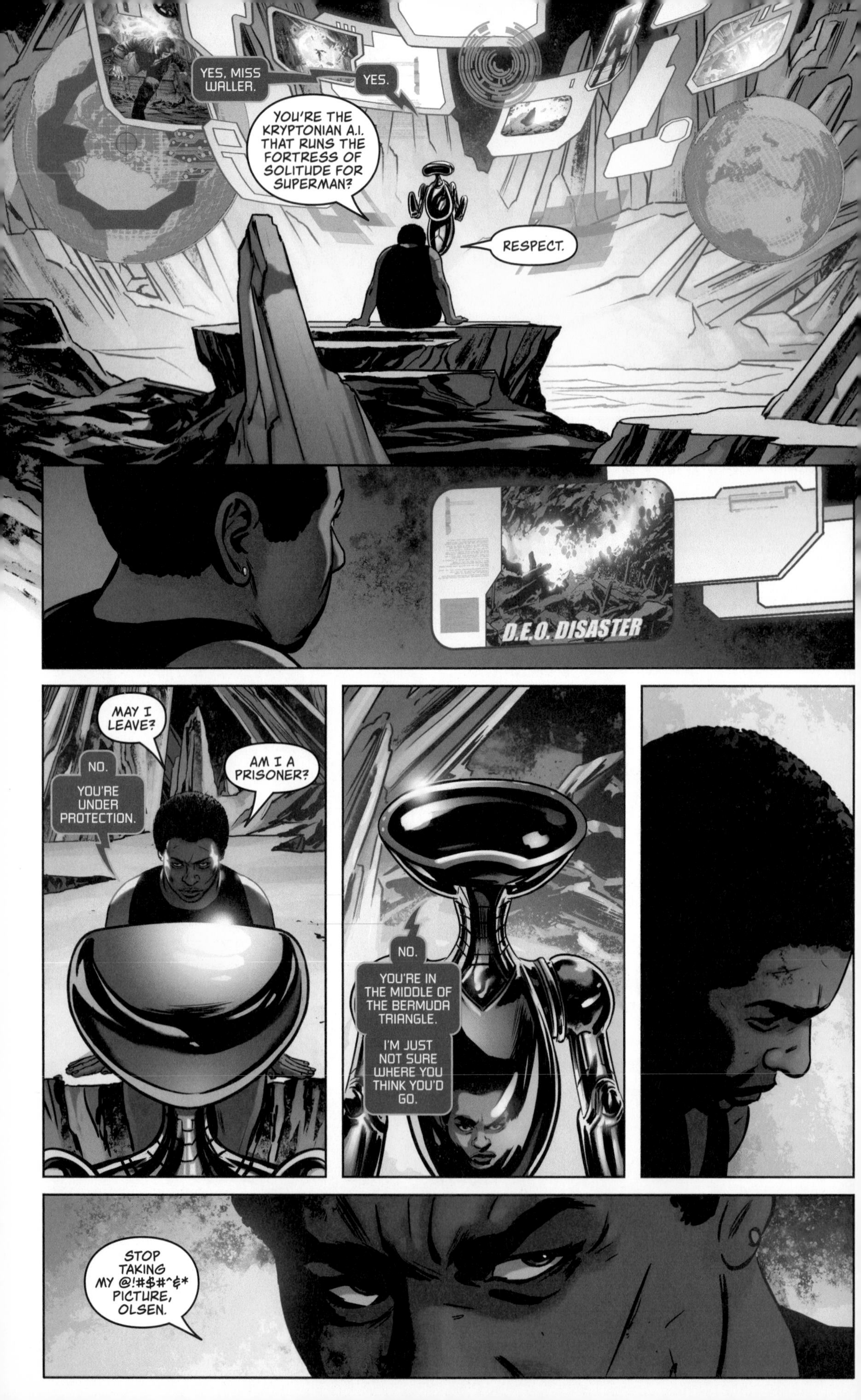
YES, MISS WALLER.
YES.
YOU'RE THE KRYPTONIAN A.I. THAT RUNS THE FORTRESS OF SOLITUDE FOR SUPERMAN?
RESPECT.
D.E.O. DISASTER
MAY I LEAVE?
NO.
YOU'RE UNDER PROTECTION.
AM I A PRISONER?
NO.
YOU'RE IN THE MIDDLE OF THE BERMUDA TRIANGLE.
I'M JUST NOT SURE WHERE YOU THINK YOU'D GO.
STOP TAKING MY @!#$#^&* PICTURE, OLSEN.

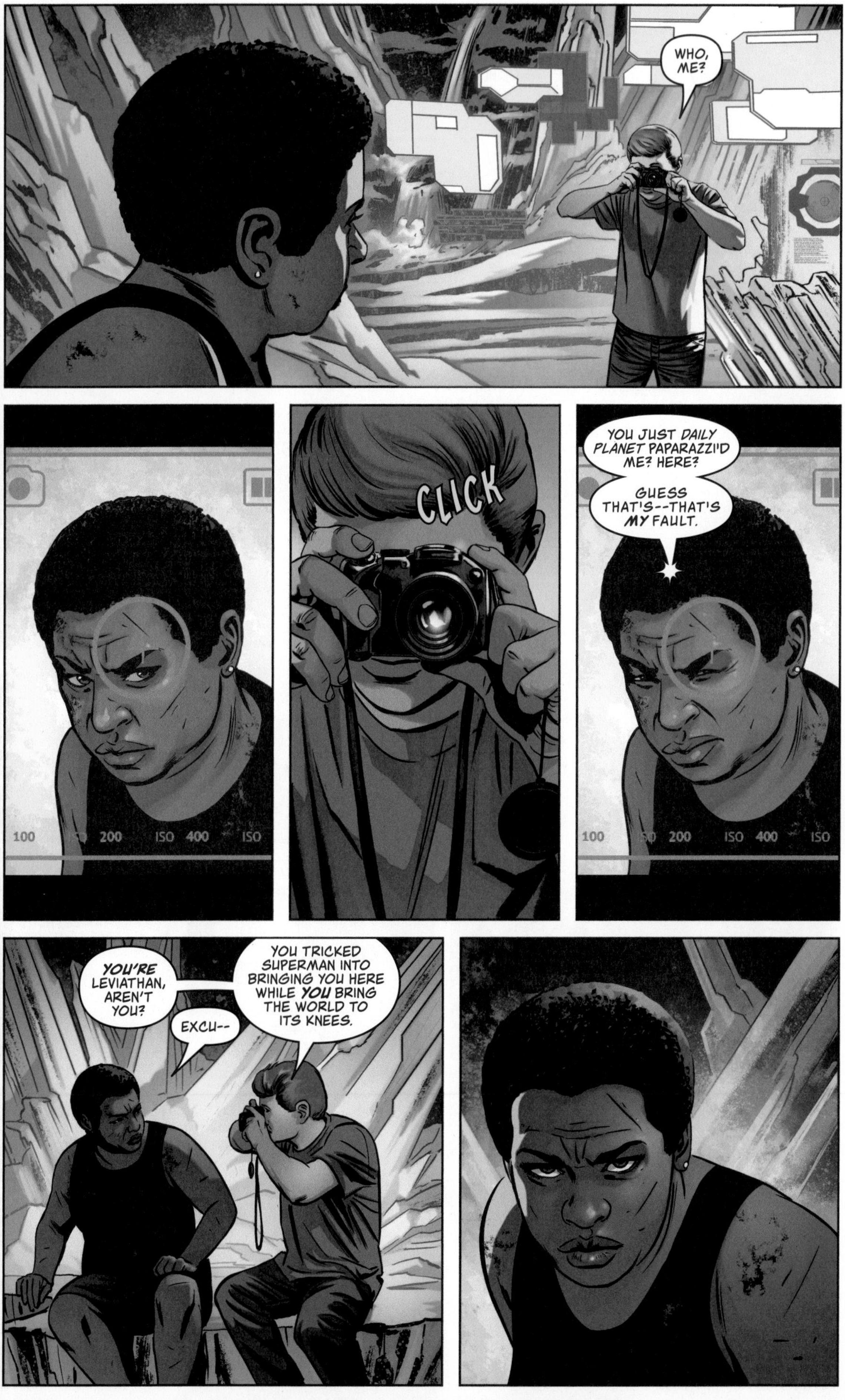
WHO, ME?
CLICK
YOU JUST *DAILY PLANET* PAPARAZZI'D ME? HERE?
GUESS THAT'S--THAT'S *MY* FAULT.
*YOU'RE* LEVIATHAN, AREN'T YOU?
EXCU--
YOU TRICKED SUPERMAN INTO BRINGING YOU HERE WHILE *YOU* BRING THE WORLD TO ITS KNEES.

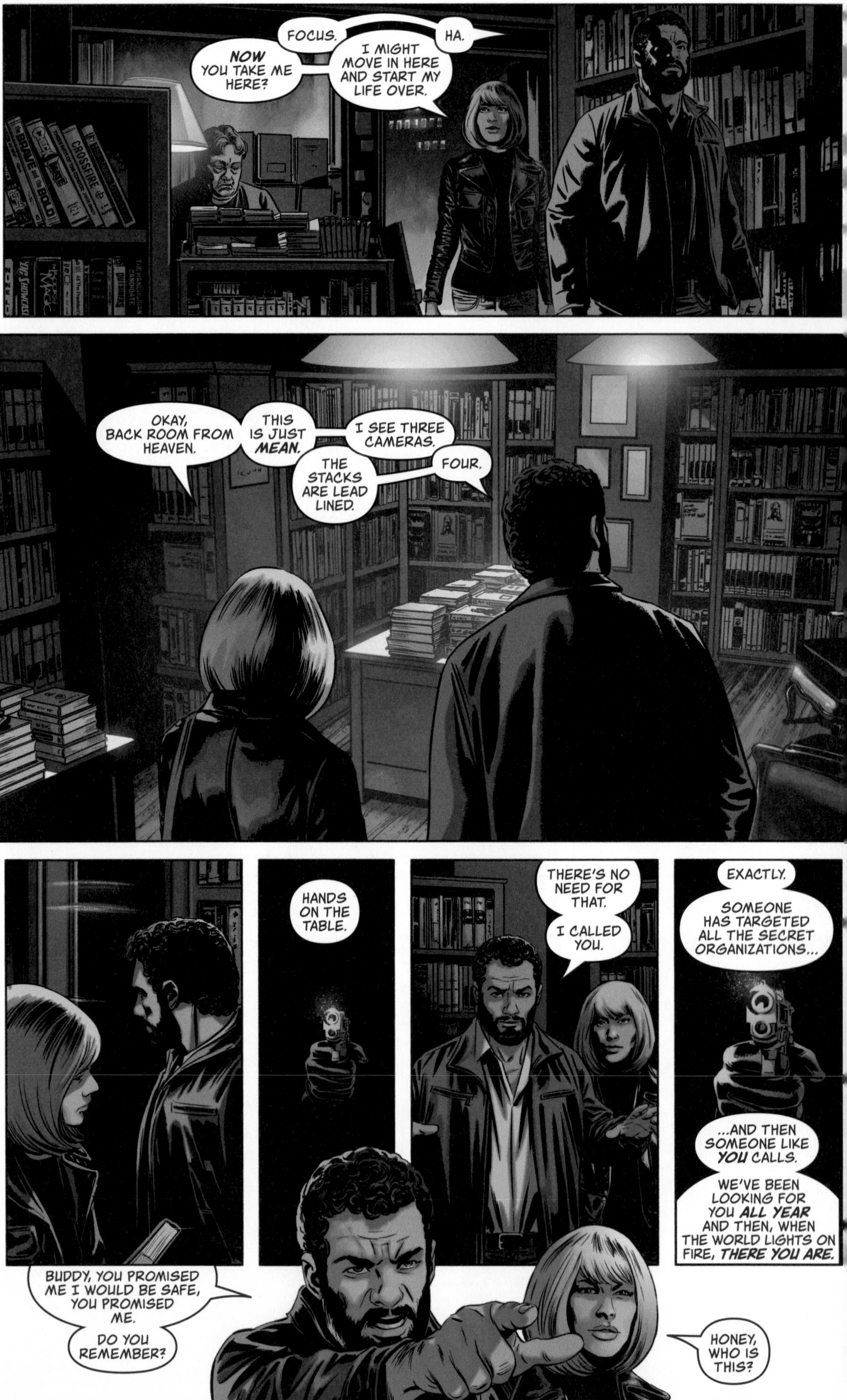
NOW YOU TAKE ME HERE?
FOCUS.
I MIGHT MOVE IN HERE AND START MY LIFE OVER.
HA.
OKAY, BACK ROOM FROM HEAVEN.
THIS IS JUST MEAN.
I SEE THREE CAMERAS.
THE STACKS ARE LEAD LINED.
FOUR.
HANDS ON THE TABLE.
THERE'S NO NEED FOR THAT.
I CALLED YOU.
EXACTLY.
SOMEONE HAS TARGETED ALL THE SECRET ORGANIZATIONS...
...AND THEN SOMEONE LIKE YOU CALLS.
WE'VE BEEN LOOKING FOR YOU ALL YEAR AND THEN, WHEN THE WORLD LIGHTS ON FIRE, THERE YOU ARE.
BUDDY, YOU PROMISED ME I WOULD BE SAFE, YOU PROMISED ME.
DO YOU REMEMBER?
HONEY, WHO IS THIS?

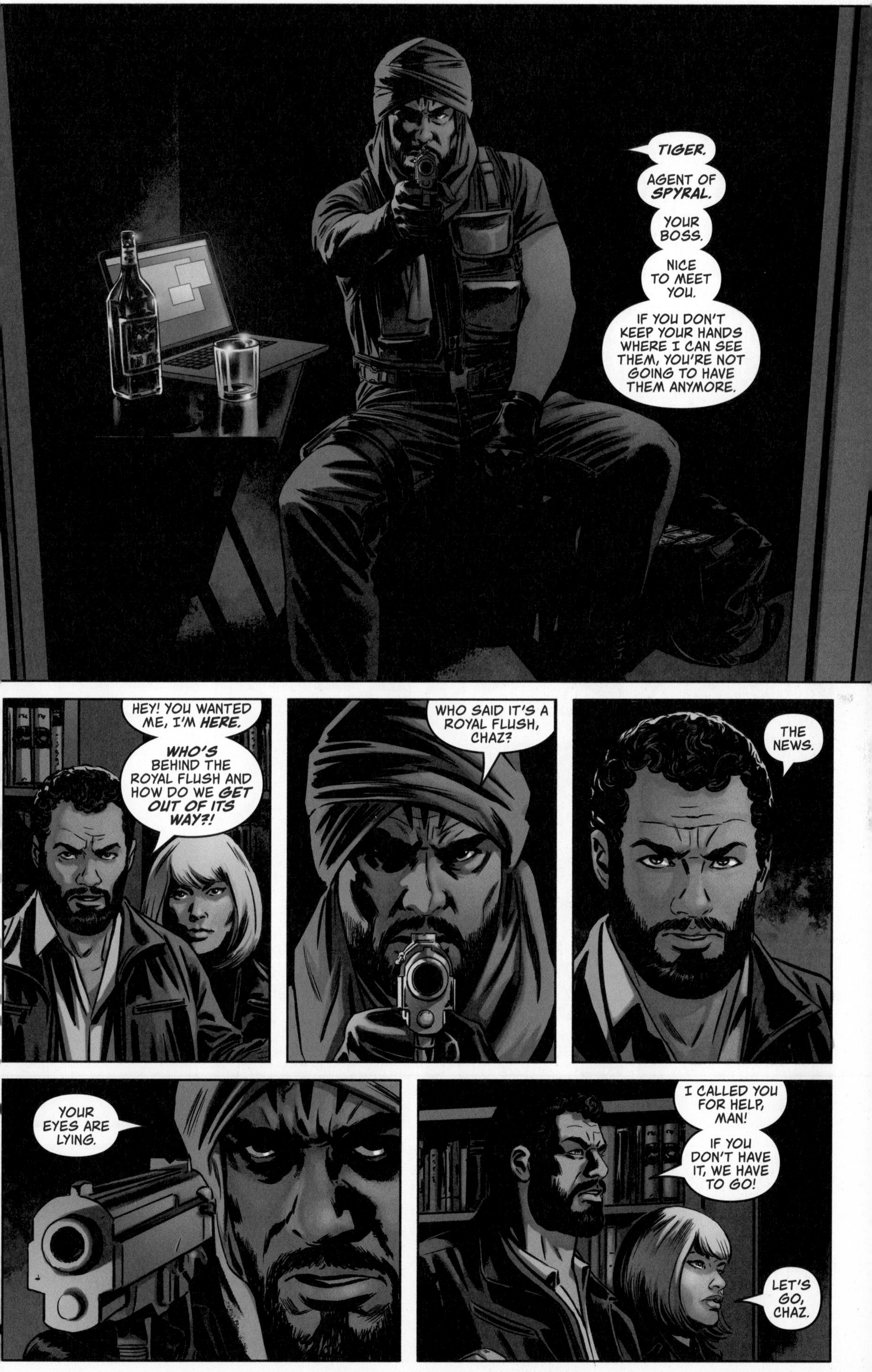
TIGER.
AGENT OF SPYRAL.
YOUR BOSS.
NICE TO MEET YOU.
IF YOU DON'T KEEP YOUR HANDS WHERE I CAN SEE THEM, YOU'RE NOT GOING TO HAVE THEM ANYMORE.
HEY! YOU WANTED ME, I'M HERE.
WHO'S BEHIND THE ROYAL FLUSH AND HOW DO WE GET OUT OF ITS WAY?!
WHO SAID IT'S A ROYAL FLUSH, CHAZ?
THE NEWS.
YOUR EYES ARE LYING.
I CALLED YOU FOR HELP, MAN!
IF YOU DON'T HAVE IT, WE HAVE TO GO!
LET'S GO, CHAZ.

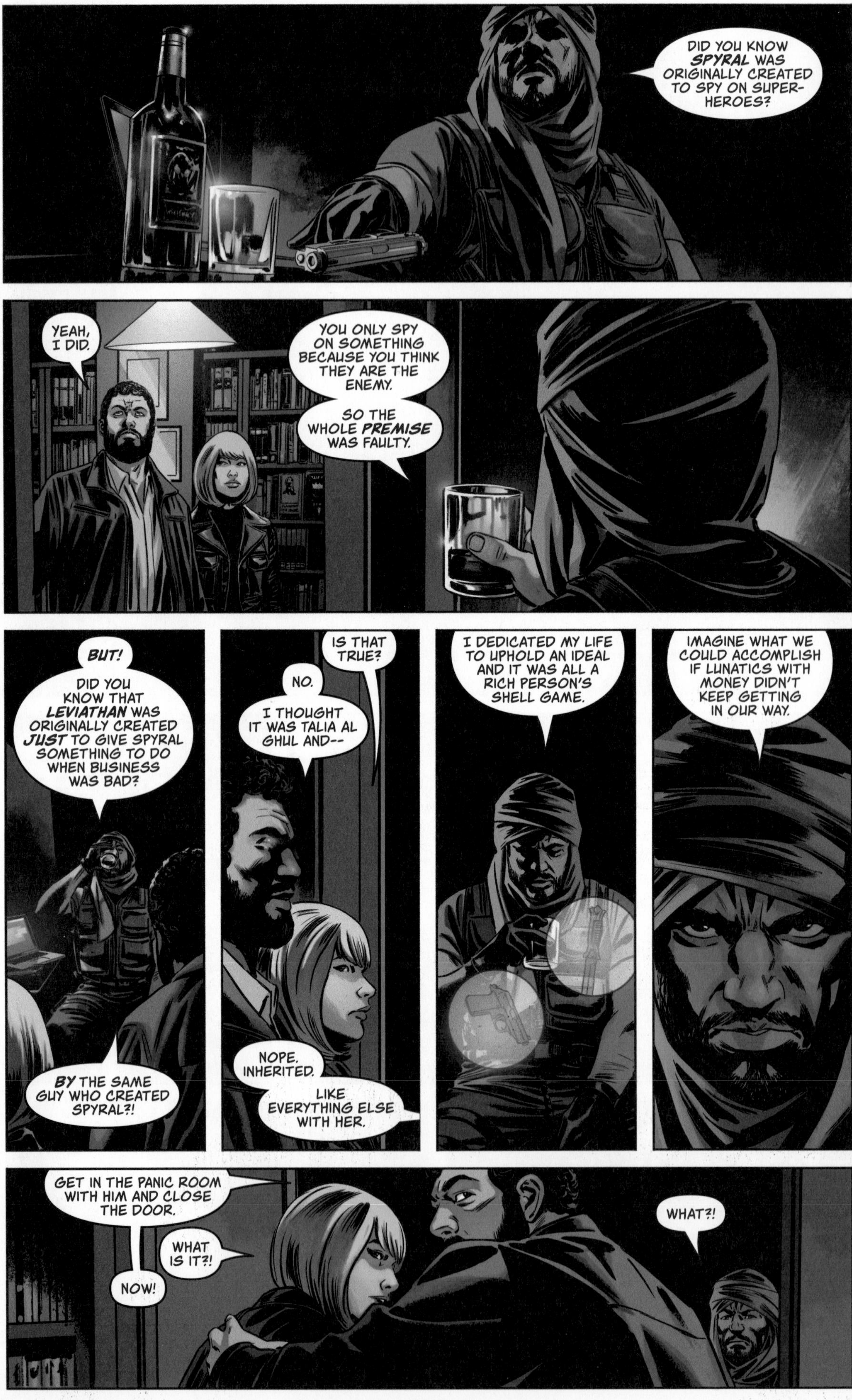
DID YOU KNOW SPYRAL WAS ORIGINALLY CREATED TO SPY ON SUPER-HEROES?
YEAH, I DID.
YOU ONLY SPY ON SOMETHING BECAUSE YOU THINK THEY ARE THE ENEMY.
SO THE WHOLE PREMISE WAS FAULTY.
BUT!
DID YOU KNOW THAT LEVIATHAN WAS ORIGINALLY CREATED JUST TO GIVE SPYRAL SOMETHING TO DO WHEN BUSINESS WAS BAD?
BY THE SAME GUY WHO CREATED SPYRAL?!
IS THAT TRUE?
NO.
I THOUGHT IT WAS TALIA AL GHUL AND--
NOPE. INHERITED.
LIKE EVERYTHING ELSE WITH HER.
I DEDICATED MY LIFE TO UPHOLD AN IDEAL AND IT WAS ALL A RICH PERSON'S SHELL GAME.
IMAGINE WHAT WE COULD ACCOMPLISH IF LUNATICS WITH MONEY DIDN'T KEEP GETTING IN OUR WAY.
GET IN THE PANIC ROOM WITH HIM AND CLOSE THE DOOR.
WHAT IS IT?!
NOW!
WHAT?!

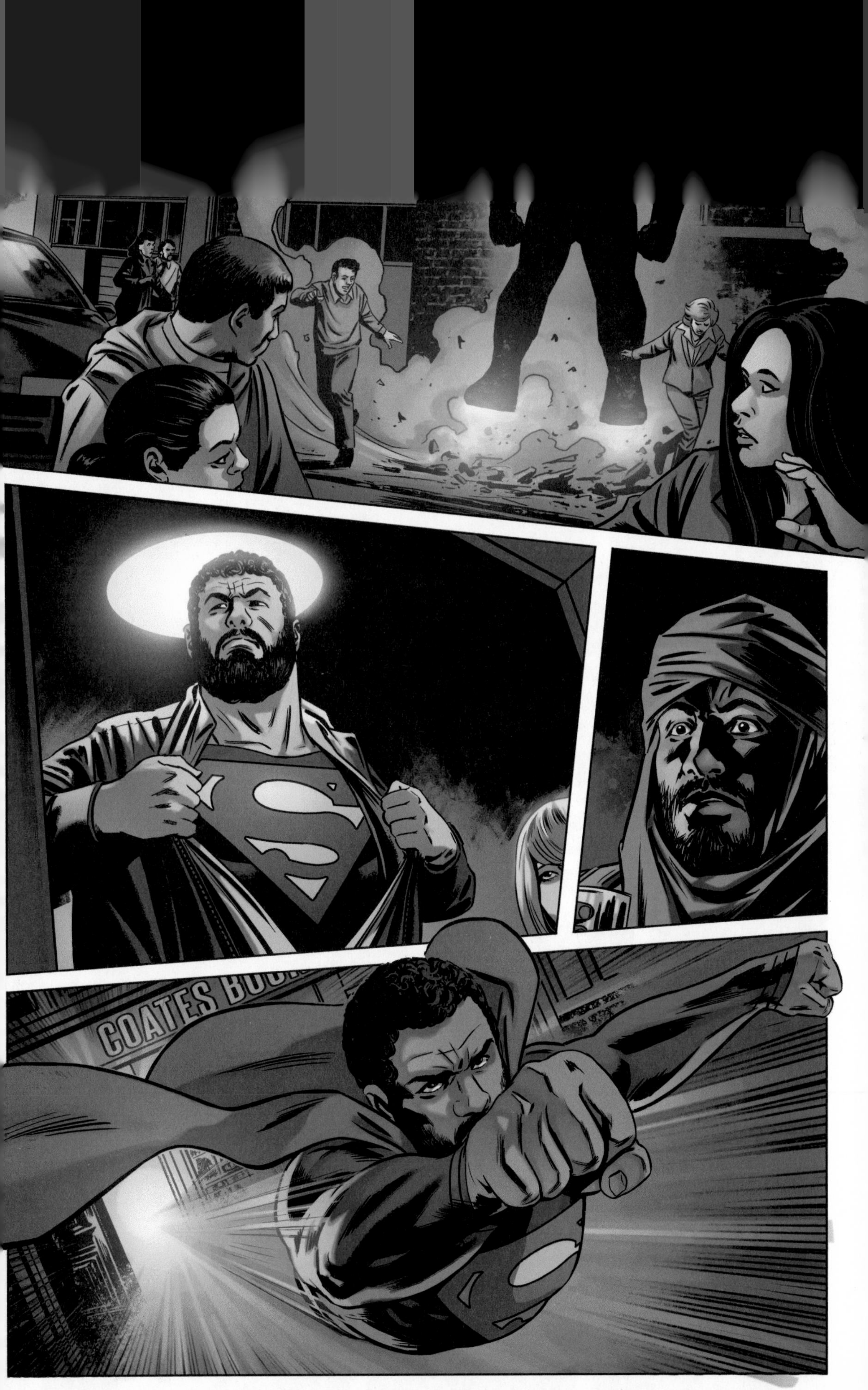
COATES BOO

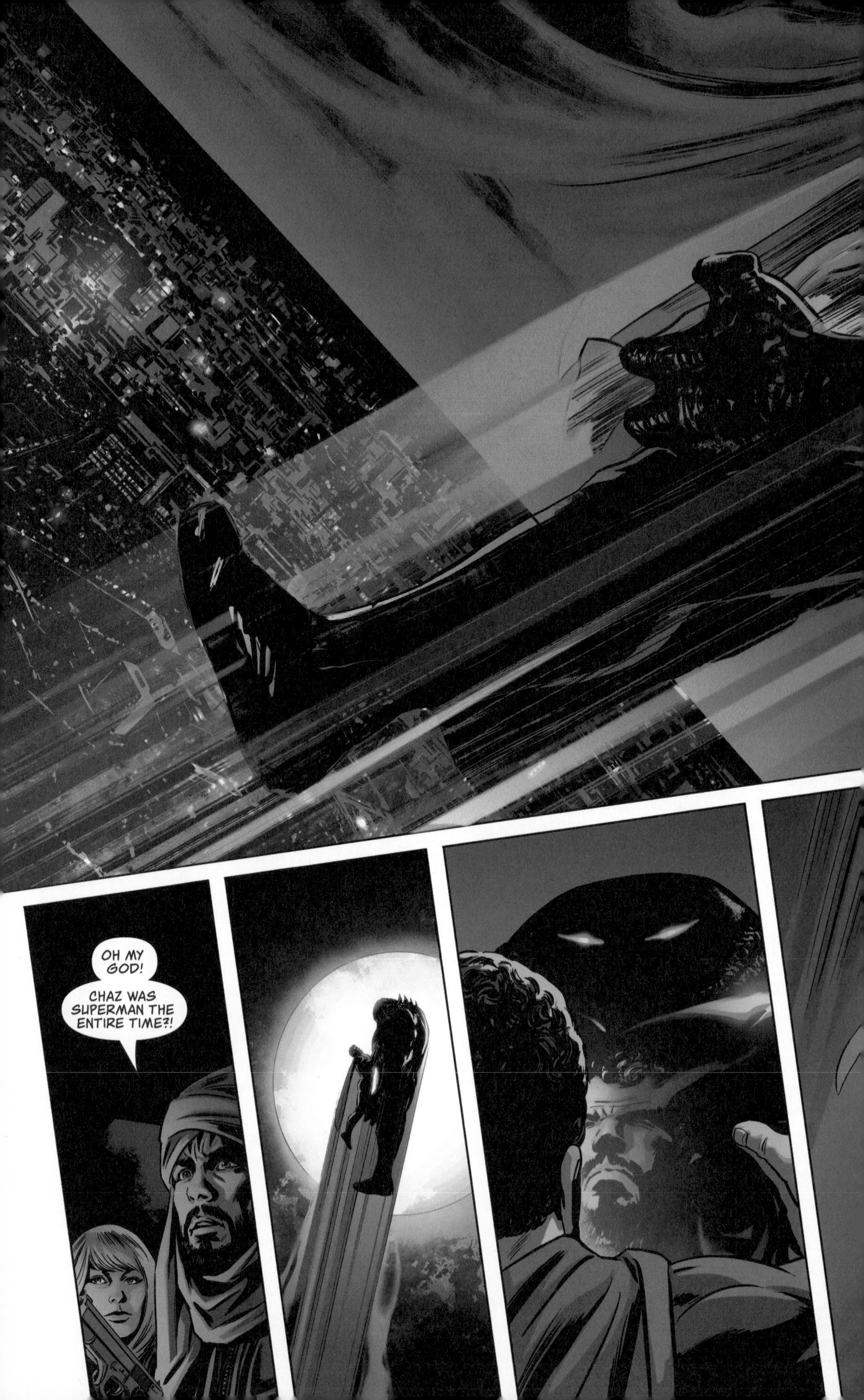
OH MY GOD!
CHAZ WAS SUPERMAN THE ENTIRE TIME?!

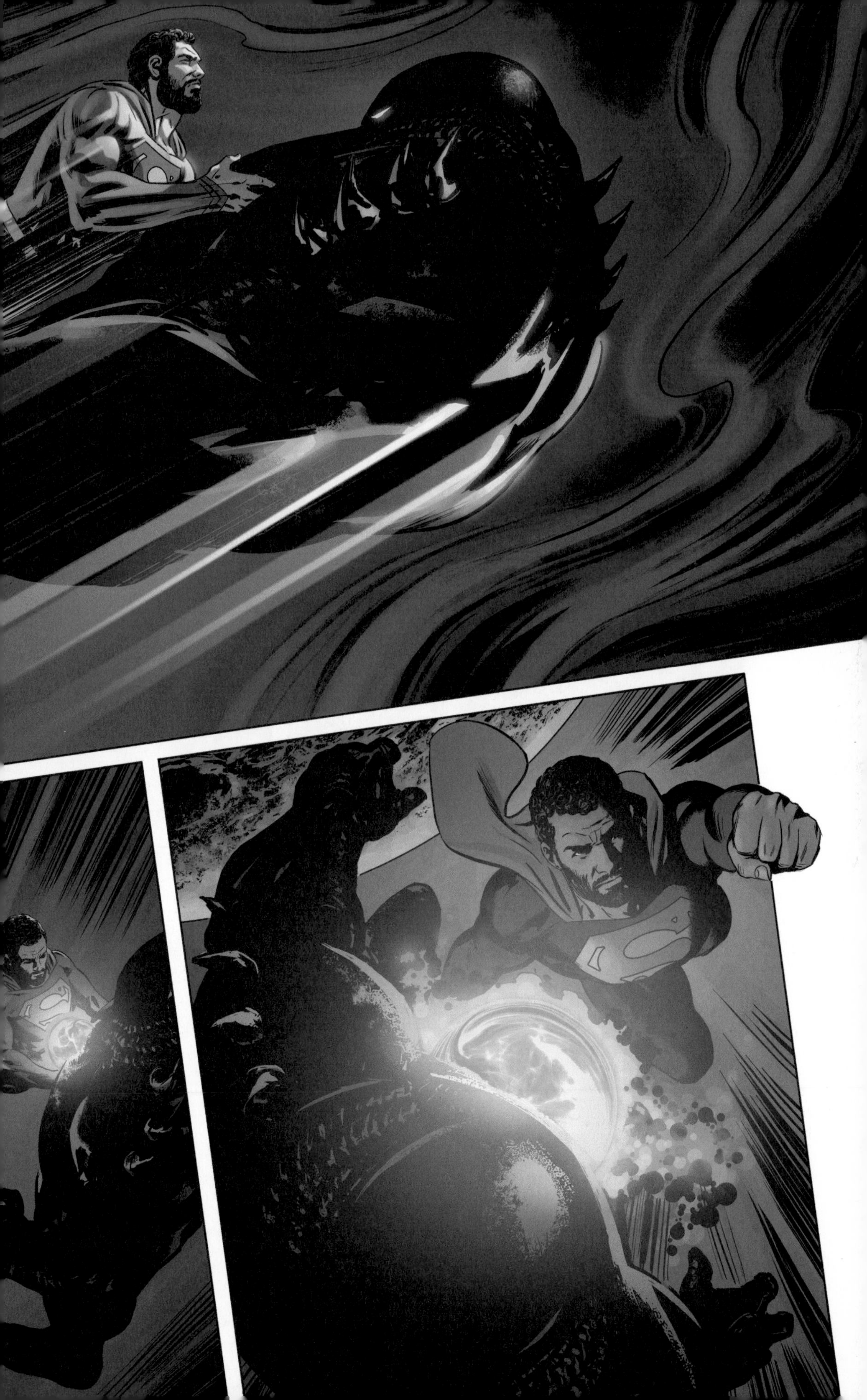

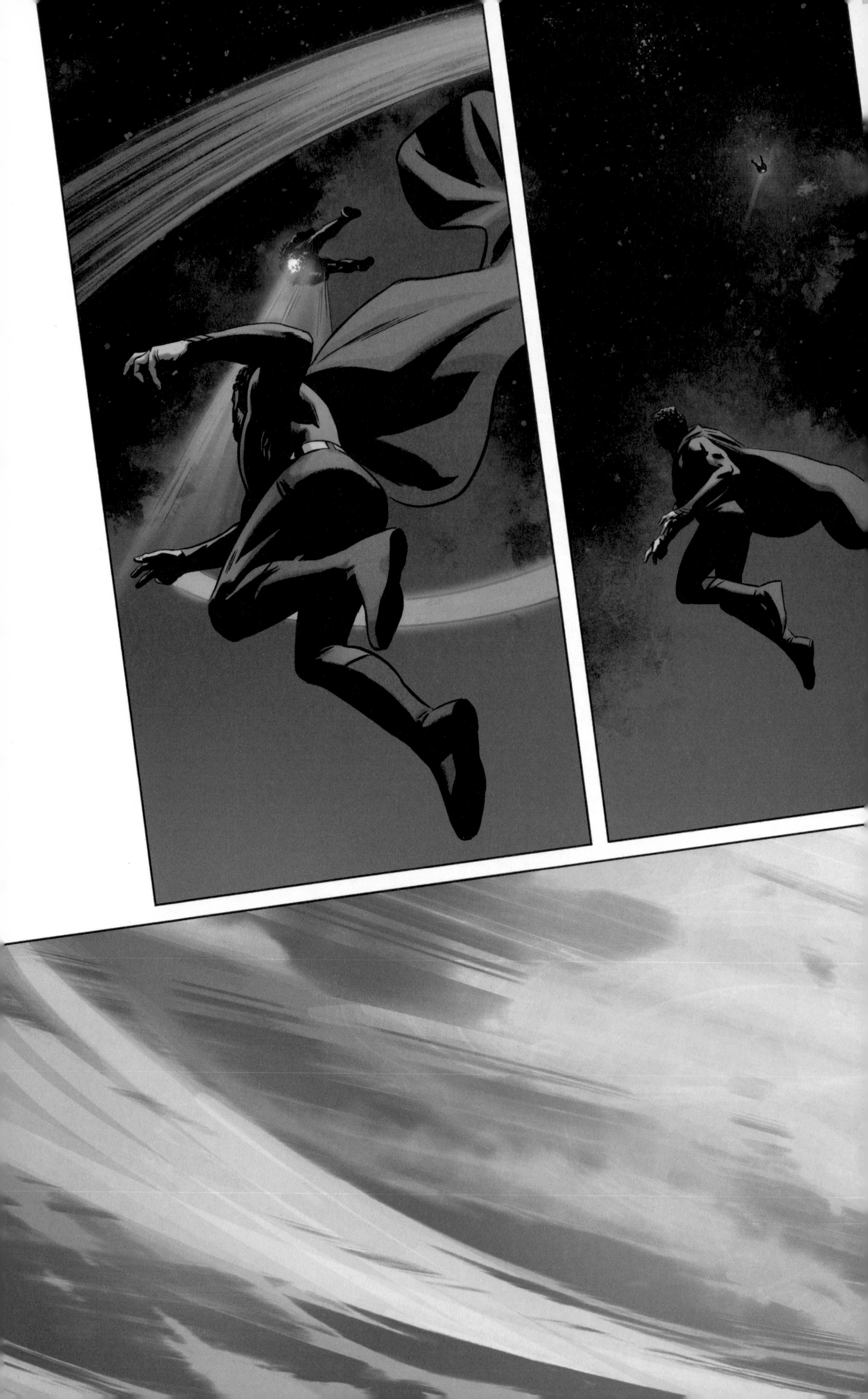

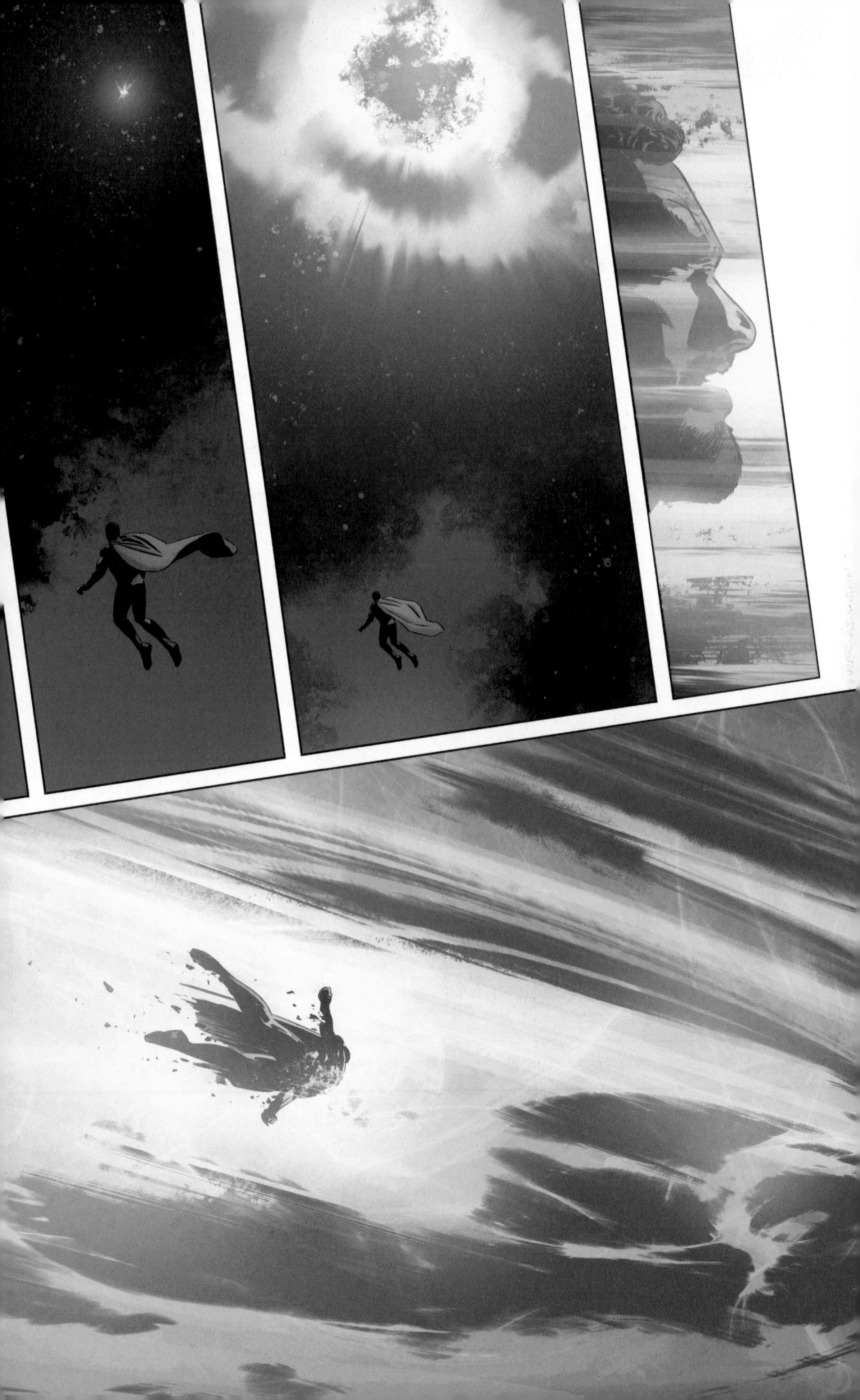

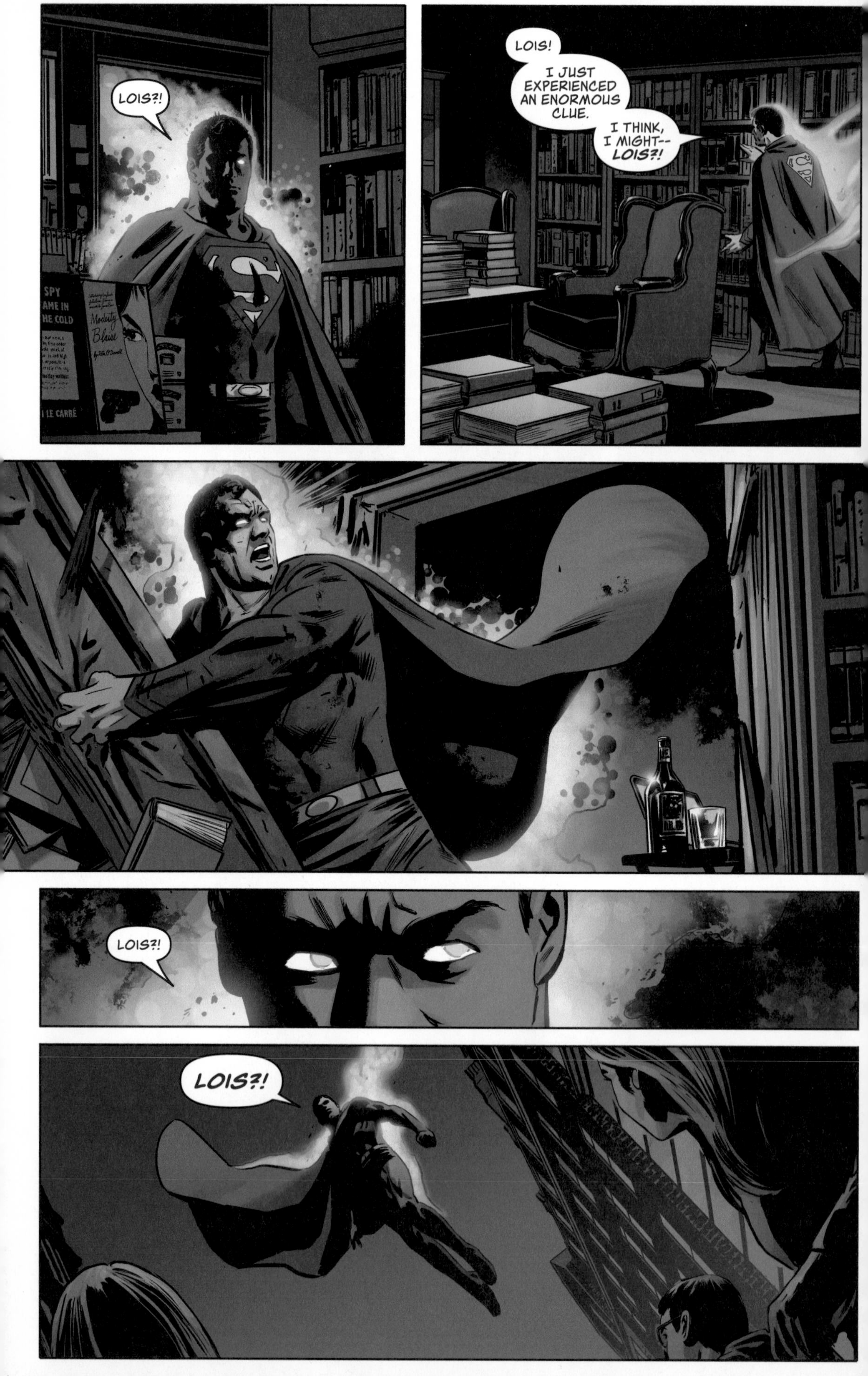
LOIS?!
Modesty Blaise
LOIS!
I JUST EXPERIENCED AN ENORMOUS CLUE.
I THINK, I MIGHT-- LOIS?!
LOIS?!
LOIS?!

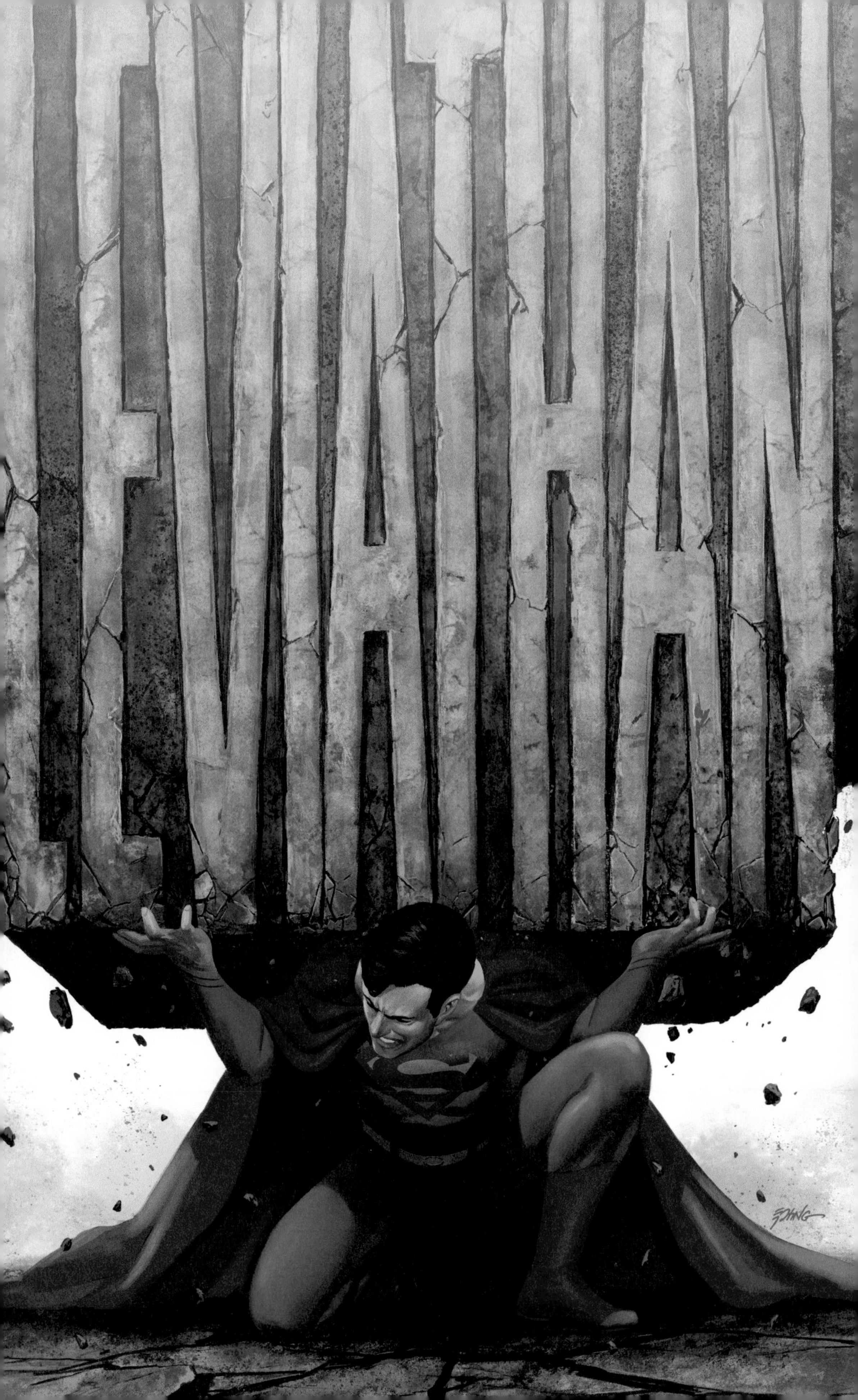

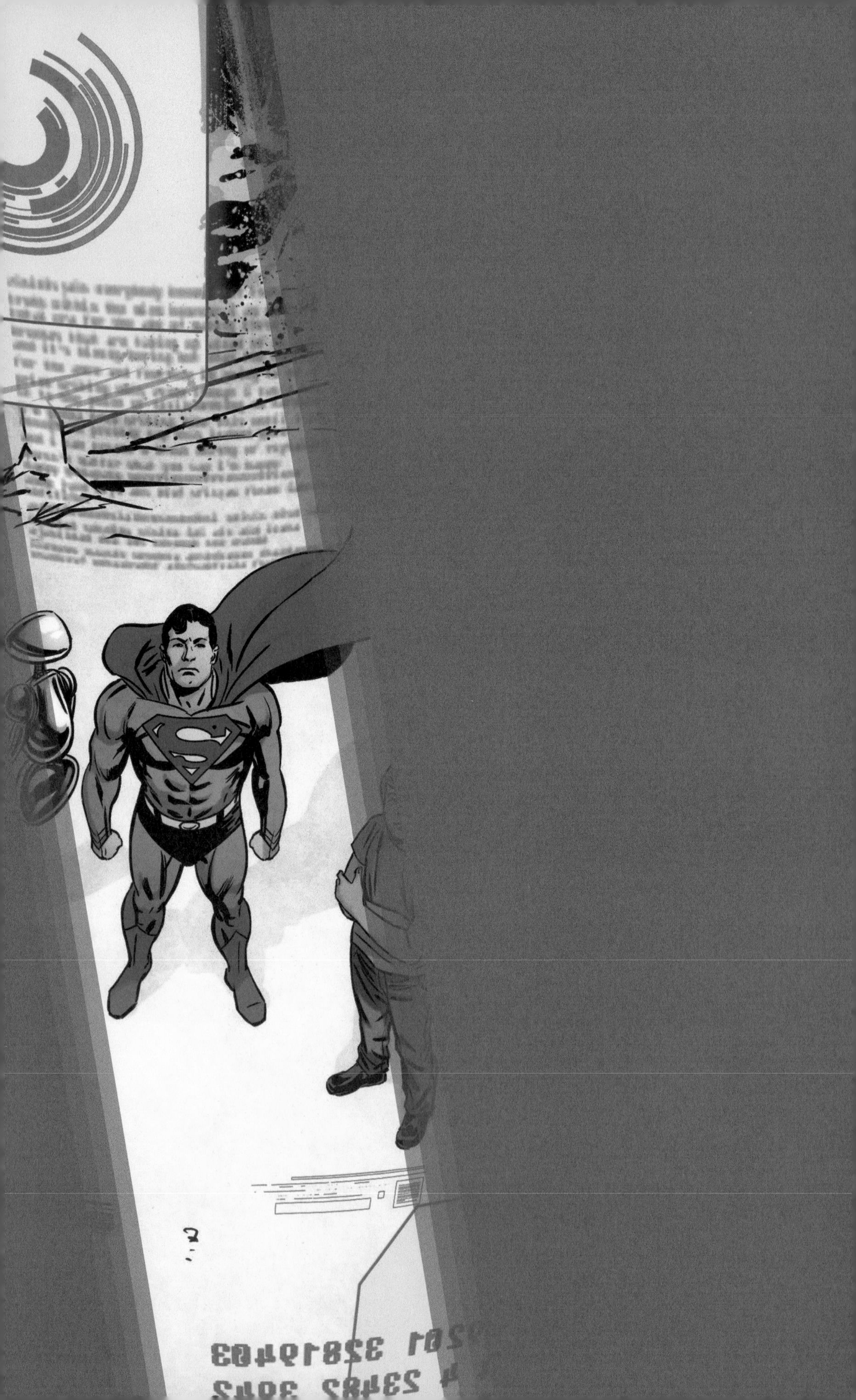

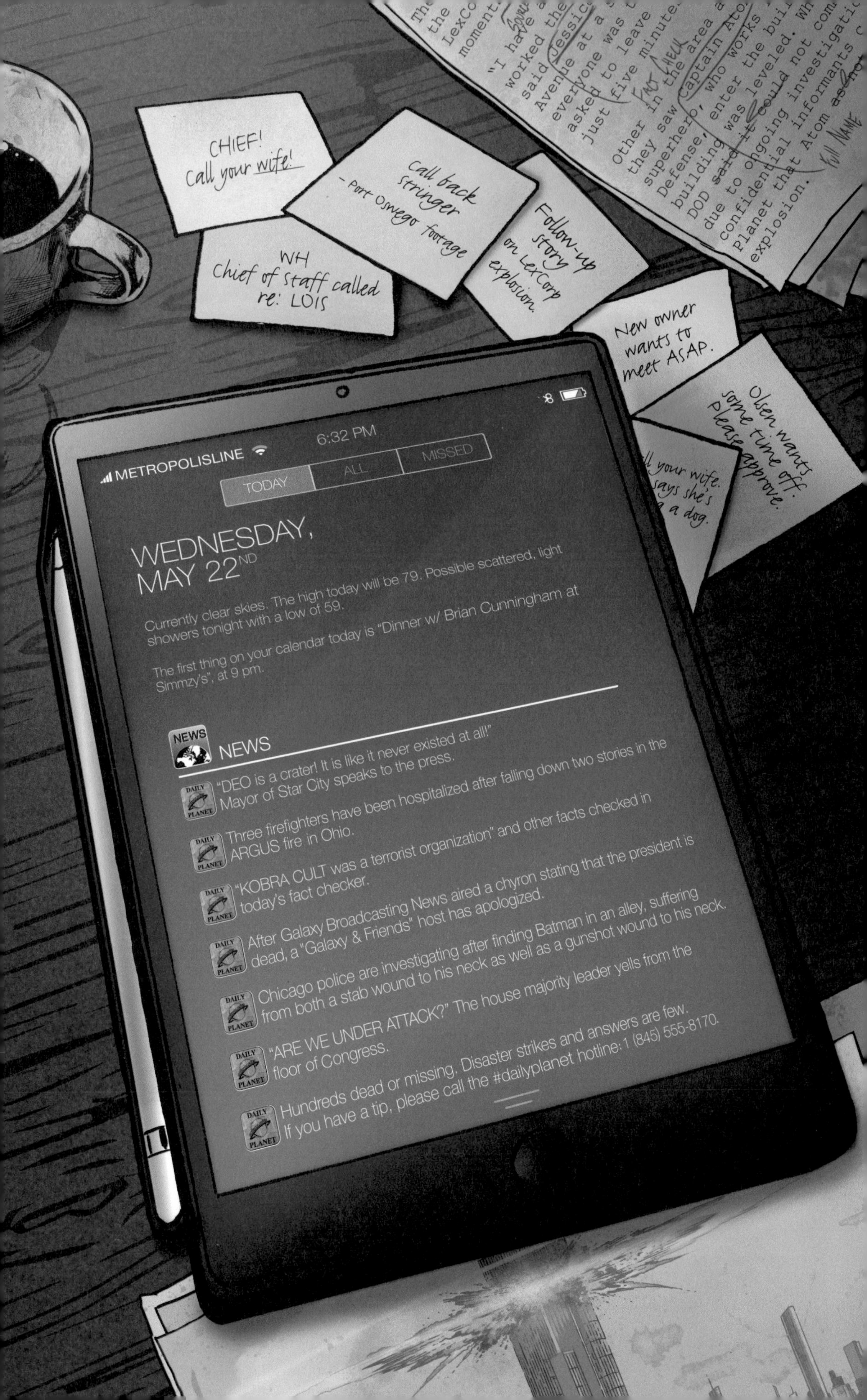
CHIEF!
Call your wife!
Call back stringer
- Port Oswego footage
WH
Chief of Staff called
re: LOIS
Follow-up story on LexCorp explosion.
New owner wants to meet ASAP.
Olsen wants some time off. Please approve.
METROPOLISLINE
6:32 PM
TODAY
ALL
MISSED
WEDNESDAY, MAY 22ND
Currently clear skies. The high today will be 79. Possible scattered, light showers tonight with a low of 59.
The first thing on your calendar today is "Dinner w/ Brian Cunningham at Simmzy's", at 9 pm.
NEWS
NEWS
"DEO is a crater! It is like it never existed at all!" Mayor of Star City speaks to the press.
Three firefighters have been hospitalized after falling down two stories in the ARGUS fire in Ohio.
"KOBRA CULT was a terrorist organization" and other facts checked in today's fact checker.
After Galaxy Broadcasting News aired a chyron stating that the president is dead, a "Galaxy & Friends" host has apologized.
Chicago police are investigating after finding Batman in an alley, suffering from both a stab wound to his neck as well as a gunshot wound to his neck.
"ARE WE UNDER ATTACK?" The house majority leader yells from the floor of Congress.
Hundreds dead or missing. Disaster strikes and answers are few. If you have a tip, please call the #dailyplanet hotline: 1 (845) 555-8170.

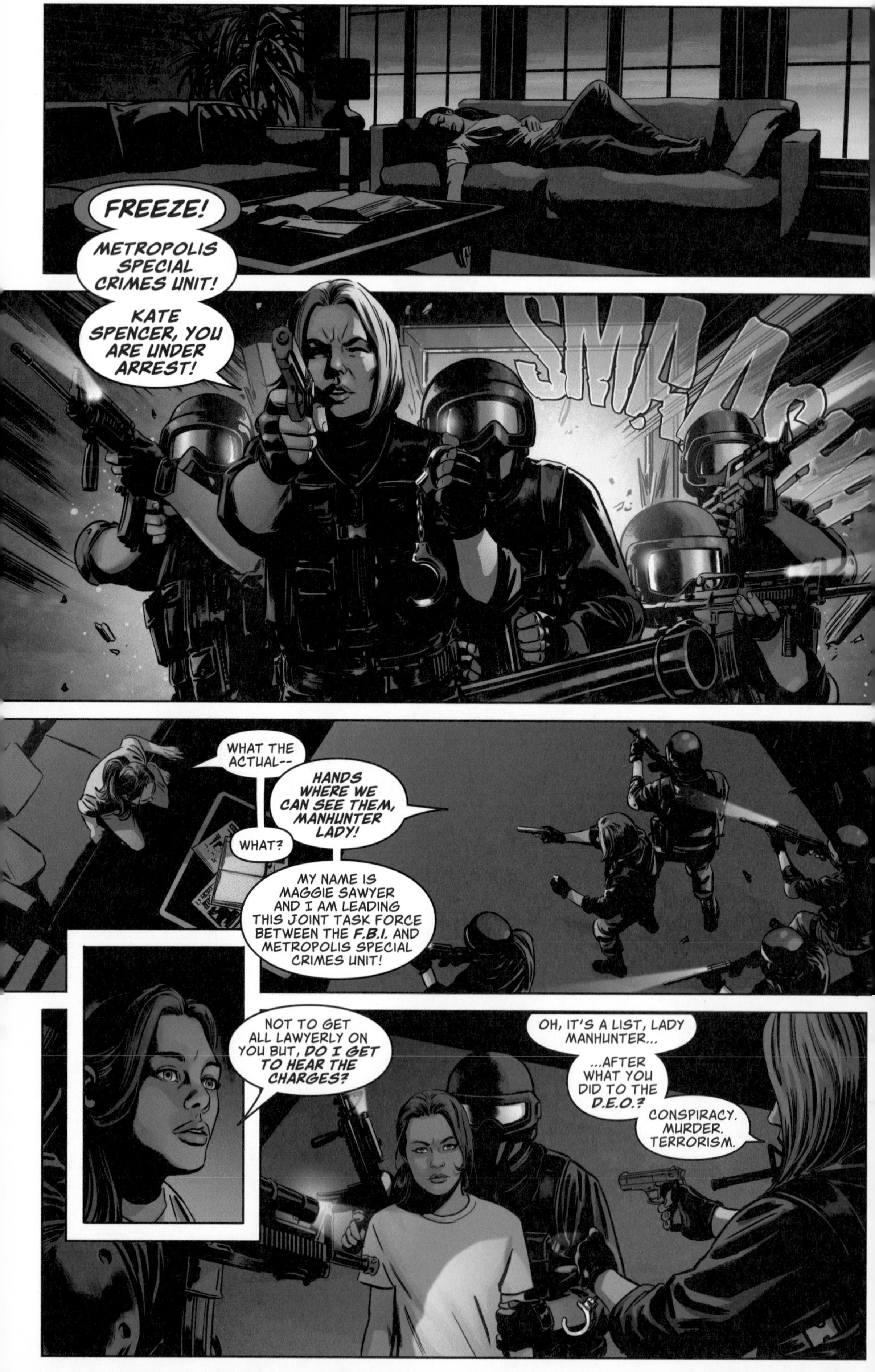
FREEZE!
METROPOLIS SPECIAL CRIMES UNIT!
KATE SPENCER, YOU ARE UNDER ARREST!
WHAT THE ACTUAL--
HANDS WHERE WE CAN SEE THEM, MANHUNTER LADY!
WHAT?
MY NAME IS MAGGIE SAWYER AND I AM LEADING THIS JOINT TASK FORCE BETWEEN THE F.B.I. AND METROPOLIS SPECIAL CRIMES UNIT!
NOT TO GET ALL LAWYERLY ON YOU BUT, DO I GET TO HEAR THE CHARGES?
OH, IT'S A LIST, LADY MANHUNTER...
...AFTER WHAT YOU DID TO THE D.E.O.?
CONSPIRACY. MURDER. TERRORISM.

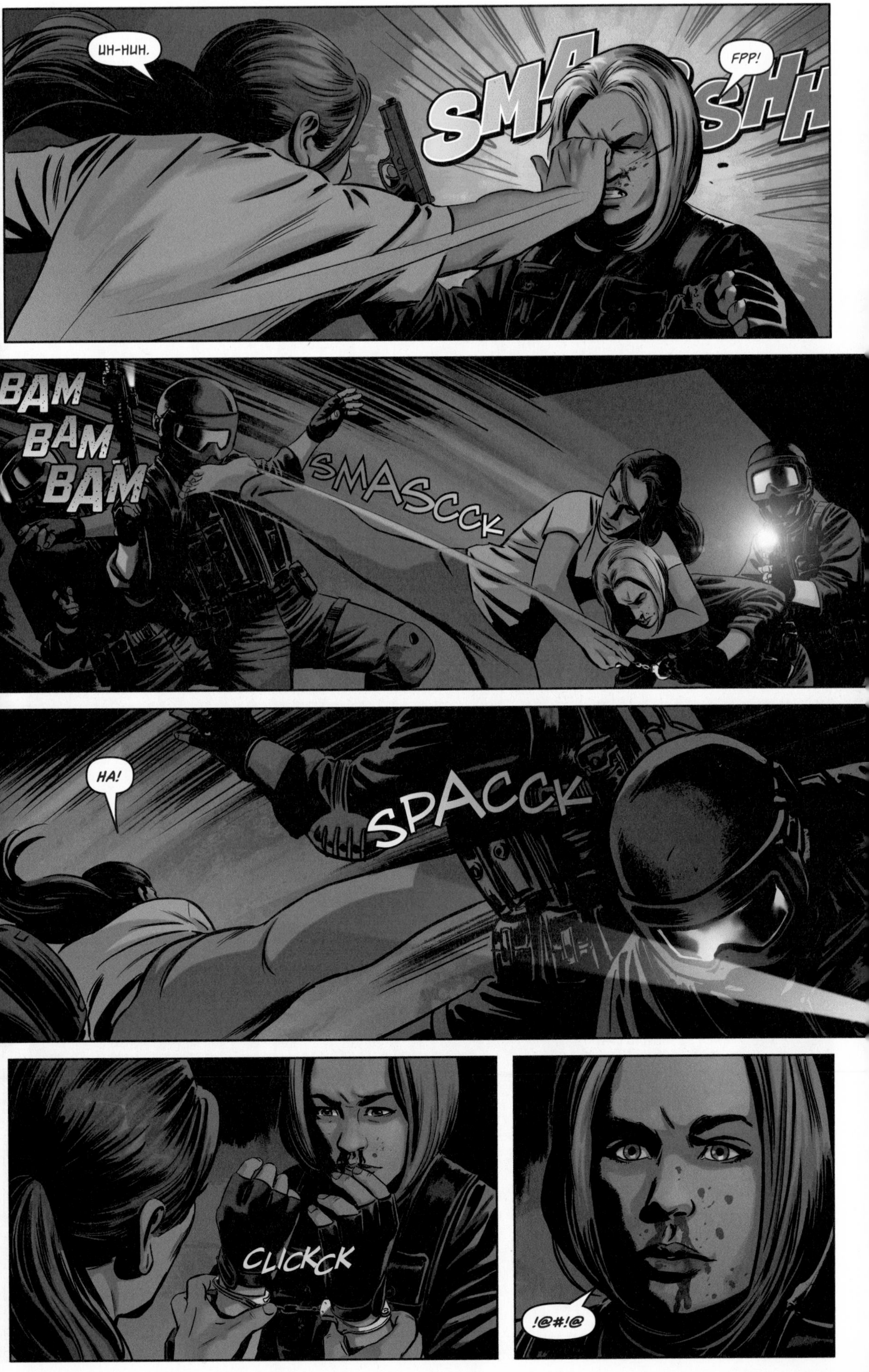
UH-HUH.
FPP!
BAM
BAM
BAM
SMASCCK
HA!
SPACCK
CLICKCK
!@#!@

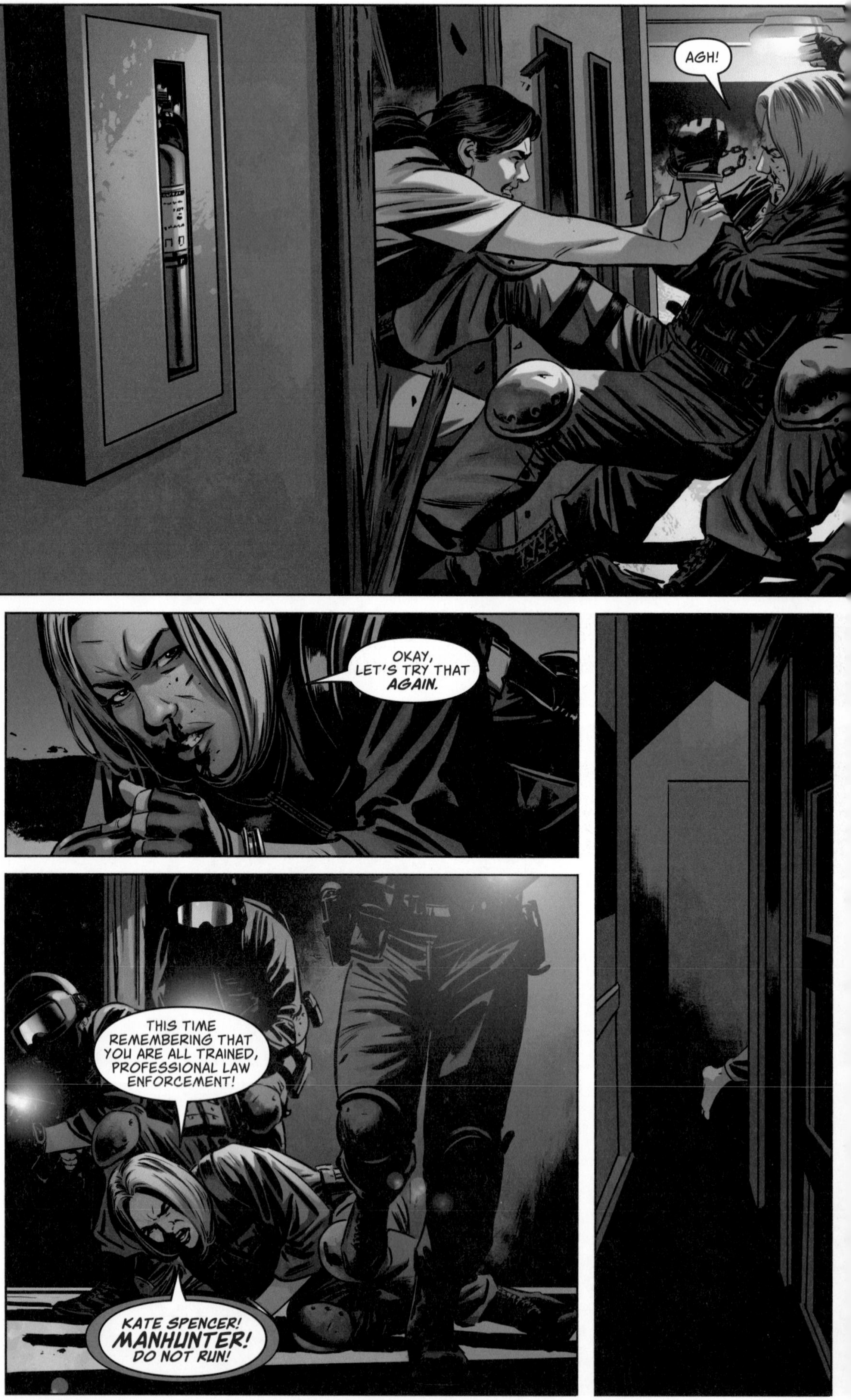
AGH!
OKAY, LET'S TRY THAT AGAIN.
THIS TIME REMEMBERING THAT YOU ARE ALL TRAINED, PROFESSIONAL LAW ENFORCEMENT!
KATE SPENCER! MANHUNTER! DO NOT RUN!

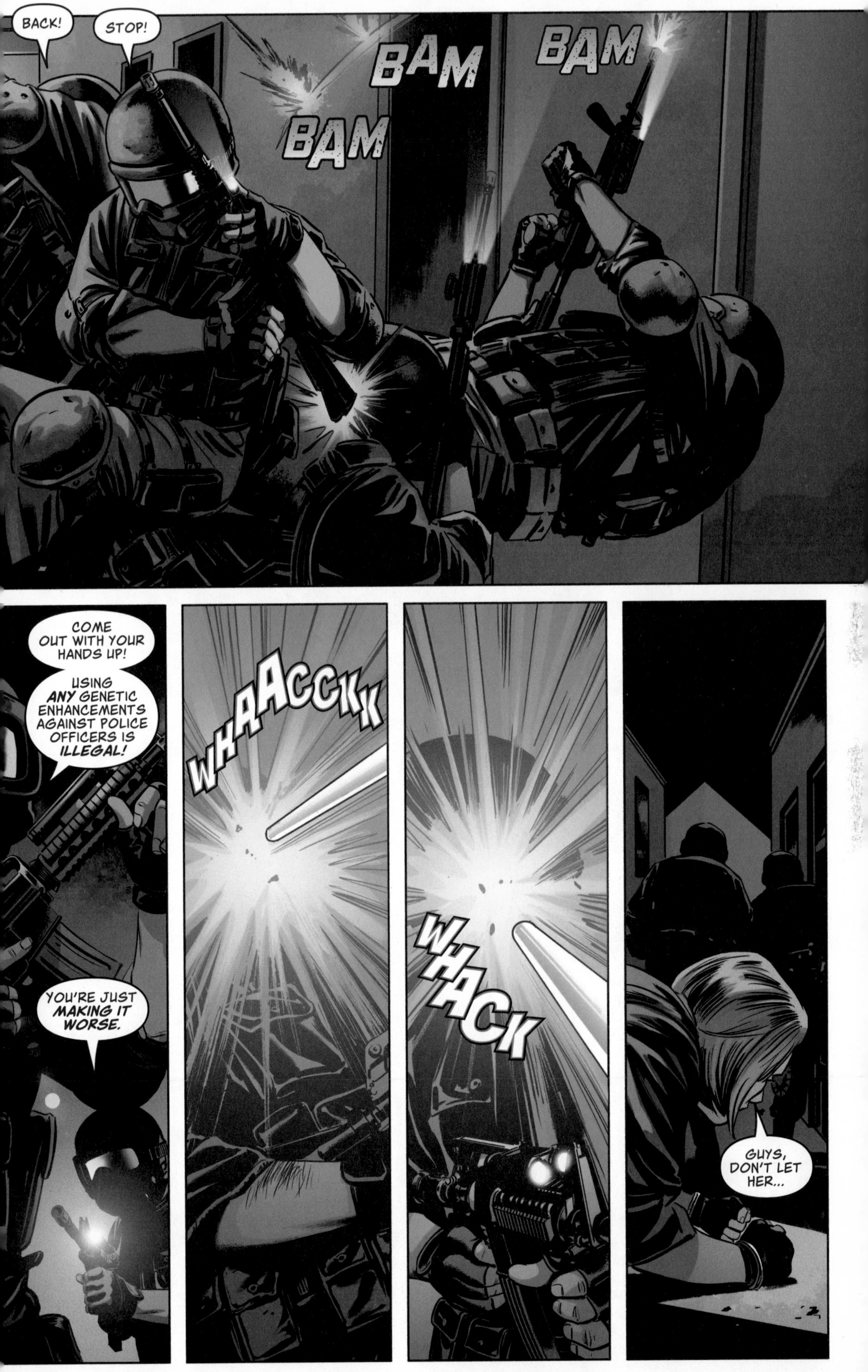
BACK!
STOP!
BAM
BAM
BAM
COME OUT WITH YOUR HANDS UP!
USING ANY GENETIC ENHANCEMENTS AGAINST POLICE OFFICERS IS ILLEGAL!
YOU'RE JUST MAKING IT WORSE.
WHAACCKK
WHACK
GUYS, DON'T LET HER...

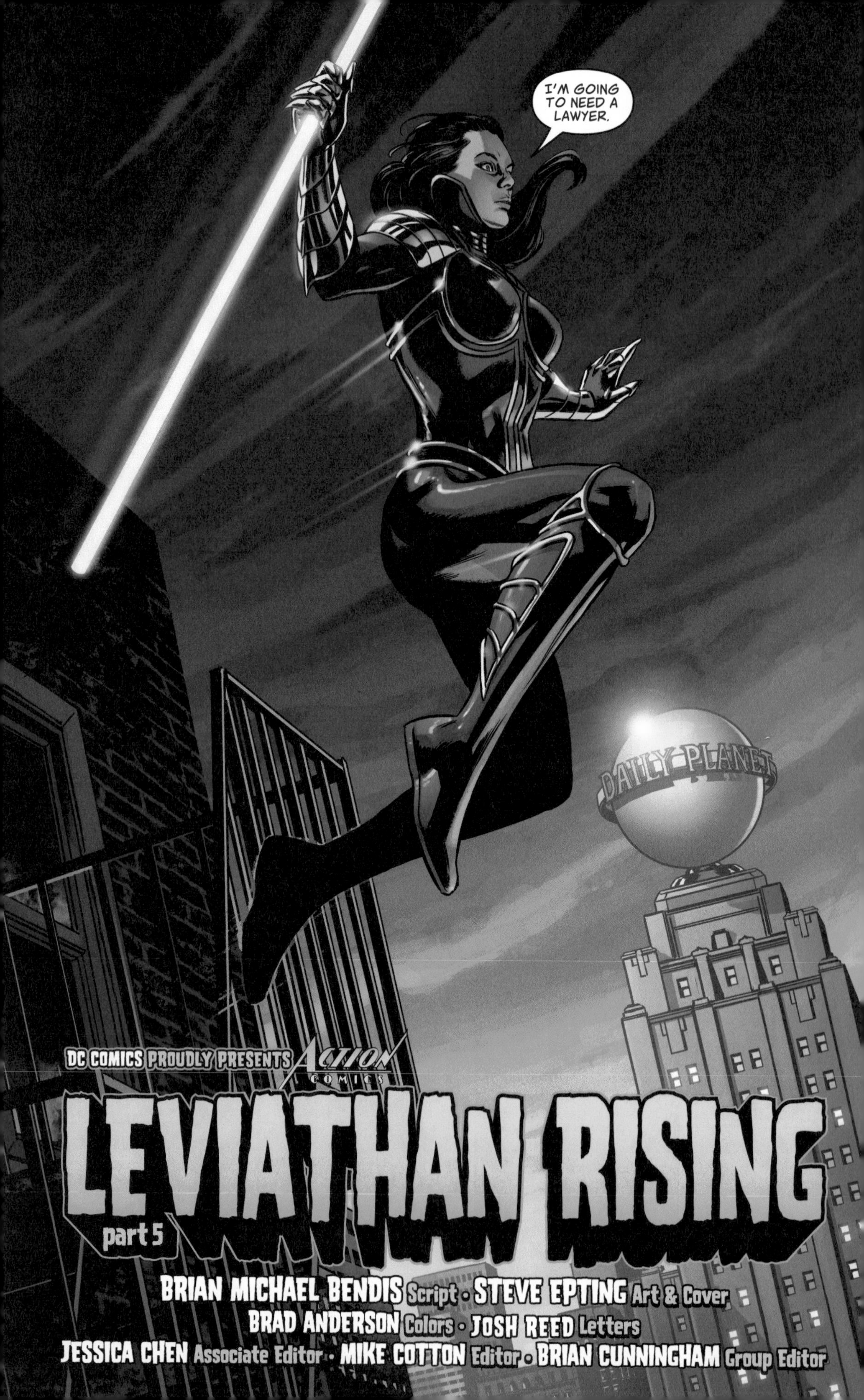

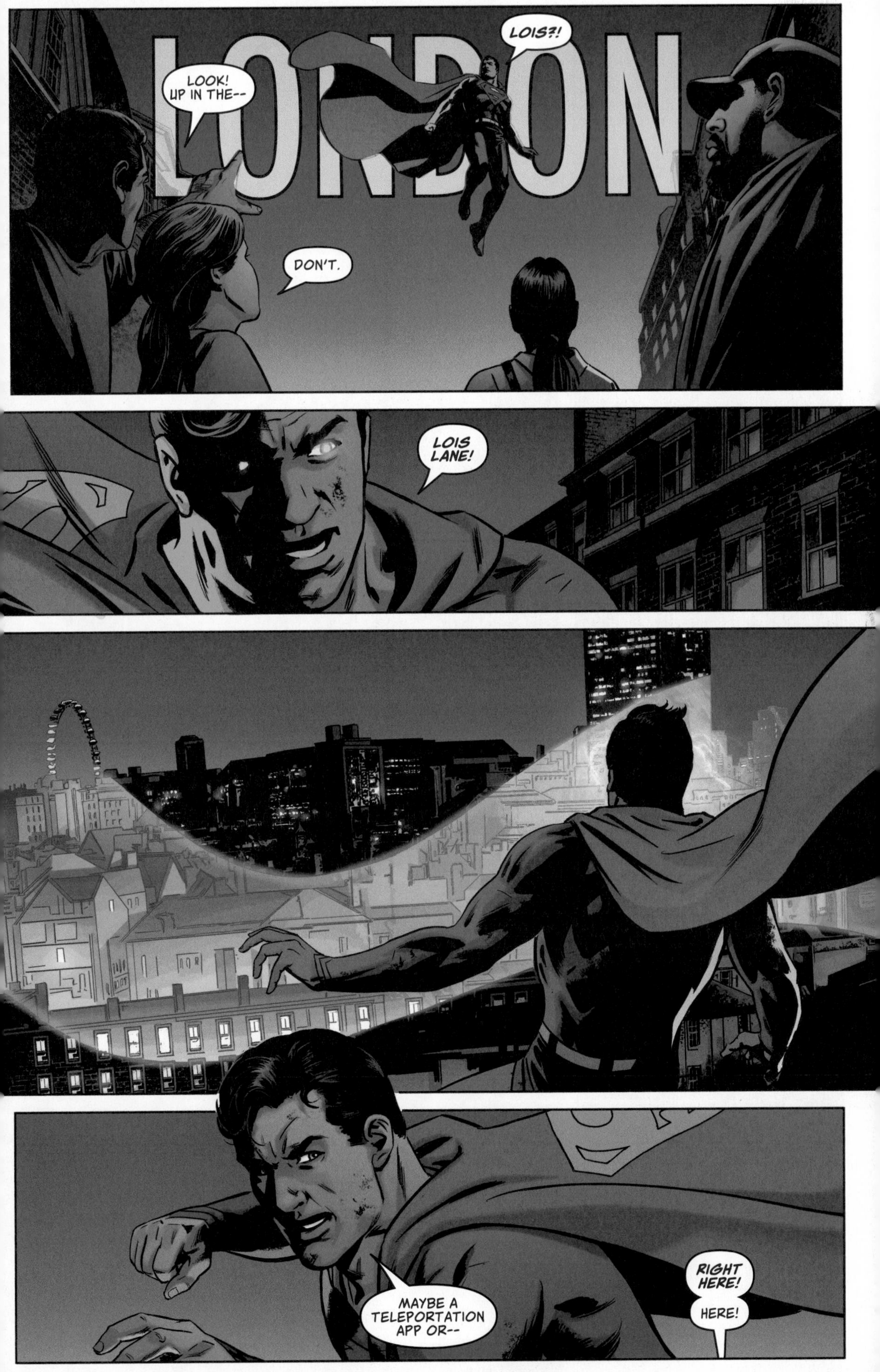
LONDON
LOIS?!
LOOK! UP IN THE--
DON'T.
LOIS LANE!
MAYBE A TELEPORTATION APP OR--
RIGHT HERE!
HERE!

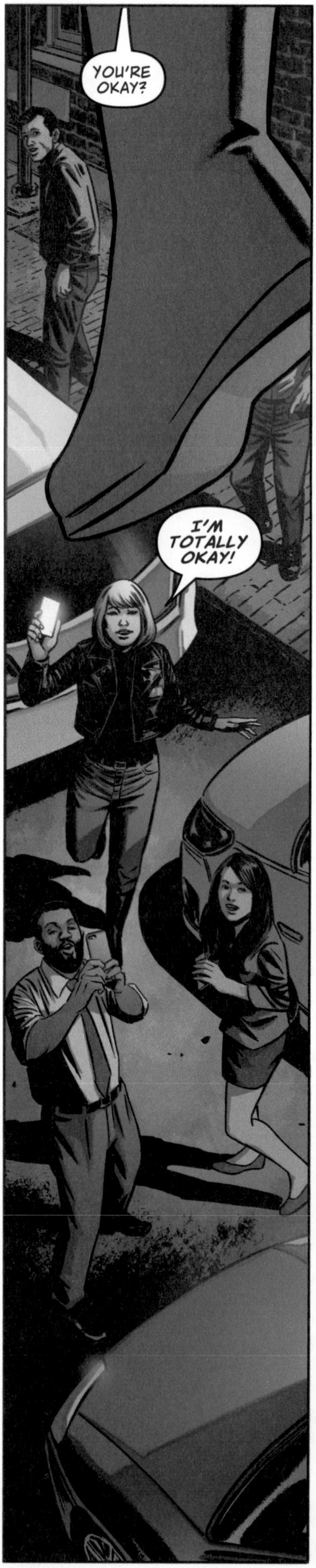
YOU'RE OKAY?
I'M TOTALLY OKAY!

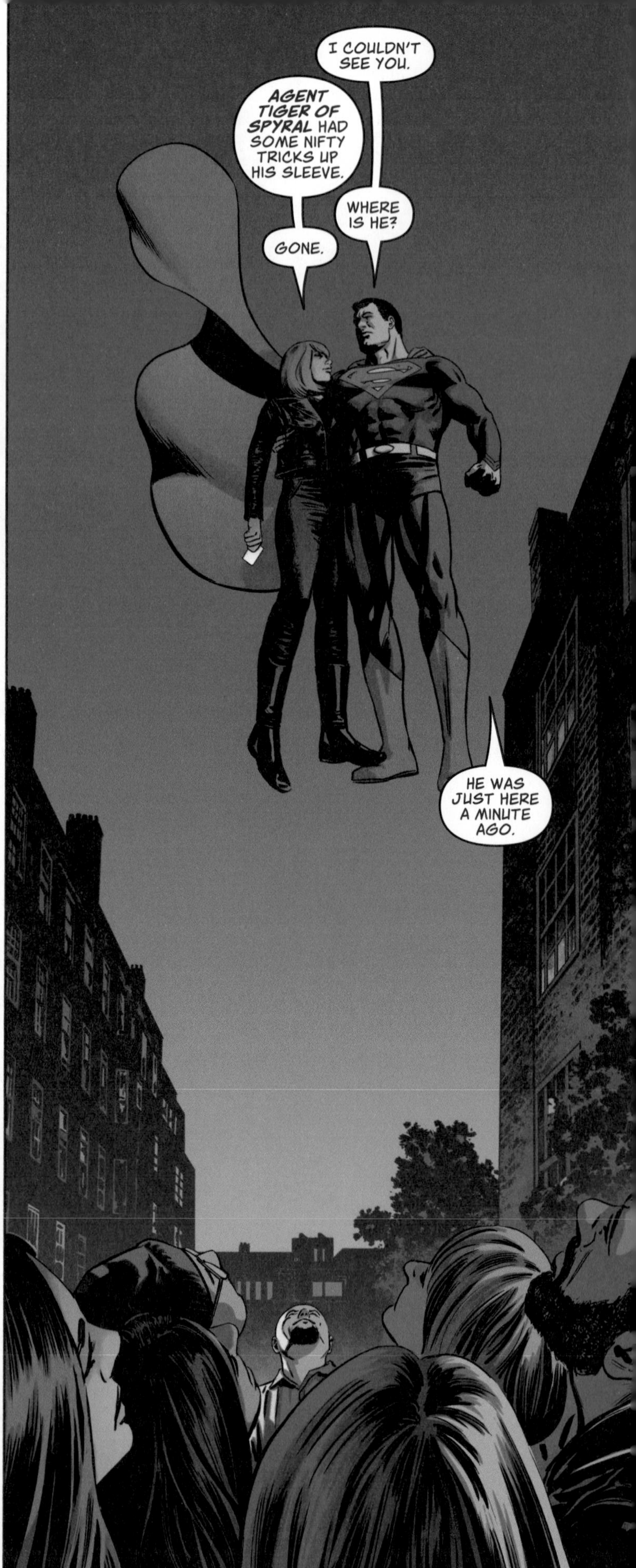
I COULDN'T SEE YOU.
AGENT TIGER OF SPYRAL HAD SOME NIFTY TRICKS UP HIS SLEEVE.
WHERE IS HE?
GONE.
HE WAS JUST HERE A MINUTE AGO.

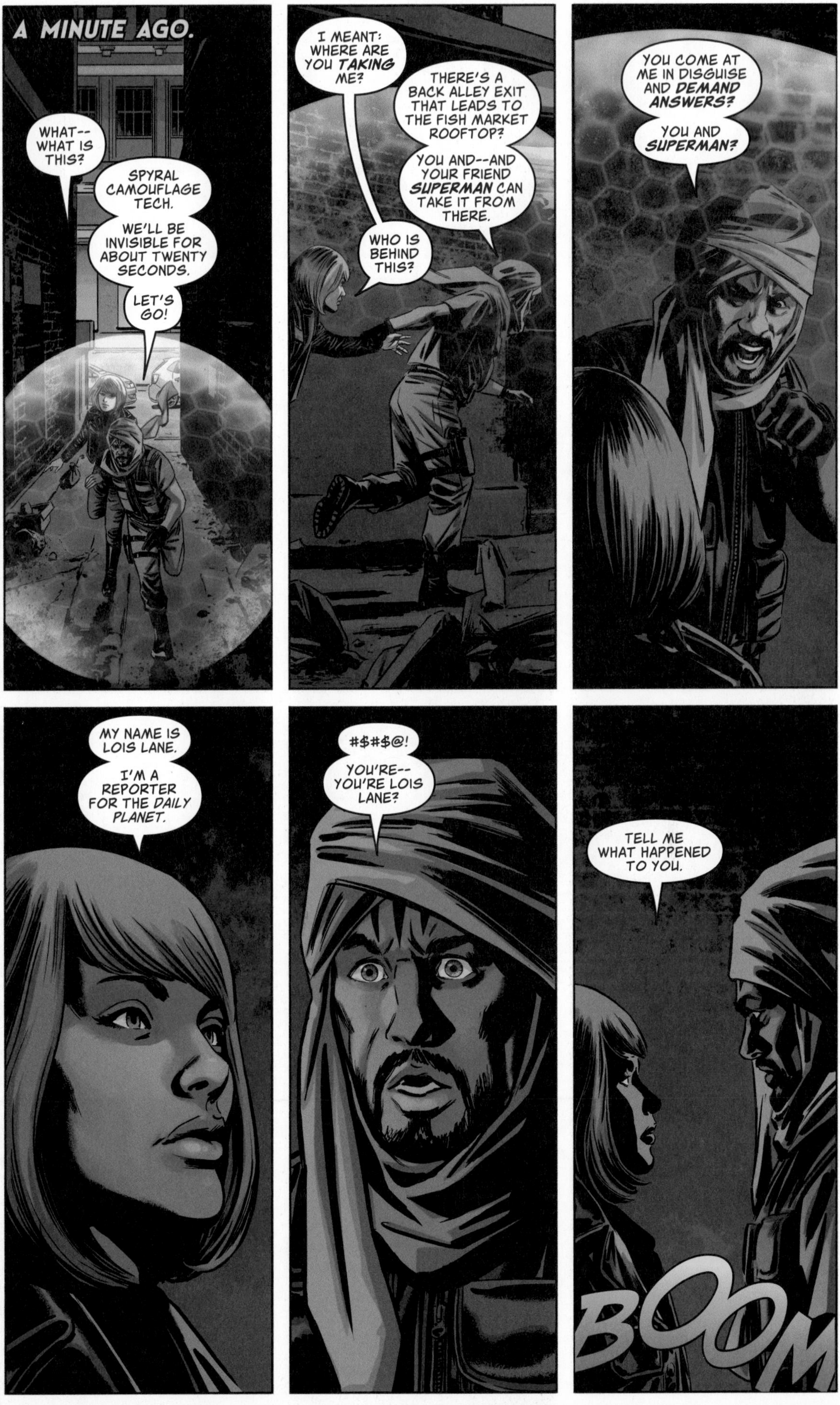
A MINUTE AGO.
WHAT-- WHAT IS THIS?
SPYRAL CAMOUFLAGE TECH.
WE'LL BE INVISIBLE FOR ABOUT TWENTY SECONDS.
LET'S GO!
I MEANT: WHERE ARE YOU TAKING ME?
THERE'S A BACK ALLEY EXIT THAT LEADS TO THE FISH MARKET ROOFTOP?
YOU AND--AND YOUR FRIEND SUPERMAN CAN TAKE IT FROM THERE.
WHO IS BEHIND THIS?
YOU COME AT ME IN DISGUISE AND DEMAND ANSWERS?
YOU AND SUPERMAN?
MY NAME IS LOIS LANE.
I'M A REPORTER FOR THE DAILY PLANET.
#$#$@!
YOU'RE-- YOU'RE LOIS LANE?
TELL ME WHAT HAPPENED TO YOU.
BOOM

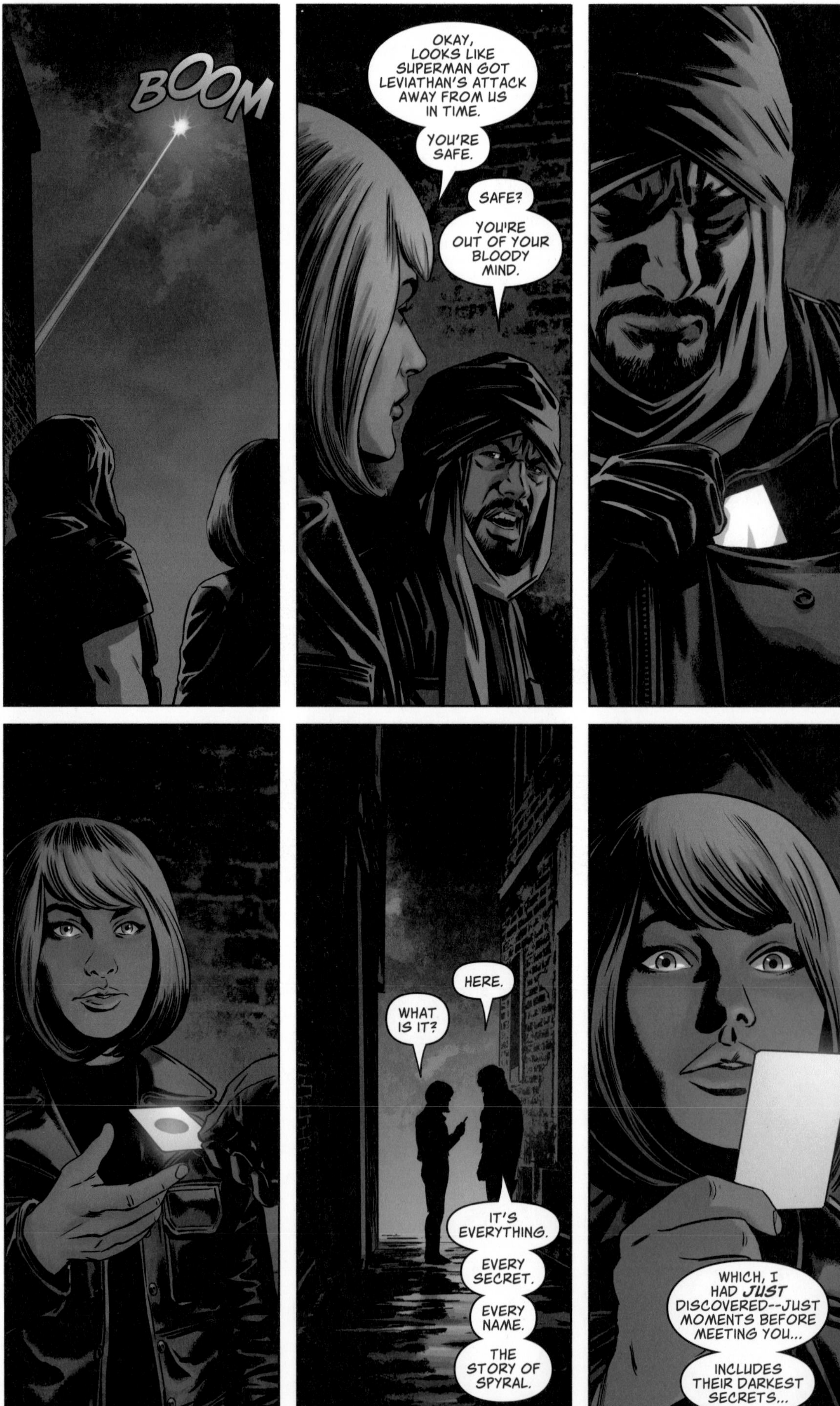
BOOM
OKAY, LOOKS LIKE SUPERMAN GOT LEVIATHAN'S ATTACK AWAY FROM US IN TIME.
YOU'RE SAFE.
SAFE?
YOU'RE OUT OF YOUR BLOODY MIND.
HERE.
WHAT IS IT?
IT'S EVERYTHING.
EVERY SECRET.
EVERY NAME.
THE STORY OF SPYRAL.
WHICH, I HAD JUST DISCOVERED--JUST MOMENTS BEFORE MEETING YOU...
INCLUDES THEIR DARKEST SECRETS...

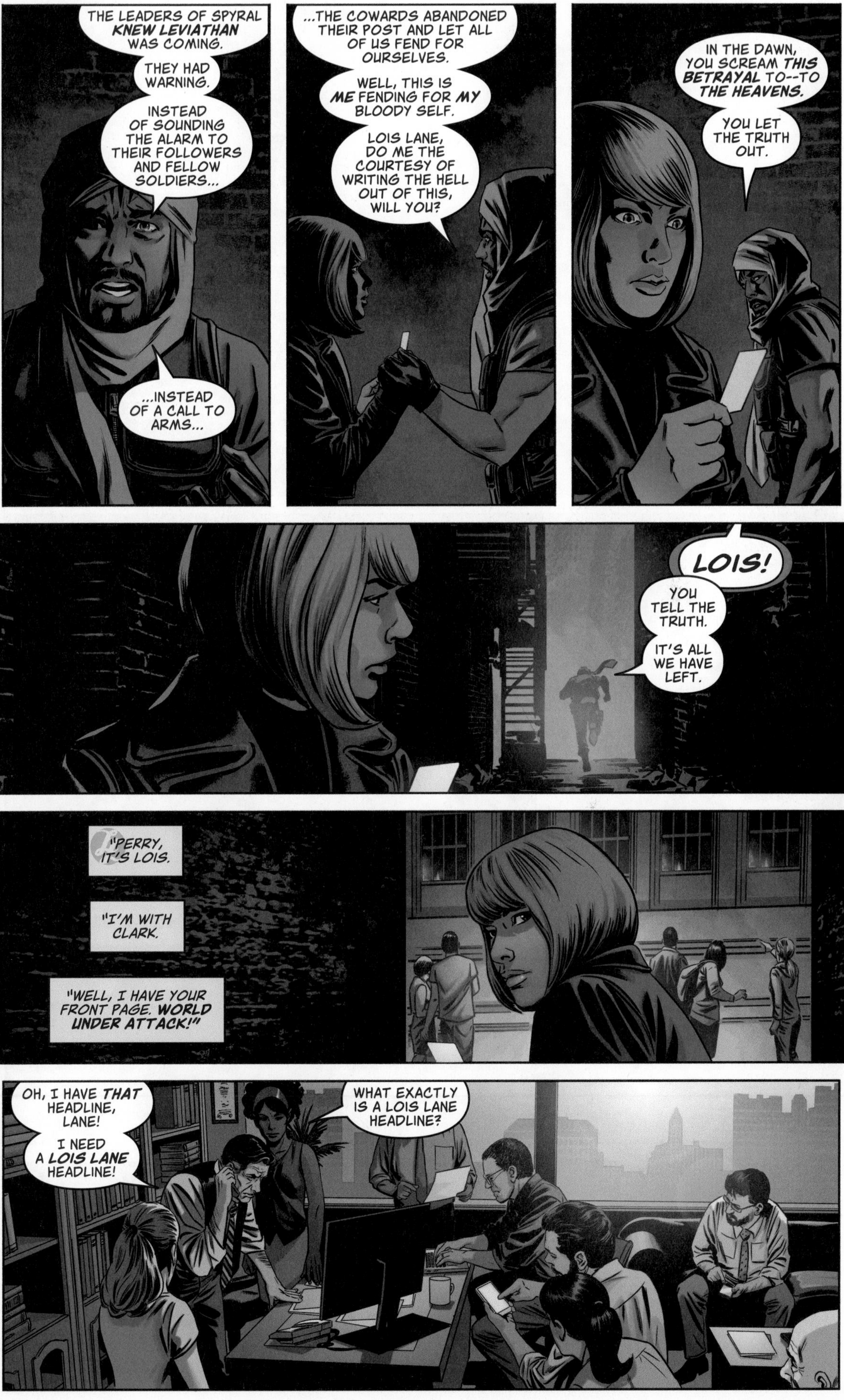
THE LEADERS OF SPYRAL KNEW LEVIATHAN WAS COMING.
THEY HAD WARNING.
INSTEAD OF SOUNDING THE ALARM TO THEIR FOLLOWERS AND FELLOW SOLDIERS...
...INSTEAD OF A CALL TO ARMS...
...THE COWARDS ABANDONED THEIR POST AND LET ALL OF US FEND FOR OURSELVES.
WELL, THIS IS ME FENDING FOR MY BLOODY SELF.
LOIS LANE, DO ME THE COURTESY OF WRITING THE HELL OUT OF THIS, WILL YOU?
IN THE DAWN, YOU SCREAM THIS BETRAYAL TO--TO THE HEAVENS.
YOU LET THE TRUTH OUT.
LOIS!
YOU TELL THE TRUTH.
IT'S ALL WE HAVE LEFT.
"PERRY, IT'S LOIS.
"I'M WITH CLARK.
"WELL, I HAVE YOUR FRONT PAGE. WORLD UNDER ATTACK!"
OH, I HAVE THAT HEADLINE, LANE!
I NEED A LOIS LANE HEADLINE!
WHAT EXACTLY IS A LOIS LANE HEADLINE?

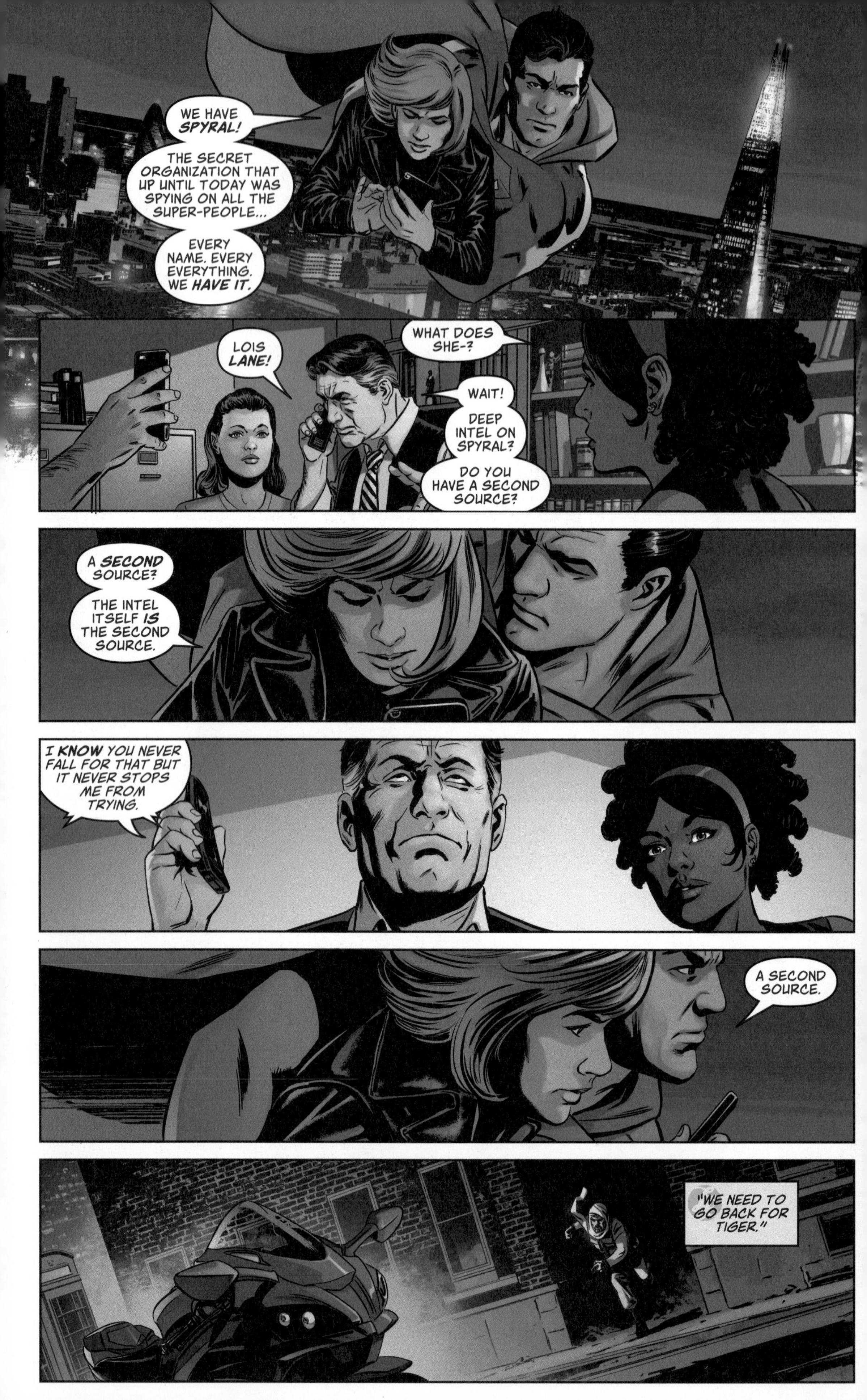
WE HAVE SPYRAL!
THE SECRET ORGANIZATION THAT UP UNTIL TODAY WAS SPYING ON ALL THE SUPER-PEOPLE...
EVERY NAME. EVERY EVERYTHING. WE HAVE IT.
LOIS LANE!
WHAT DOES SHE-?
WAIT!
DEEP INTEL ON SPYRAL?
DO YOU HAVE A SECOND SOURCE?
A SECOND SOURCE?
THE INTEL ITSELF IS THE SECOND SOURCE.
I KNOW YOU NEVER FALL FOR THAT BUT IT NEVER STOPS ME FROM TRYING.
A SECOND SOURCE.
"WE NEED TO GO BACK FOR TIGER."

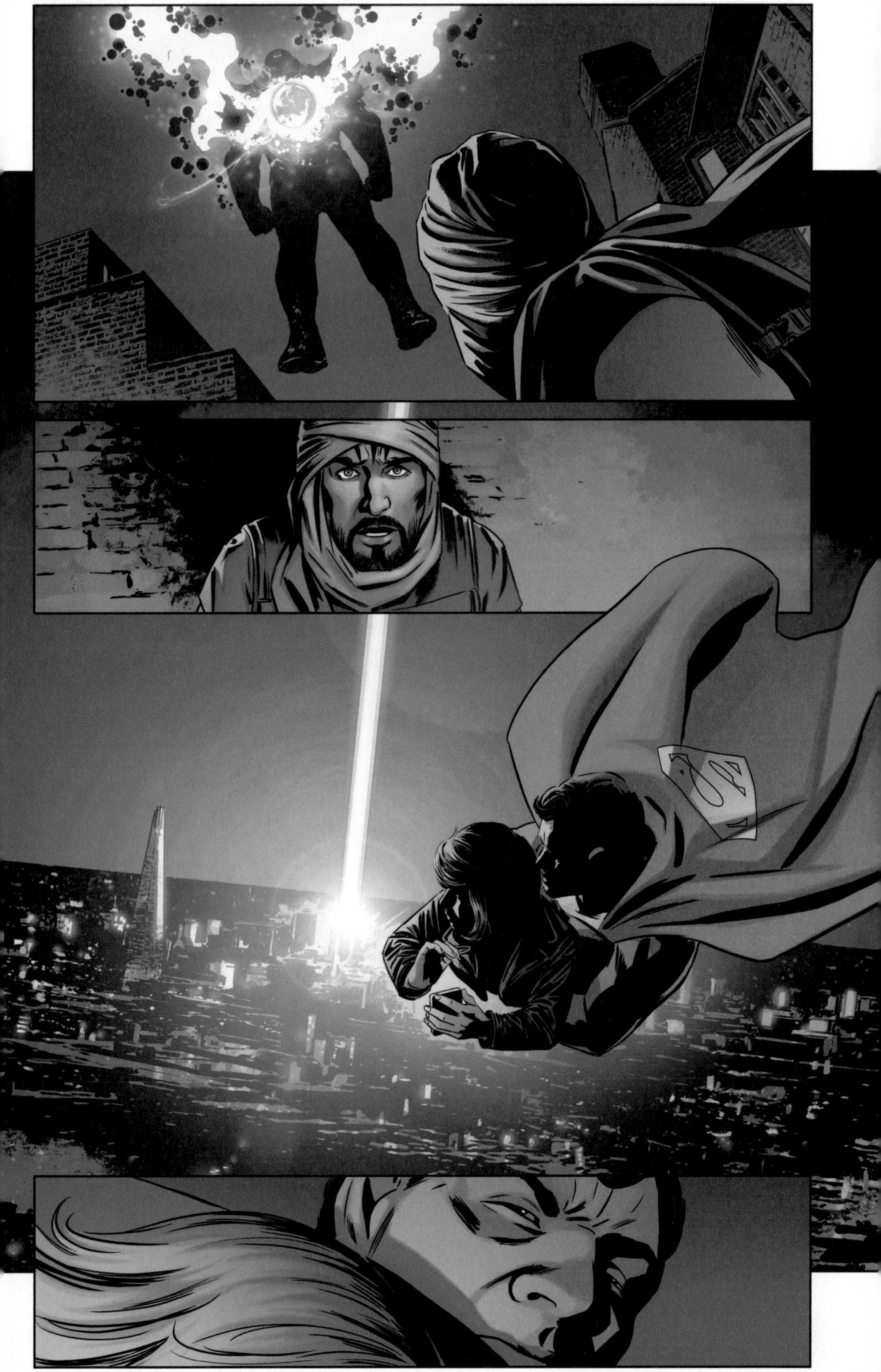

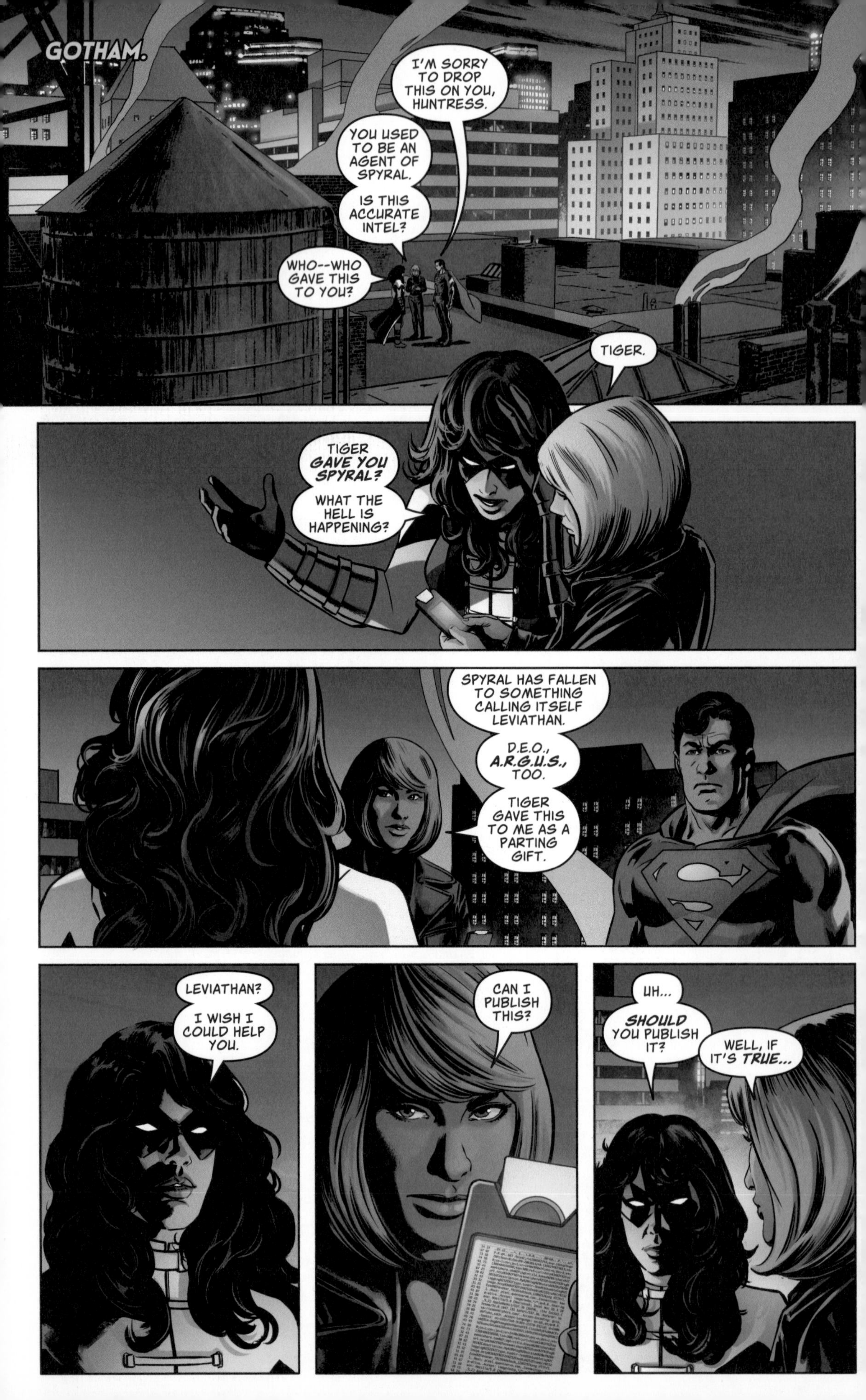
GOTHAM.
I'M SORRY TO DROP THIS ON YOU, HUNTRESS.
YOU USED TO BE AN AGENT OF SPYRAL.
IS THIS ACCURATE INTEL?
WHO--WHO GAVE THIS TO YOU?
TIGER.
TIGER GAVE YOU SPYRAL?
WHAT THE HELL IS HAPPENING?
SPYRAL HAS FALLEN TO SOMETHING CALLING ITSELF LEVIATHAN.
D.E.O., A.R.G.U.S., TOO.
TIGER GAVE THIS TO ME AS A PARTING GIFT.
LEVIATHAN?
I WISH I COULD HELP YOU.
CAN I PUBLISH THIS?
UH...
SHOULD YOU PUBLISH IT?
WELL, IF IT'S TRUE...

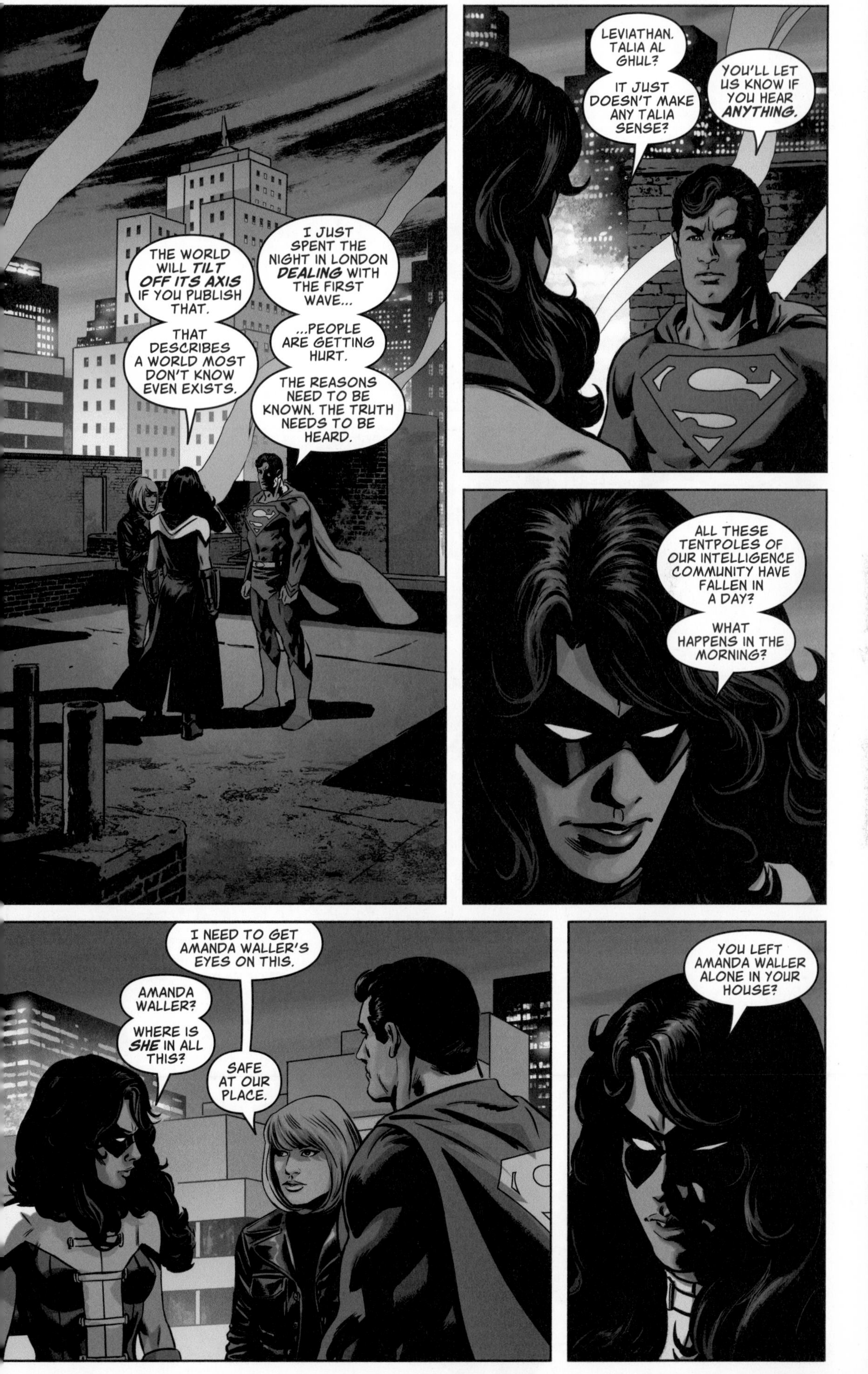
THE WORLD WILL TILT OFF ITS AXIS IF YOU PUBLISH THAT.
I JUST SPENT THE NIGHT IN LONDON DEALING WITH THE FIRST WAVE...
THAT DESCRIBES A WORLD MOST DON'T KNOW EVEN EXISTS.
...PEOPLE ARE GETTING HURT.
THE REASONS NEED TO BE KNOWN. THE TRUTH NEEDS TO BE HEARD.
LEVIATHAN. TALIA AL GHUL?
IT JUST DOESN'T MAKE ANY TALIA SENSE?
YOU'LL LET US KNOW IF YOU HEAR ANYTHING.
ALL THESE TENTPOLES OF OUR INTELLIGENCE COMMUNITY HAVE FALLEN IN A DAY?
WHAT HAPPENS IN THE MORNING?
I NEED TO GET AMANDA WALLER'S EYES ON THIS.
AMANDA WALLER?
WHERE IS SHE IN ALL THIS?
SAFE AT OUR PLACE.
YOU LEFT AMANDA WALLER ALONE IN YOUR HOUSE?

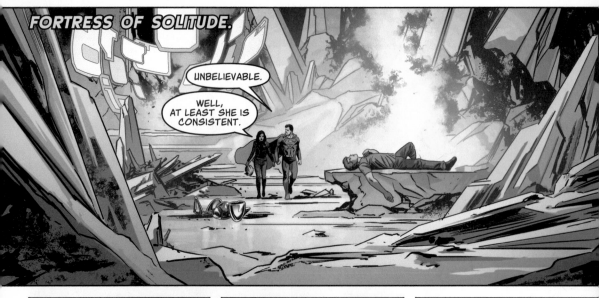

UNBELIEVABLE.

WELL, AT LEAST SHE IS CONSISTENT.

JIMMY.

AMANDA WALLER?

OH--GREAT CAESAR'S SALAD!

OH, UH, I THINK SHE MAY HAVE LEFT.

HOW? WE'RE IN THE MIDDLE OF THE BERMUDA TRIANGLE.

I AM KELEX.

I AM BACK ONLINE.

MY CONTROLS WERE OVERRIDDEN.

KELEX, WHERE DID AMANDA WALLER GO?

SHE TOOK BATMAN'S SPARE LIFE-POD IN GARAGE DECK THREE.

YOU OKAY, LOIS?

THAT WAS A LOT OF AROUND-THE-WORLD FLYING, SMALLVILLE.

I JUST NEED A SECOND.

BATMAN KEEPS A POD HERE?

HE LEAVES STUFF EVERYWHERE.

YOU OKAY?

CAN YOU TRACK THE POD?

IT WENT OFFLINE OVER MEXICO.

OF COURSE IT DID.

KELEX, I NEED MY WRITING PROGRAM.

AND YOU, SUPERMAN, HAVE BETTER THINGS TO DO BUT THAT REALLY DID HELP.

I TYPE FASTER THAN YOU.

FASTER ISN'T BETTER.

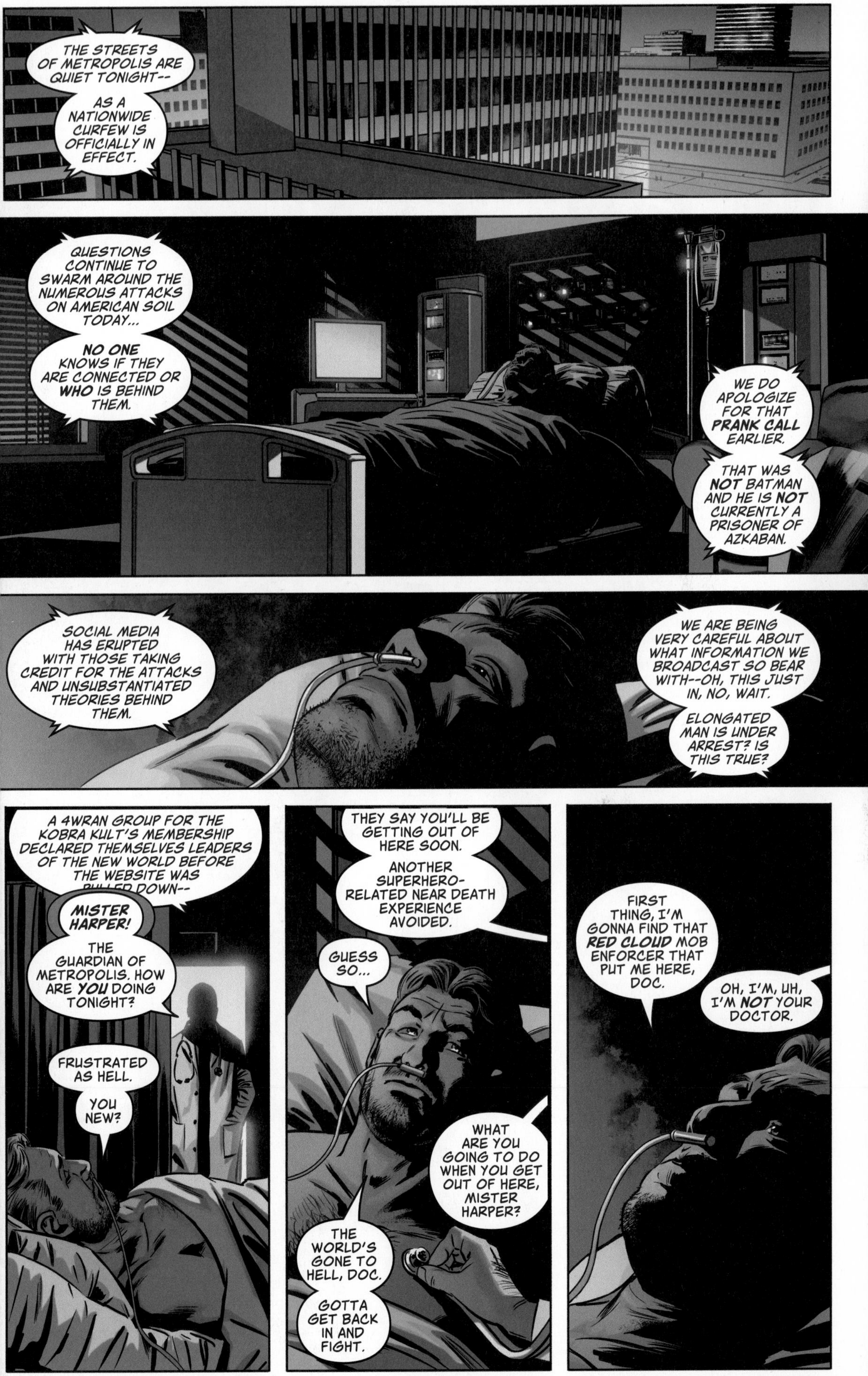
THE STREETS OF METROPOLIS ARE QUIET TONIGHT--
AS A NATIONWIDE CURFEW IS OFFICIALLY IN EFFECT.
QUESTIONS CONTINUE TO SWARM AROUND THE NUMEROUS ATTACKS ON AMERICAN SOIL TODAY...
NO ONE KNOWS IF THEY ARE CONNECTED OR WHO IS BEHIND THEM.
WE DO APOLOGIZE FOR THAT PRANK CALL EARLIER.
THAT WAS NOT BATMAN AND HE IS NOT CURRENTLY A PRISONER OF AZKABAN.
SOCIAL MEDIA HAS ERUPTED WITH THOSE TAKING CREDIT FOR THE ATTACKS AND UNSUBSTANTIATED THEORIES BEHIND THEM.
WE ARE BEING VERY CAREFUL ABOUT WHAT INFORMATION WE BROADCAST SO BEAR WITH--OH, THIS JUST IN, NO, WAIT.
ELONGATED MAN IS UNDER ARREST? IS THIS TRUE?
A 4WRAN GROUP FOR THE KOBRA KULT'S MEMBERSHIP DECLARED THEMSELVES LEADERS OF THE NEW WORLD BEFORE THE WEBSITE WAS
DOWN--
MISTER HARPER!
THE GUARDIAN OF METROPOLIS. HOW ARE YOU DOING TONIGHT?
FRUSTRATED AS HELL.
YOU NEW?
THEY SAY YOU'LL BE GETTING OUT OF HERE SOON.
ANOTHER SUPERHERO-RELATED NEAR DEATH EXPERIENCE AVOIDED.
GUESS SO...
WHAT ARE YOU GOING TO DO WHEN YOU GET OUT OF HERE, MISTER HARPER?
THE WORLD'S GONE TO HELL, DOC.
GOTTA GET BACK IN AND FIGHT.
FIRST THING, I'M GONNA FIND THAT RED CLOUD MOB ENFORCER THAT PUT ME HERE, DOC.
OH, I'M, UH, I'M NOT YOUR DOCTOR.

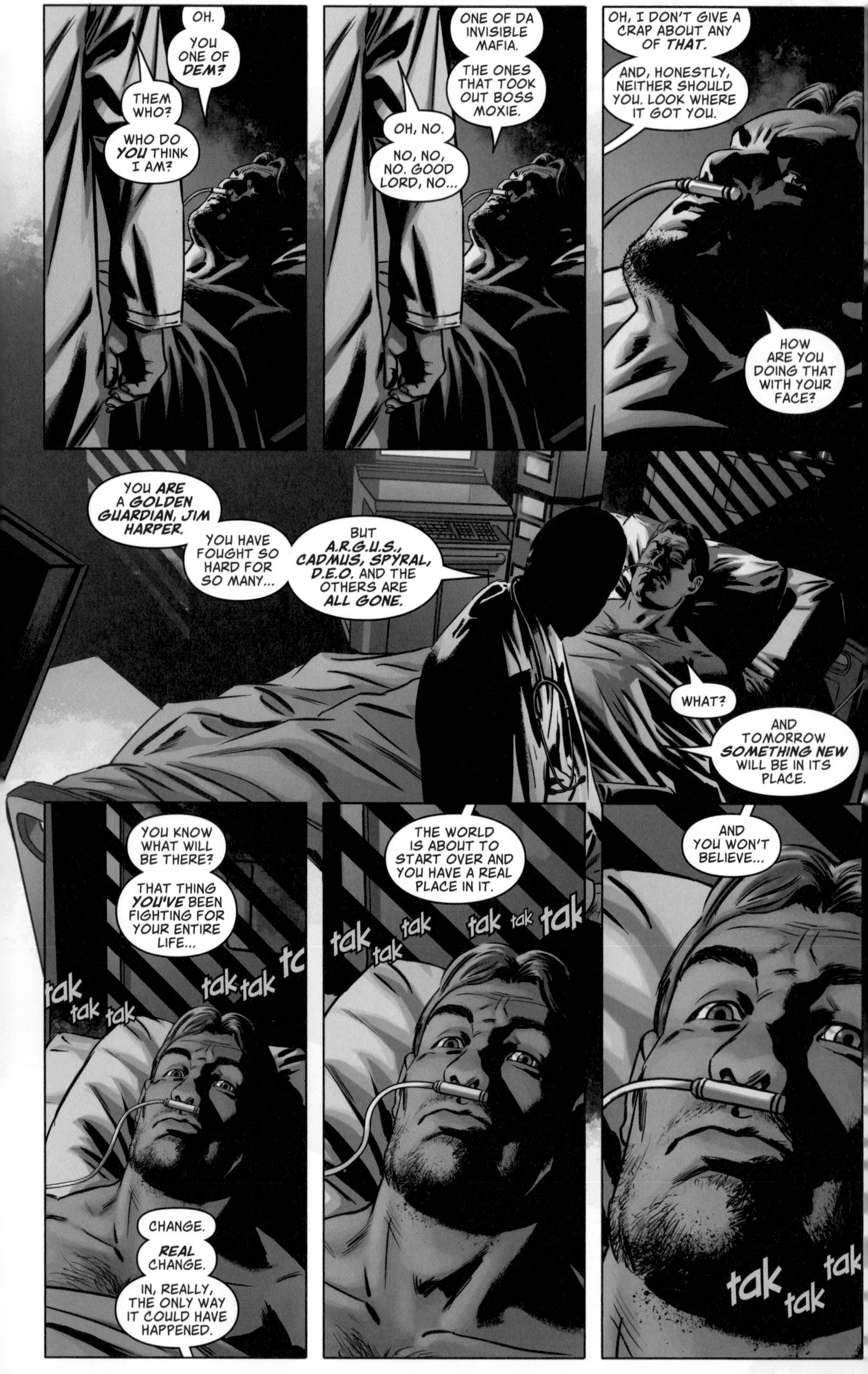
OH.
YOU ONE OF DEM?
THEM WHO?
WHO DO YOU THINK I AM?
ONE OF DA INVISIBLE MAFIA.
THE ONES THAT TOOK OUT BOSS MOXIE.
OH, NO.
NO, NO, NO. GOOD LORD, NO...
OH, I DON'T GIVE A CRAP ABOUT ANY OF THAT.
AND, HONESTLY, NEITHER SHOULD YOU. LOOK WHERE IT GOT YOU.
HOW ARE YOU DOING THAT WITH YOUR FACE?
YOU ARE A GOLDEN GUARDIAN, JIM HARPER.
YOU HAVE FOUGHT SO HARD FOR SO MANY...
BUT A.R.G.U.S., CADMUS, SPYRAL, D.E.O. AND THE OTHERS ARE ALL GONE.
WHAT?
AND TOMORROW SOMETHING NEW WILL BE IN ITS PLACE.
YOU KNOW WHAT WILL BE THERE?
THAT THING YOU'VE BEEN FIGHTING FOR YOUR ENTIRE LIFE...
tak tak tak
tak tak
CHANGE.
REAL CHANGE.
IN, REALLY, THE ONLY WAY IT COULD HAVE HAPPENED.
THE WORLD IS ABOUT TO START OVER AND YOU HAVE A REAL PLACE IN IT.
tak tak tak
tak tak tak
AND YOU WON'T BELIEVE...
tak tak tak

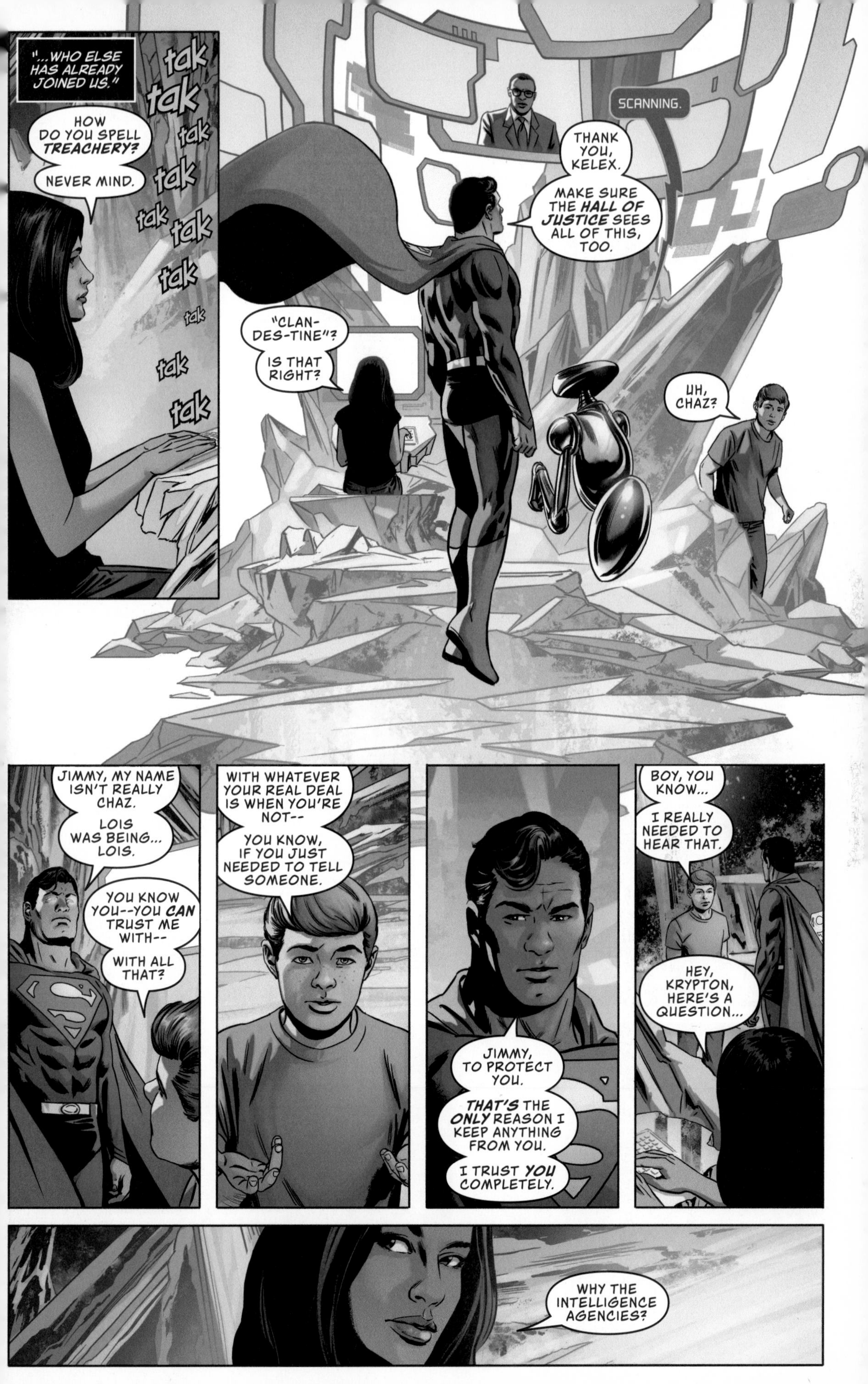
"...WHO ELSE HAS ALREADY JOINED US."
tak tak tak tak tak tak tak tak tak tak
HOW DO YOU SPELL TREACHERY?
NEVER MIND.
SCANNING.
THANK YOU, KELEX.
MAKE SURE THE HALL OF JUSTICE SEES ALL OF THIS, TOO.
"CLAN-DES-TINE"?
IS THAT RIGHT?
UH, CHAZ?
JIMMY, MY NAME ISN'T REALLY CHAZ.
LOIS WAS BEING... LOIS.
YOU KNOW YOU--YOU CAN TRUST ME WITH--
WITH ALL THAT?
WITH WHATEVER YOUR REAL DEAL IS WHEN YOU'RE NOT--
YOU KNOW, IF YOU JUST NEEDED TO TELL SOMEONE.
JIMMY, TO PROTECT YOU.
THAT'S THE ONLY REASON I KEEP ANYTHING FROM YOU.
I TRUST YOU COMPLETELY.
BOY, YOU KNOW...
I REALLY NEEDED TO HEAR THAT.
HEY, KRYPTON, HERE'S A QUESTION...
WHY THE INTELLIGENCE AGENCIES?

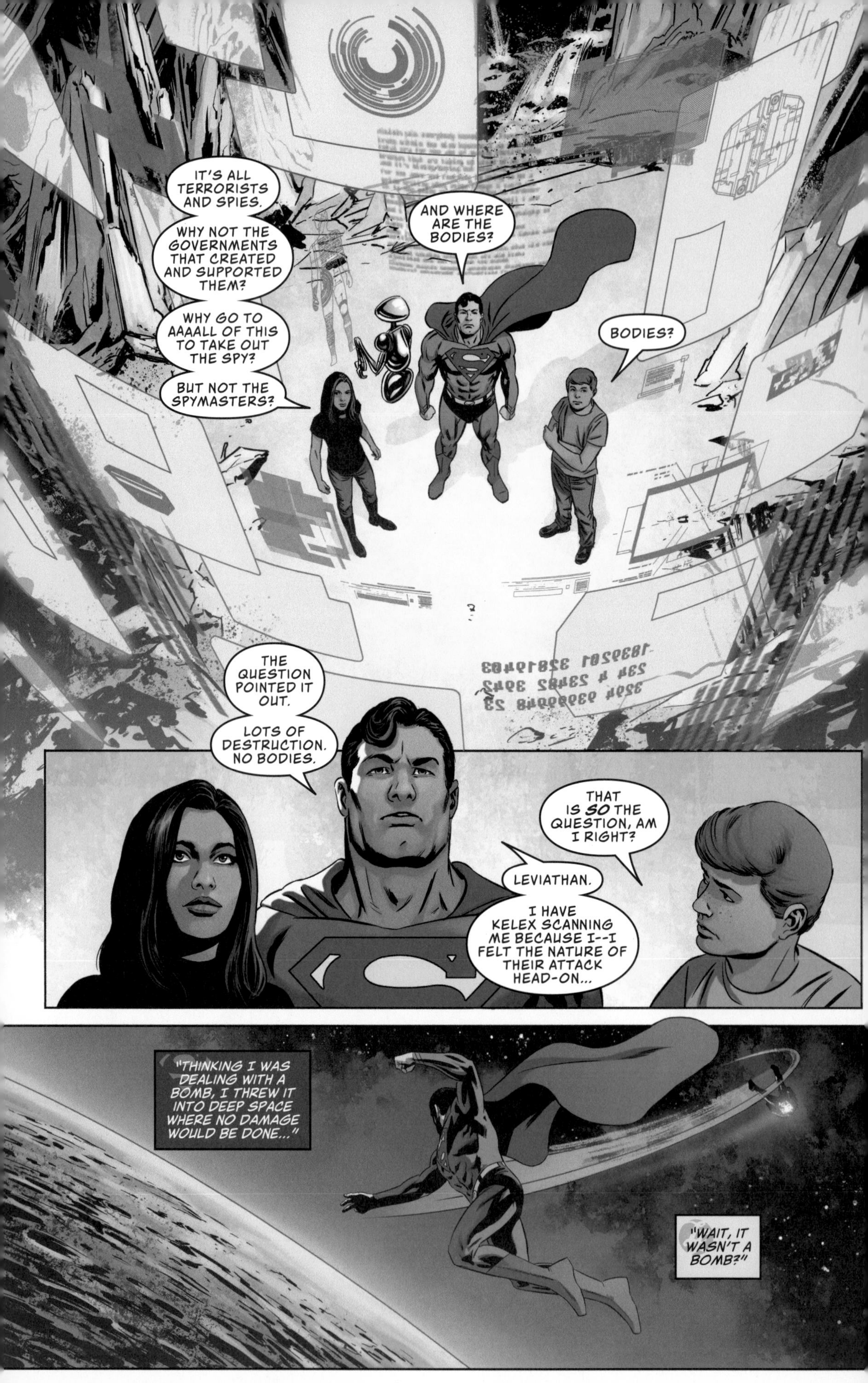
IT'S ALL TERRORISTS AND SPIES.
WHY NOT THE GOVERNMENTS THAT CREATED AND SUPPORTED THEM?
WHY GO TO AAAALL OF THIS TO TAKE OUT THE SPY?
BUT NOT THE SPYMASTERS?
AND WHERE ARE THE BODIES?
BODIES?
THE QUESTION POINTED IT OUT.
LOTS OF DESTRUCTION. NO BODIES.
THAT IS SO THE QUESTION, AM I RIGHT?
LEVIATHAN.
I HAVE KELEX SCANNING ME BECAUSE I--I FELT THE NATURE OF THEIR ATTACK HEAD-ON...
"THINKING I WAS DEALING WITH A BOMB, I THREW IT INTO DEEP SPACE WHERE NO DAMAGE WOULD BE DONE..."
"WAIT, IT WASN'T A BOMB?"

"IT WASN'T ANY KIND OF DESTRUCTIVE MATRIX DESIGNED TO EXPLODE ON IMPACT--

"SO NO.

"IT ERUPTED BUT--

"IT WAS SOMETHING ELSE.

"I PURPOSELY EXPERIENCED IT IN SUPER-SPEED.

"IT WAS THEN I COULD SEE--IT WAS AS IF THE SPACE IT WAS TOUCHING WAS JUST NOT THERE ANYMORE.

"AS IF THE ENERGY FIELD JUST MADE THINGS NOT BE.

"IT WASN'T DESTRUCTION, IT WASN'T DISINTEGRATION, IT WAS...SOMETHING ELSE."

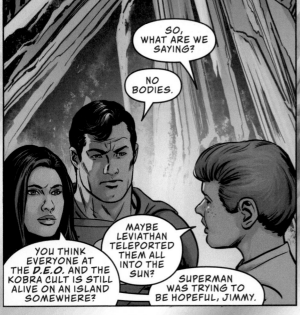

SO, WHAT ARE WE SAYING?

NO BODIES.

YOU THINK EVERYONE AT THE *D.E.O.* AND THE KOBRA CULT IS STILL ALIVE ON AN ISLAND SOMEWHERE?

MAYBE LEVIATHAN TELEPORTED THEM ALL INTO THE SUN?

SUPERMAN WAS TRYING TO BE HOPEFUL, JIMMY.

MAN...

YOU KNOW...

I'M *REALLY* SORRY I ACCUSED AMANDA WALLER OF *RUNNING LEVIATHAN* AND THEN LETTING HER GET AWAY.

YOU--YOU SAID *WHAT* TO AMANDA WALLER NOW?

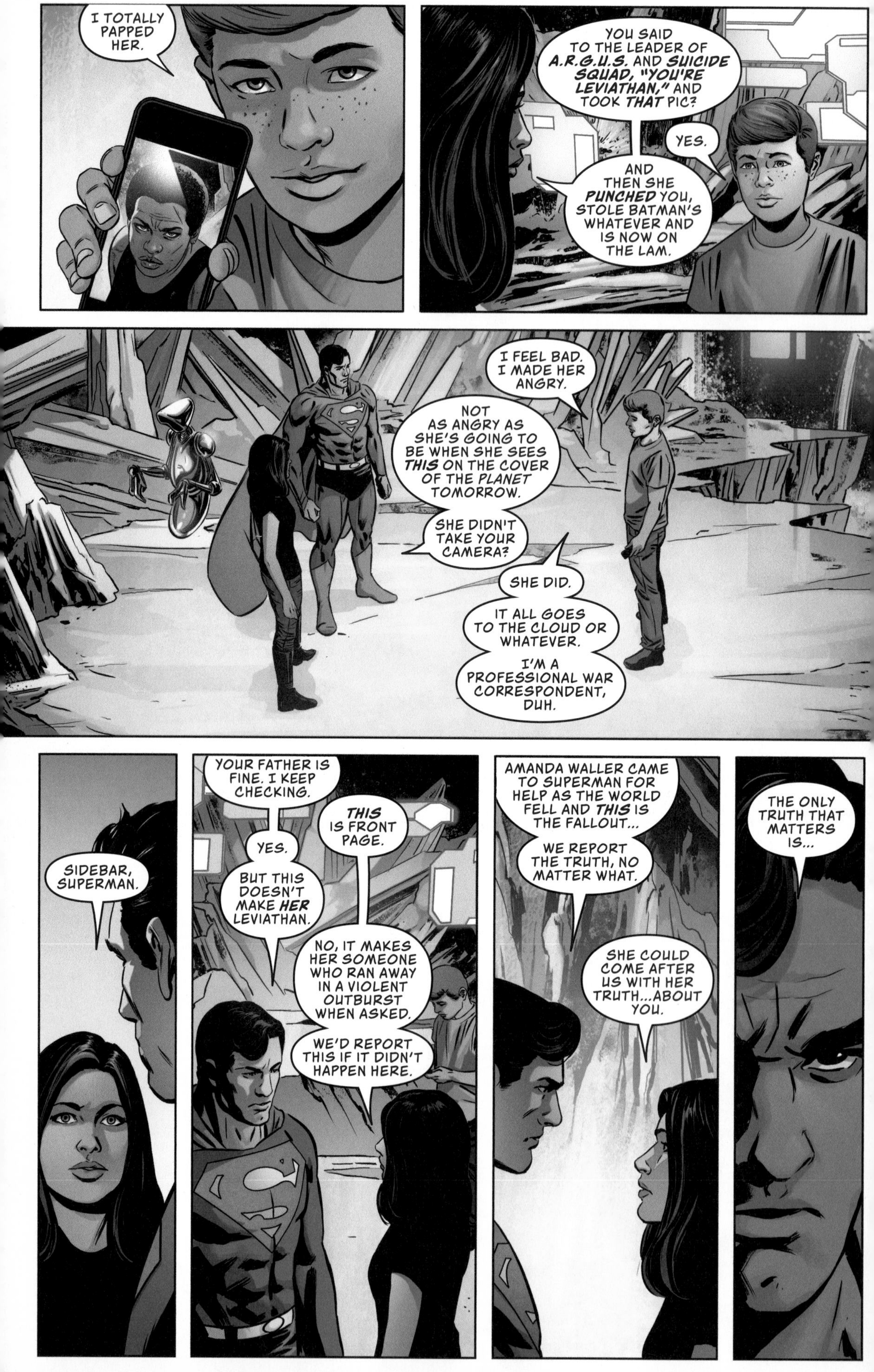
I TOTALLY PAPPED HER.
YOU SAID TO THE LEADER OF A.R.G.U.S. AND SUICIDE SQUAD, "YOU'RE LEVIATHAN," AND TOOK THAT PIC?
YES.
AND THEN SHE PUNCHED YOU, STOLE BATMAN'S WHATEVER AND IS NOW ON THE LAM.
I FEEL BAD. I MADE HER ANGRY.
NOT AS ANGRY AS SHE'S GOING TO BE WHEN SHE SEES THIS ON THE COVER OF THE PLANET TOMORROW.
SHE DIDN'T TAKE YOUR CAMERA?
SHE DID.
IT ALL GOES TO THE CLOUD OR WHATEVER.
I'M A PROFESSIONAL WAR CORRESPONDENT, DUH.
SIDEBAR, SUPERMAN.
YOUR FATHER IS FINE. I KEEP CHECKING.
YES.
BUT THIS DOESN'T MAKE HER LEVIATHAN.
THIS IS FRONT PAGE.
NO, IT MAKES HER SOMEONE WHO RAN AWAY IN A VIOLENT OUTBURST WHEN ASKED.
WE'D REPORT THIS IF IT DIDN'T HAPPEN HERE.
AMANDA WALLER CAME TO SUPERMAN FOR HELP AS THE WORLD FELL AND THIS IS THE FALLOUT...
WE REPORT THE TRUTH, NO MATTER WHAT.
SHE COULD COME AFTER US WITH HER TRUTH...ABOUT YOU.
THE ONLY TRUTH THAT MATTERS IS...

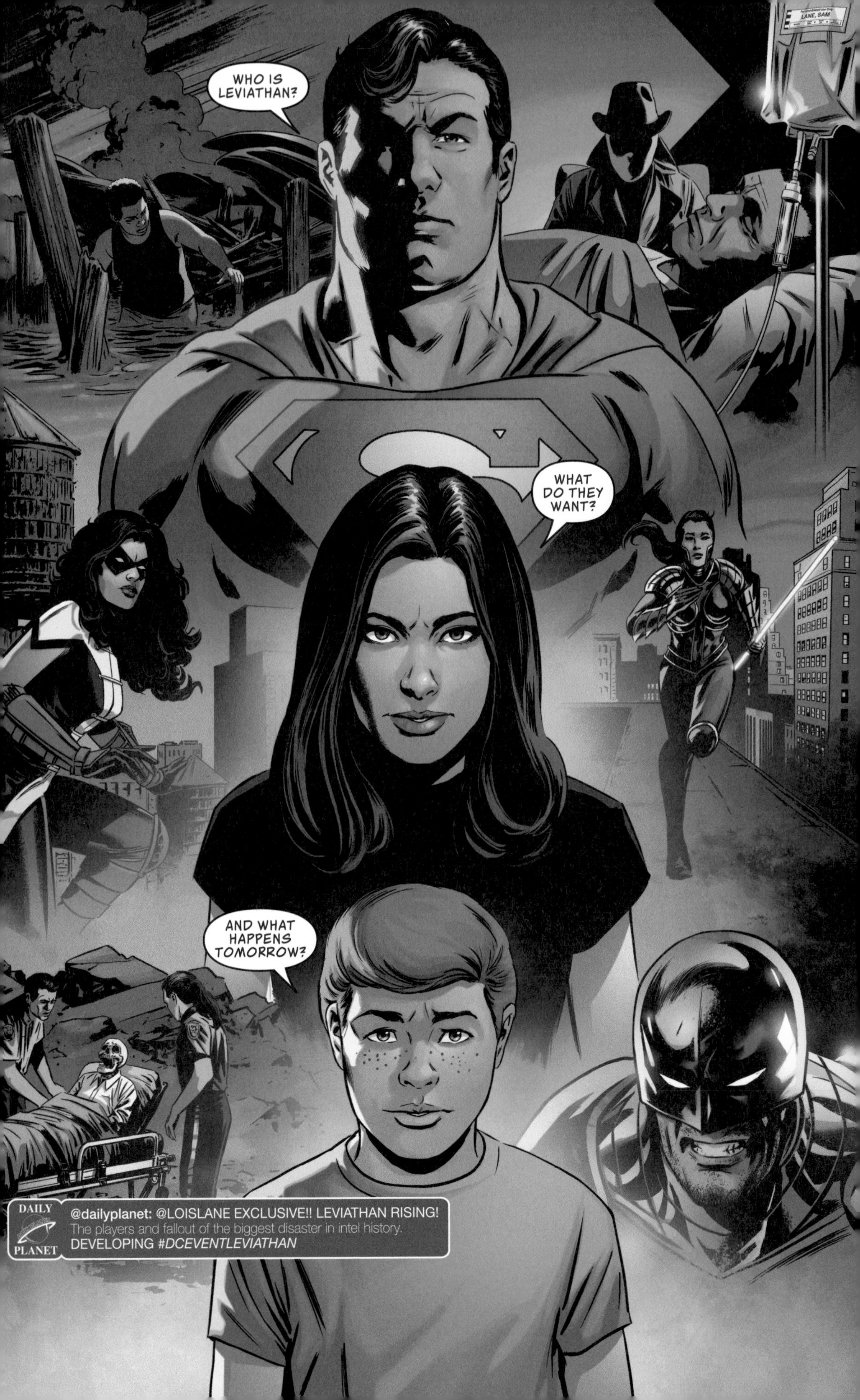
LANE, SAM
WHO IS LEVIATHAN?
WHAT DO THEY WANT?
AND WHAT HAPPENS TOMORROW?
DAILY PLANET
@dailyplanet: @LOISLANE EXCLUSIVE!! LEVIATHAN RISING!
The players and fallout of the biggest disaster in intel history.
DEVELOPING #DCEVENTLEVIATHAN

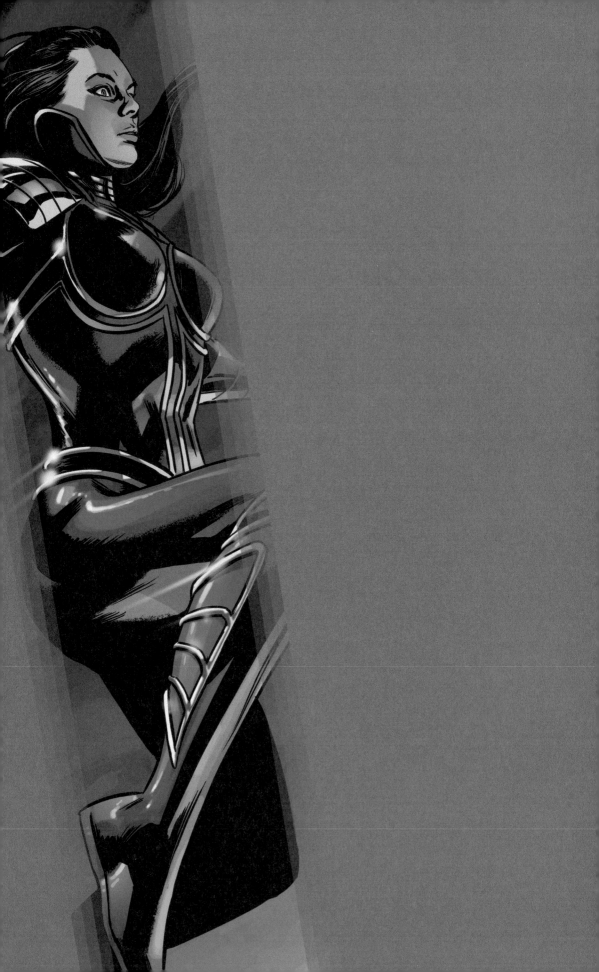

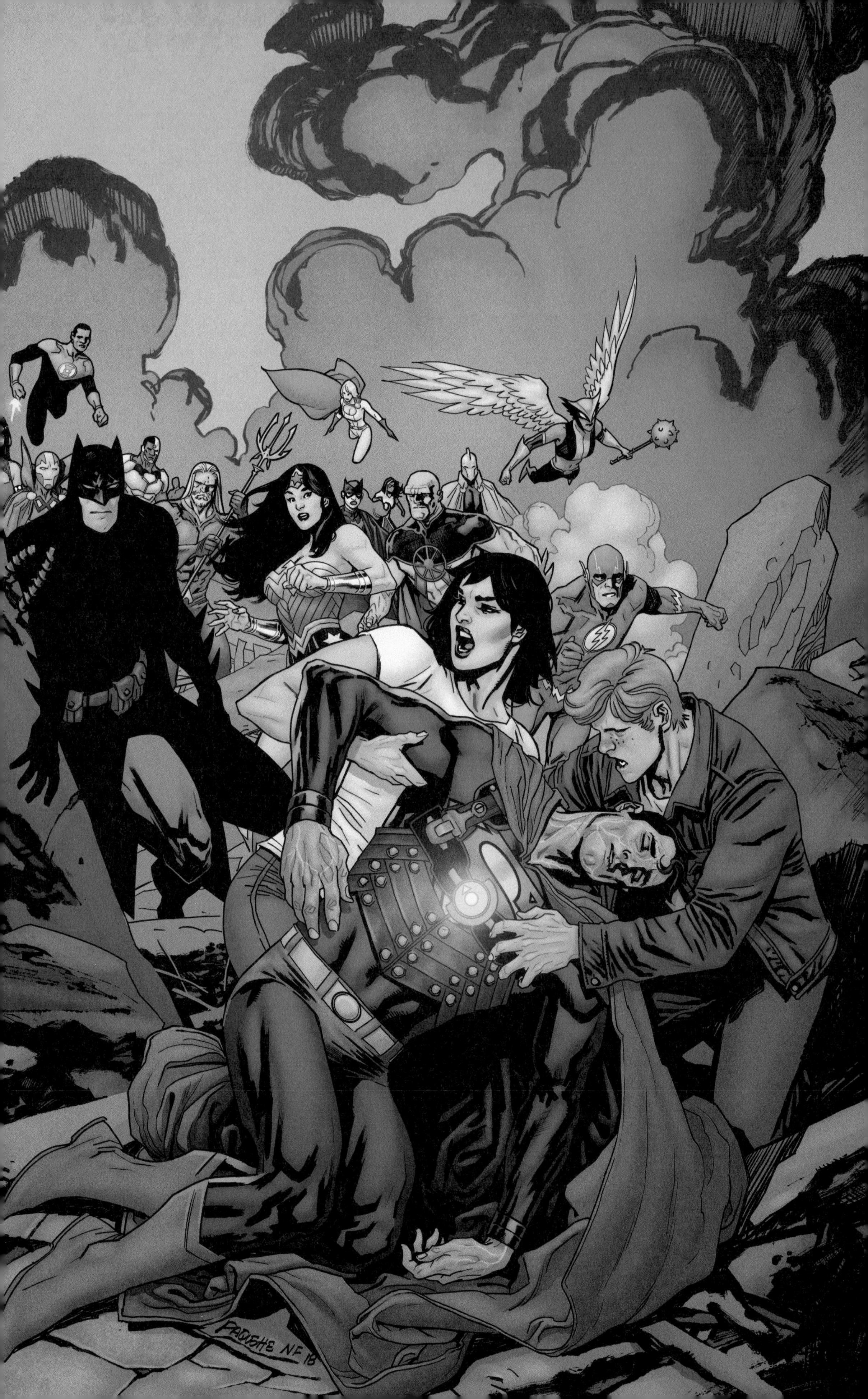
PAQUETTE NF 18

DC COMICS PRESENTS:
# LEVIATHAN RISING

**BRIAN MICHAEL BENDIS**
writer

**YANICK PAQUETTE**
artist

**NATHAN FAIRBAIRN**
colorist

**DAVE SHARPE**
**ALW'S TROY PETERI**
letterers

**YANICK PAQUETTE**
**and NATHAN FAIRBAIRN**
cover

**JESSICA CHEN**
associate editor

**MIKE COTTON**
editor

**BRIAN CUNNINGHAM**
group editor

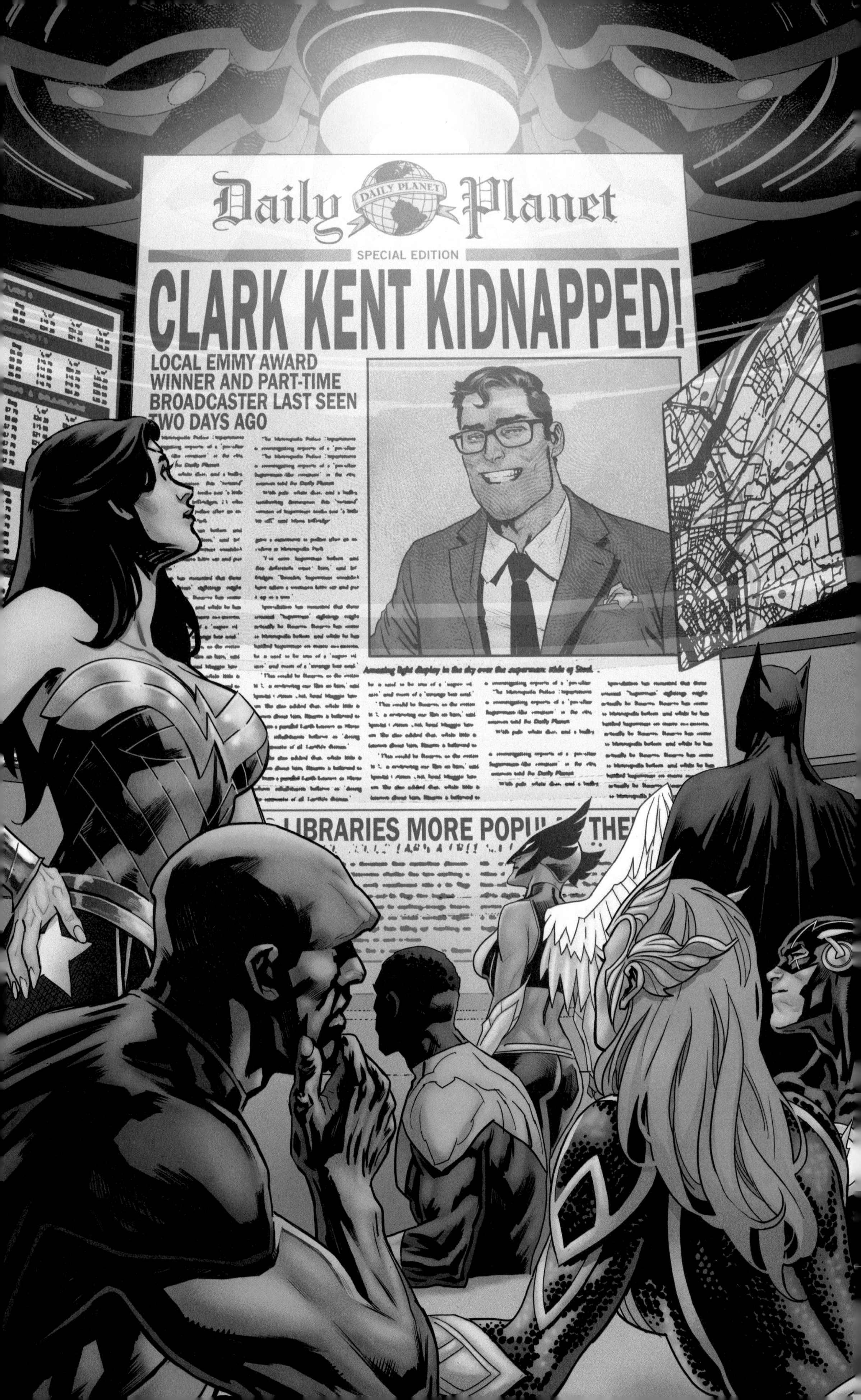
Daily Planet
DAILY PLANET
SPECIAL EDITION
CLARK KENT KIDNAPPED!
LOCAL EMMY AWARD WINNER AND PART-TIME BROADCASTER LAST SEEN TWO DAYS AGO
LIBRARIES MORE POPU THE

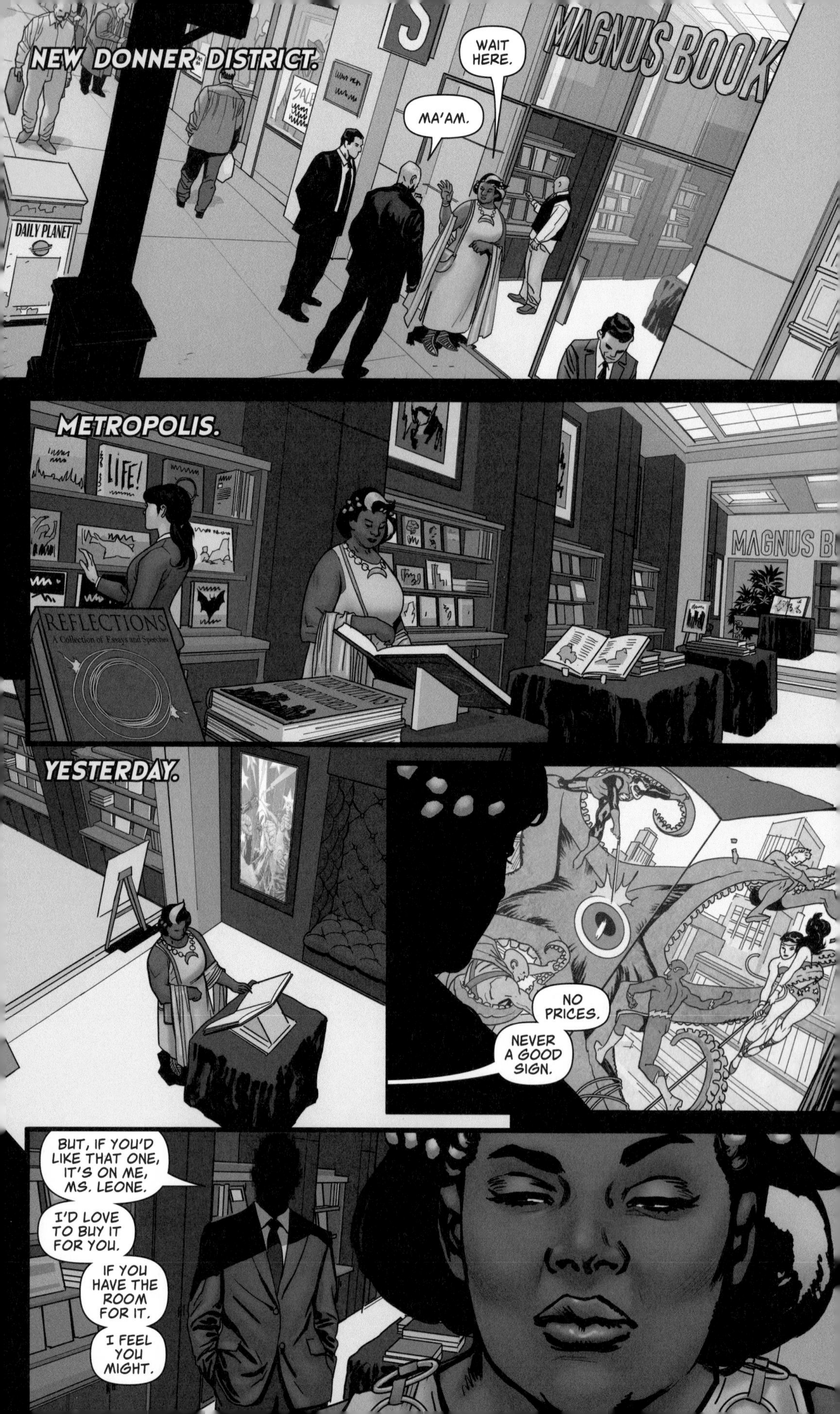
NEW DONNER DISTRICT.
MAGNUS BOOK
DAILY PLANET
SALE
WAIT HERE.
MA'AM.
METROPOLIS.
LIFE!
REFLECTIONS
A Collection of Essays and Speeches
MAGNUS B
YESTERDAY.
NO PRICES.
NEVER A GOOD SIGN.
BUT, IF YOU'D LIKE THAT ONE, IT'S ON ME, MS. LEONE.
I'D LOVE TO BUY IT FOR YOU.
IF YOU HAVE THE ROOM FOR IT.
I FEEL YOU MIGHT.

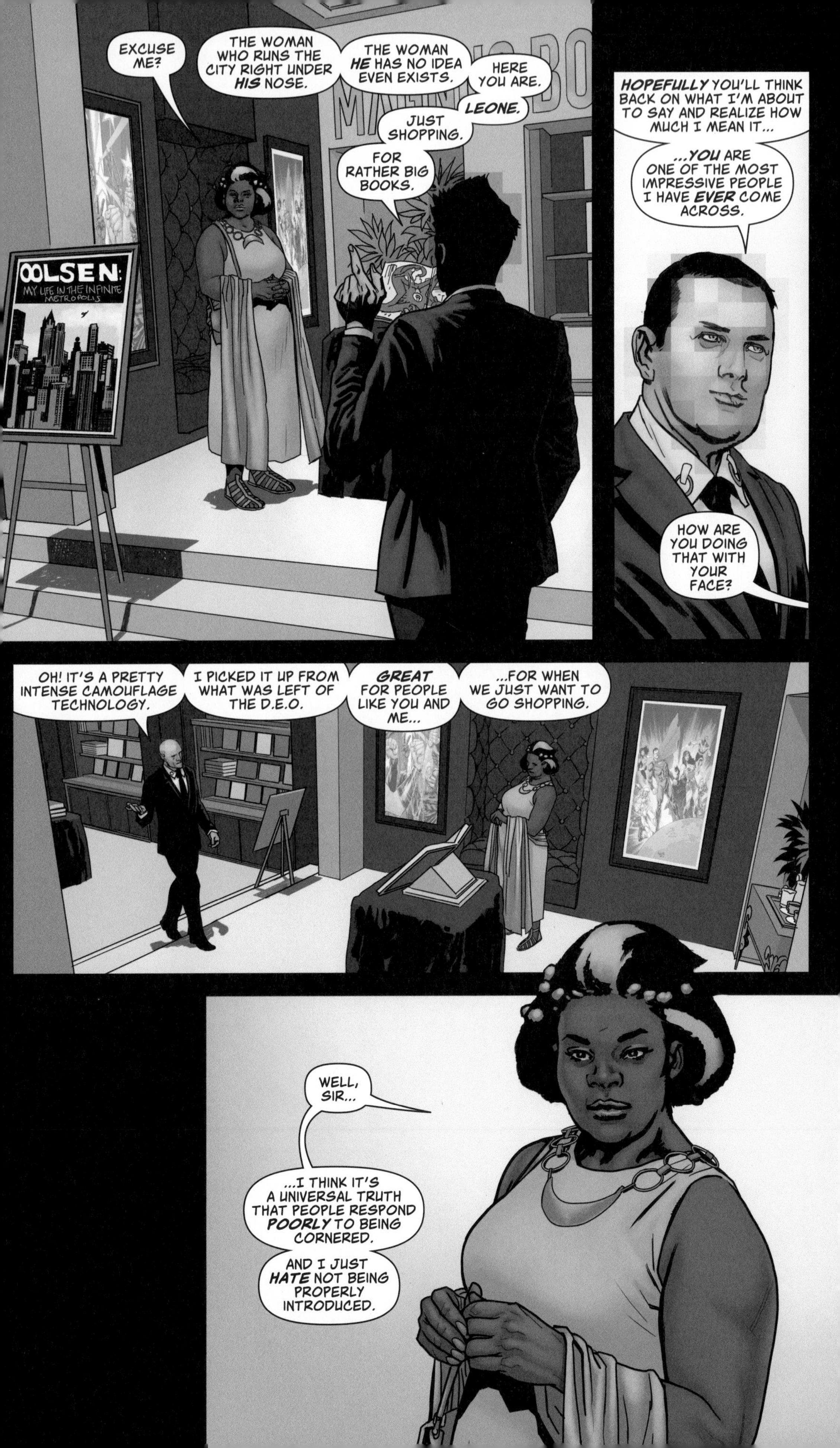
EXCUSE ME?
THE WOMAN WHO RUNS THE CITY RIGHT UNDER HIS NOSE.
THE WOMAN HE HAS NO IDEA EVEN EXISTS.
HERE YOU ARE.
LEONE.
JUST SHOPPING.
FOR RATHER BIG BOOKS.
OLSEN: MY LIFE IN THE INFINITE METROPOLIS
HOPEFULLY YOU'LL THINK BACK ON WHAT I'M ABOUT TO SAY AND REALIZE HOW MUCH I MEAN IT...
...YOU ARE ONE OF THE MOST IMPRESSIVE PEOPLE I HAVE EVER COME ACROSS.
HOW ARE YOU DOING THAT WITH YOUR FACE?
OH! IT'S A PRETTY INTENSE CAMOUFLAGE TECHNOLOGY.
I PICKED IT UP FROM WHAT WAS LEFT OF THE D.E.O.
GREAT FOR PEOPLE LIKE YOU AND ME...
...FOR WHEN WE JUST WANT TO GO SHOPPING.
WELL, SIR...
...I THINK IT'S A UNIVERSAL TRUTH THAT PEOPLE RESPOND POORLY TO BEING CORNERED.
AND I JUST HATE NOT BEING PROPERLY INTRODUCED.

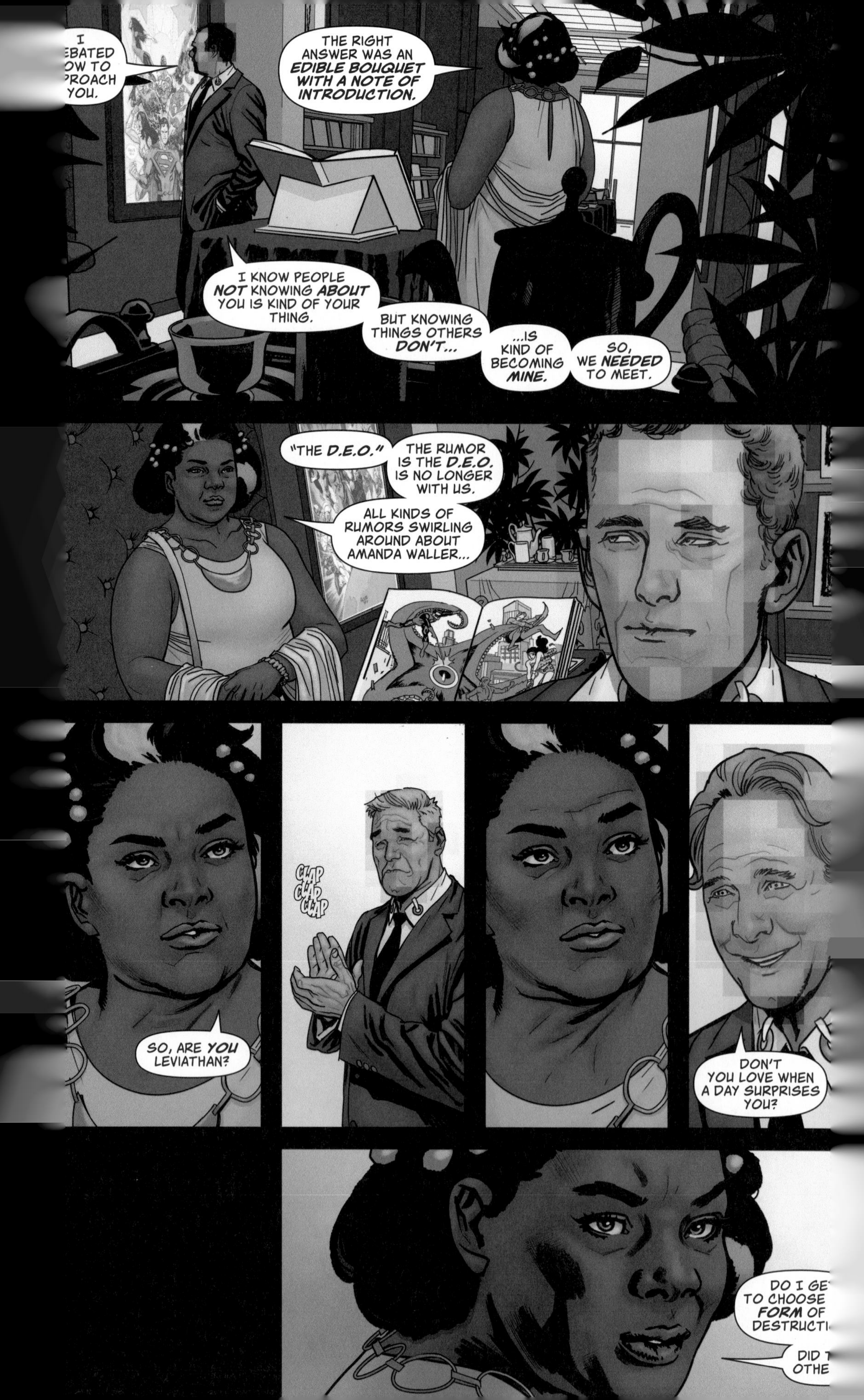
I EBATED OW TO PROACH YOU.
THE RIGHT ANSWER WAS AN EDIBLE BOUQUET WITH A NOTE OF INTRODUCTION.
I KNOW PEOPLE NOT KNOWING ABOUT YOU IS KIND OF YOUR THING.
BUT KNOWING THINGS OTHERS DON'T...
...IS KIND OF BECOMING MINE.
SO, WE NEEDED TO MEET.
"THE D.E.O."
THE RUMOR IS THE D.E.O. IS NO LONGER WITH US.
ALL KINDS OF RUMORS SWIRLING AROUND ABOUT AMANDA WALLER...
SO, ARE YOU LEVIATHAN?
CLAP CLAP CLAP
DON'T YOU LOVE WHEN A DAY SURPRISES YOU?
DO I GE TO CHOOSE FORM OF DESTRUCTI
DID T OTHE

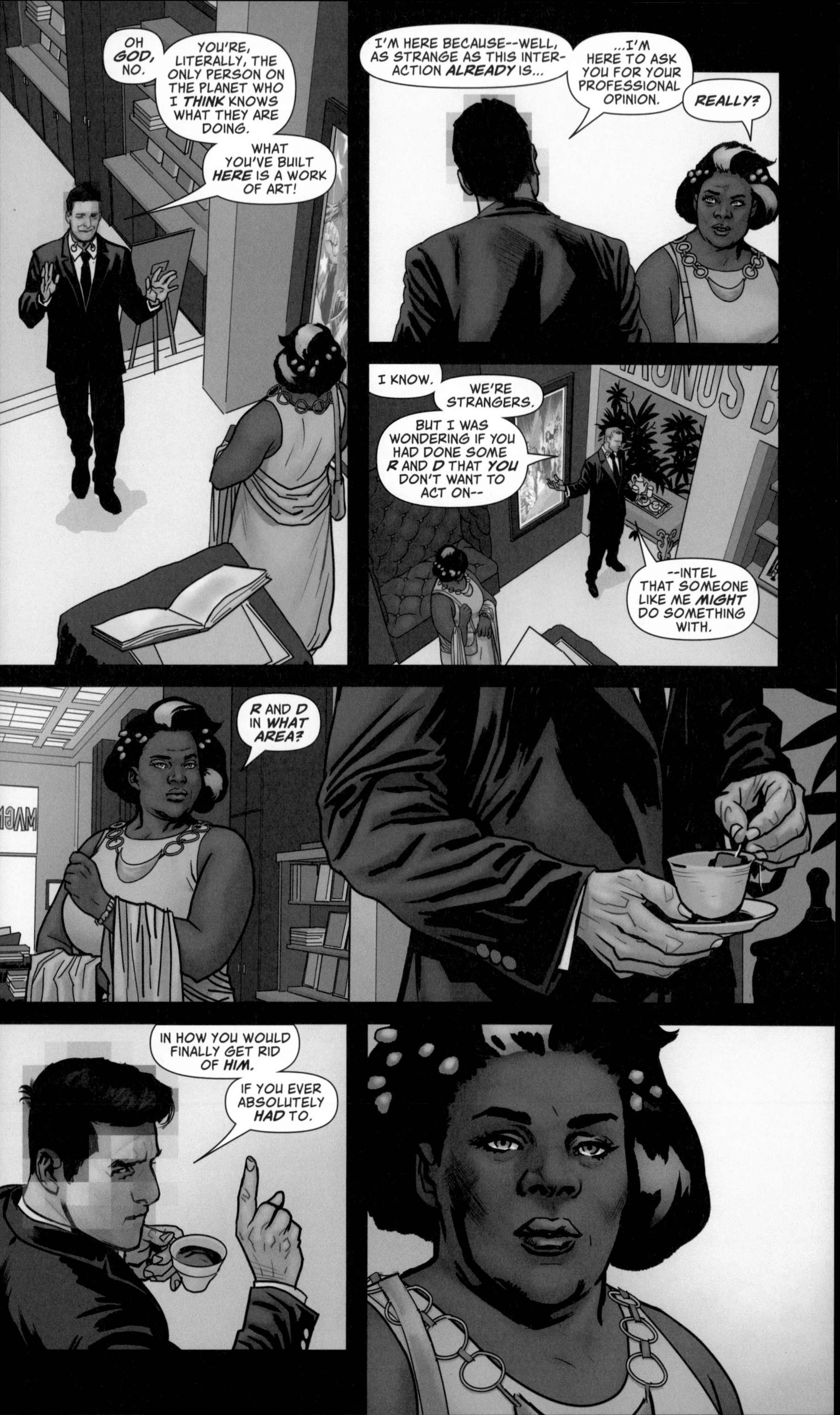

OH GOD, NO.
YOU'RE, LITERALLY, THE ONLY PERSON ON THE PLANET WHO I THINK KNOWS WHAT THEY ARE DOING.
WHAT YOU'VE BUILT HERE IS A WORK OF ART!
I'M HERE BECAUSE--WELL, AS STRANGE AS THIS INTER-ACTION ALREADY IS...
...I'M HERE TO ASK YOU FOR YOUR PROFESSIONAL OPINION.
REALLY?
I KNOW.
WE'RE STRANGERS.
BUT I WAS WONDERING IF YOU HAD DONE SOME R AND D THAT YOU DON'T WANT TO ACT ON--
--INTEL THAT SOMEONE LIKE ME MIGHT DO SOMETHING WITH.
R AND D IN WHAT AREA?
IN HOW YOU WOULD FINALLY GET RID OF HIM.
IF YOU EVER ABSOLUTELY HAD TO.

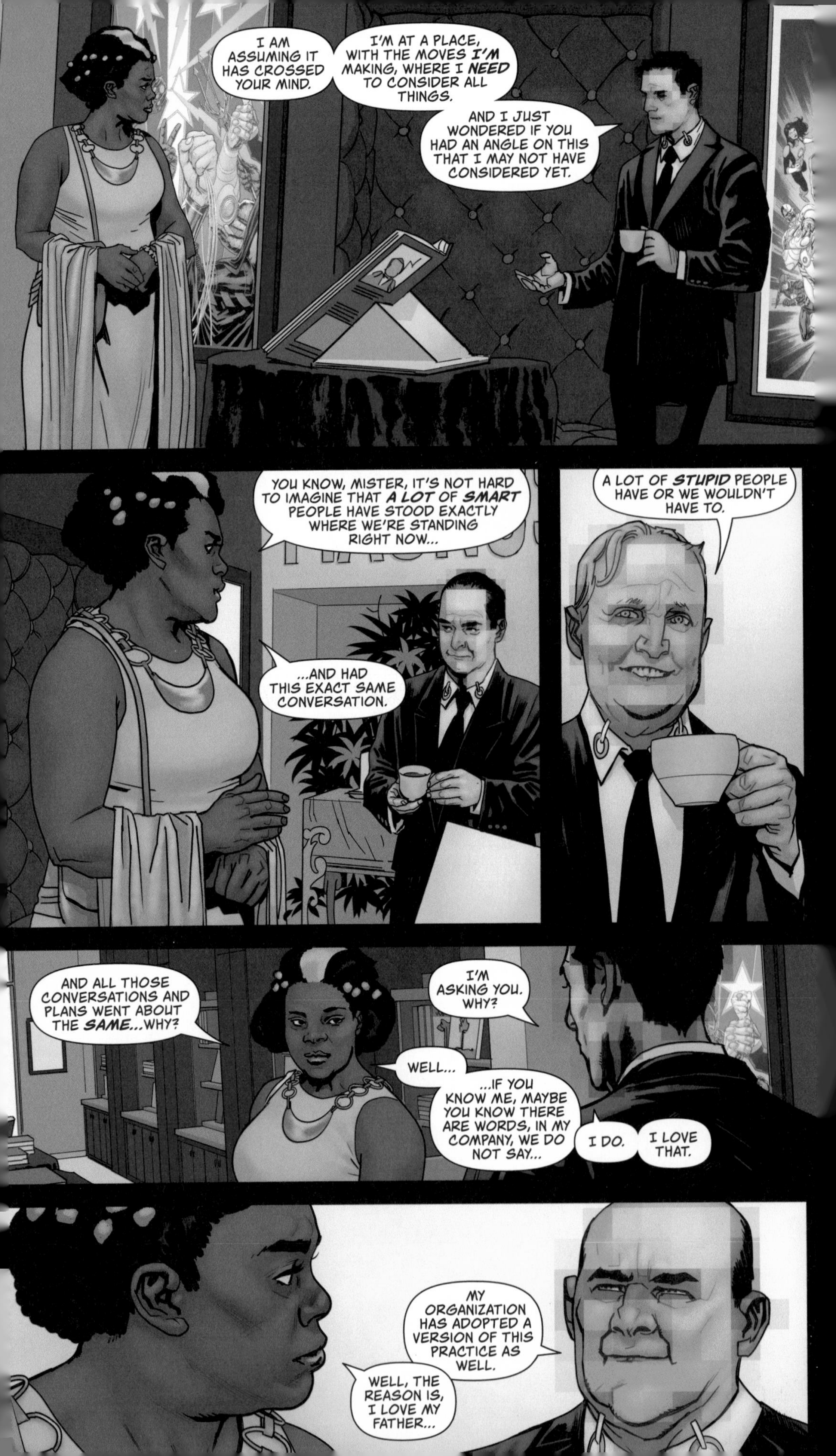

I AM ASSUMING IT HAS CROSSED YOUR MIND.
I'M AT A PLACE, WITH THE MOVES *I'M* MAKING, WHERE I *NEED* TO CONSIDER ALL THINGS.
AND I JUST WONDERED IF YOU HAD AN ANGLE ON THIS THAT I MAY NOT HAVE CONSIDERED YET.
YOU KNOW, MISTER, IT'S NOT HARD TO IMAGINE THAT *A LOT* OF *SMART* PEOPLE HAVE STOOD EXACTLY WHERE WE'RE STANDING RIGHT NOW...
...AND HAD THIS EXACT SAME CONVERSATION.
A LOT OF *STUPID* PEOPLE HAVE OR WE WOULDN'T HAVE TO.
AND ALL THOSE CONVERSATIONS AND PLANS WENT ABOUT THE *SAME*...WHY?
I'M ASKING YOU. WHY?
WELL...
...IF YOU KNOW ME, MAYBE YOU KNOW THERE ARE WORDS, IN MY COMPANY, WE DO NOT SAY...
I DO.
I LOVE THAT.
MY ORGANIZATION HAS ADOPTED A VERSION OF THIS PRACTICE AS WELL.
WELL, THE REASON IS, I LOVE MY FATHER...

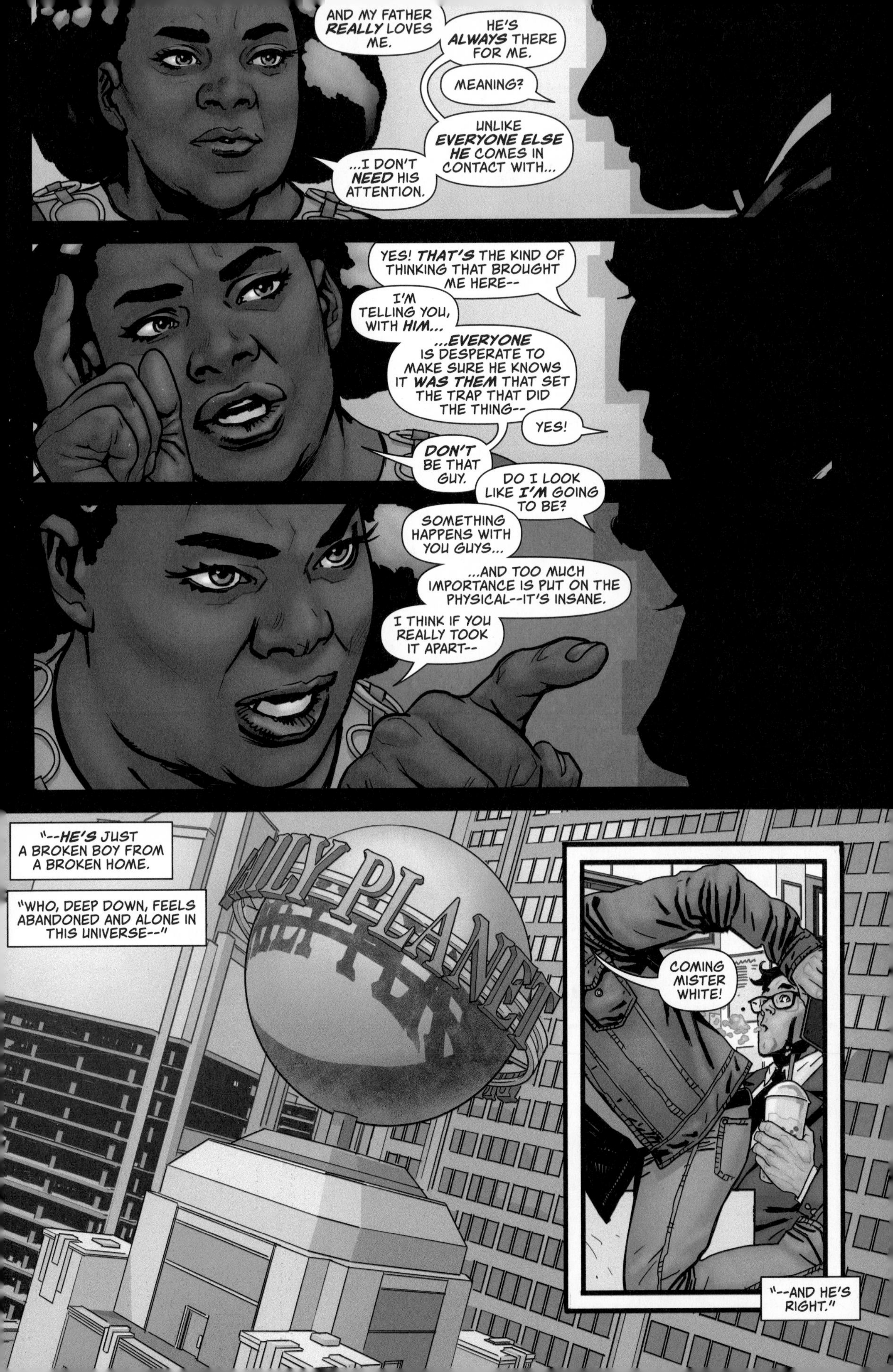
AND MY FATHER REALLY LOVES ME.
HE'S ALWAYS THERE FOR ME.
MEANING?
UNLIKE EVERYONE ELSE HE COMES IN CONTACT WITH...
...I DON'T NEED HIS ATTENTION.
YES! THAT'S THE KIND OF THINKING THAT BROUGHT ME HERE--
I'M TELLING YOU, WITH HIM...
...EVERYONE IS DESPERATE TO MAKE SURE HE KNOWS IT WAS THEM THAT SET THE TRAP THAT DID THE THING--
YES!
DON'T BE THAT GUY.
DO I LOOK LIKE I'M GOING TO BE?
SOMETHING HAPPENS WITH YOU GUYS...
...AND TOO MUCH IMPORTANCE IS PUT ON THE PHYSICAL--IT'S INSANE.
I THINK IF YOU REALLY TOOK IT APART--
"--HE'S JUST A BROKEN BOY FROM A BROKEN HOME.
"WHO, DEEP DOWN, FEELS ABANDONED AND ALONE IN THIS UNIVERSE--"
DAILY PLANET
COMING MISTER WHITE!
"--AND HE'S RIGHT."

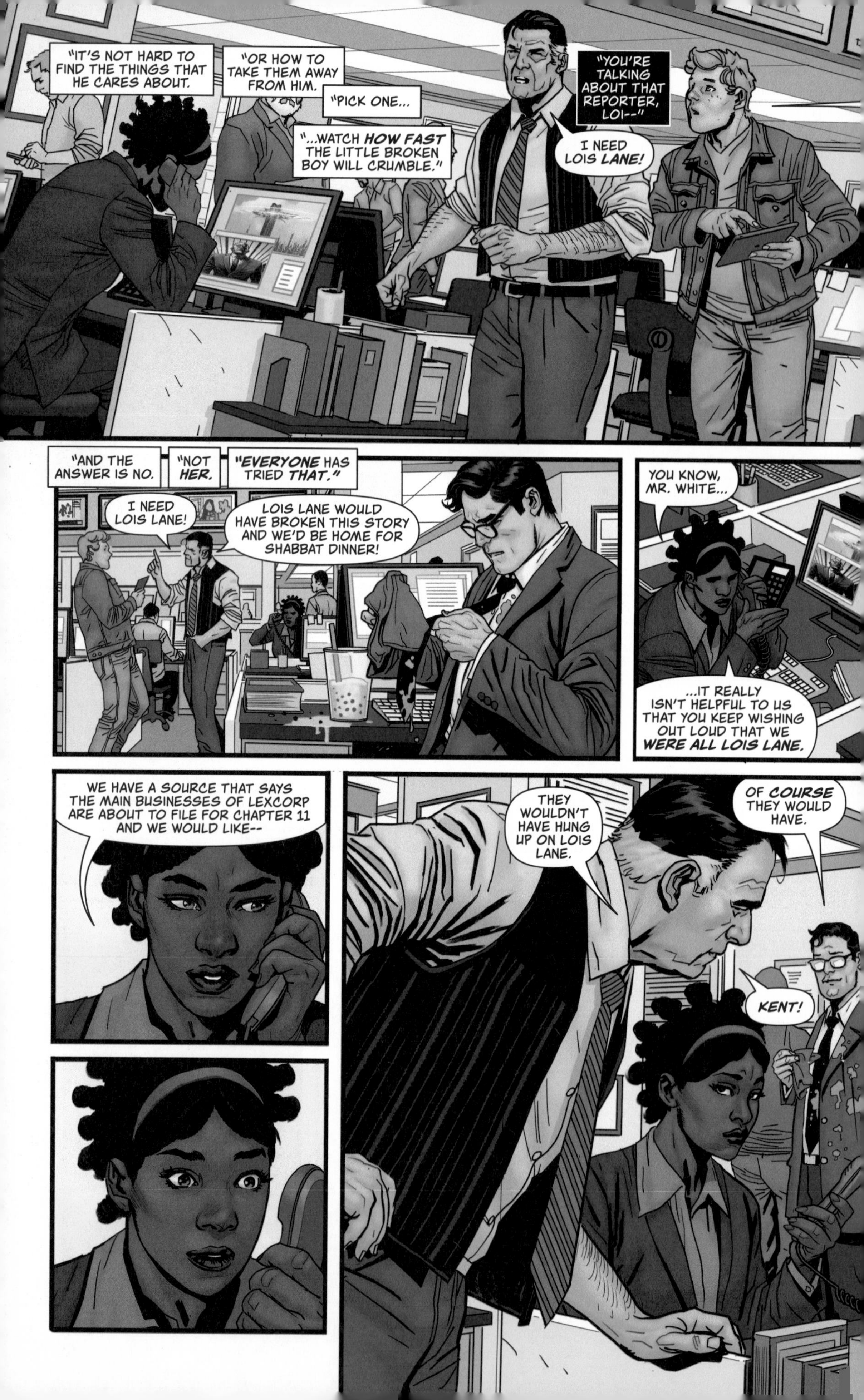
"IT'S NOT HARD TO FIND THE THINGS THAT HE CARES ABOUT.
"OR HOW TO TAKE THEM AWAY FROM HIM.
"PICK ONE...
"...WATCH HOW FAST THE LITTLE BROKEN BOY WILL CRUMBLE."
"YOU'RE TALKING ABOUT THAT REPORTER, LOI--"
I NEED LOIS LANE!
"AND THE ANSWER IS NO.
"NOT HER.
"EVERYONE HAS TRIED THAT."
I NEED LOIS LANE!
LOIS LANE WOULD HAVE BROKEN THIS STORY AND WE'D BE HOME FOR SHABBAT DINNER!
YOU KNOW, MR. WHITE...
...IT REALLY ISN'T HELPFUL TO US THAT YOU KEEP WISHING OUT LOUD THAT WE WERE ALL LOIS LANE.
WE HAVE A SOURCE THAT SAYS THE MAIN BUSINESSES OF LEXCORP ARE ABOUT TO FILE FOR CHAPTER 11 AND WE WOULD LIKE--
THEY WOULDN'T HAVE HUNG UP ON LOIS LANE.
OF COURSE THEY WOULD HAVE.
KENT!

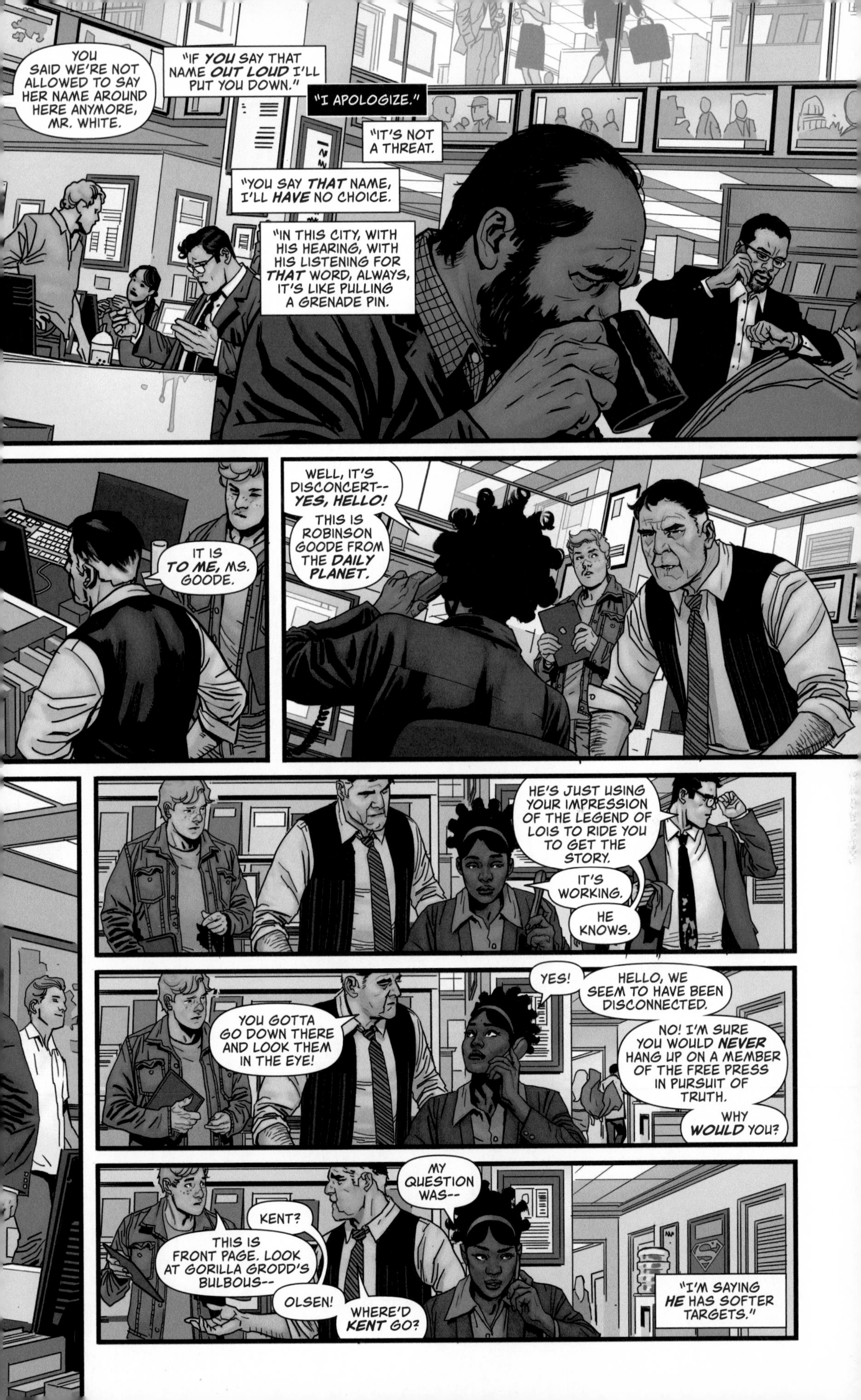
YOU SAID WE'RE NOT ALLOWED TO SAY HER NAME AROUND HERE ANYMORE, MR. WHITE.
"IF YOU SAY THAT NAME OUT LOUD I'LL PUT YOU DOWN."
"I APOLOGIZE."
"IT'S NOT A THREAT.
"YOU SAY THAT NAME, I'LL HAVE NO CHOICE.
"IN THIS CITY, WITH HIS HEARING, WITH HIS LISTENING FOR THAT WORD, ALWAYS, IT'S LIKE PULLING A GRENADE PIN.
WELL, IT'S DISCONCERT-- YES, HELLO!
THIS IS ROBINSON GOODE FROM THE DAILY PLANET.
IT IS TO ME, MS. GOODE.
HE'S JUST USING YOUR IMPRESSION OF THE LEGEND OF LOIS TO RIDE YOU TO GET THE STORY.
IT'S WORKING.
HE KNOWS.
YES!
HELLO, WE SEEM TO HAVE BEEN DISCONNECTED.
YOU GOTTA GO DOWN THERE AND LOOK THEM IN THE EYE!
NO! I'M SURE YOU WOULD NEVER HANG UP ON A MEMBER OF THE FREE PRESS IN PURSUIT OF TRUTH.
WHY WOULD YOU?
MY QUESTION WAS--
KENT?
THIS IS FRONT PAGE. LOOK AT GORILLA GRODD'S BULBOUS--
OLSEN!
WHERE'D KENT GO?
"I'M SAYING HE HAS SOFTER TARGETS."

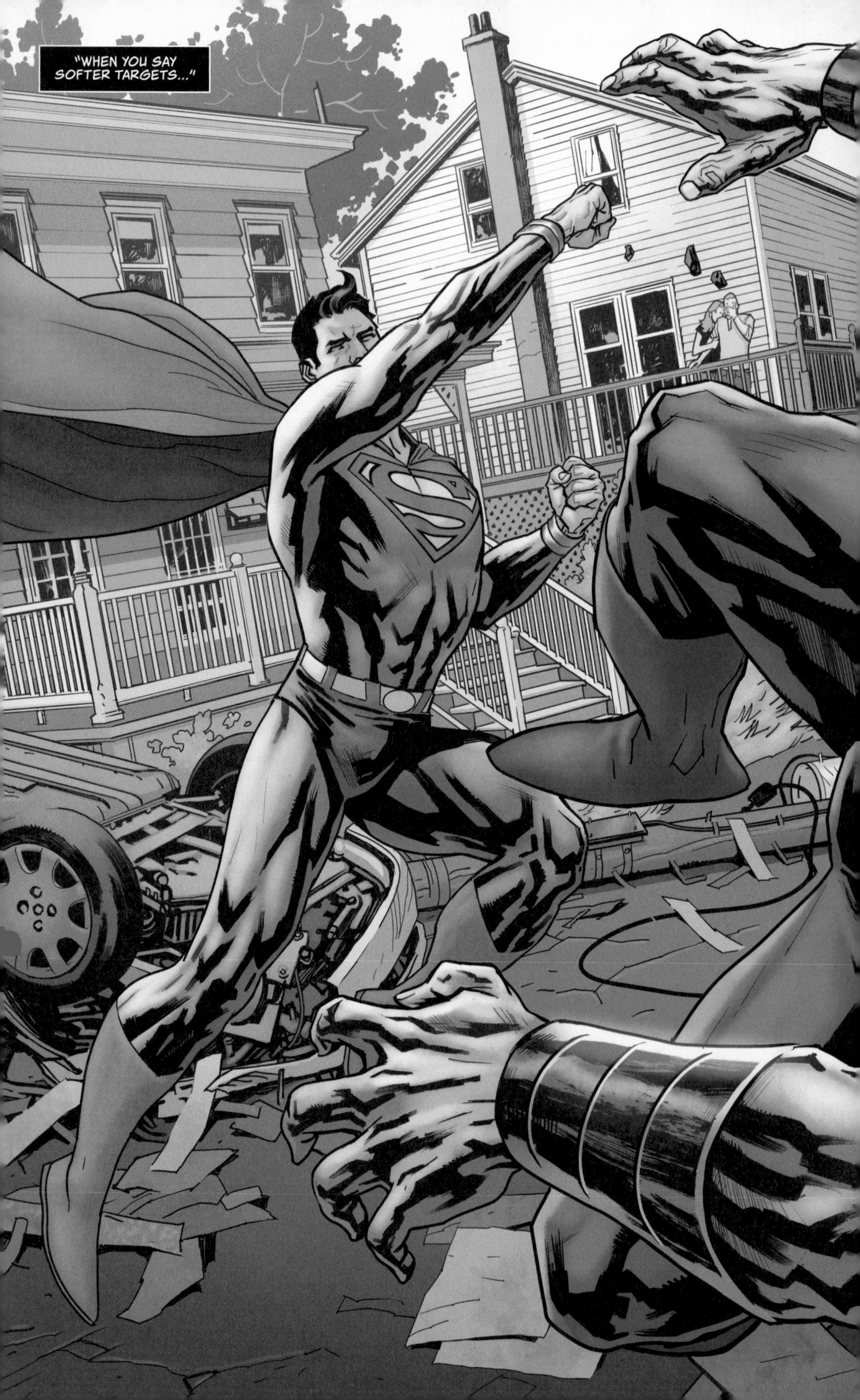
"WHEN YOU SAY
SOFTER TARGETS..."

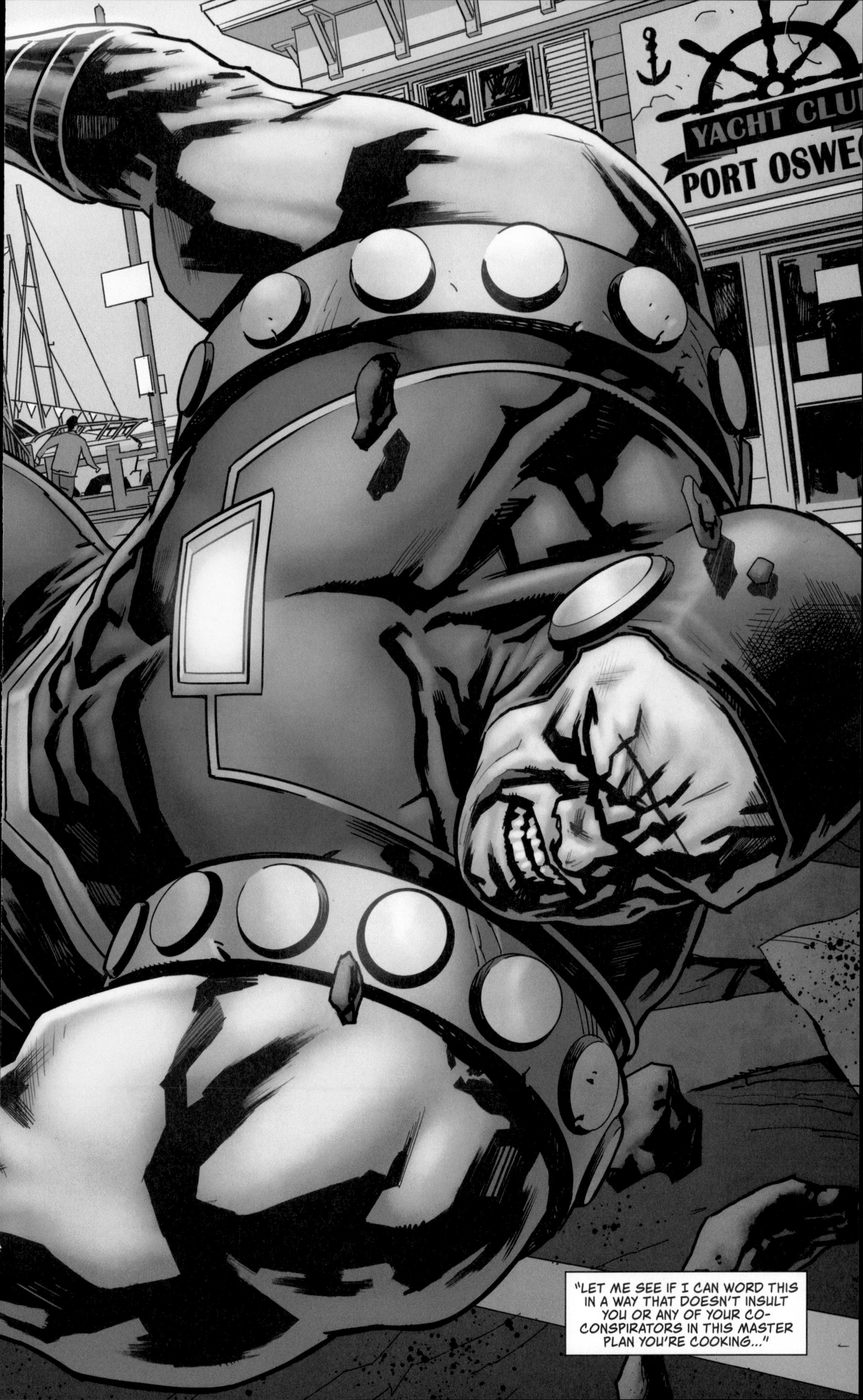
YACHT CLU
PORT OSWE
"LET ME SEE IF I CAN WORD THIS IN A WAY THAT DOESN'T INSULT YOU OR ANY OF YOUR CO-CONSPIRATORS IN THIS MASTER PLAN YOU'RE COOKING..."

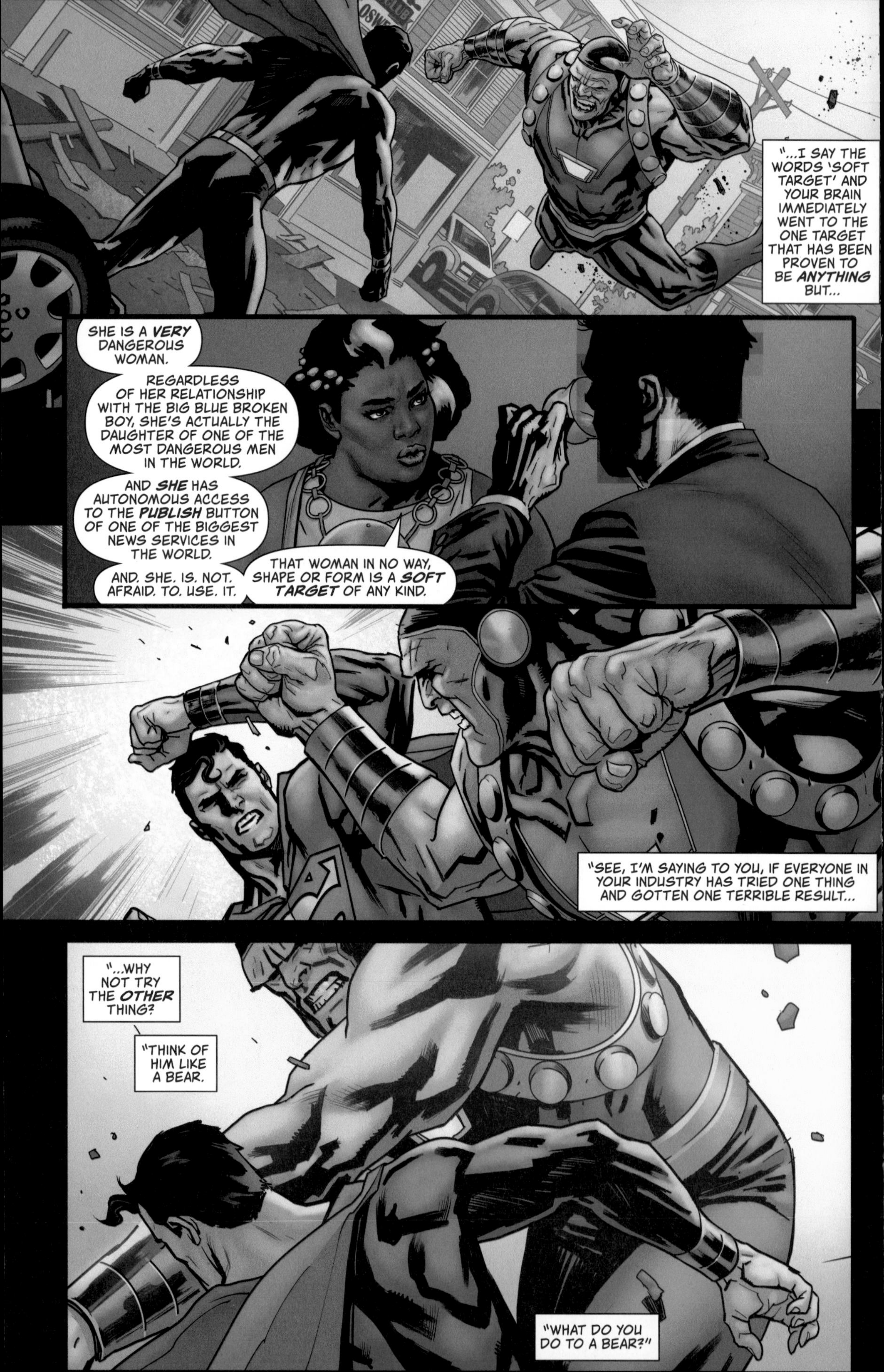

"...I SAY THE WORDS 'SOFT TARGET' AND YOUR BRAIN IMMEDIATELY WENT TO THE ONE TARGET THAT HAS BEEN PROVEN TO BE ANYTHING BUT...
SHE IS A VERY DANGEROUS WOMAN.
REGARDLESS OF HER RELATIONSHIP WITH THE BIG BLUE BROKEN BOY, SHE'S ACTUALLY THE DAUGHTER OF ONE OF THE MOST DANGEROUS MEN IN THE WORLD.
AND SHE HAS AUTONOMOUS ACCESS TO THE PUBLISH BUTTON OF ONE OF THE BIGGEST NEWS SERVICES IN THE WORLD.
AND. SHE. IS. NOT. AFRAID. TO. USE. IT.
THAT WOMAN IN NO WAY, SHAPE OR FORM IS A SOFT TARGET OF ANY KIND.
"SEE, I'M SAYING TO YOU, IF EVERYONE IN YOUR INDUSTRY HAS TRIED ONE THING AND GOTTEN ONE TERRIBLE RESULT...
"...WHY NOT TRY THE OTHER THING?
"THINK OF HIM LIKE A BEAR.
"WHAT DO YOU DO TO A BEAR?"

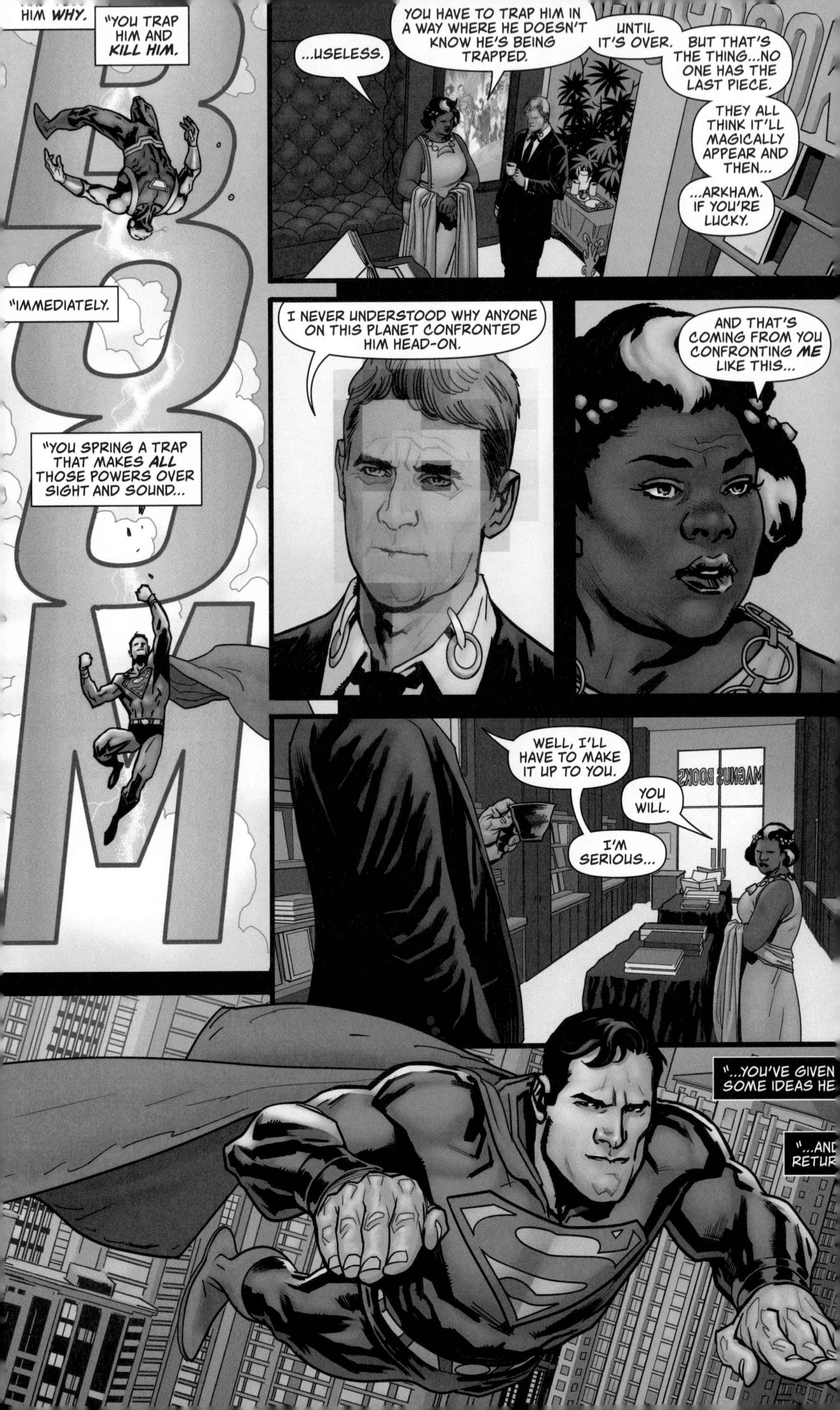

HIM WHY.
"YOU TRAP HIM AND KILL HIM.
...USELESS.
YOU HAVE TO TRAP HIM IN A WAY WHERE HE DOESN'T KNOW HE'S BEING TRAPPED.
UNTIL IT'S OVER.
BUT THAT'S THE THING...NO ONE HAS THE LAST PIECE.
THEY ALL THINK IT'LL MAGICALLY APPEAR AND THEN...
...ARKHAM. IF YOU'RE LUCKY.
"IMMEDIATELY.
I NEVER UNDERSTOOD WHY ANYONE ON THIS PLANET CONFRONTED HIM HEAD-ON.
AND THAT'S COMING FROM YOU CONFRONTING ME LIKE THIS...
"YOU SPRING A TRAP THAT MAKES ALL THOSE POWERS OVER SIGHT AND SOUND...
WELL, I'LL HAVE TO MAKE IT UP TO YOU.
YOU WILL.
I'M SERIOUS...
"...YOU'VE GIVEN SOME IDEAS HE
"...AND RETUR

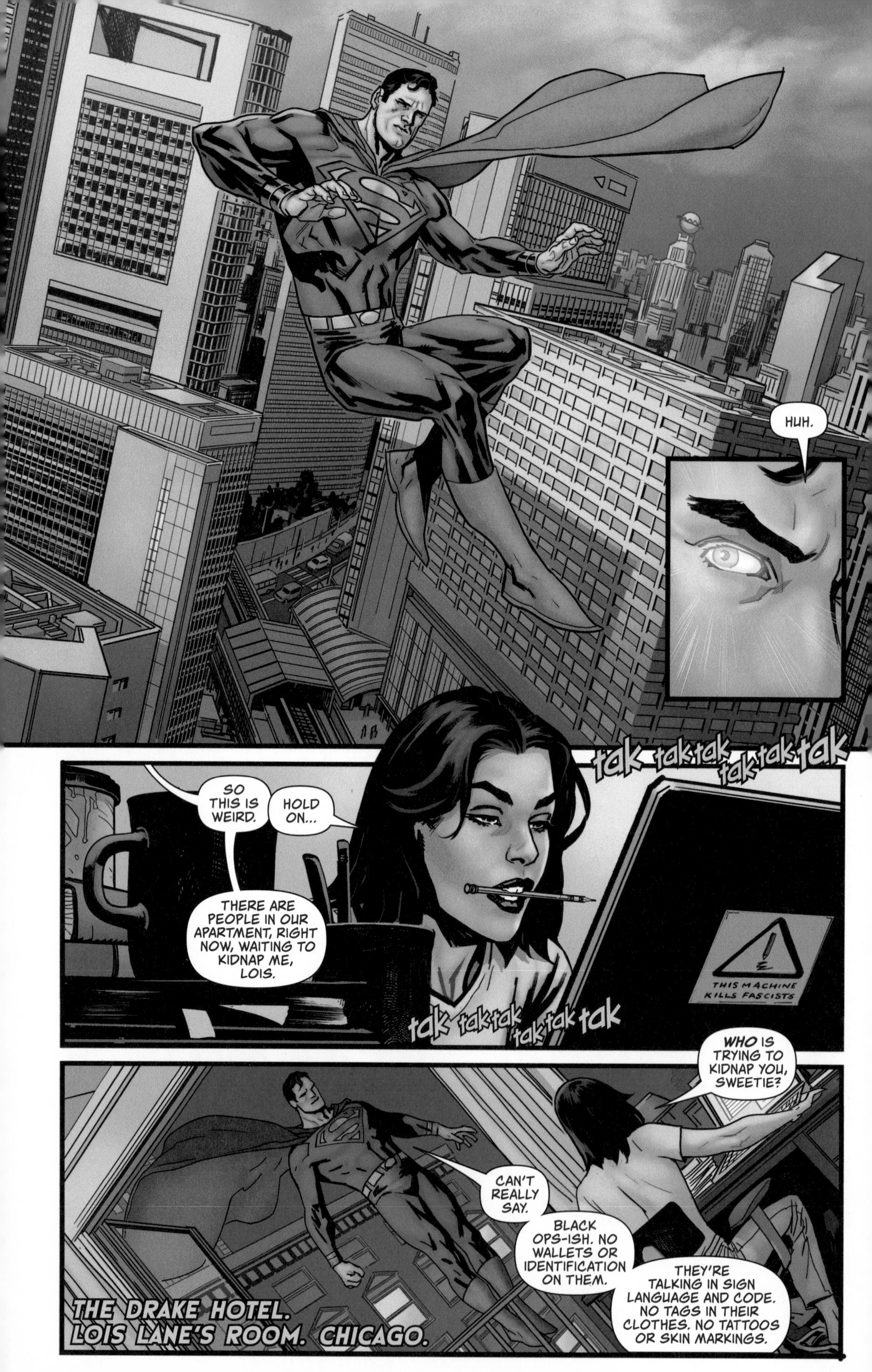
HUH.
tak taktak taktaktak
SO THIS IS WEIRD.
HOLD ON...
THERE ARE PEOPLE IN OUR APARTMENT, RIGHT NOW, WAITING TO KIDNAP ME, LOIS.
THIS MACHINE KILLS FASCISTS
tak taktak taktak tak
THE DRAKE HOTEL. LOIS LANE'S ROOM. CHICAGO.
WHO IS TRYING TO KIDNAP YOU, SWEETIE?
CAN'T REALLY SAY.
BLACK OPS-ISH. NO WALLETS OR IDENTIFICATION ON THEM.
THEY'RE TALKING IN SIGN LANGUAGE AND CODE. NO TAGS IN THEIR CLOTHES. NO TATTOOS OR SKIN MARKINGS.

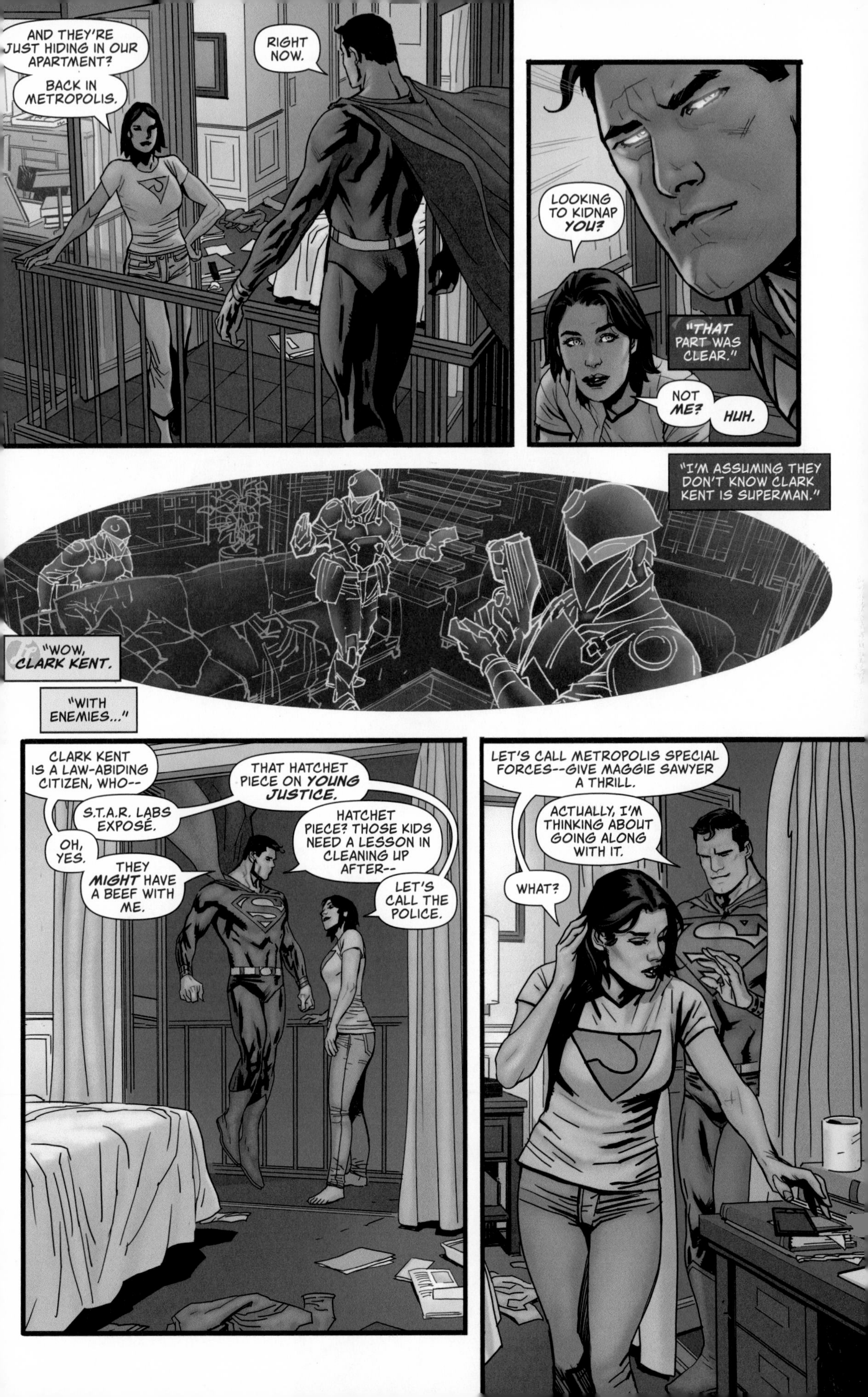
AND THEY'RE JUST HIDING IN OUR APARTMENT?
RIGHT NOW.
BACK IN METROPOLIS.
LOOKING TO KIDNAP *YOU?*
"*THAT* PART WAS CLEAR."
NOT *ME?*
*HUH.*
"I'M ASSUMING THEY DON'T KNOW CLARK KENT IS SUPERMAN."
"WOW, *CLARK KENT.*
"WITH ENEMIES..."
CLARK KENT IS A LAW-ABIDING CITIZEN, WHO--
THAT HATCHET PIECE ON *YOUNG JUSTICE.*
S.T.A.R. LABS EXPOSÉ.
OH, YES.
HATCHET PIECE? THOSE KIDS NEED A LESSON IN CLEANING UP AFTER--
THEY *MIGHT* HAVE A BEEF WITH ME.
LET'S CALL THE POLICE.
LET'S CALL METROPOLIS SPECIAL FORCES--GIVE MAGGIE SAWYER A THRILL.
ACTUALLY, I'M THINKING ABOUT GOING ALONG WITH IT.
WHAT?

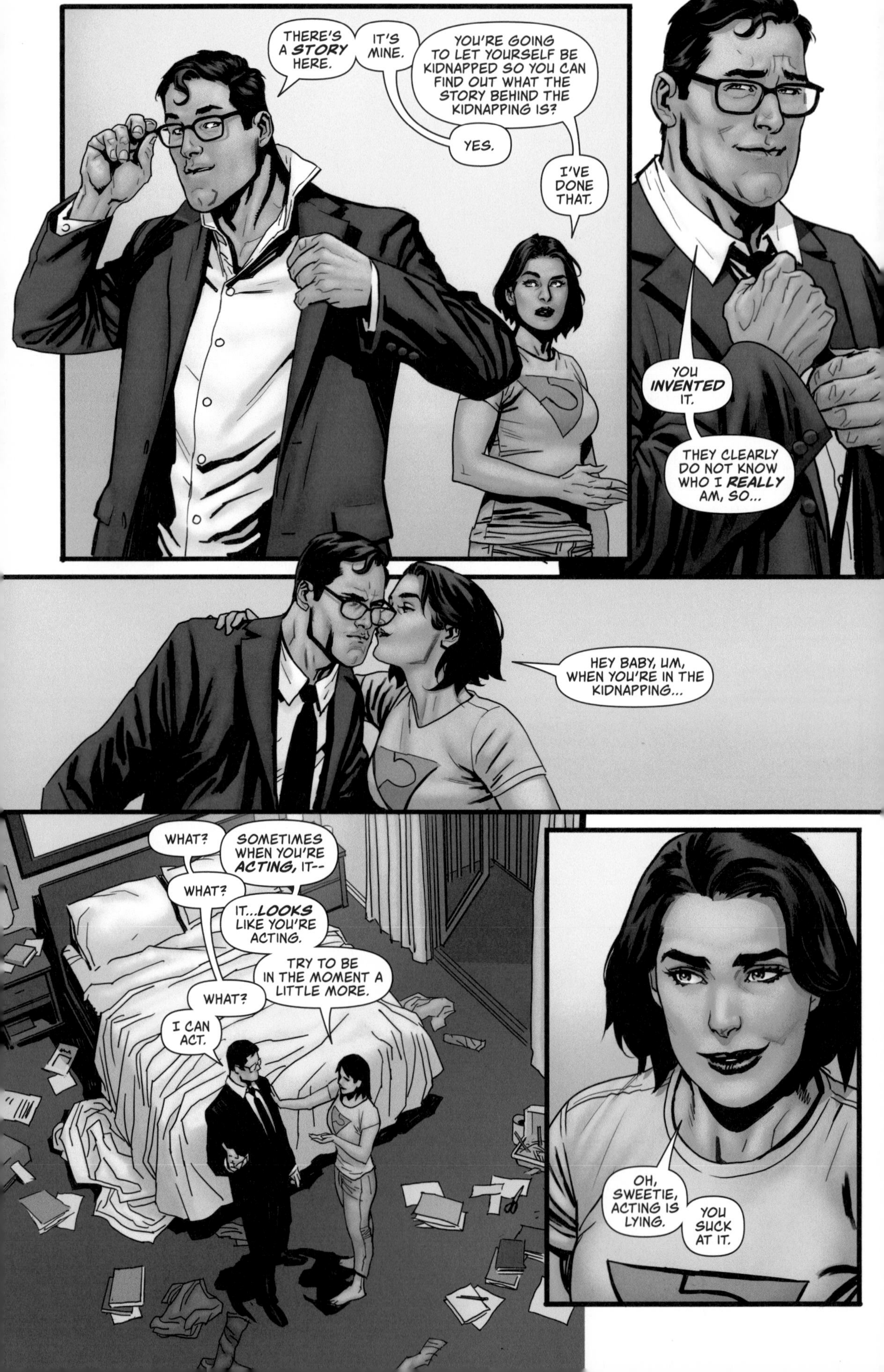
THERE'S A STORY HERE.
IT'S MINE.
YOU'RE GOING TO LET YOURSELF BE KIDNAPPED SO YOU CAN FIND OUT WHAT THE STORY BEHIND THE KIDNAPPING IS?
YES.
I'VE DONE THAT.
YOU INVENTED IT.
THEY CLEARLY DO NOT KNOW WHO I REALLY AM, SO...
HEY BABY, UM, WHEN YOU'RE IN THE KIDNAPPING...
WHAT?
SOMETIMES WHEN YOU'RE ACTING, IT--
WHAT?
IT...LOOKS LIKE YOU'RE ACTING.
TRY TO BE IN THE MOMENT A LITTLE MORE.
WHAT?
I CAN ACT.
OH, SWEETIE, ACTING IS LYING.
YOU SUCK AT IT.

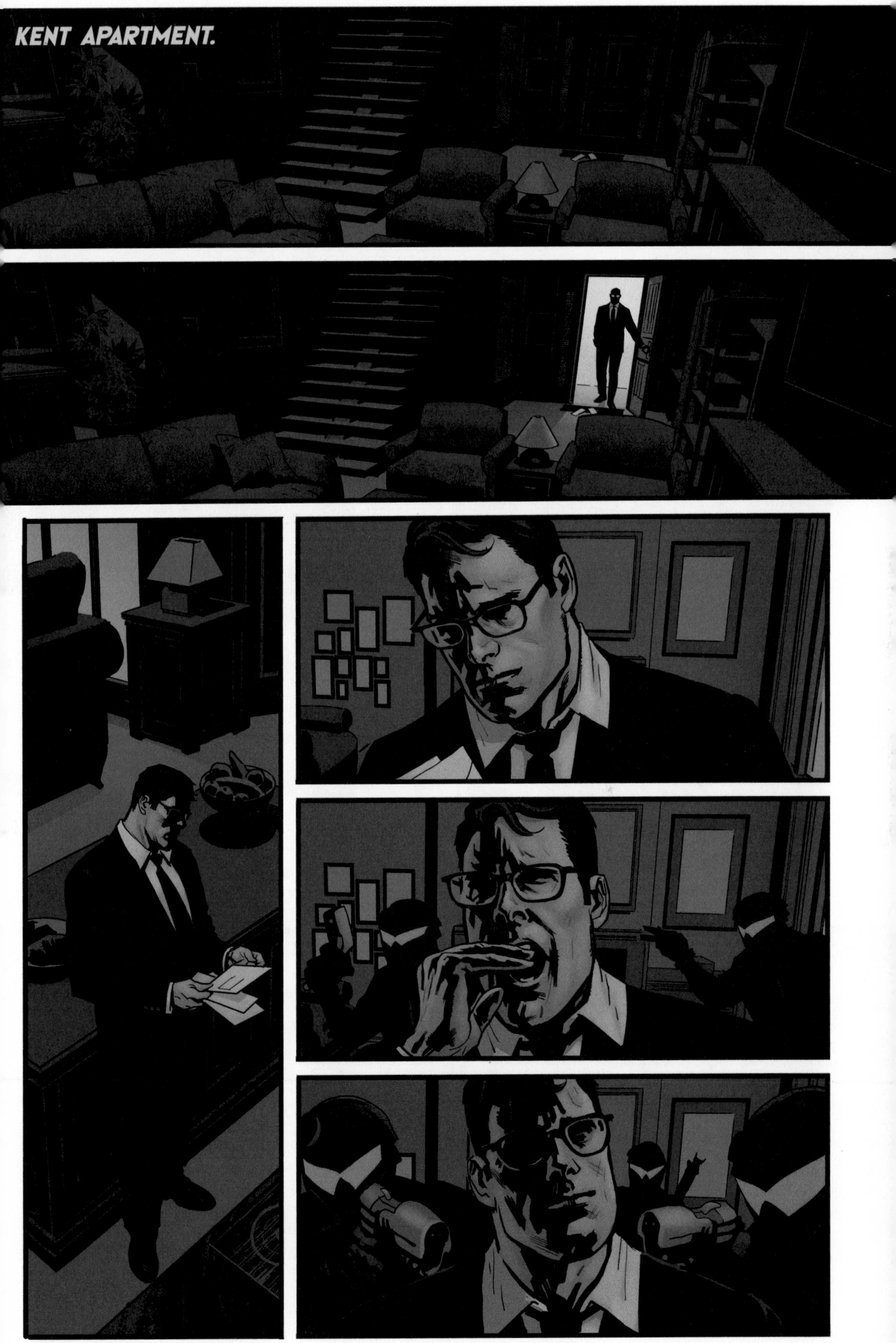
KENT APARTMENT.

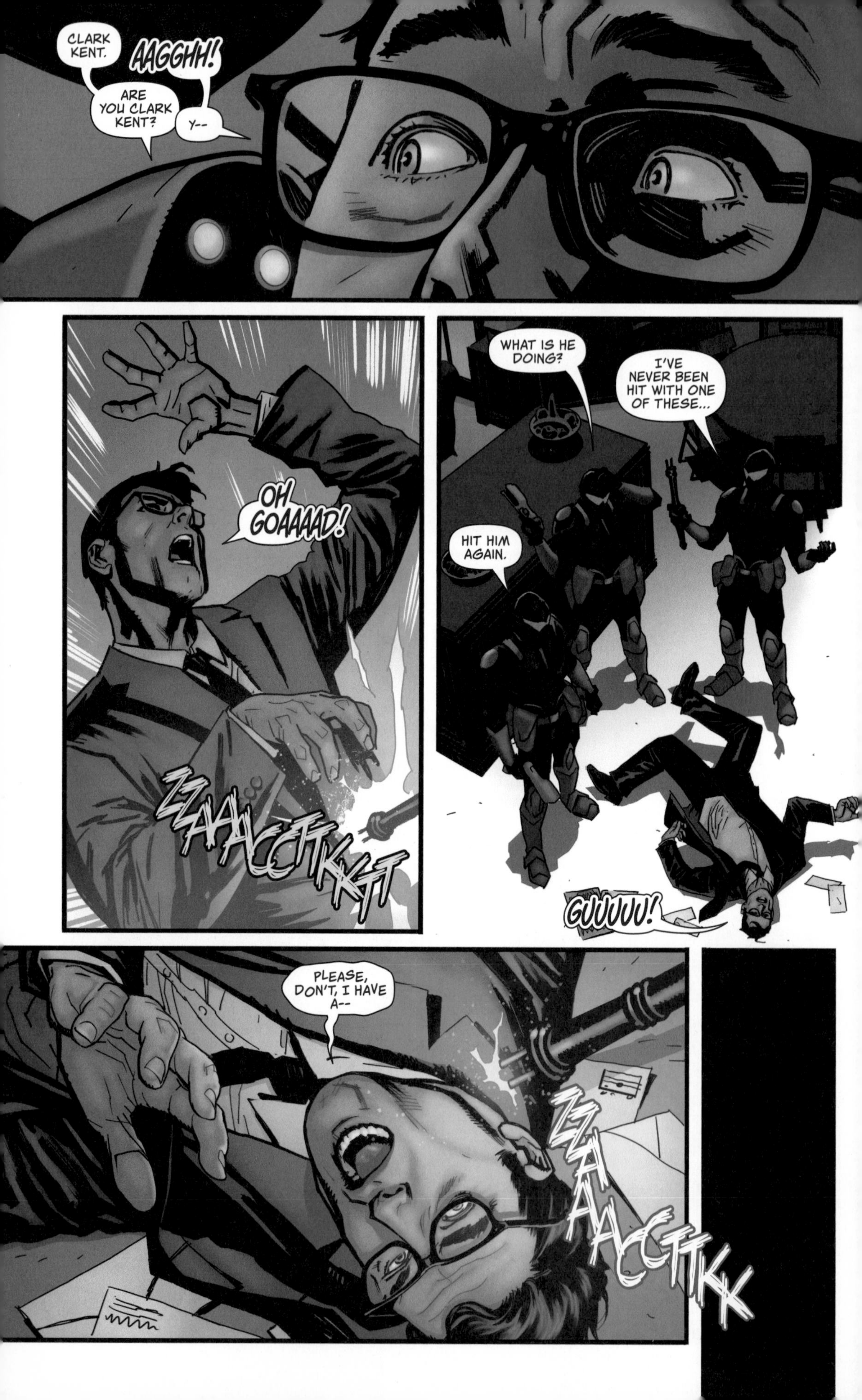
CLARK KENT.
ARE YOU CLARK KENT?
AAGGHH!
Y--
OH GOAAAAD!
ZZAAACCTTKKTT
WHAT IS HE DOING?
I'VE NEVER BEEN HIT WITH ONE OF THESE...
HIT HIM AGAIN.
GUUUUU!
PLEASE, DON'T, I HAVE A--
ZZAAACCTTKK

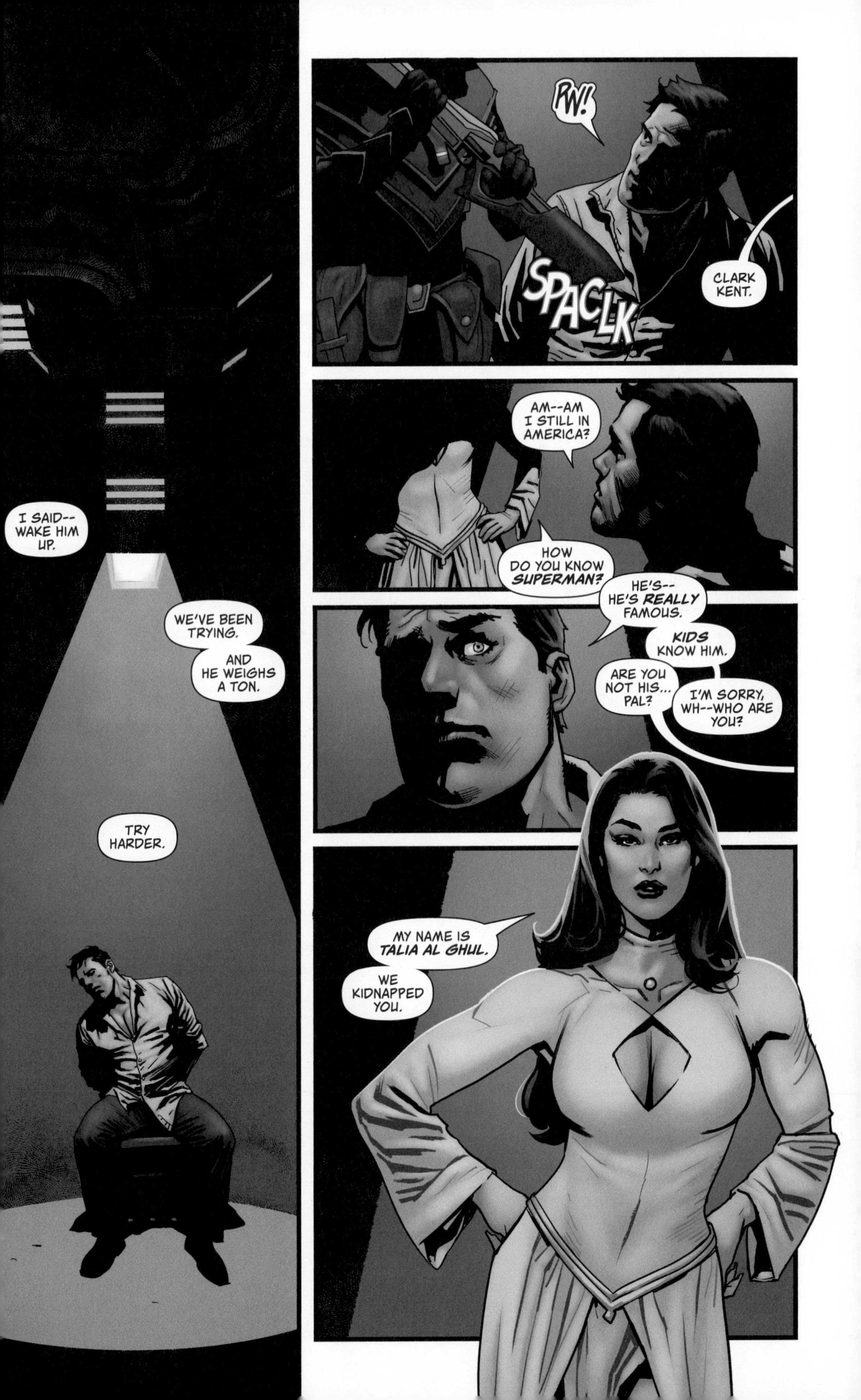
I SAID-- WAKE HIM UP.
WE'VE BEEN TRYING.
AND HE WEIGHS A TON.
TRY HARDER.
PW!
SPACLK
CLARK KENT.
AM--AM I STILL IN AMERICA?
HOW DO YOU KNOW *SUPERMAN?*
HE'S-- HE'S *REALLY* FAMOUS.
*KIDS* KNOW HIM.
ARE YOU NOT HIS... PAL?
I'M SORRY, WH--WHO ARE YOU?
MY NAME IS *TALIA AL GHUL.*
WE KIDNAPPED YOU.

DO--DO YOU HAVE MY GLASSES?

I GET MIGRAINES.

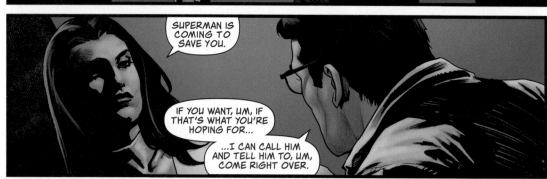

I INTERVIEWED YOUR FATHER ONCE.

IT WAS... UNPLEASANT.

SUPERMAN IS COMING TO SAVE YOU.

IF YOU WANT, UM, IF THAT'S WHAT YOU'RE HOPING FOR...

...I CAN CALL HIM AND TELL HIM TO, UM, COME RIGHT OVER.

WHEN HE DOES, YOU'RE GOING TO GET THE STORY OF YOUR LIFE.

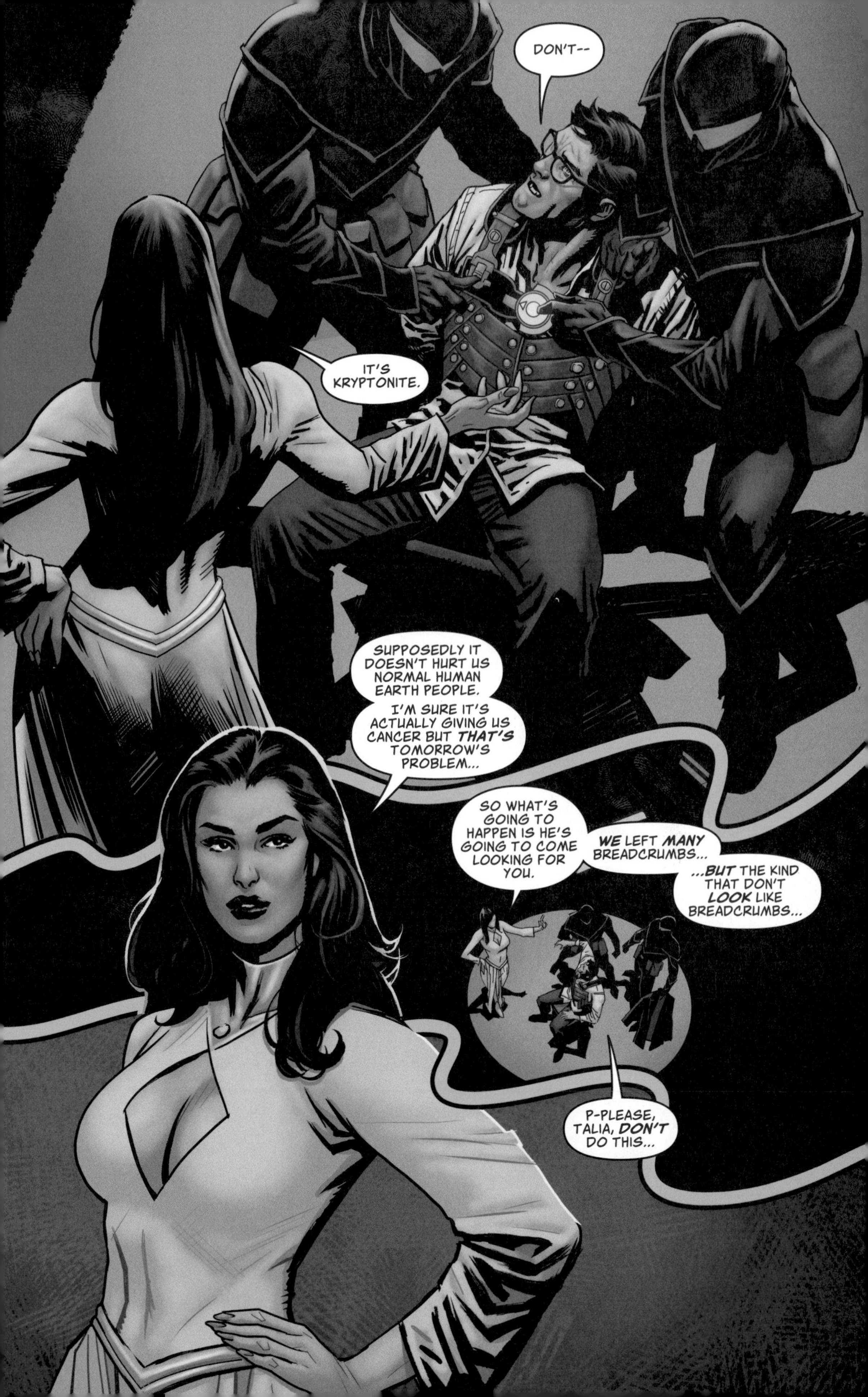
DON'T--
IT'S KRYPTONITE.
SUPPOSEDLY IT DOESN'T HURT US NORMAL HUMAN EARTH PEOPLE.
I'M SURE IT'S ACTUALLY GIVING US CANCER BUT THAT'S TOMORROW'S PROBLEM...
SO WHAT'S GOING TO HAPPEN IS HE'S GOING TO COME LOOKING FOR YOU.
WE LEFT MANY BREADCRUMBS...
...BUT THE KIND THAT DON'T LOOK LIKE BREADCRUMBS...
P-PLEASE, TALIA, DON'T DO THIS...

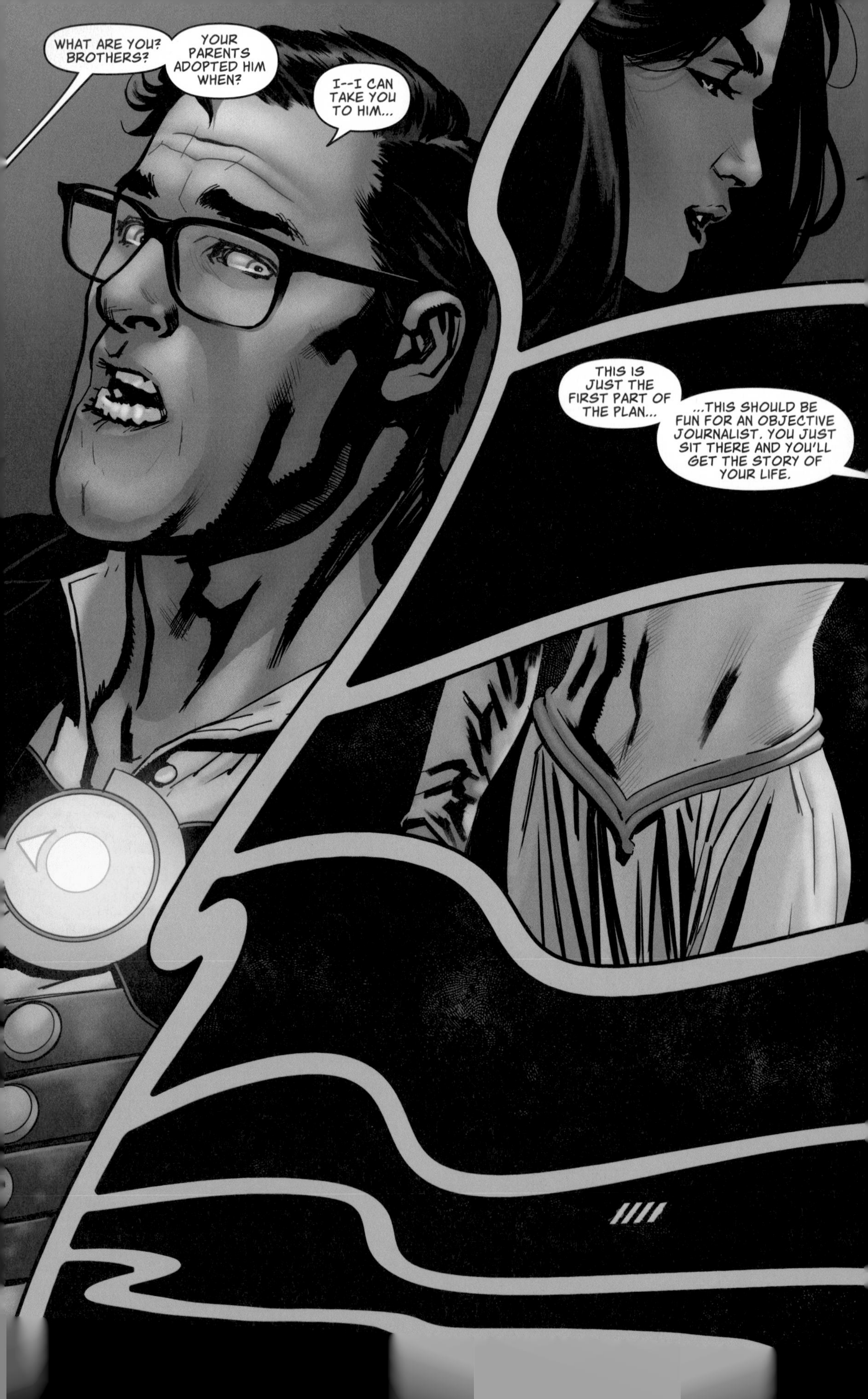
WHAT ARE YOU? BROTHERS?
YOUR PARENTS ADOPTED HIM WHEN?
I--I CAN TAKE YOU TO HIM...
THIS IS JUST THE FIRST PART OF THE PLAN...
...THIS SHOULD BE FUN FOR AN OBJECTIVE JOURNALIST. YOU JUST SIT THERE AND YOU'LL GET THE STORY OF YOUR LIFE.

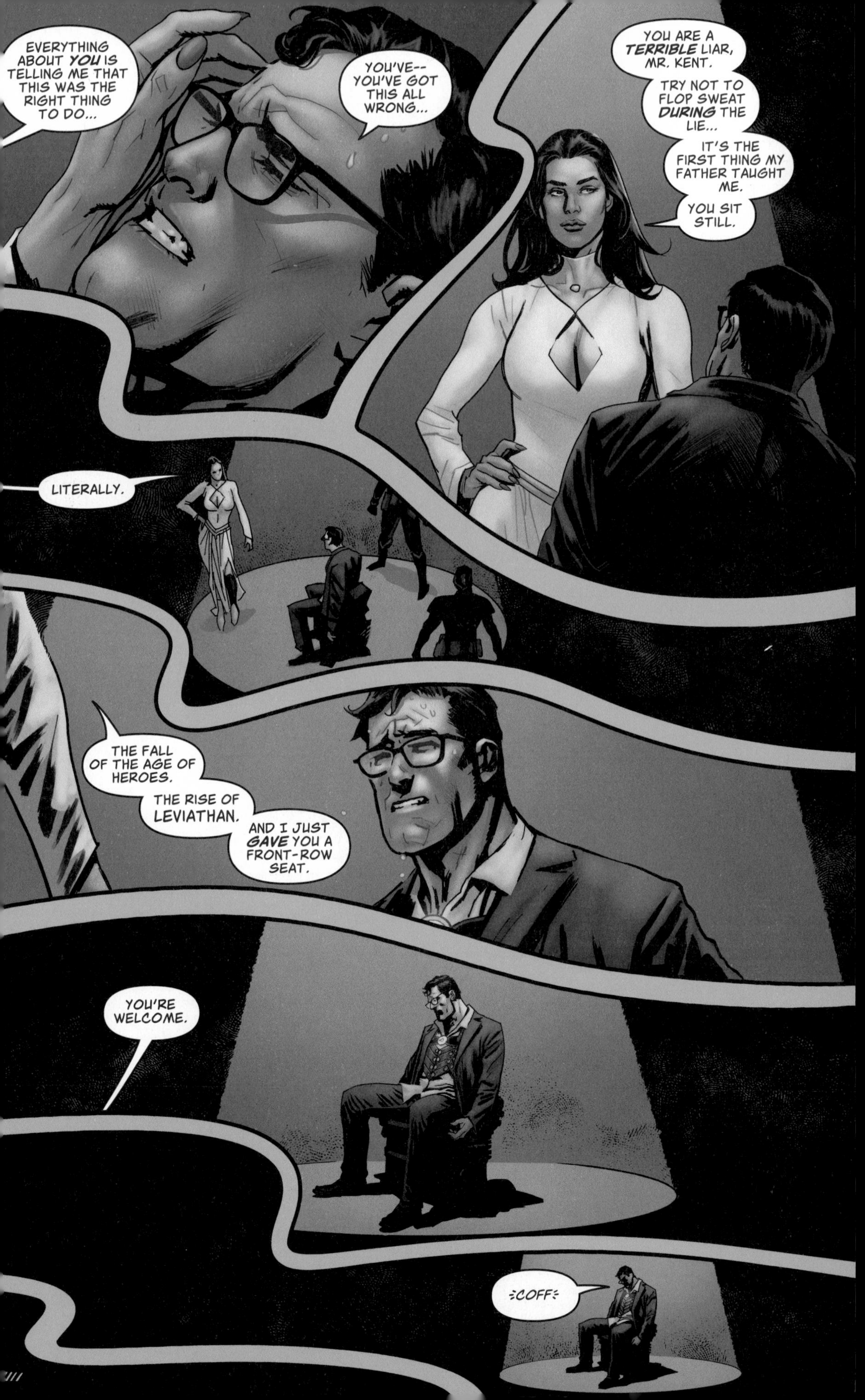
EVERYTHING ABOUT YOU IS TELLING ME THAT THIS WAS THE RIGHT THING TO DO...
YOU'VE-- YOU'VE GOT THIS ALL WRONG...
YOU ARE A TERRIBLE LIAR, MR. KENT.
TRY NOT TO FLOP SWEAT DURING THE LIE...
IT'S THE FIRST THING MY FATHER TAUGHT ME.
YOU SIT STILL.
LITERALLY.
THE FALL OF THE AGE OF HEROES.
THE RISE OF LEVIATHAN.
AND I JUST GAVE YOU A FRONT-ROW SEAT.
YOU'RE WELCOME.
COFF

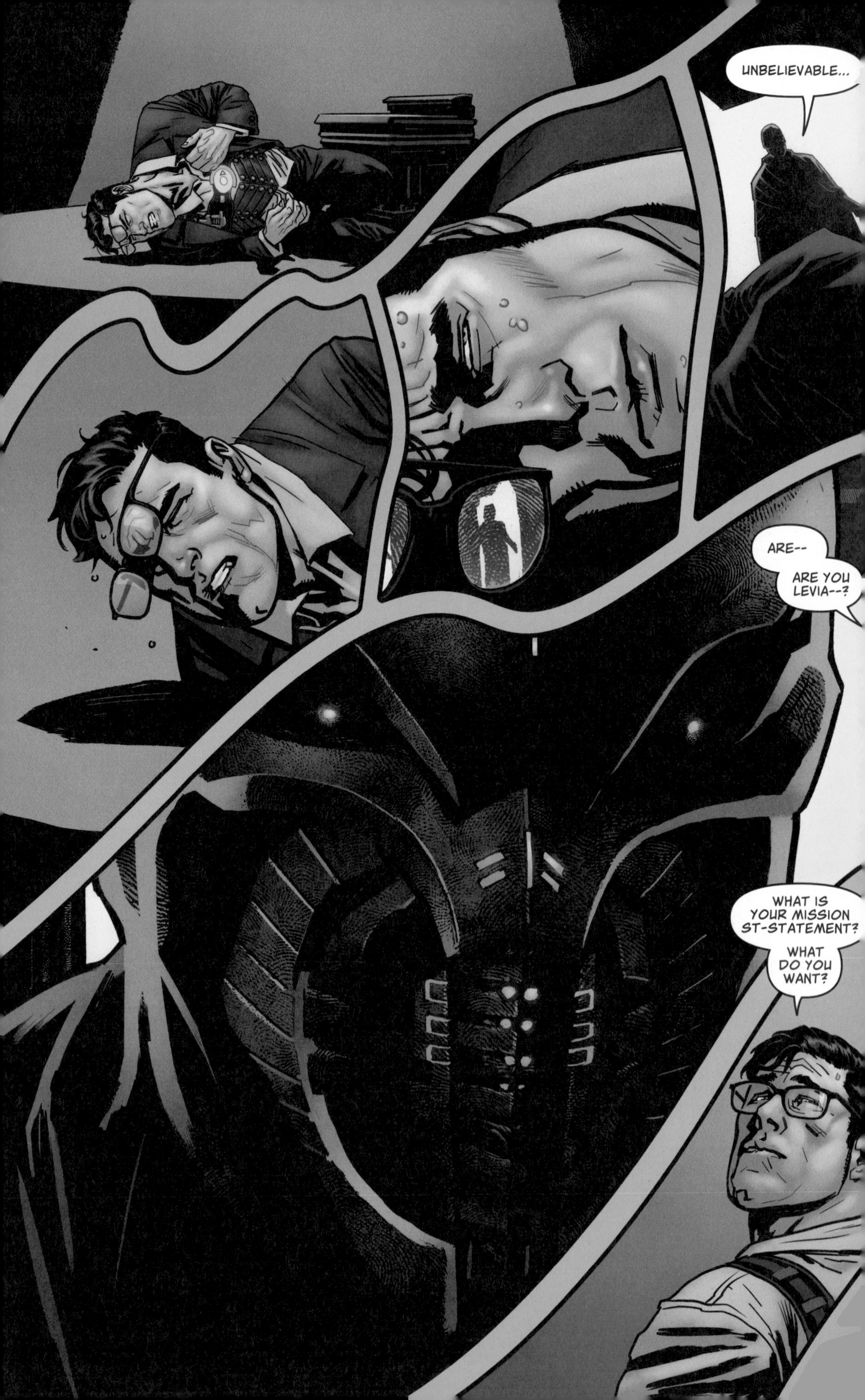
UNBELIEVABLE...
ARE--
ARE YOU LEVIA--?
WHAT IS YOUR MISSION ST-STATEMENT?
WHAT DO YOU WANT?

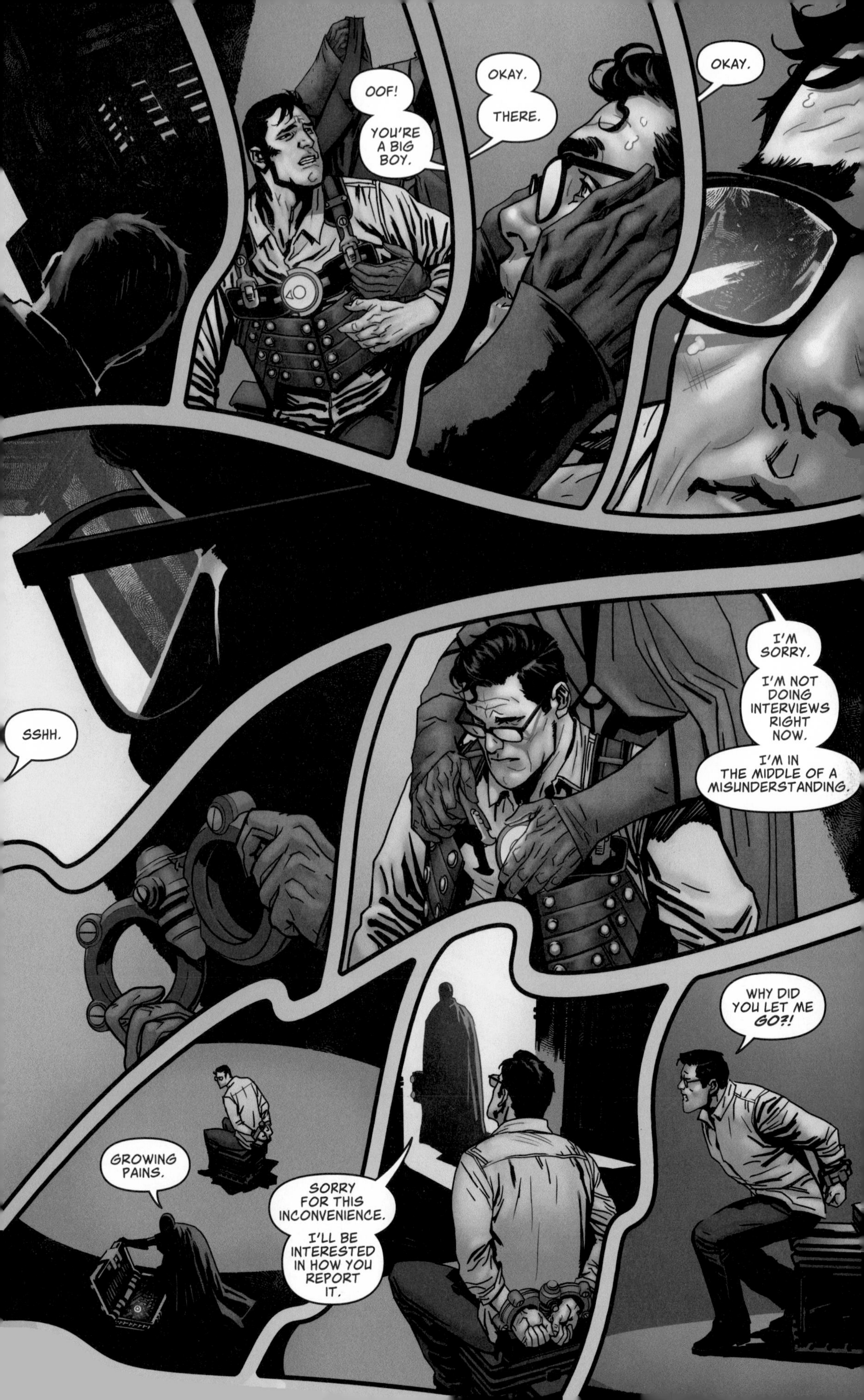
OOF!
YOU'RE A BIG BOY.
OKAY.
THERE.
OKAY.
SSHH.
I'M SORRY.
I'M NOT DOING INTERVIEWS RIGHT NOW.
I'M IN THE MIDDLE OF A MISUNDERSTANDING.
GROWING PAINS.
SORRY FOR THIS INCONVENIENCE.
I'LL BE INTERESTED IN HOW YOU REPORT IT.
WHY DID YOU LET ME GO?!

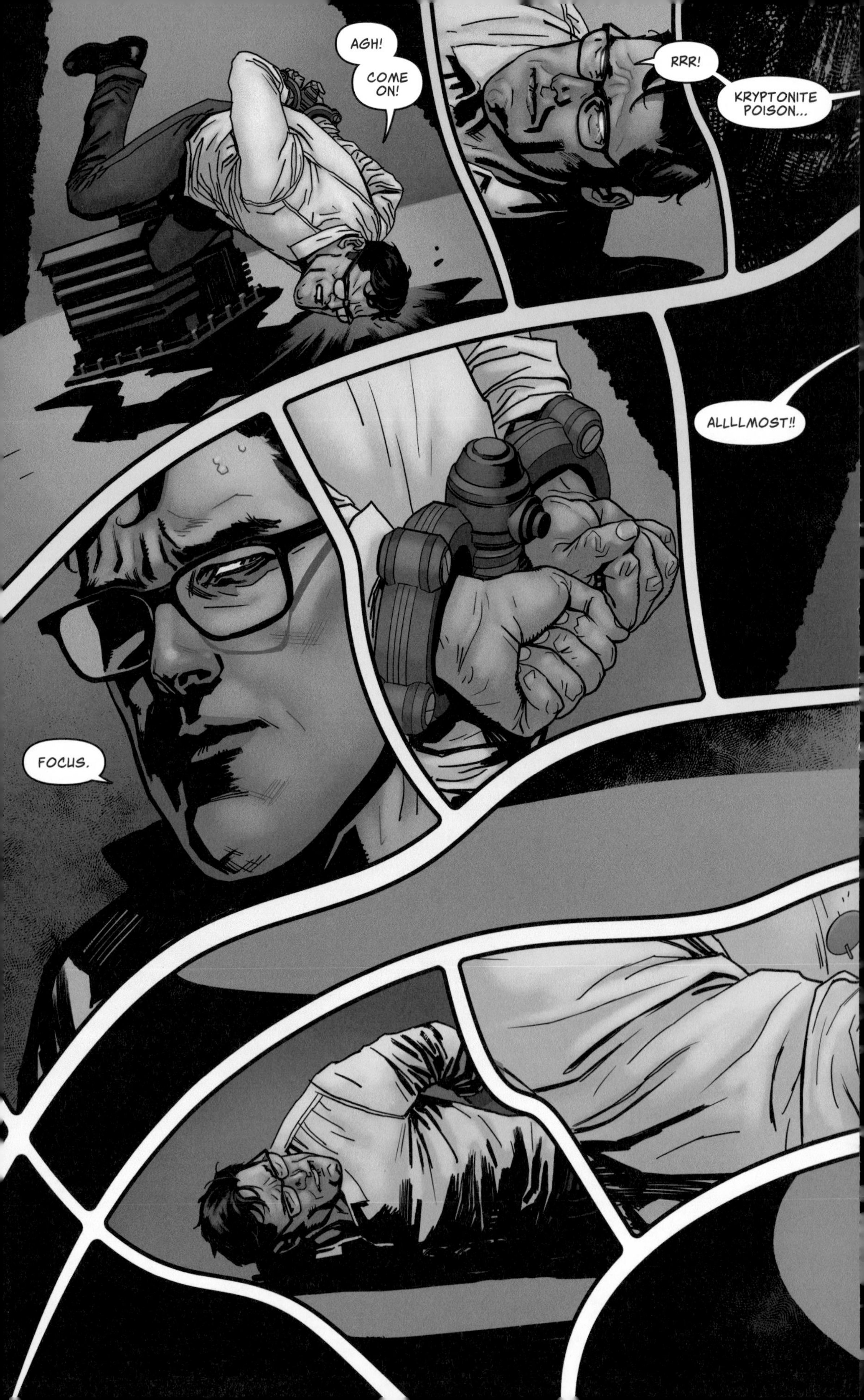
AGH!
COME ON!
RRR!
KRYPTONITE POISON...
ALLLLMOST!!
FOCUS.

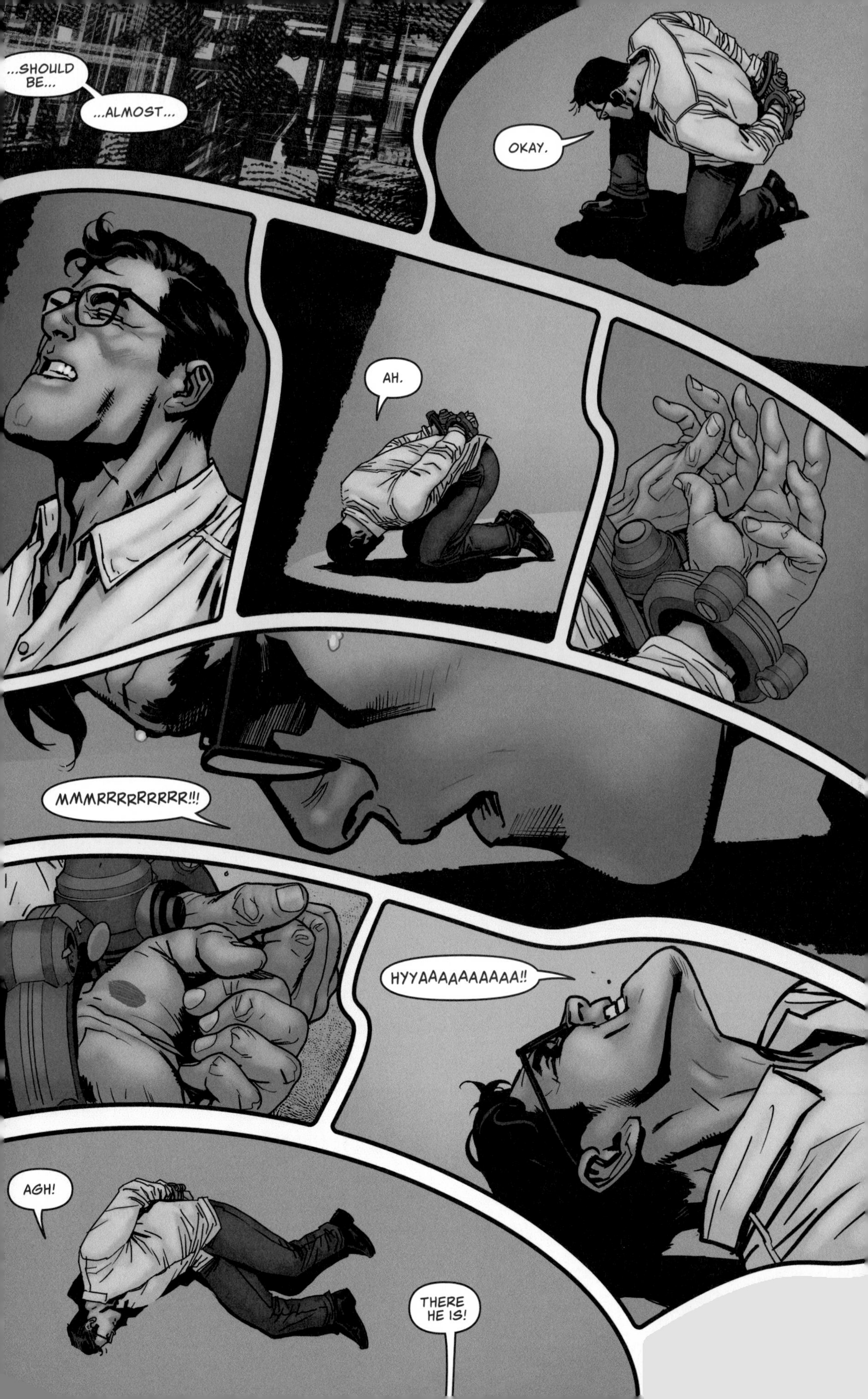
...SHOULD BE...
...ALMOST...
OKAY.
AH.
MMMRRRRRRRR!!!
HYYAAAAAAAAAA!!
AGH!
THERE HE IS!

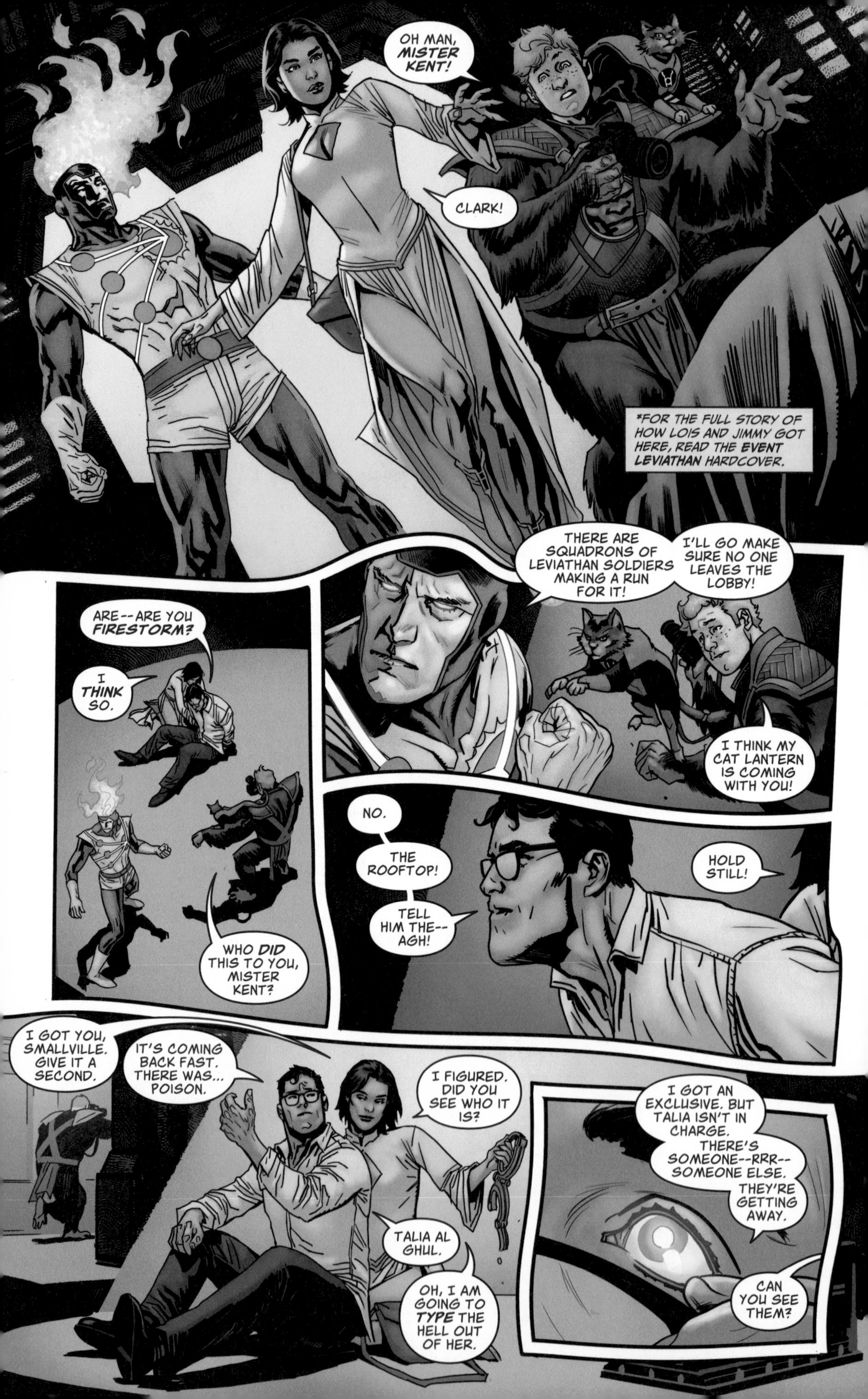
OH MAN, MISTER KENT!
CLARK!
*FOR THE FULL STORY OF HOW LOIS AND JIMMY GOT HERE, READ THE EVENT LEVIATHAN HARDCOVER.
ARE--ARE YOU FIRESTORM?
I THINK SO.
WHO DID THIS TO YOU, MISTER KENT?
THERE ARE SQUADRONS OF LEVIATHAN SOLDIERS MAKING A RUN FOR IT!
I'LL GO MAKE SURE NO ONE LEAVES THE LOBBY!
I THINK MY CAT LANTERN IS COMING WITH YOU!
NO.
THE ROOFTOP!
TELL HIM THE-- AGH!
HOLD STILL!
I GOT YOU, SMALLVILLE. GIVE IT A SECOND.
IT'S COMING BACK FAST. THERE WAS... POISON.
I FIGURED. DID YOU SEE WHO IT IS?
TALIA AL GHUL.
OH, I AM GOING TO TYPE THE HELL OUT OF HER.
I GOT AN EXCLUSIVE. BUT TALIA ISN'T IN CHARGE.
THERE'S SOMEONE--RRR-- SOMEONE ELSE.
THEY'RE GETTING AWAY.
CAN YOU SEE THEM?

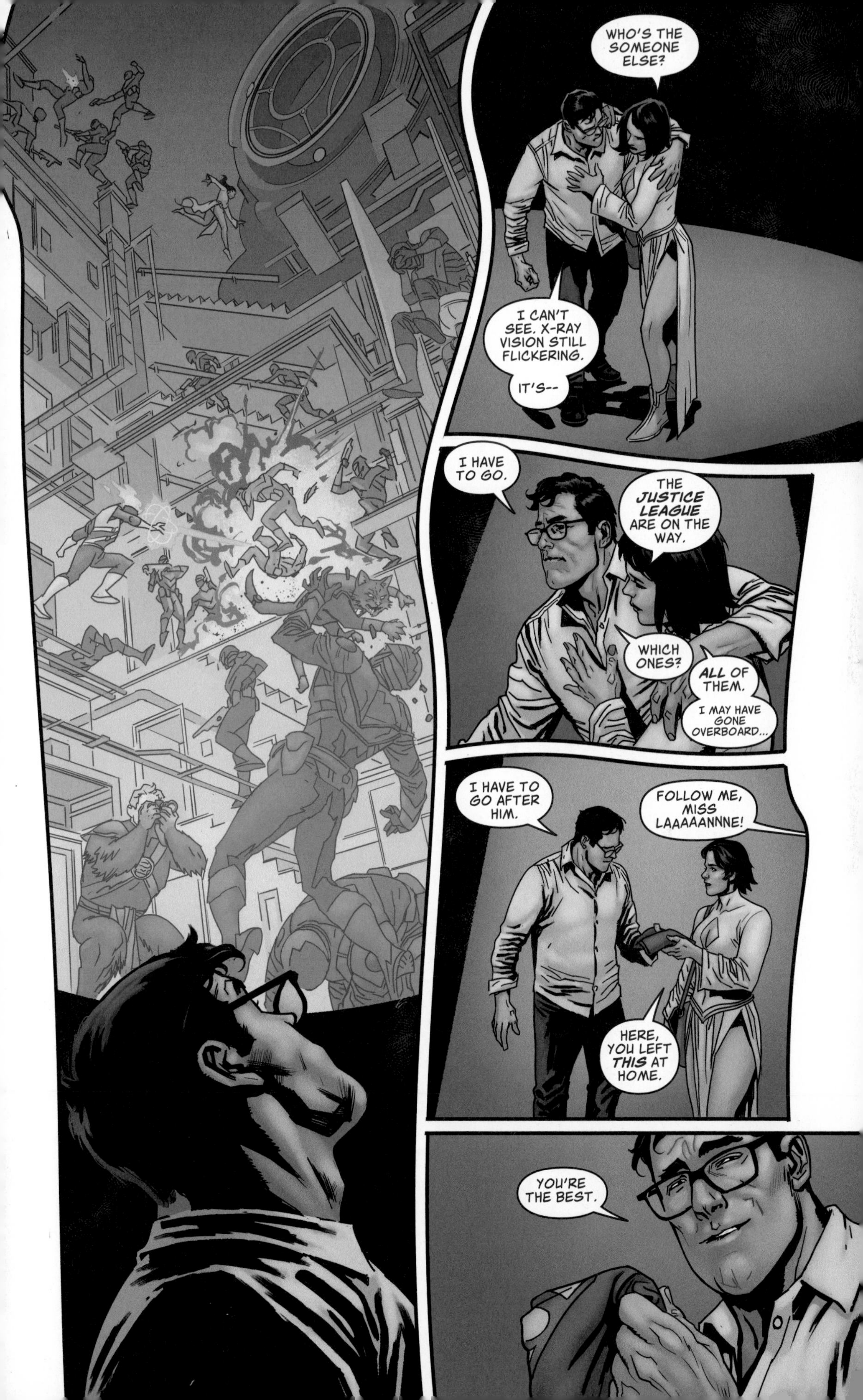
WHO'S THE SOMEONE ELSE?
I CAN'T SEE. X-RAY VISION STILL FLICKERING.
IT'S--
I HAVE TO GO.
THE *JUSTICE LEAGUE* ARE ON THE WAY.
WHICH ONES?
*ALL* OF THEM.
I MAY HAVE GONE OVERBOARD...
I HAVE TO GO AFTER HIM.
FOLLOW ME, MISS LAAAAANNNE!
HERE, YOU LEFT *THIS* AT HOME.
YOU'RE THE BEST.

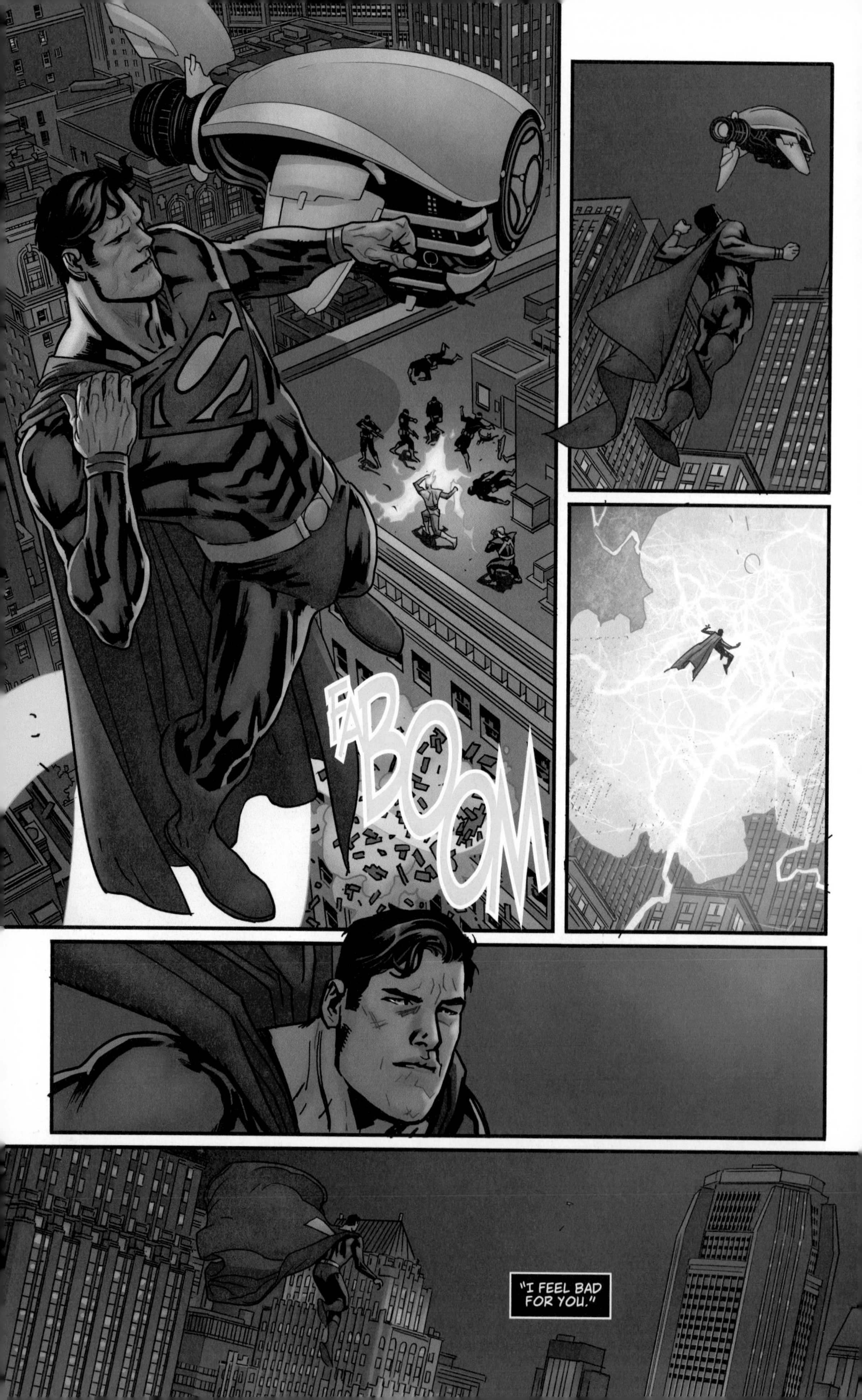
FABOOOM
"I FEEL BAD FOR YOU."

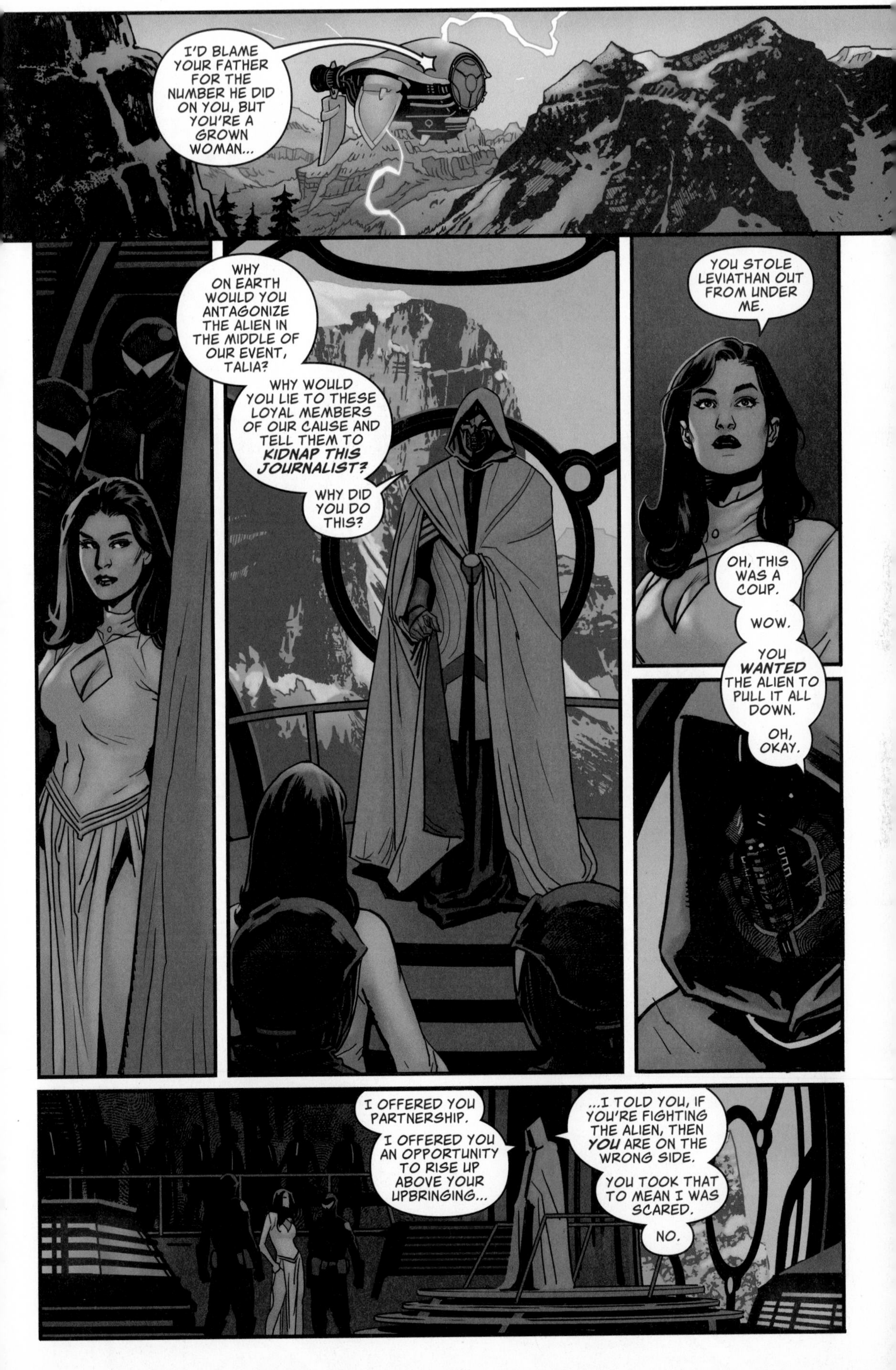

I'D BLAME YOUR FATHER FOR THE NUMBER HE DID ON YOU, BUT YOU'RE A GROWN WOMAN...
WHY ON EARTH WOULD YOU ANTAGONIZE THE ALIEN IN THE MIDDLE OF OUR EVENT, TALIA?
WHY WOULD YOU LIE TO THESE LOYAL MEMBERS OF OUR CAUSE AND TELL THEM TO KIDNAP THIS JOURNALIST?
WHY DID YOU DO THIS?
YOU STOLE LEVIATHAN OUT FROM UNDER ME.
OH, THIS WAS A COUP.
WOW.
YOU WANTED THE ALIEN TO PULL IT ALL DOWN.
OH, OKAY.
I OFFERED YOU PARTNERSHIP.
I OFFERED YOU AN OPPORTUNITY TO RISE UP ABOVE YOUR UPBRINGING...
...I TOLD YOU, IF YOU'RE FIGHTING THE ALIEN, THEN YOU ARE ON THE WRONG SIDE.
YOU TOOK THAT TO MEAN I WAS SCARED.
NO.

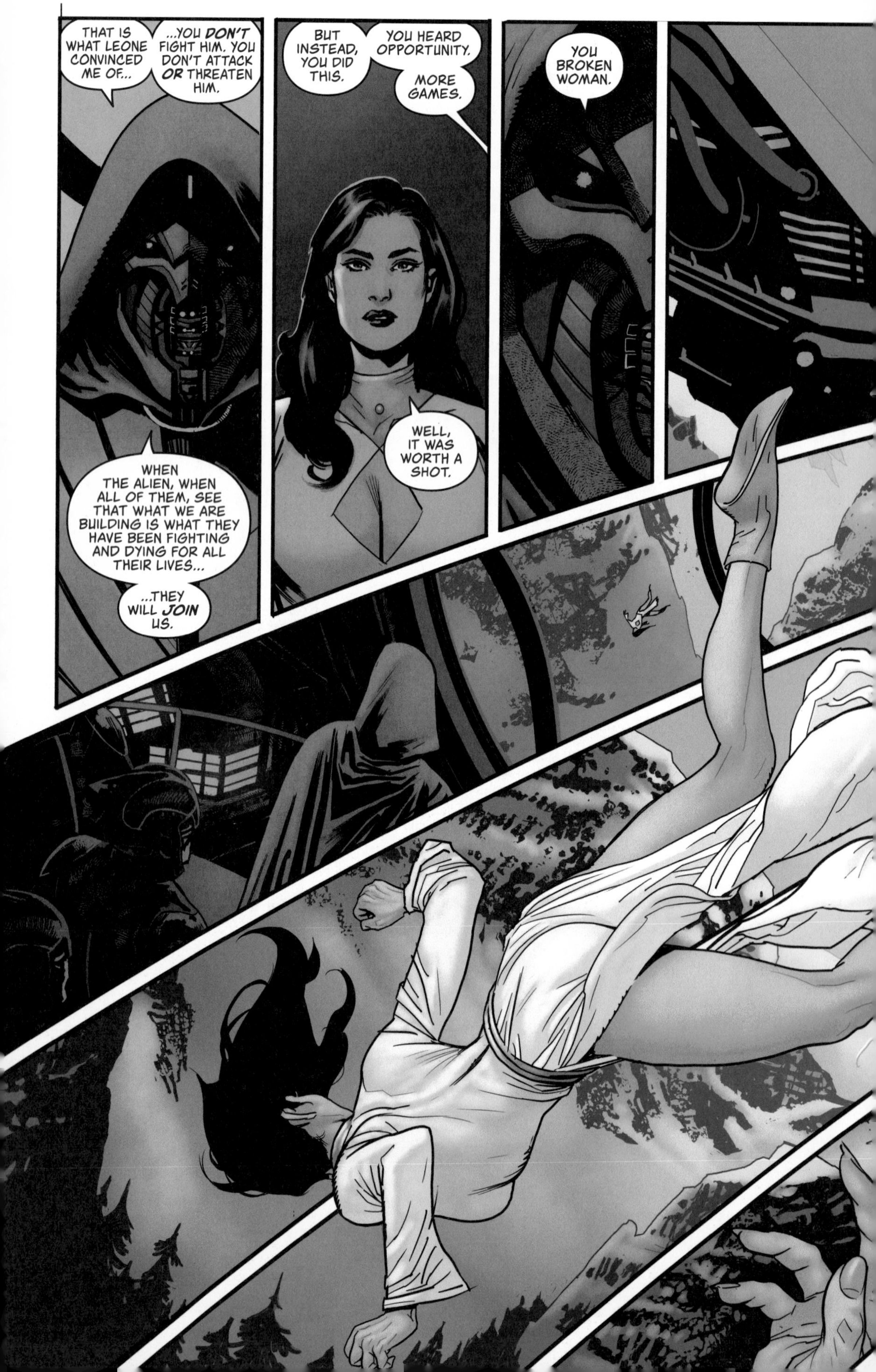
THAT IS WHAT LEONE CONVINCED ME OF...
...YOU DON'T FIGHT HIM. YOU DON'T ATTACK OR THREATEN HIM.
WHEN THE ALIEN, WHEN ALL OF THEM, SEE THAT WHAT WE ARE BUILDING IS WHAT THEY HAVE BEEN FIGHTING AND DYING FOR ALL THEIR LIVES...
...THEY WILL JOIN US.
BUT INSTEAD, YOU DID THIS.
YOU HEARD OPPORTUNITY.
MORE GAMES.
WELL, IT WAS WORTH A SHOT.
YOU BROKEN WOMAN.

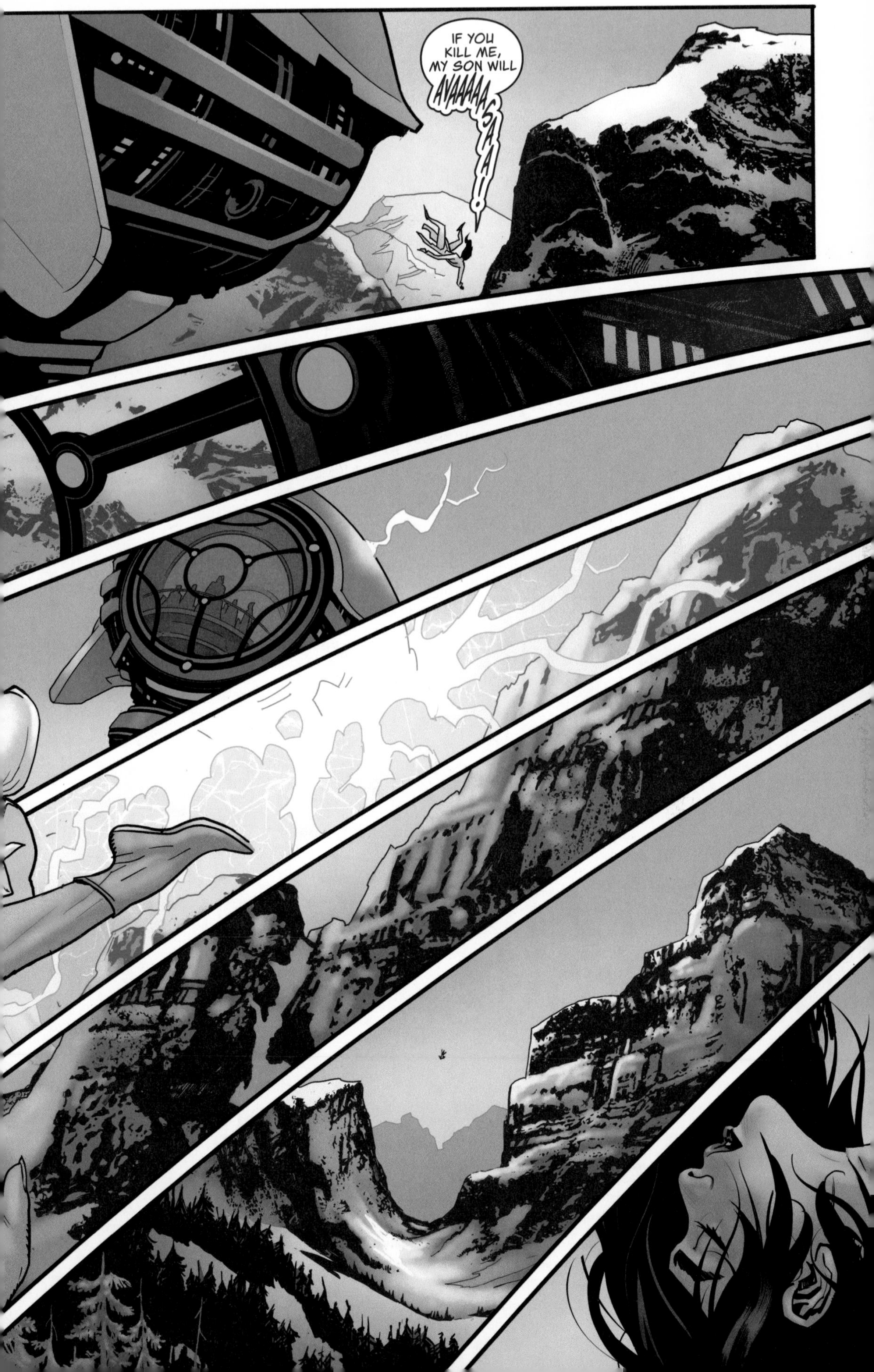
IF YOU KILL ME, MY SON WILL
AVAAAAASAA!

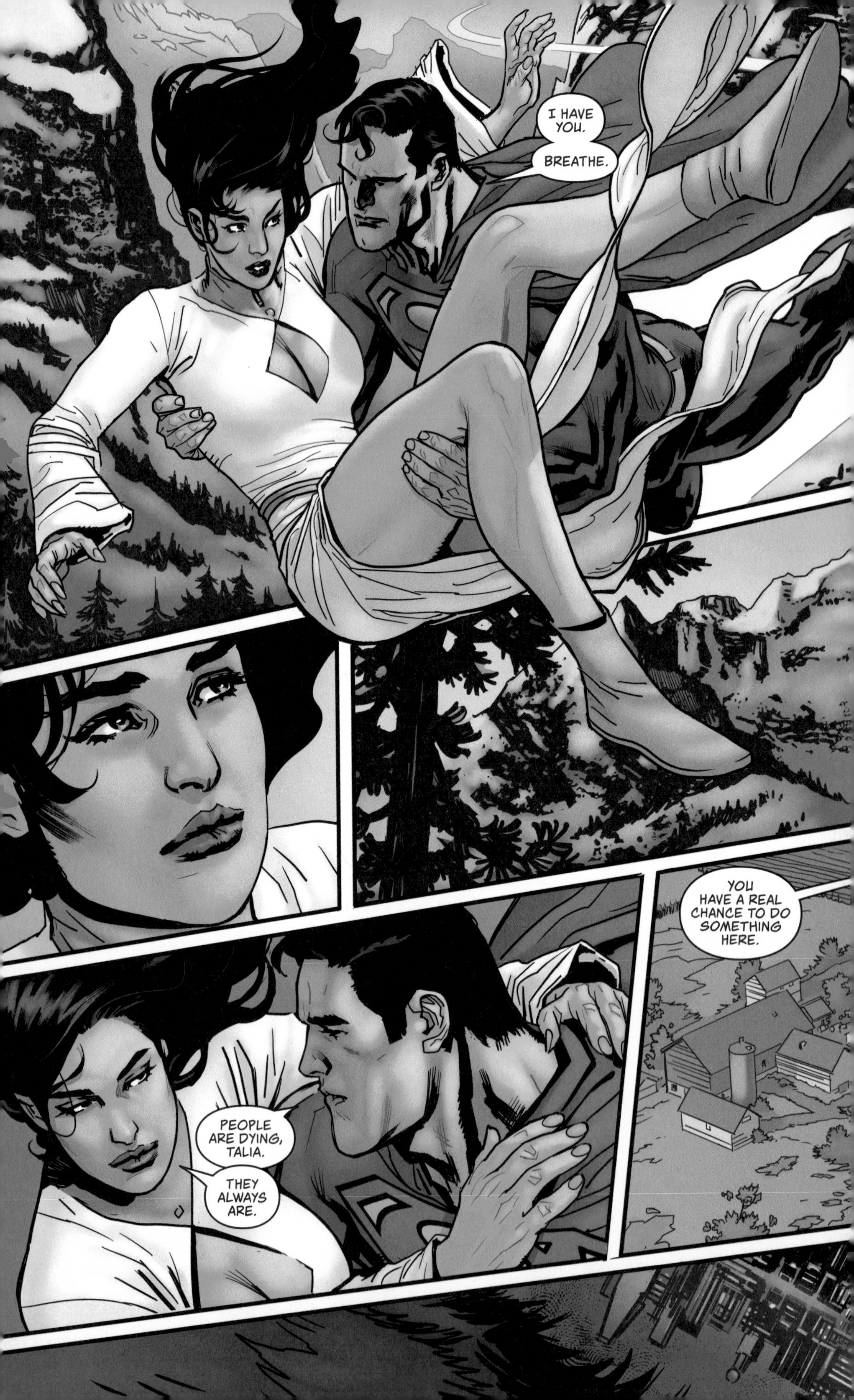
I HAVE YOU.
BREATHE.
YOU HAVE A REAL CHANCE TO DO SOMETHING HERE.
PEOPLE ARE DYING, TALIA.
THEY ALWAYS ARE.

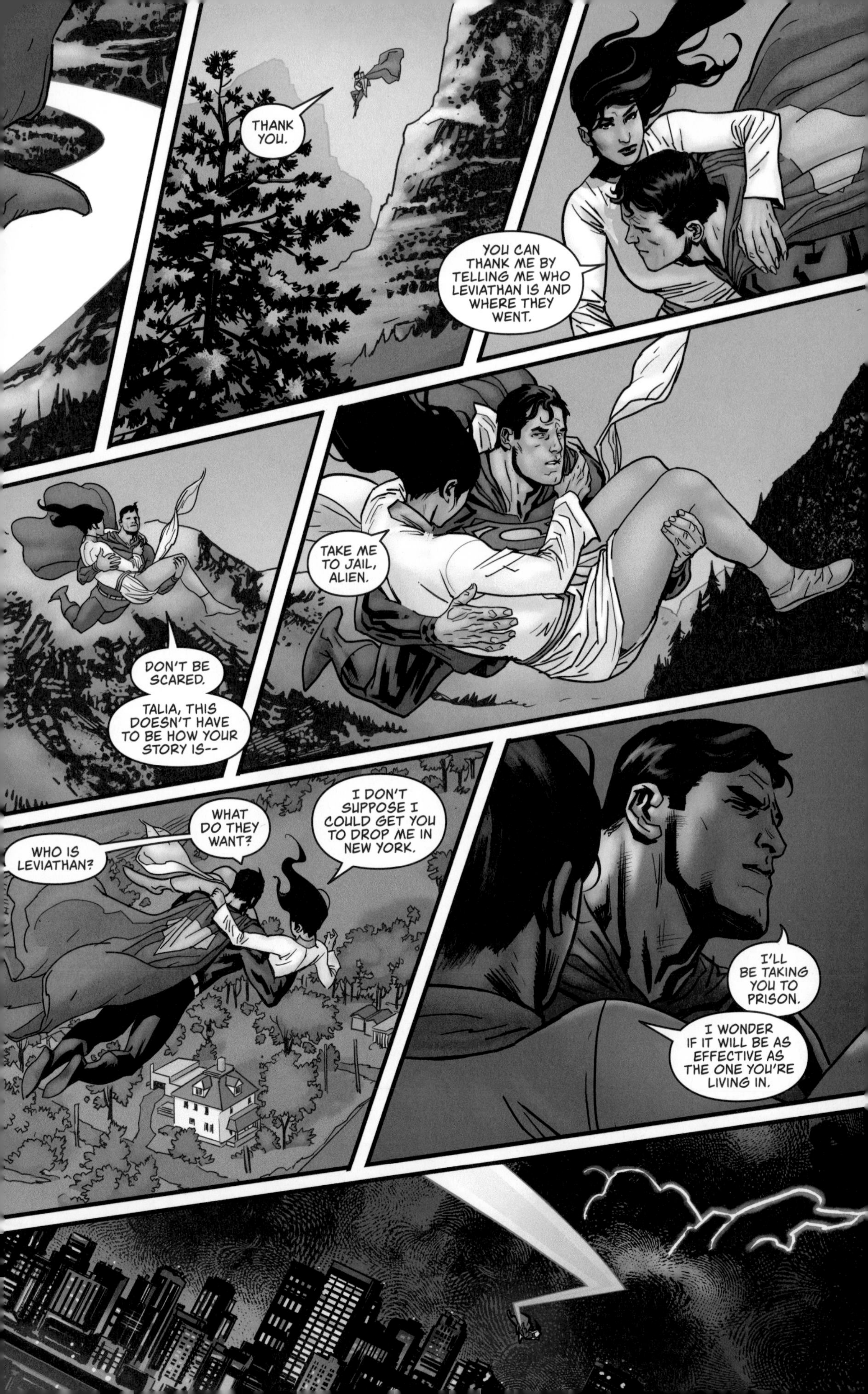
THANK YOU.
YOU CAN THANK ME BY TELLING ME WHO LEVIATHAN IS AND WHERE THEY WENT.
DON'T BE SCARED.
TALIA, THIS DOESN'T HAVE TO BE HOW YOUR STORY IS--
TAKE ME TO JAIL, ALIEN.
WHO IS LEVIATHAN?
WHAT DO THEY WANT?
I DON'T SUPPOSE I COULD GET YOU TO DROP ME IN NEW YORK.
I'LL BE TAKING YOU TO PRISON.
I WONDER IF IT WILL BE AS EFFECTIVE AS THE ONE YOU'RE LIVING IN.

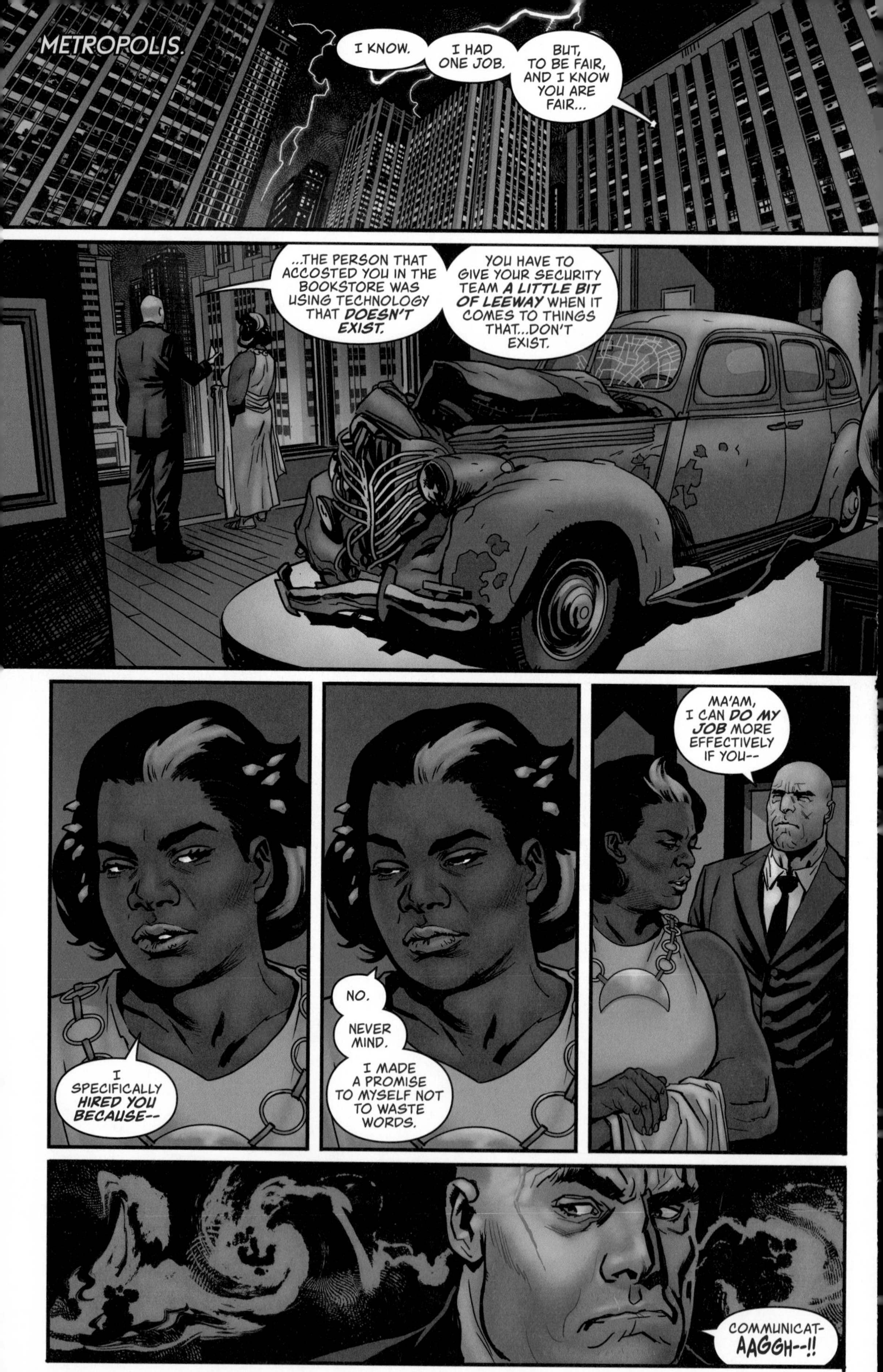
METROPOLIS.
I KNOW.
I HAD ONE JOB.
BUT, TO BE FAIR, AND I KNOW YOU ARE FAIR...
...THE PERSON THAT ACCOSTED YOU IN THE BOOKSTORE WAS USING TECHNOLOGY THAT DOESN'T EXIST.
YOU HAVE TO GIVE YOUR SECURITY TEAM A LITTLE BIT OF LEEWAY WHEN IT COMES TO THINGS THAT...DON'T EXIST.
I SPECIFICALLY HIRED YOU BECAUSE--
NO.
NEVER MIND.
I MADE A PROMISE TO MYSELF NOT TO WASTE WORDS.
MA'AM, I CAN DO MY JOB MORE EFFECTIVELY IF YOU--
COMMUNICAT-AAGGH--!!

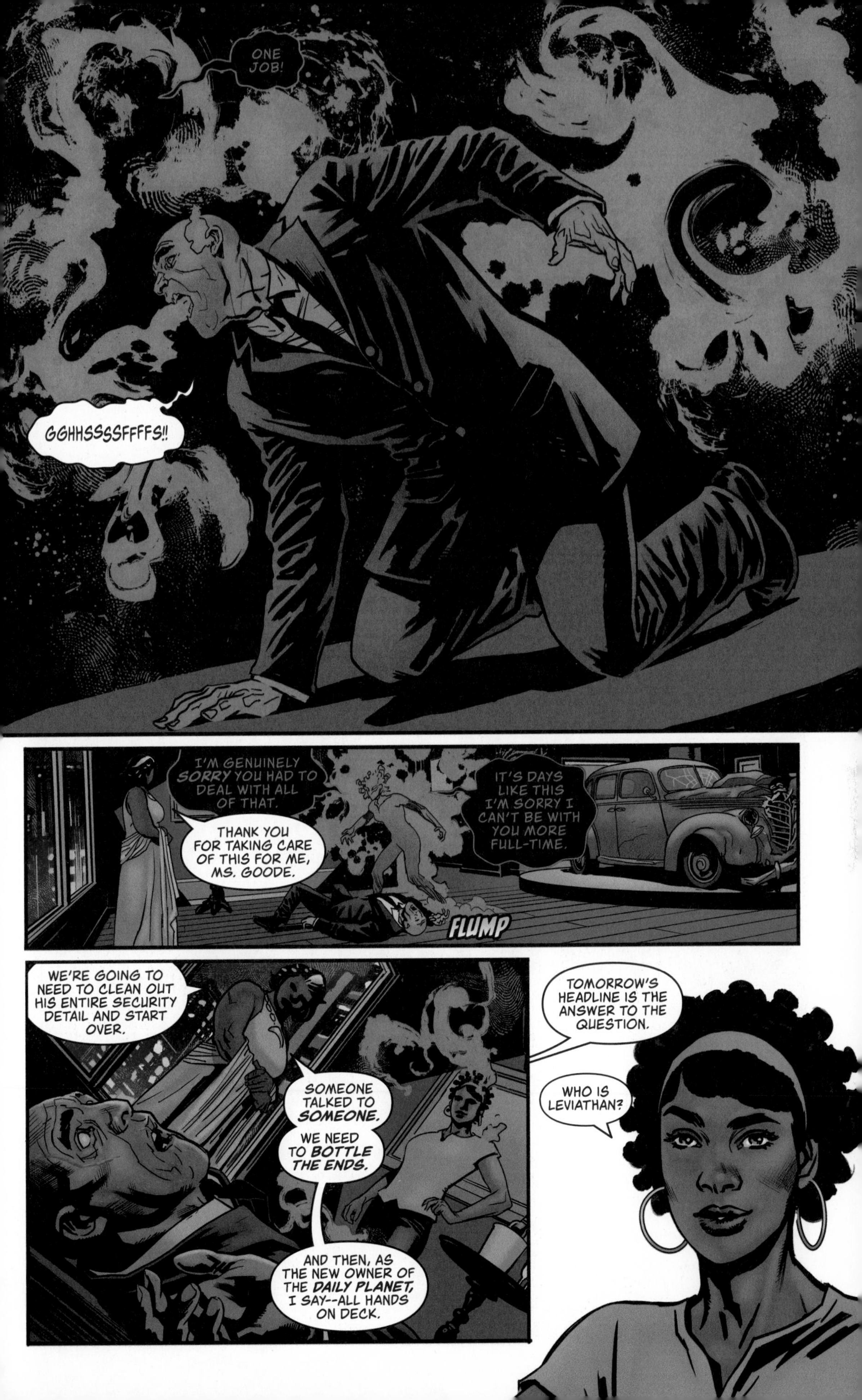

ONE JOB!
GGHHSSSSFFFFS!!
I'M GENUINELY SORRY YOU HAD TO DEAL WITH ALL OF THAT.
THANK YOU FOR TAKING CARE OF THIS FOR ME, MS. GOODE.
IT'S DAYS LIKE THIS I'M SORRY I CAN'T BE WITH YOU MORE FULL-TIME.
FLUMP
WE'RE GOING TO NEED TO CLEAN OUT HIS ENTIRE SECURITY DETAIL AND START OVER.
SOMEONE TALKED TO SOMEONE.
WE NEED TO BOTTLE THE ENDS.
AND THEN, AS THE NEW OWNER OF THE DAILY PLANET, I SAY--ALL HANDS ON DECK.
TOMORROW'S HEADLINE IS THE ANSWER TO THE QUESTION.
WHO IS LEVIATHAN?

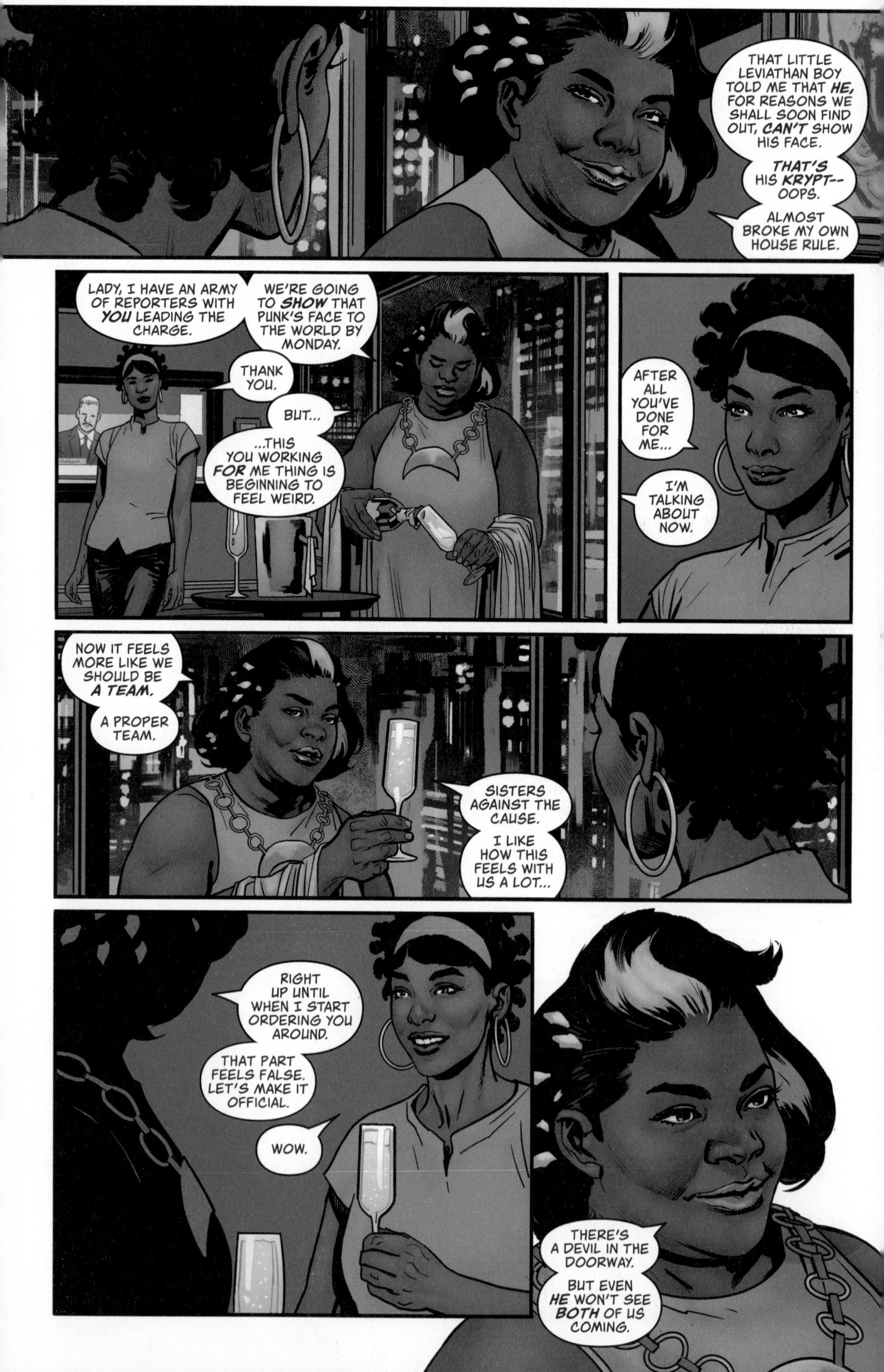
THAT LITTLE LEVIATHAN BOY TOLD ME THAT HE, FOR REASONS WE SHALL SOON FIND OUT, CAN'T SHOW HIS FACE.
THAT'S HIS KRYPT-- OOPS.
ALMOST BROKE MY OWN HOUSE RULE.
LADY, I HAVE AN ARMY OF REPORTERS WITH YOU LEADING THE CHARGE.
WE'RE GOING TO SHOW THAT PUNK'S FACE TO THE WORLD BY MONDAY.
THANK YOU.
BUT...
...THIS YOU WORKING FOR ME THING IS BEGINNING TO FEEL WEIRD.
AFTER ALL YOU'VE DONE FOR ME...
I'M TALKING ABOUT NOW.
NOW IT FEELS MORE LIKE WE SHOULD BE A TEAM.
A PROPER TEAM.
SISTERS AGAINST THE CAUSE.
I LIKE HOW THIS FEELS WITH US A LOT...
RIGHT UP UNTIL WHEN I START ORDERING YOU AROUND.
THAT PART FEELS FALSE. LET'S MAKE IT OFFICIAL.
WOW.
THERE'S A DEVIL IN THE DOORWAY.
BUT EVEN HE WON'T SEE BOTH OF US COMING.

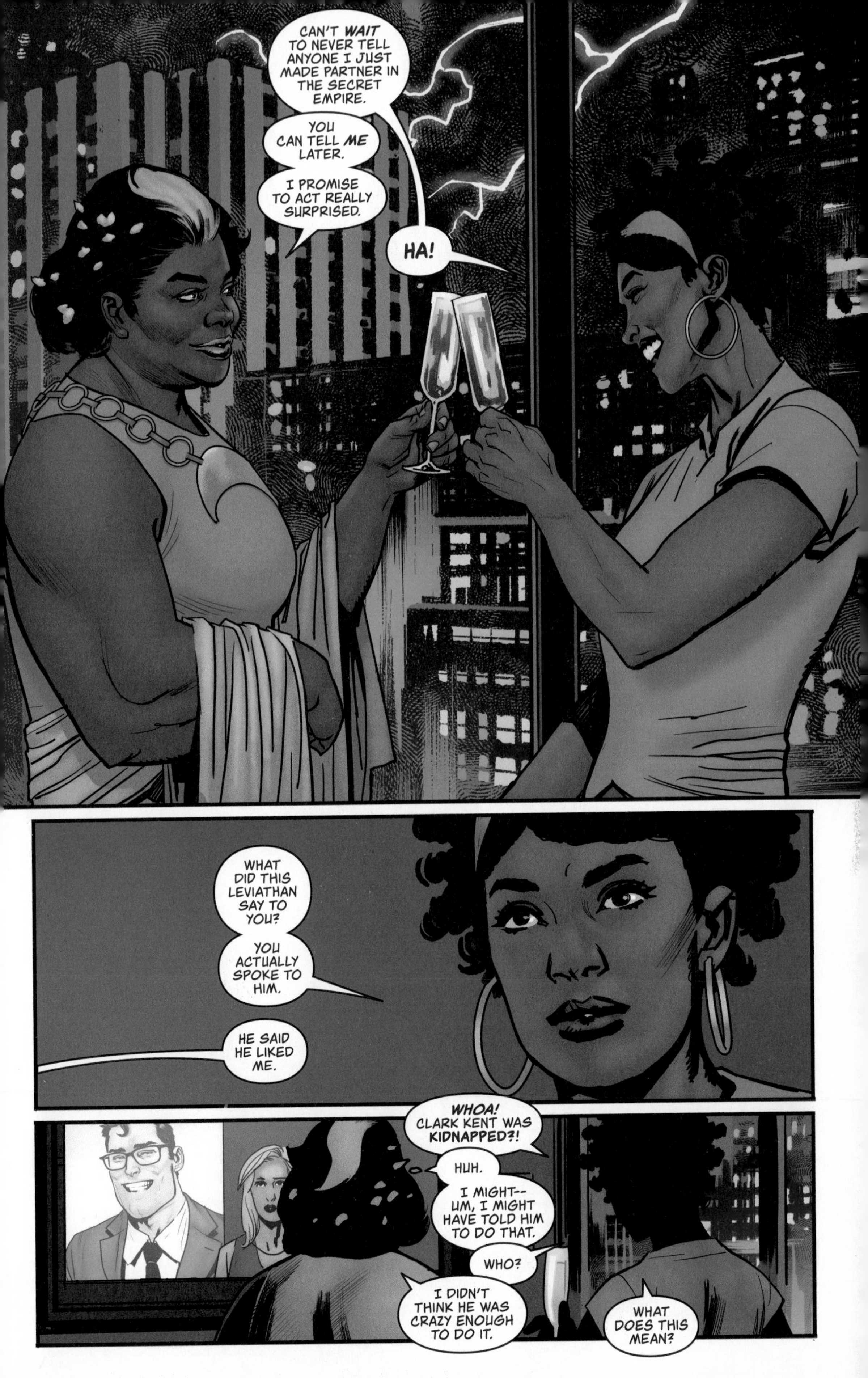
CAN'T WAIT TO NEVER TELL ANYONE I JUST MADE PARTNER IN THE SECRET EMPIRE.
YOU CAN TELL ME LATER.
I PROMISE TO ACT REALLY SURPRISED.
HA!
WHAT DID THIS LEVIATHAN SAY TO YOU?
YOU ACTUALLY SPOKE TO HIM.
HE SAID HE LIKED ME.
WHOA! CLARK KENT WAS KIDNAPPED?!
HUH.
I MIGHT-- UM, I MIGHT HAVE TOLD HIM TO DO THAT.
WHO?
I DIDN'T THINK HE WAS CRAZY ENOUGH TO DO IT.
WHAT DOES THIS MEAN?

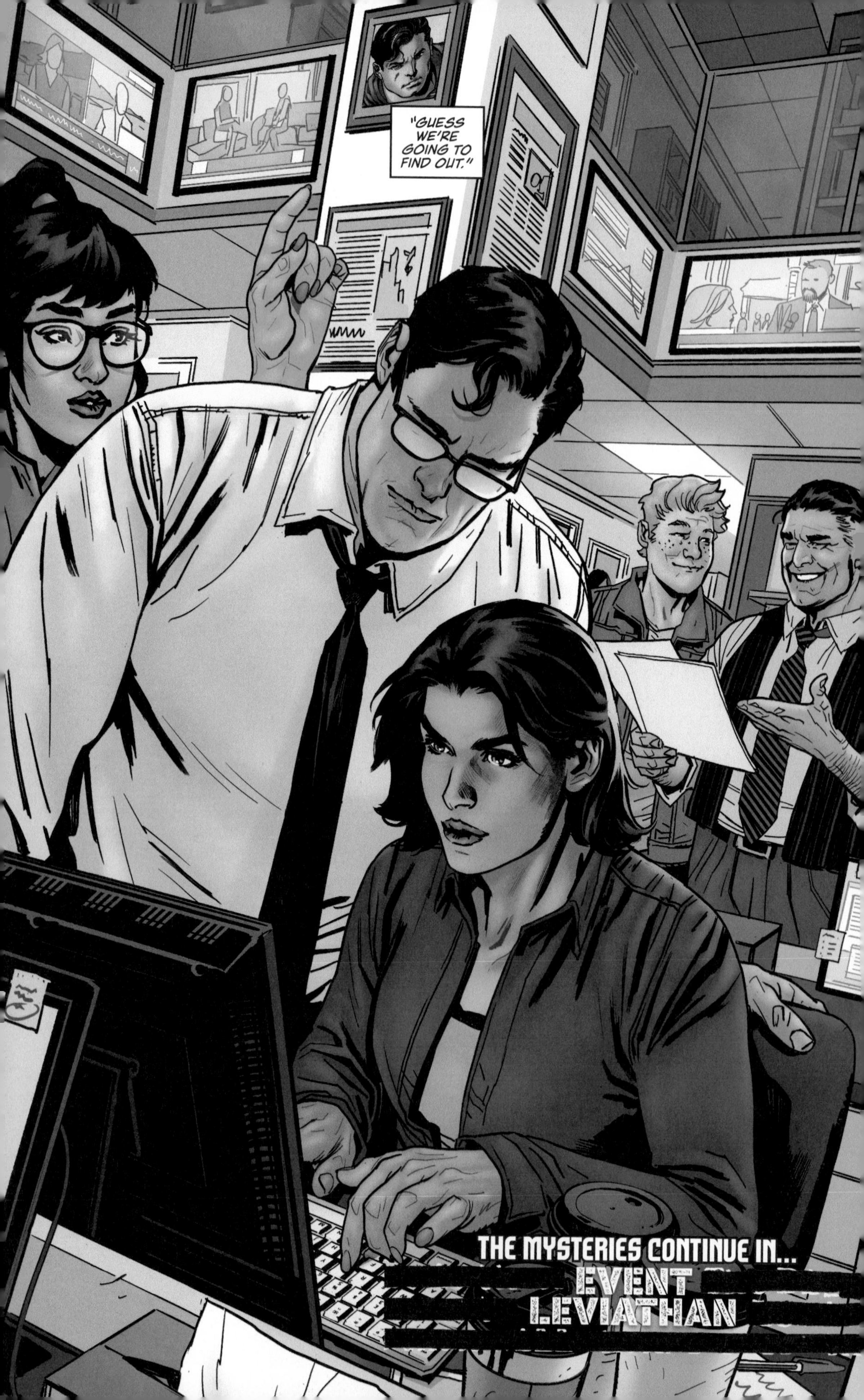
"GUESS WE'RE GOING TO FIND OUT."
THE MYSTERIES CONTINUE IN...
[redacted] EVENT [redacted]
[redacted] LEVIATHAN [redacted]

VARIANT COVER GALLERY

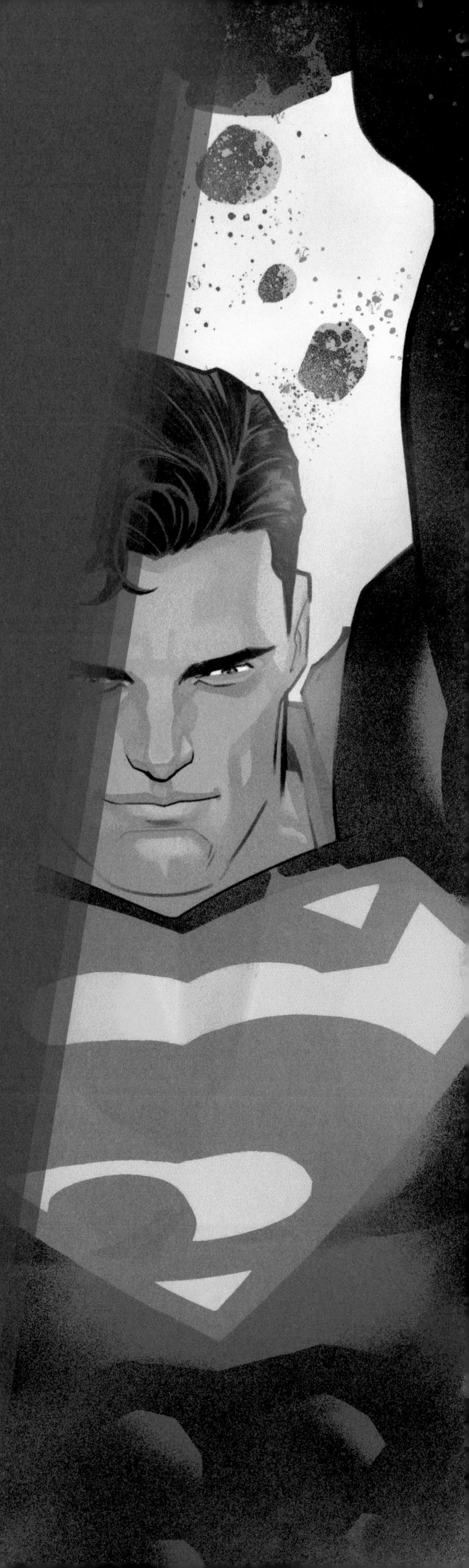

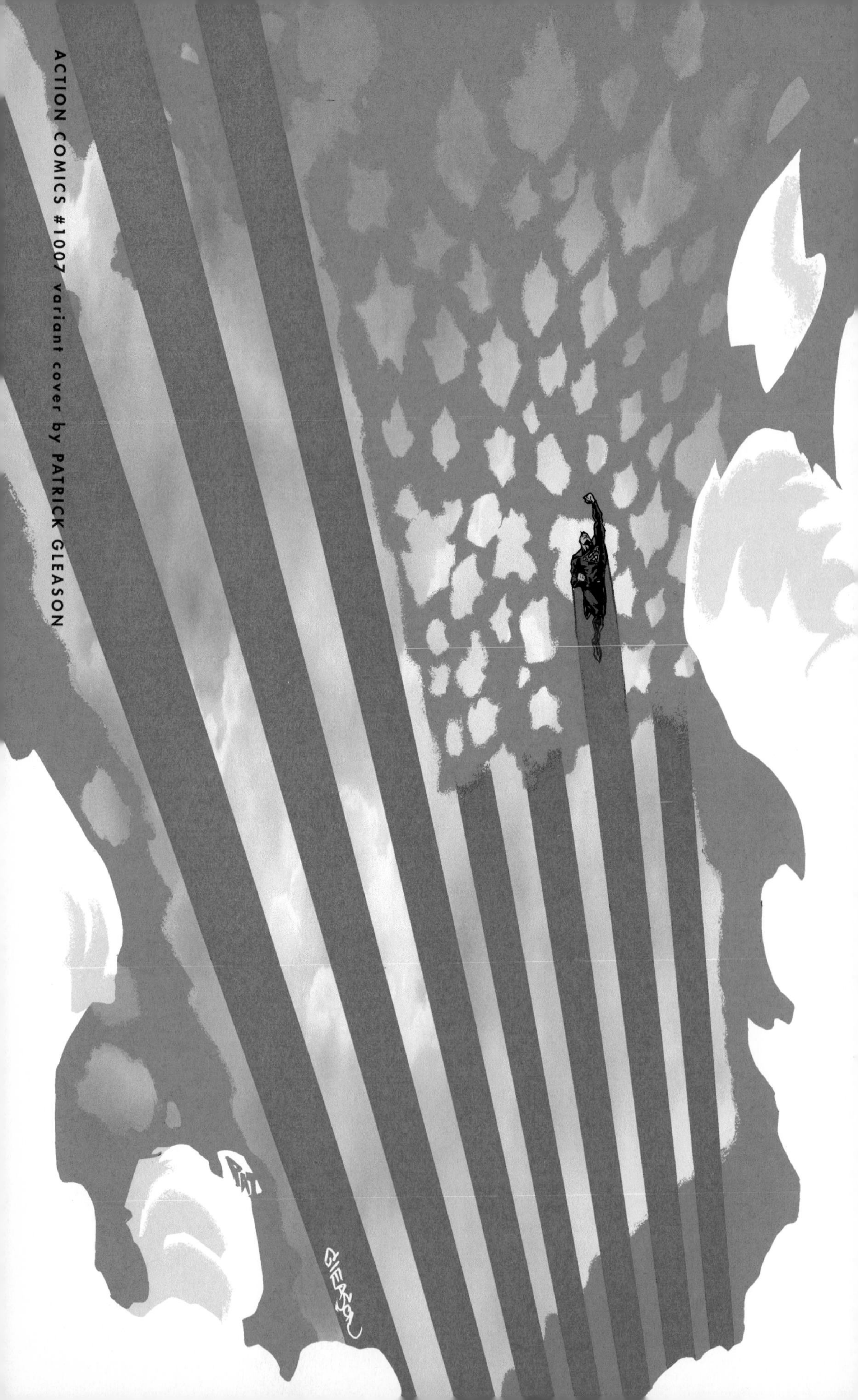

ACTION COMICS #1007 variant cover by PATRICK GLEASON

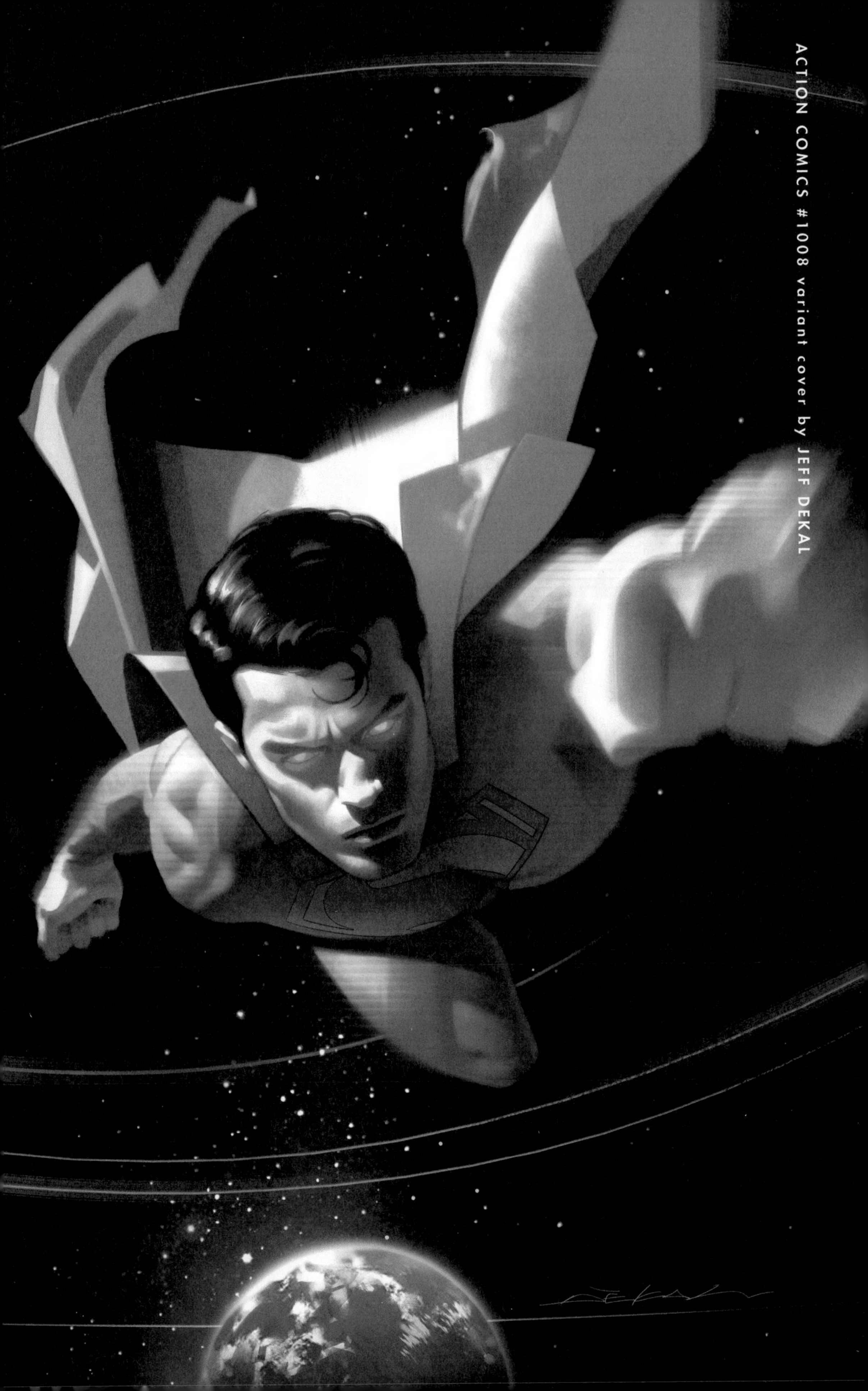

ACTION COMICS #1008 variant cover by JEFF DEKAL

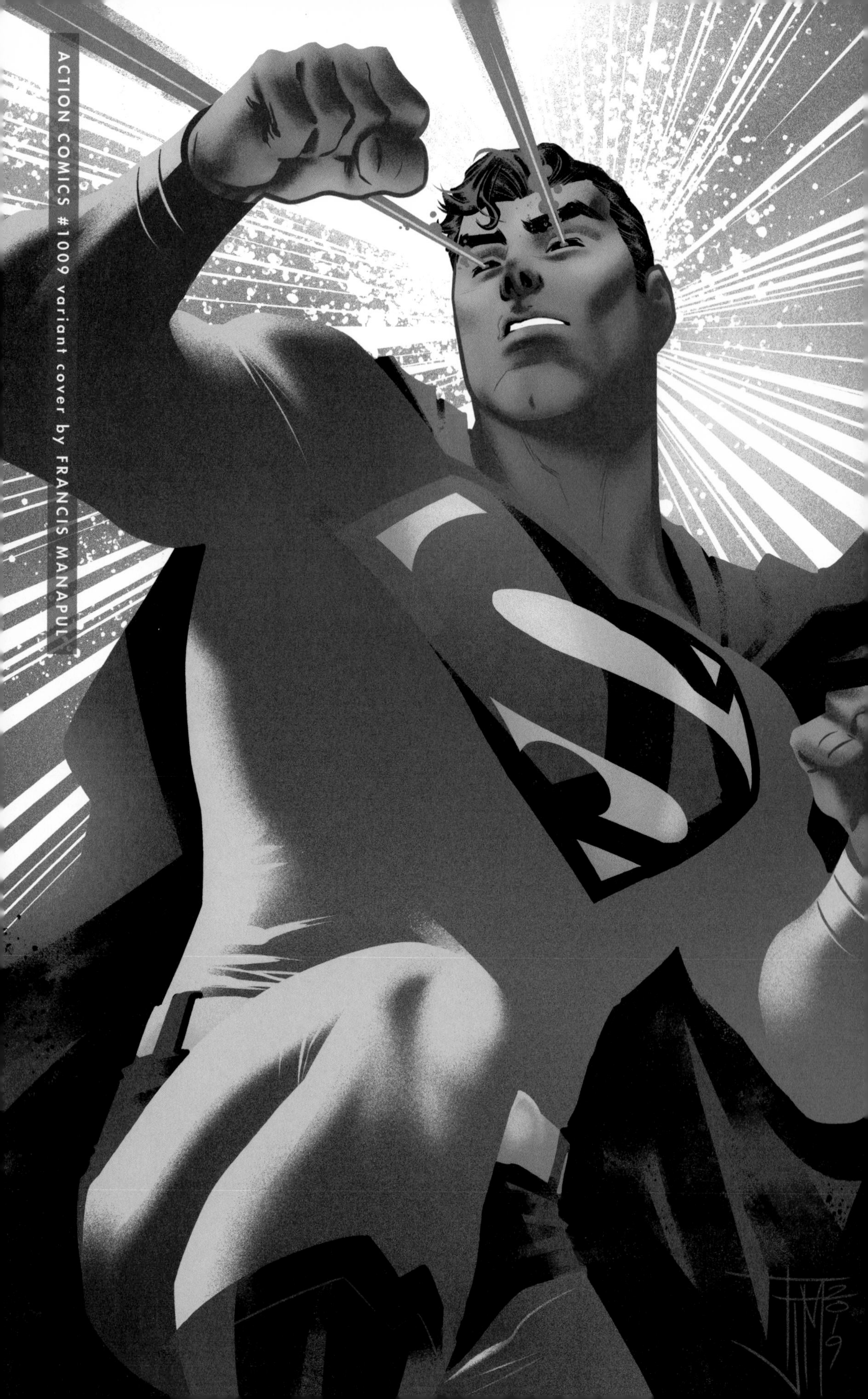

ACTION COMICS #1009 variant cover by FRANCIS MANAPUL

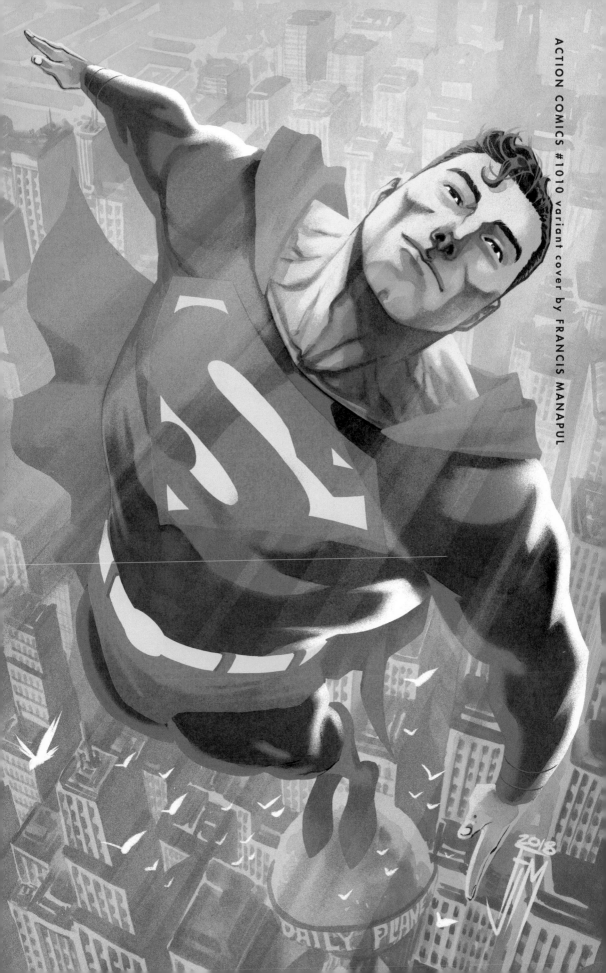

ACTION COMICS #1010 variant cover by FRANCIS MANAPUL

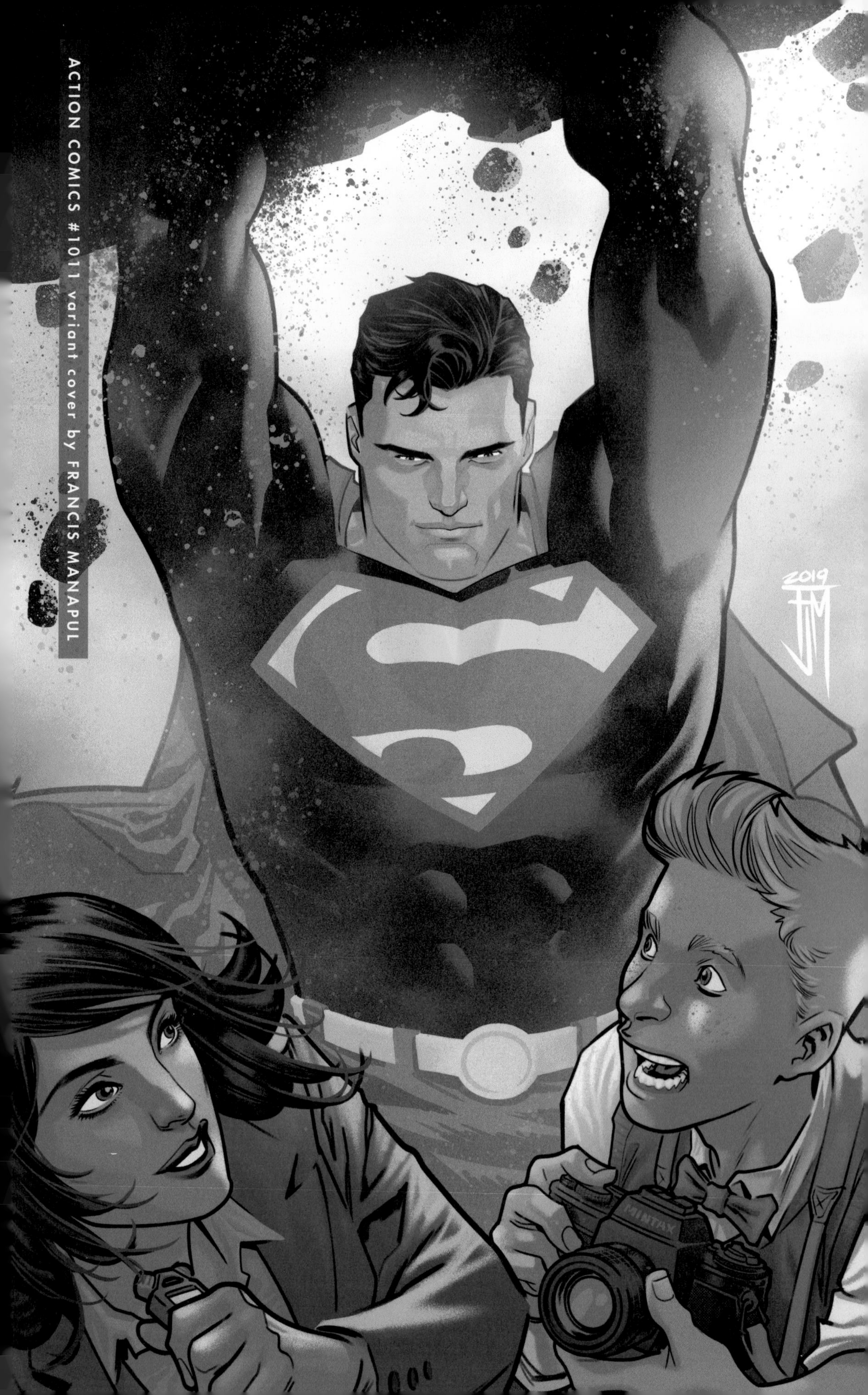
ACTION COMICS #1011 variant cover by FRANCIS MANAPUL
2019
MINTAX

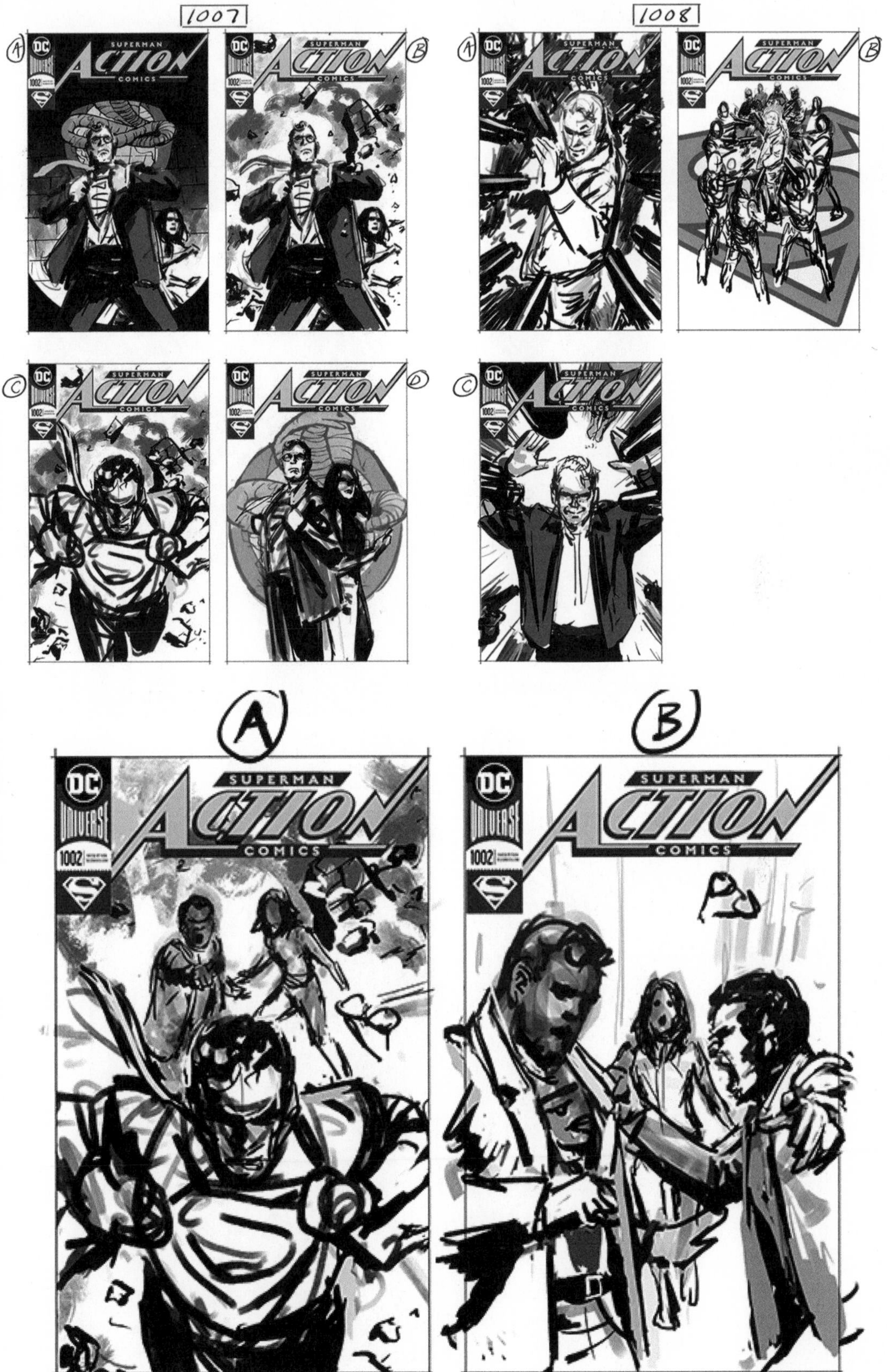
1007
1008
A
B
C
D
DC
UNIVERSE
SUPERMAN
ACTION
COMICS
1002

Cover sketches for ACTION COMICS #1007-1009 by STEVE EPTING

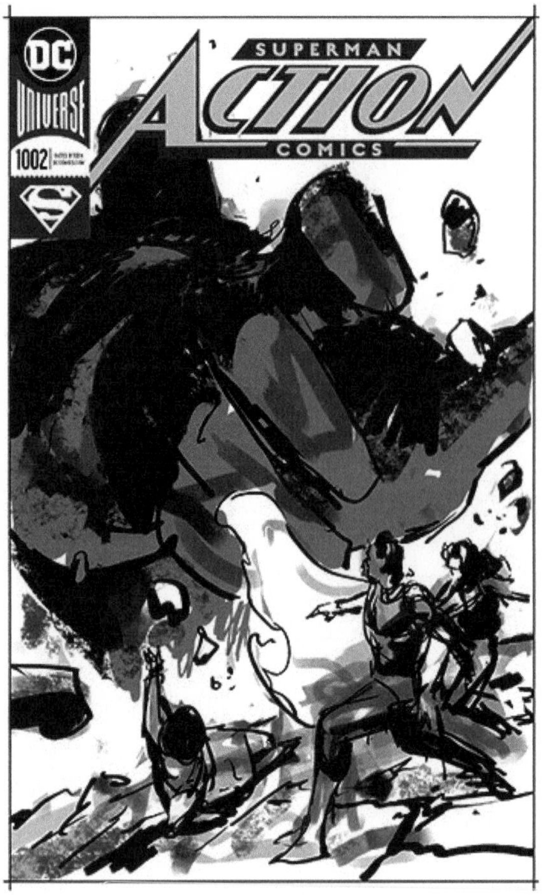
DC
UNIVERSE
1002
SUPERMAN
ACTION
COMICS

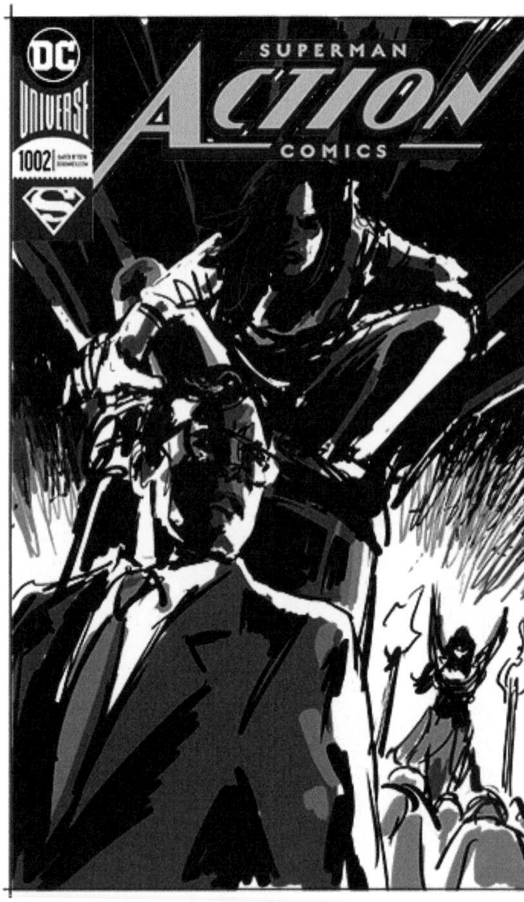
DC
UNIVERSE
1002
SUPERMAN
ACTION
COMICS

A

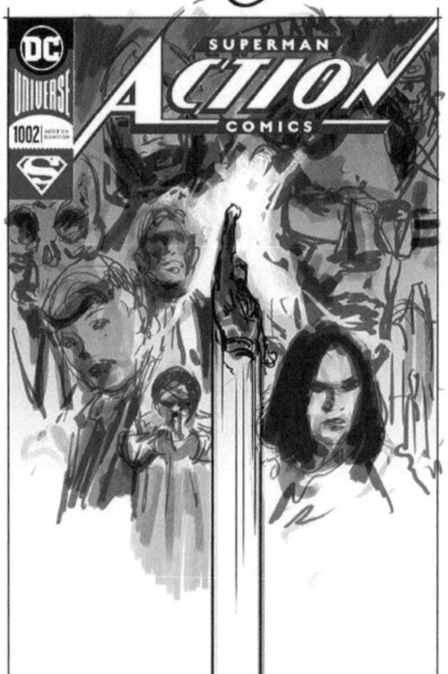
DC
UNIVERSE
1002
SUPERMAN
ACTION
COMICS

B

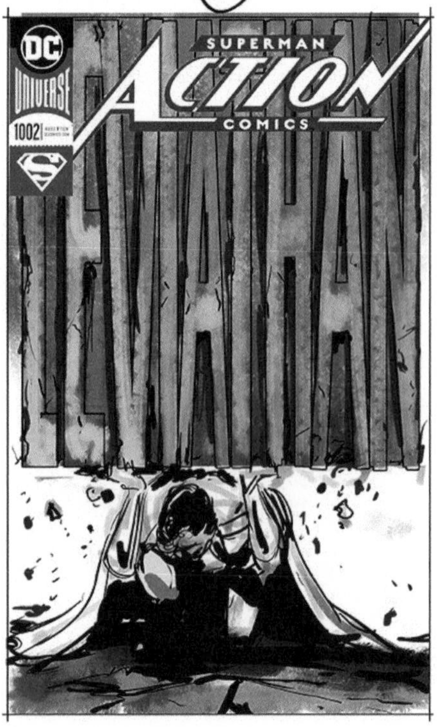
DC
UNIVERSE
1002
SUPERMAN
ACTION
COMICS

**Cover sketches for ACTION COMICS #1010-1011 by STEVE EPTING**

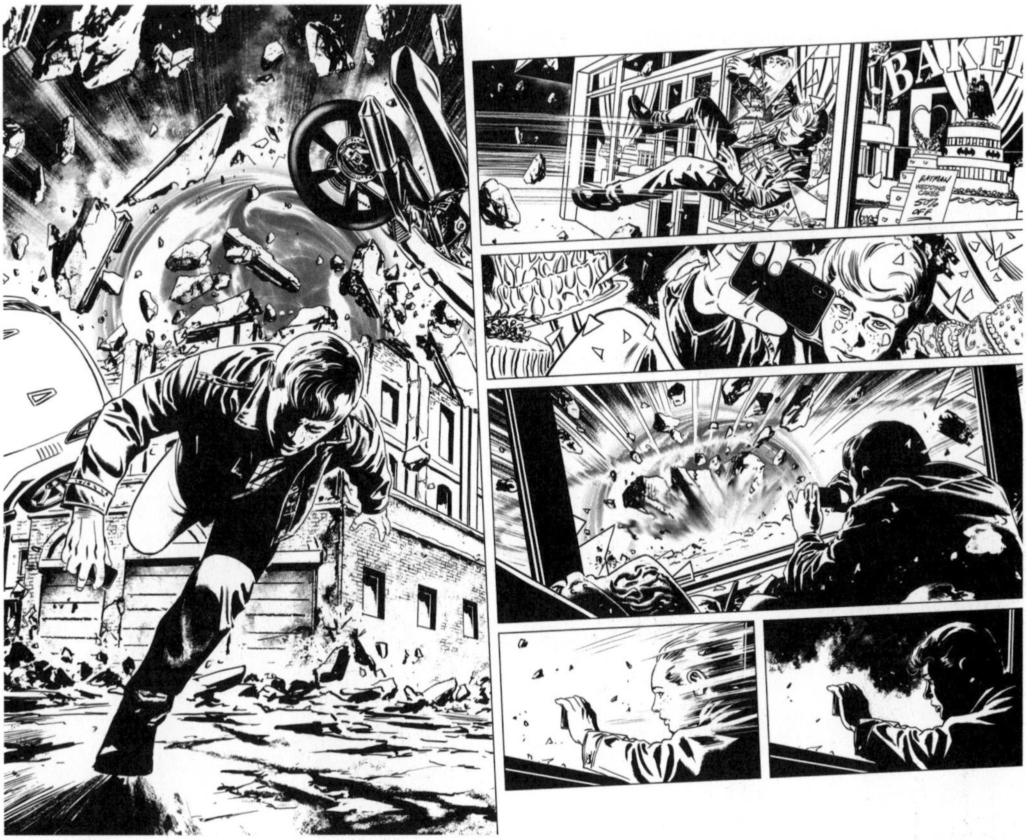
BATMAN
WEDDING CAKES
50% OFF

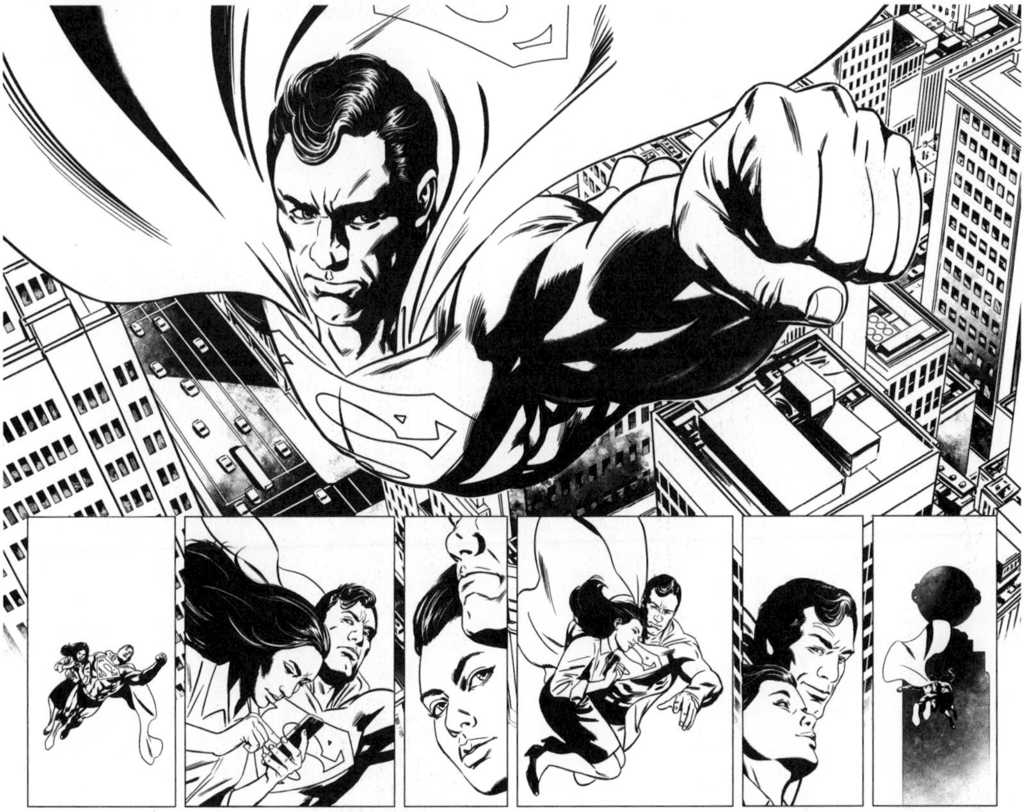

Line art for ACTION COMICS #1007
pages 8-9 and ACTION COMICS #1008
pages 10-11 by STEVE EPTING

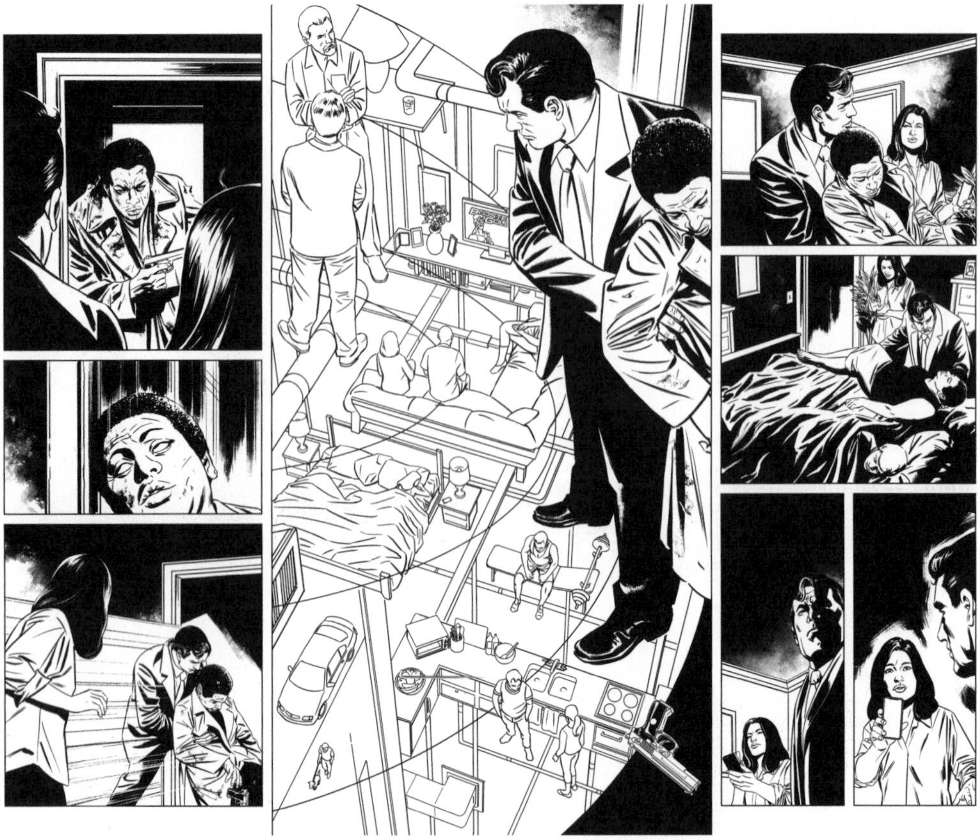

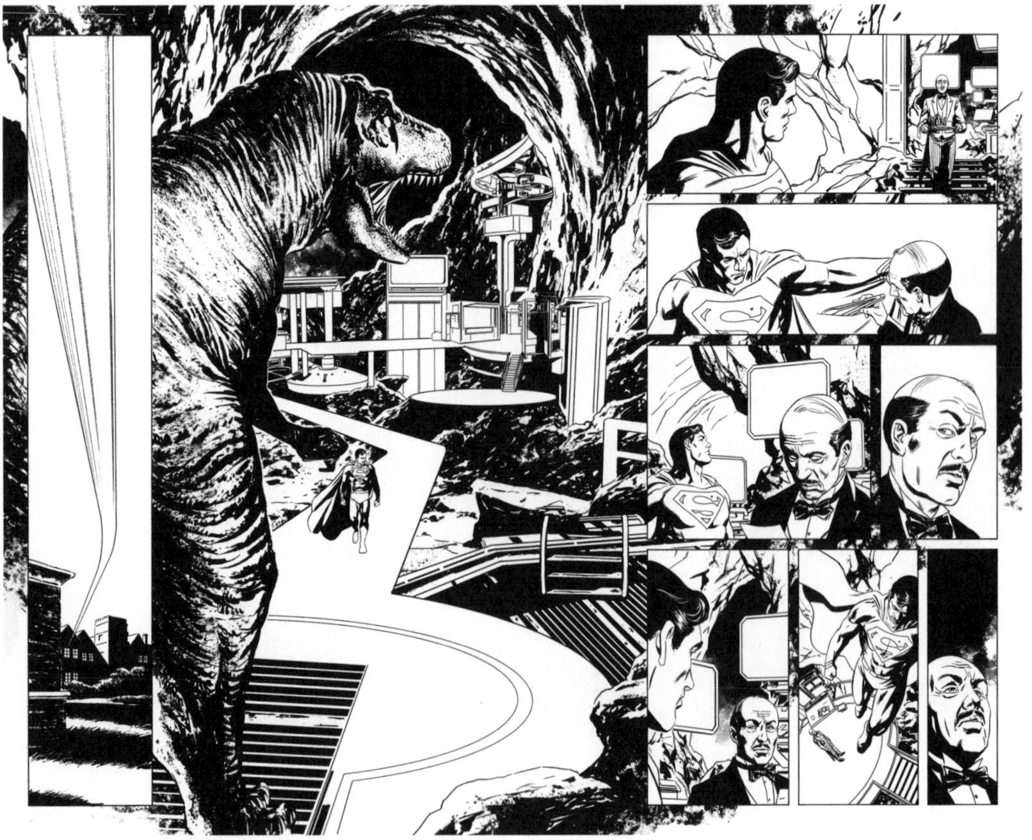

**Line art for ACTION COMICS #1009 pages 4-5 and 16-17 by STEVE EPTING**

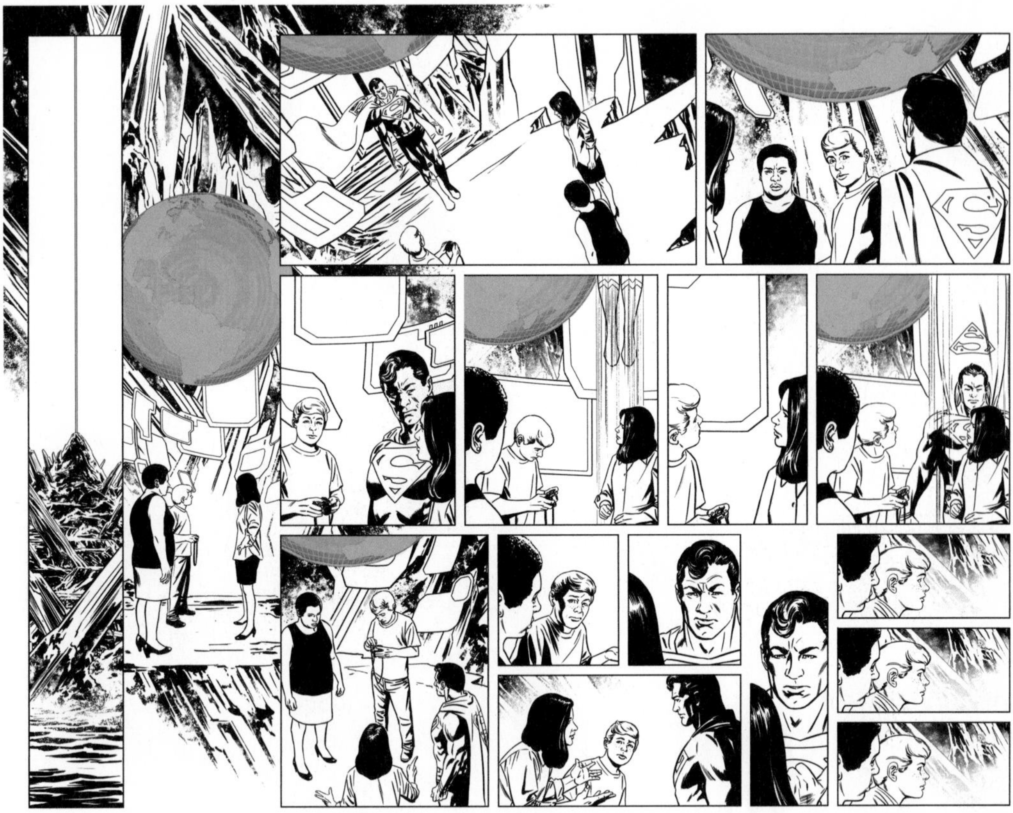

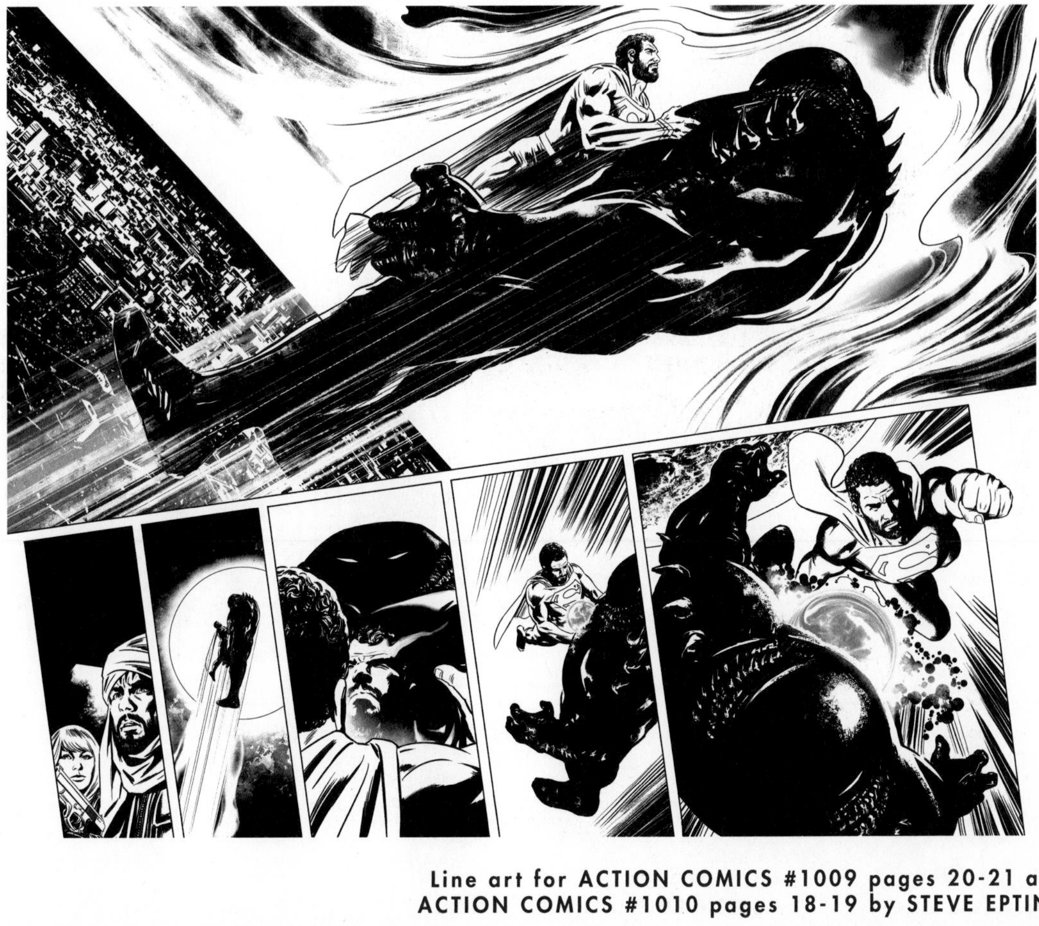

Line art for ACTION COMICS #1009 pages 20-21 and ACTION COMICS #1010 pages 18-19 by STEVE EPTING

"That gorgeous spectacle is an undeniable part of Superman's appeal, but the family dynamics are what make it such an engaging read."
**– A.V. CLUB**

"Head and shoulders above the rest."
**– NEWSARAMA**

## DC UNIVERSE REBIRTH
# SUPERMAN
### VOL. 1: SON OF SUPERMAN

PETER J. TOMASI with PATRICK GLEASON,
DOUG MAHNKE & JORGE JIMENEZ

**VOL.1 SON OF SUPERMAN**
PETER J.TOMASI ★ PATRICK GLEASON ★ DOUG MAHNKE ★ JORGE JIMENEZ ★ MICK GRAY

**SUPERGIRL VOL. 1:
REIGN OF THE SUPERMEN**

**ACTION COMICS VOL. 1:
PATH OF DOOM**

**BATMAN VOL. 1:
I AM GOTHAM**

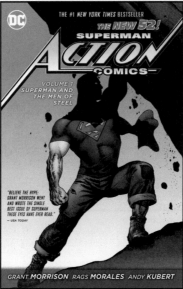
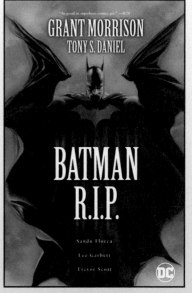

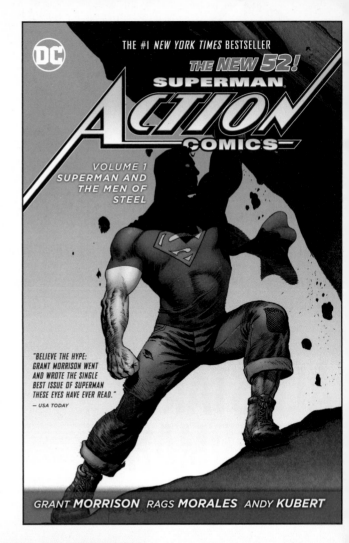
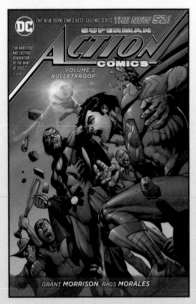